Media Pluralism and European Law

Information Law Series

VOLUME 26

General Editor

Prof. P. Bernt Hugenholtz
Institute for Information Law
University of Amsterdam

The titles published in this series are listed at the back of this volume.

Media Pluralism and European Law

Ewa Komorek

Wolters Kluwer
Law & Business

Published by:
Kluwer Law International
PO Box 316
2400 AH Alphen aan den Rijn
The Netherlands
E-mail: sales@kluwerlaw.com
Website: www.kluwerlaw.com

Sold and distributed in North, Central and South America by:
Aspen Publishers, Inc.
7201 McKinney Circle
Frederick, MD 21704
United States of America
Email: customer.service@aspenpublishers.com

Sold and distributed in all other countries by:
Turpin Distribution Services Ltd
Stratton Business Park
Pegasus Drive, Biggleswade
Bedfordshire SG18 8TQ
United Kingdom
Email: kluwerlaw@turpin-distribution.com

Printed on acid-free paper.

ISBN 978-90-411-3894-1

For My Family

Table of Contents

List of Abbreviations

API	Application Programming Interface
AVMS	Audiovisual Media Services (Directive)
CAS	Conditional Access System
DG	Directorate General
ECHR	European Convention on Human Rights
ECJ	European Court of Justice
EPG	Electronic Programme Guide
EU	European Union
MS	Member State
NRA	National Regulatory Authority
PSB	Public Service Broadcaster
SMP	Significant Market Power
STB	Set-Top-Box
TEU	Treaty on European Union
TFEU	Treaty on the Functioning of the European Union
TVWF	Television Without Frontiers (Directive)

Preface

This book examines European regulation of media pluralism and diversity. It analyses both the law of the European Union, as well as the case-law of the European Court of Human Rights and the work of the Council of Europe in the area. The phenomena of digitalization and the resulting technological convergence stimulate the minds of regulators in Europe and underlie the Audiovisual Media Services Directive. Despite development of technology and rapid changes in the sector, there are still concerns for safeguarding freedom and pluralism of the media which, according to Article 11(2) of the Charter of Fundamental Rights of the European Union, deserve respect at the European Union level. Meanwhile there is no binding legislation on media pluralism in the EU law. An attempt to introduce a media concentration directive in the mid-1990s is a story of missed opportunity. The directive tried to reconcile too many conflicting interests, tried to impose a 'one size fits all' solution and did not take account of changes in the sector.

The controversies surrounding the need for media pluralism legislation derive from a 'culture/commodity' policy dilemma associated with the media sector. On the one hand, there are views that media is a sector like any other and does not require additional regulation in the public interest. On the other hand, there are still advocates of the need to protect media pluralism as an established common European value.

The European Parliament has consistently called for coming back to the debate on a positive action on media pluralism at the EU level. However, the European Commission's stance over the past decade has been that the current regulatory regime, consisting of several EU measures complemented by national law, is satisfactory and sufficient. The European instruments for the protection of structural pluralism include competition law and the possibility of obliging network operators with significant market power to grant access to their networks on fair and non-discriminatory terms. The country of origin principle, which is the cornerstone of the Audiovisual Media Services

Directive is also believed to actively promote structural media pluralism. Internal pluralism is supported by the European Union with the must-carry rules, as well as requirements on independent and European production quotas. The above measures are complemented by national media concentration legislations.

With regard to the national instruments, the liberalization sentiments which have taken over media regulators in Europe mean that the rules are being relaxed or, in some cases, done away with completely. This, combined with the weaknesses and fragmentation of the currently available EU level legislative tools supporting media pluralism has led to one conclusion: there is a need for positive additional action at the EU level aimed at safeguarding media pluralism in the European media market. However, it is highly unlikely that the additional action will take a form of a *binding* legislative intervention in the near future. There is no firm legal basis in the Treaties for the EU legislative action aimed specifically at the protecting pluralism, and there is also no political will to introduce it.

However, even if the political climate for legislative intervention is currently unfavourable, the topic should not be abandoned. Awareness raising should continue in order to keep the matter on the agenda since there is a case for more EU rules on media pluralism. Therefore, in light of the EU's current competence, it is possible to suggest some solutions which could be introduced *now* to provide additional safeguards at every level of 'diversity chain'. This book examines several possible solutions including strengthening of transparency and monitoring, adopting 'soft law with hard statements', introduction of media specific merger review by including a 'pluralism test' in the EU Merger Regulation, more active promotion of public service media and fostering media literacy.

Constant raising of awareness of the need to safeguard pluralism in the European media is vital. Current reluctance of the European Commission to introduce any strong-worded recommendations, much less a legislation in this area, should not prevent searching for ways to augment the currently utilized tools aimed at safeguarding media pluralism. Situations such as the continuing 'Italian anomaly', the Hungarian media law of 2010 or the hacking scandal in the UK in 2011 indicate that a stronger EU voice in this area is needed.

I would like to express my gratitude to Dr Eoin O'Dell (Trinity College Dublin) for his support and guidance.

I would also like to thank Dr Daithí Mac Síthigh (University of Edinburgh) for stimulating discussions, Tarlach McGonagle of the Institute for Information Law, University of Amsterdam for inspiring my interest in the European media regulation, as well as Kevin Coates and Torben Toft of the European Commission for guiding me through the nuances of the European Union's policy in the media sector.

Every effort has been made to ensure that the law is as stated in June 2012. Any mistakes or omissions remain my own.

Ewa Komorek
Dublin, June 2012

Chapter 1
Introduction

1.1. CULTURE/COMMODITY DILEMMA

The purpose of this book is to examine the existing European regulatory framework contributing to the protection of pluralism and diversity in the media sector, with particular focus on broadcasting. The question being asked is whether there is a case for additional European-level measures aimed at protection of freedom and pluralism of the media, which, according to Article 11(2) of the Charter of Fundamental Rights of the European Union,[1] 'shall be respected' at the European Union level. An attempt to introduce a media pluralism directive in the mid-1990s is a story of missed opportunity,[2] and as a result there is currently no binding legislation provided by the EU law dealing specifically with this issue.

In fact, the term 'media pluralism' has not featured in the Treaty for a long time. It was only introduced in 1997 when the Treaty of Amsterdam annexed the Protocol on the system of public broadcasting in the Member States.[3] The Protocol emphasizes that 'the system of public broadcasting in the Member States is directly related to the democratic, social and cultural needs of each society and to the need to preserve *media pluralism*'. With the Charter of Fundamental Rights of the European Union receiving binding legal effect equal to the Treaties as of the date of the entry into force of the

---

1. Charter of Fundamental Rights of the European Union, OJ (2000) C-364/1.
2. See Ch. 2.2.1 below.
3. Treaty of Amsterdam amending the Treaty on European Union, The Treaties establishing the European communities and related acts, OJ [1997] C-340/109; currently annexed to the Treaty on the Functioning of the European Union, OJ [2010] C-83/1.

Lisbon Treaty, the place of media pluralism seems to be now firmly secured in the catalogue of main principles of EU law. In addition, some authors even believe that with the introduction of paragraph 2 to Article 11, the freedom and pluralism of the media became fundamental rights on equal footing with the other two established rights of freedom of expression and the free flow of information.[4] However, it is worth noting that the wording of Article 11(2) changed from '*guaranteed*' to '*respected*' as a result of a pressure from some Member States at a late stage of the drafting process.

This change is an indication of underlying clash of rationales and values characterizing the media pluralism debate at the EU level. The lack of regulation and coherent approach by the European Union to the issue of media pluralism derives from a 'culture/commodity' policy dilemma[5] which renders the sector a 'particularly complex object for legal regulation'.[6] Discussions on media pluralism trigger economic, political and cultural concerns, and tackling these problems independently from one another is simply impossible. Therefore, the debate has been marked by a 'power struggle' between actors in the media arena and regulators, which has centred on deciding which of these interests should take the priority.[7] Klimkiewicz observes that this clash of arguments results essentially from five types of tensions pertinent to the media pluralism debate. These are tensions between: (i) processes of media concentration and the citizens' rights to receive information from diverse and independent sources; (ii) status of public service broadcasting (PSB) and EU competition and state aid policy; (iii) structural media diversity and high costs of market entry; (iv) unequal representation of minorities and pressure from advertisers in favour of mainstream audiences; and (v) journalistic autonomy and political influences.[8]

4. Haraszti, M., 'Media Pluralism and Human Rights', discussion paper prepared for the Council's of Europe Commissioner for Human Rights, 6 December 2011.
5. The 'culture/commodity' struggle in media is well considered *inter alia* in the UNESCO Convention on Cultural Diversity; EBU 'Position Paper on the Commission Proposal for a Directive on services in the internal market', 8 December 2004 (accessed 8 April 2008); see also Marsden, C., Verhulst, S., 'Convergence: A Framework for Discussion', in Marsden, C., Verhulst, S. (eds) *Convergence in European Digital TV Regulation* (Blackstone Press Limited, 1999), 2; Goldberg, D., Prosser, T., Verhulst, S. (eds), *Regulating the Changing Media. A Comparative Study* (Clarendon Press,1998), 145.
6. Goldberg, D., Prosser, T., Verhulst, S., *EC Media Law and Policy* (Longman, 1998), 1.
7. Feintuck, M., Varney, M., *Media Regulation, Public Interest and the Law* (Edinburgh University Press, 2006), 40, 74.
8. Klimkiewicz, B., 'Is the Clash of Rationalities Leading Nowhere? Media Pluralism in European Regulatory Policies', in Czepek, A., Hellwig, M., Nowak, E. (eds), *Press Freedom and Pluralism in Europe: Concepts and Conditions* (Intellect Books, 2009), 59.

Therefore, on the one hand there are arguments put forward for a liberal approach and the need to support further growth of big European media companies to make them able to compete in the global market. On the other hand, the pluralism, as an established common European value, must be respected and protected which requires a regulatory intervention. This clash between liberal and more protective regulatory approach has become nothing short of the 'war of the values'.

Some argue that media are business like any other.[9] In this sense, concentration may be desirable and commercially justified. In the current situation in the media sector characterized by rapid changes, convergence of technologies and inflated costs of premium media content, big horizontal and vertically integrated media conglomerates provide for a range of benefits. It is often argued that only the 'big ones' can take full advantage of the recent changes and reap the economies of scale and scope inherent in the sector. Cross-media mergers and diagonal concentrations between different sectors help media operators minimize the risks of failure in one of their markets. Concentration in the media industry may thus be seen as a natural and positive development.[10]

However, information which is the main product of the media industry is so much more than just a commercial commodity,[11] and the media should not be treated as just another market.[12] Media are often referred to as the Fourth Estate.[13] Therefore, it is essential that the media industry in Europe remains pluralistic and diverse. Only then, can the members of a democratic society 'make an informed choice on a variety of public matters'.[14] As illustrated by Craufurd Smith:

> Media ownership controls remain necessary because the media industry is unlike any other, in that it has a unique capacity to promote or damage those goods, services, persons, or organisations that come within its sights. Whether particular events are reported or not, and how they are reported, affect how people perceive the world around them, it can

9. Zeno-Zencovich, V., 'Plurality of Political Opinions and the Concentration of Media', Italia National Reports to the XVIIIth International Congress of the International Academy of Comparative Law, Washington 2010, The Cardozo Electronic Law Bulletin, 16(1) Special Issue.
10. McGonagle, M., *Media Law*, 2nd edn (Thomson, Round Hall, 2002), 426.
11. Goldberg, D., Prosser, T., Verhulst, S., *EC Media Law and Policy*, 3.
12. Haraszti, M., 'Media Pluralism and Human Rights'.
13. Feintuck, M., Varney, M., *Media Regulation, Public Interest and the Law*, 17.
14. Ward, D., 'Media Concentration and Pluralism: Regulation, Realties and the Council of Europe's Standards in the Television Sector', UNIDEM Campus Trieste Seminar 'The Role of Media Freedom and Pluralism in Strengthening Democracy', Trieste, Italy, 24–28 January 2005.

> determine whether they turn out to vote in national or regional elections, and their level of participation in the society around them.[15]

In addition, not only news programmes, but also entertainment programmes contribute to the formation of public opinion. Therefore, as observed by Hoffman-Riem:

> ' … the calls for pluralism are by no means limited to informational diversity in special news and current affairs programmes, but rather relate as well to the operation of broadcasting as a whole'.[16]

1.2. DEFINITIONS

Before turning to present in more detail the recent trends in the sector and the arguments for and against the need to regulate for pluralism, it is essential to briefly define the notions of media pluralism, diversity and concentration, which are central to this book.

There have been numerous definitions and classifications of media pluralism provided. In general, it is possible to distinguish between two main types of media pluralism: internal (content diversity) and external (structural or media diversity). Within each society there is a plurality of political, social and religious points of view and a diversity of cultures, interests, hobbies and passions. Media pluralism can therefore be best defined as 'the scope for a wide range of social, political and cultural values, opinions, information and interests to find expression through the media'.[17] Therefore protecting pluralism means ensuring that 'many, if not all, points of view are represented in the marketplace of ideas'.[18] However, this is only one 'face' of media pluralism – the internal one, sometimes also called content diversity. The second face is external or structural, relating to the existence of a number of media suppliers.[19] Apart from the external/internal face of

15. Craufurd Smith, R., 'Rethinking European Union Competence in the Field of Media Ownership: The Internal Market, Fundamental Rights and European Citizenship', (2004) European Law Review 29, 652–673, 655.
16. Hoffman-Riem, W., *Regulating Media. The Licensing and Supervision of Broadcasting in Six Countries* (The Guilford Press, 1996), 298; see also Alger, D., *Megamedia. How Giant Corporations Dominate Mass Media, Distort Competition, and Endanger Democracy* (Rowman & Littlefield Publishers, 1998), 1.
17. This is Council of Europe's 'working definition' of media pluralism Council of Europe; See Council of Europe, Explanatory memorandum to Recommendation R(99) 1 on Measures to promote Media Pluralism, (1999) paras 3 and 4; Cavallin, J., 'European Policies and Regulations on Media Concentration', (1998) International Journal of Communications Law and Policy 1.
18. Organisation for Economic Co-operation and development 'Media Mergers', 19 September 2003.
19. In this book, I use the term structural pluralism in reference to external/structural pluralism and the terms internal pluralism or diversity in reference to internal pluralism.

media pluralism, the Council of Europe further defines two aspects of pluralism, which I would be inclined to more precisely call two aspects of *internal* pluralism: political and cultural. The former is the reflection of a 'wide range of political opinions and viewpoints to be represented in the media', and the latter represents 'the need for a variety of cultures which reflect the diversity within society to find expression in and to find themselves represented in the media'.

It must be borne in mind that neither external nor internal nature of pluralism taken separately can guarantee a fully and genuinely pluralistic media market.[20] As noted by Gibbons 'neither diversity of source nor of outlet can be guaranteed to produce diversity of content'.[21] In the socialist regimes of Central and Eastern Europe, for example, external pluralism often existed – there were numerous 'producers' of media content. However, there was no doubt about what point of view was presented in Central and Eastern European media at that time. This continues to be true nowadays in the era of free media – diversity of ownership *may* contribute, but does not necessarily have to result in the breadth and diversity of programming content. There is a need for additional regulation on content requirements for that to happen. However, internal pluralism within one media company is hard to achieve without the imposition of regulations, codes of practice or internal regulations aimed at guaranteeing the provision of diversified and unbiased content.[22] Therefore, for pluralism to exist both of its key attributes must come together; there must be both diversified ownership of media companies and different views and opinions being expressed.

In addition, the changing media environment requires that for any given media market to be truly pluralistic and diverse, safeguards are needed at each level of the 'diversity chain', as identified by Napoli[23] and Valcke.[24] The three links of the chain can in simplified terms be described as: (i) source/supplier diversity (structural pluralism); (ii) content diversity (internal

20. Ward, D., *The European Union Democratic Deficit and the Public Sphere. An Evaluation of EU Media Policy* (IOS Press, 2004), 125; Klimkiewicz, B., 'Is the Clash of Rationalities Leading Nowhere? Media Pluralism in European Regulatory Policies'.
21. Gibbons, T., 'Concentrations of Ownership and Control in a Converging Media Industry', in Marsden, C., Verhulst, S. (eds), *Press Freedom and Pluralism in Europe: Concepts and Conditions* (Blackstone Press Limited, 1999), 30.
22. Hoffman-Riem, W., *Regulating Media. The Licensing and Supervision of Broadcasting in Six Countries*, 284.
23. Napoli, P.M., 'Deconstructing the Diversity Principle', (1999) Journal of Communication 49(4), 7–34; Valcke, P., 'Looking for the User in Media Pluralism Regulation: Unraveling the Traditional Diversity Chain and Recent Trends of User Empowerment in European Media Regulation', (2011) Journal of Information Policy 1, 287–320.
24. Valcke, P., 'Looking for the User in Media Pluralism Regulation: Unraveling the Traditional Diversity Chain and Recent Trends of User Empowerment in European Media Regulation'.

pluralism); and (iii) and exposure diversity (diverse content actually 'consumed' by the users).

Also with great simplification, one may say that there are basically three models of ensuring pluralism and diversity in media:[25] (i) market model (competition law is sufficient to guarantee plurality of providers and diversity of content); (ii) new media model (pluralism and diversity are 'natural' consequences of economic growth and technical development); and (iii) public policy model (favours state intervention). The European Union currently presents a mixed model, since market and new media models intertwine with scraps of the public policy model.

There is a widespread agreement that there is a potential danger for media pluralism when media power is concentrated in the hands of just a few companies. Such concentration of power may take place through a natural growth of a company (through adding new channels or new subscribers and, thus, eliminating other companies from the market), but most frequently by integration of media companies. The terms of media integration and concentration are often mixed up and used incorrectly as synonyms of each other, when in fact there are important differences between them. Media integration or industrial concentration can be defined as 'all forms of more or less far-reaching combination of power and control over the activities of a company or a group of companies'[26] and is a concept which should be applied at the company level. Media concentration, however, happens at the relevant market level and can be defined as 'an increase in the presence of one or handful of media companies in any market as a result of various possible processes: acquisitions, mergers, deals with other companies, or even the disappearance of competitors'.[27] Therefore, integration of media companies is only one of the possible reasons for the concentration of the media market (the other being natural growth of a company and elimination of competitors).

The fact that a media company integrates by expanding into other media of a similar or different type, or into other countries or into different levels of the production process does not necessarily lead to concentration in industry. In fact, the expansion into other geographic markets may lead to increased numbers of media companies and less concentration at national level, but greater concentration at EU level. Due to the complexity of media markets, it is very difficult to pinpoint exactly when media integration reached such a level that the market became concentrated. As will be explained below, in the media industry, the possession of power and the risk

---

25. Jakubowicz, K., 'Legislative Guarantees of Plurality of Information Sources', Implementation of Constitutional Provisions Regarding Mass Media in a Pluralist Society, (1994) Collection Science and Technique of Democracy 13, 81–86.
26. Lange, A., Van Loon, A., *Multimedia Concentration Regulation in Europe* (IDATE, Montpelier and Institute for Information Law, 1990), 8.
27. Sanchez-Tabernero, A., *Media Concentration in Europe. Commercial Enterprise and the Public Interest* (The European Institute for the Media, 1993).

of its abuse is in itself dangerous for pluralism and diversity. Therefore, no matter what the reasons are for excessive concentration of the media market, the attempts to prevent it have focused on the search for this threshold point when concentration starts acting against the public interest.

There are several types of integration of media companies, which in turn may lead to five different forms of concentration of the media market. They include horizontal, vertical, multi-media (cross-media) and multi-sectoral (diagonal) integration/concentration. It is vital to differentiate between these different forms since each of them affects pluralism and diversity in a different way and raises different competition problems.

Horizontal integration takes place within one and the same media sector, for example when two television stations merge.[28] This type of integration is the quickest way to a concentrated media market, and its impact on pluralism and diversity can be very detrimental. The disappearance of media outlets diminishes external pluralism and may in turn lead to decreased diversity of content. However, competition problems arising from this type of media concentration are no different than in other industries (creating market power in the form of single or joint dominance, raising barriers to entry, etc.).

It is vertical integration which creates competition problems characteristic to the media sector. A media company integrates vertically when it strives to control, partially or completely, the channels of production and distribution of a particular media market. For example, a cable TV company that engages not only in channel distribution but also in content production. This gives a company greater market autonomy and insulates it from the pressures of downstream or upstream markets. This type of integration may not necessarily lead to market concentration. However, it is a logical step for horizontally integrated companies to expand into different levels of production and distribution. In fact this has been the most common trend in the recent years. The result is that very few vertically integrated companies exist in any given media market. The effect on pluralism and diversity is detrimental since the company controls both the content production and distribution. Moreover, the competition concerns are particularly serious (gate-keeper issue, foreclosure of the content markets, leveraging of market power and network effects).[29]

In multi-media or cross-media integration, a media company gains control of different media products in different media sectors. These days, it is difficult to find genuine television or press companies. These are usually

28. For the European Commission's position on the assessment of horizontal mergers, see Guidelines on the assessment of horizontal mergers under the Council Regulation between undertakings, OJ (2004) C-31/5.
29. For the European Commission's position on the assessment of vertical mergers, see Guidelines on the assessment of non-horizontal mergers under the Council Regulation on the control of concentrations between undertakings, paras 28–90.

large vertically integrated conglomerates active in most media markets. For example, Rupert Murdoch's News Corporation has operations in eight industry segments: filmed entertainment, television, cable network programming, direct broadcast satellite television, magazines and inserts, newspapers and book publishing.[30] One owner decides on the editorial line and content of a great number and multiplicity of media products. The potential threat to pluralism and diversity is, therefore, apparent. Moreover, the combination of the deregulation of the audiovisual industry in Europe with the increased attractiveness, influence and profitability of the media business, has resulted in firms that are active in other sectors of the economy gaining control of media companies.[31] This so-called multi-sectoral or diagonal integration is not necessarily harmful for competition.[32] However, the support of vast resources of big businesses significantly strengthens the power of media companies. Strong media arms become in turn a source of influence and political power of potent business owners.[33]

The phenomenon of global media concentration is fairly recent. Up until the 1980s, media was owned and regulated at national level; hence, media companies had no interest and no way of entering into international mergers and alliances. Everything changed with deregulation and privatization of the sector in the late 1980s, which coincided with the development of commercial television and satellite transmission technology.[34] Since then, there has been a notable trend of a few media companies 'that are increasingly demonstrating pan-European structural features' to gain control over media sector.[35] These days, therefore, while the communications devices get smaller, the companies that utilize them enlarge, 'forging production, distribution and transmission enterprises into global conglomerates'.[36] As a result, currently only approximately fifty media firms provide

30. http://www.newscorp.com.
31. One of the examples is General Electric (GE). Media arm NBC Universal operates alongside divisions including GE Commercial Finance, GE Industrial, GE Infrastructure, GE Consumer Finance or GE Healthcare.
32. For the European Commission's position on the assessment of conglomerate mergers, see Guidelines on the assessment of non-horizontal mergers under the Council Regulation on the control of concentrations between undertakings, paras 91–121; See also leading cases of the European Court of Justice and Court of First Instance on conglomerate mergers: Case C-12/03 P, *Commission v. Tetra Laval* [2005] 4 CMLR 8; Case T-210/01, *General Electric v. Commission* [2005] ECR II-5527.
33. For instance, there have been instances of NBC news reports from the war in Iraq with tanks, helicopters and weapons operating on GE technology featured in the background.
34. McChesney, R.W., 'The Nine Firms That Dominate the World', Global Policy Forum, August 2003.
35. Ward, D., *The European Union Democratic Deficit and the Public Sphere. An Evaluation of EU Media Policy*, 72.
36. Noveck, B.S., 'Thinking Analogue about Digital Television? Bringing European Content Regulation into the Information Age', in Marsden, C., Verhulst, S. (eds), *Convergence in European Digital TV Regulation* (Blackstone Press Limited, 1999), 37.

the bulk (in revenue terms) of the world's media content production, and they own an overwhelming majority of cable channels and, cable and satellite transmission systems.[37] An even smaller number, only the first nine firms on the list of world' biggest media companies,[38] occupy dominant positions in many media markets. Moreover, these firms almost on a daily basis enter into joint ventures and agreements with each other.

As will be presented in more detail in Chapters 4 and 5, the European legislation currently in force does not sufficiently address this development. Chapter 4 deals with application of competition law to the television broadcasting sector and concludes that competition law by virtue of its focus on markets efficiency cannot be used as the only tool of EU intervention in media concentration which necessarily must also involve consideration of public interest. Chapter 5 analyses existing EU-level legislative measures contributing to the maintenance of pluralism and diversity in the sector, contained in the E-Communications framework (requirements of access, must-carry rules, or principles of interoperability) and the Audiovisual Media Services Directive (country of origin principle, lists of events of major importance, European production quotas). The Chapter concludes that the measures do present some benefits, but overall they are fragmented and insufficient.

This book places itself on the culture side of the dilemma and attempts to demonstrate why it is vital for regulators to preserve media pluralism by counteracting excessive media concentration and safeguarding media freedom as well as quality and diversity of content. There are various examples of how dangerous the lack of or disrespect of the rules aimed at protection of media pluralism can be. In Europe, two most prominent examples concern the media empires of Rupert Murdoch and Silvio Berlusconi. Rupert Murdoch owns, among other media, a staggering number of 175 newspapers around the world, all of which present almost exactly the same editorial line. For example, in 2003 they all advocated for the war in Iraq.[39] Silvio Berlusconi is not only an influential politician and three times the Prime Minister of Italy, but he is also the richest man in the country and a media monarch. He or his relatives own or control three of Italy's four commercial television networks, two big publishing houses, two national newspapers, fifty magazines, the largest Italian movie production and distribution

37. McChesney, R.W., 'The Nine Firms That Dominate the World'.
38. TimeWarner, Disney, Bertelsmann, Viacom, News Corporation, Comcast, GE, Sony & Seagram; see McChesney, R.W., 'The Nine Firms That Dominate the World'; Alger, D., *Megamedia. How Giant Corporations Dominate Mass Media, Distort Competition, and Endanger Democracy*, 33, 217.
39. Kumar, D., 'Media, War, and Propaganda: Strategies of Information Management During the 2003 Iraq War', (2006) Communication and Critical/Cultural Studies 3(1); Greenslade, R., 'Their Master's Voice', The Guardian, 17 February 2003.

company and a big portion of the country's internet services.[40] He exploits the media dominance to boost his political campaigns and uses his political influence to promote his commercial interests.

1.3. RECENT TRENDS

This book concentrates on the risks the lack of protection for pluralism brings mainly for one sector – audiovisual. Notwithstanding its relatively short history – the technology on which it is based was developed early in the twentieth century – television is without a doubt the most significant medium of all. The industry is characterized by a complexity of functions and relations. It involves content creation, publishing, delivery and reception, whilst the products vary from content through channels and means of delivery, to reception equipment. Television companies are classified by the European Audiovisual Observatory[41] into the following main categories: (i) public radio-television companies; (ii) private television companies; (iii) pay-TV; (iv) programme packagers (offering programme packages via cable, satellite or terrestrially); and (v) thematic television companies.

The opinion forming power of television broadcasting continues to be much greater than any other medium. It is ubiquitous,[42] worldwide in scope and reach; it gives the viewers 'a sense of participating in unfolding human events and provides a link and a social bond between men and nations'[43] – as a well-known saying goes 'one picture is worth a thousand words'. Concentration in this sector is all the more problematic because television is still the primary source of knowledge about the world for the majority of people.[44] As noted by Noveck, 'in the reflection of the television screen, we constitute ourselves as individuals; and this screen is a window through which we view our world'.[45] Therefore, because people still rely on television as the principal source of information external to their own

40. Moyers, B., 'Keynote Address to the National Conference on Media Reform', Madison, Wisconsin (8 November 2003).
41. European Audiovisual Observatory, 'The financial situation of television companies in the European Union (1999–2004)', prepared by Andre Lange, September 2005.
42. Trager, R., Dickerson, D.L., *Freedom of Expression in the 21st Century* (Pine Forge Press, Inc., 1999), 154.
43. Confalonieri, F., the Chair of Mediaset, speech at the second United Nations World Television Forum, 1997.
44. Open Society Institute, 'Television across Europe: Regulation, Policy and Independence', '4000 Channels in Europe, but What's on TV', Press Release, 11 October 2005; Verhulst, S., 'Convergence: A Framework for Discussion', 2; Tongue, C., 'Culture or Monoculture? The European Audiovisual Challenge', in Marsden, C., Verhulst, S. (eds), *Convergence in European Digital TV Regulation* (Blackstone Press Limited, 1999), 135; McGonagle, M., *Media Law*, 387.
45. Noveck, B.S., 'Thinking Analogue about Digital Television? Bringing European Content Regulation into the Information Age', 63.

experience, it is vital to ensure that television owners 'do not exclude alternative possibilities'.[46]

Television broadcasting is currently undergoing substantial and rapid changes. In the 1990s, the main trends were privatization and commercialization. The disappearance of public service monopolies operating on the basis of the licensee fees only, marked the end of the first phase in the development of the television in Europe. The structure of the television landscape in Europe has changed drastically and irreversibly.

When dual systems of public and commercial systems are well established and dominate European countries, as is currently the case, the main trends in the European television broadcasting sector can be described as consisting of: growing commercialization, digitalization, rapid technological change and convergence, inflation of content costs, liberalization and deregulation.[47]

The most talked about recent trend in the media sector has without a doubt been the digitalization of media content. The European Commission set a deadline of 2012 for 'digital switchover', that is complete replacement of traditional analogue terrestrial broadcasting.[48] Thus, the introduction and growing expansion of digital television, marks the third phase in the development of European television.[49]

The possibility of dematerializing media products and their transformation into packages of bytes, allows the transmission of audiovisual content via different networks, i.e., mobile, Internet, cable, satellite. Digital television allows for the proliferation of channels beyond the capacities of terrestrial frequencies, and it renders the problem of the scarcity of frequencies a thing of the past. The resulting expansion of pay-television has induced competitive pressure. This in turn has lead to the inflation of costs caused by exceptional increases in prices paid for premium television content. For example, while the cumulative price paid for the broadcasting rights to the Football World Cups of 1990, 1994 and 1998 amounted to EUR241 million, the price paid for the same rights just to the World Cup of 2010 increased to a whopping EUR 1.8 billion.[50]

---

46. Gibbons, T., 'Concentrations of Ownership and Control in a Converging Media Industry', 157.
47. Goldberg, D., Prosser, T., Verhulst, S., 'Regulating the Changing Media', 8, 9.
48. European Commission, 'Commission expects most broadcasting in the EU to be digital by 2010', Press Release, IP/05/595, 24 May 2005.
49. McQuail, D., Siune, K. (eds), *Media Policy. Convergence, Concentration and Commerce* (SAGE Publication, 1998), 72.
50. Mendes Pereira, M., 'Vertical and Horizontal Integration in the Media Sector and EU Competition Law', Conference on the ICT and Media Sector within the EU Policy Framework, Brussels, 7 April 2003.

Digital technology has lead to the phenomenon of convergence, which has in the recent years stimulated the imagination of the owners of television companies and regulators alike. It has even become 'something of a catchphrase when speaking about recent trends in the communications sector'.[51] The coming together of traditionally separate media which has resulted in text, sound, video and voice becoming one 'multimedia' product, has created seemingly endless possibilities. Convergence has led to the belief that the Internet will soon render other media forms obsolete. Furthermore, the unprecedented wave of investment into IT companies resulted in the creation of the 'dotcom bubble', which spectacularly burst in the early 2000. Now it is all about the Web 2.0 – audiences taking control, grass-root contributors making their views known on numerous blogs and sites like YouTube, Facebook or Twitter. The Time magazine announced Person of the Year 2006 to be YOU. That is everyone who 'seizes the reins of the global media, founds and frames the new digital democracy, works for nothing and beats the pros at their own game'.[52] Overall, in the era of 'dotcom bubble', it was very popular to proclaim the imminent death of television as we knew it, that is as a traditional 'point-to-multipoint' transmission of content,[53] and the dawn of the era of Internet and interactive services. New technologies were expected to take over, and our children were apparently not known what broadcasting meant. Now the term 'convergence' has transformed to mean the paradigm shift which has taken place in the media sector, with audiences evolving from passive receivers of media message to active creators of content. And, while it seems that television remains the primary source of news and information for the majority of Europeans,[54] the Internet is quickly closing this gap.[55] The change in the media sector is undeniable, and the co-existence of 'old' and 'new' media poses particular challenges for regulators.

Another current trend associated with digitalization, convergence and the proliferation of 'new media outlets' is a shift in focus noted by Valcke, 'from traditional command-and-control regulation, imposed on suppliers,

51. Ward, D., *The European Union Democratic Deficit and the Public Sphere. An Evaluation of EU Media Policy*, 107.
52. Time Magazine, 'Person of the Year', 15 December 2006 / 1 January 2007, 31.
53. Bratkowski, P., 'Death of television', *Newsweek Poland* 30/2004; see also Graham, A., Davies, G., *Broadcasting, Society and Policy in the Multimedia Age* (John Libbey Media, 1997).
54. Open Society Institute, 'Television across Europe: Regulation, Policy and Independence', '4000 Channels in Europe, but What's on TV', Press Release, 11 October 2005; see also Marsden, C., Verhulst, S., 'Convergence: A Framework for Discussion', 2; Tongue, C., 'Culture or Monoculture? The European Audiovisual Challenge', 135; McGonagle, M., *Media Law*, 387.
55. 'Web to Overtake Printed Press as Source of EU Information: Survey', EurActiv, 8 March 2011.

towards more decentralized forms of regulation (such as co- and self-regulation) and increased attention on audience empowerment and media literacy'.[56] Valcke adds that:

> The new enthusiasm for the responsible and sovereign viewer can be seen as part of a broader trend to transfer some of the regulatory responsibility from governments and suppliers to consumers and citizens.[57]

This in turn has lead to liberalization and deregulation trends in the European television sector. Many Member States have for the most part relaxed their national anti-concentration rules and continue to answer the persistent industrial calls for further deregulation. In addition, Valcke observes that 'the growing role of the user is frequently used as an argument to relax existing regulations in the area of source and content diversity'.[58]

All the above recent developments have led to an increased tolerance towards concentration in the media sector. As noted by the former Competition Commissioner Mario Monti 'the sector has moved towards the concentration which seems inevitably to accompany globalization'.[59] Convergence allows television companies to seek not only economies of scale but for the first time, economies of scope. The result is that it is now possible to use the same product in a number of different ways. In the era of the 'dotcom bubble', the 'Create once, Place everywhere (COPE)' motto dominated the media sector.[60] Media companies embarked on unprecedented processes of vertical integration with content providers and telecommunications companies. This meant that they could exploit their products at every single level of the value chain. The renowned mergers between AOL and Time Warner, Vivendi and Vodafone or Endemol and Telefonica happened during that time. As observed by Business Week Online in the beginning of 2004:

---

56. Valcke, P., 'Looking for the User in Media Pluralism Regulation: Unraveling the Traditional Diversity Chain and Recent Trends of User Empowerment in European Media Regulation', 307.
57. Valcke, P., 'Looking for the User in Media Pluralism Regulation: Unraveling the Traditional Diversity Chain and Recent Trends of User Empowerment in European Media Regulation', 307.
58. Valcke, P., 'Looking for the User in Media Pluralism Regulation: Unraveling the Traditional Diversity Chain and Recent Trends of User Empowerment in European Media Regulation', 307.
59. Monti, M., 'Does EC Competition Policy Help or Hinder the European Audiovisual and Telecoms Industries?', British Screen Advisory Council, The Cavendish Conference Centre, London, 26 November 2001.
60. Mendes Pereira, M., 'Vertical and Horizontal Integration in the Media Sector and EU Competition Law'.

> Apart from a brief respite in the post-September 11 economy, the media business has been consolidating steadily for more than a decade. But the deals of the past few months have upped the stakes. It's not longer enough to have more content than the other guy. You need distribution to win.[61]

However, as the belief in the endless potential of the Internet proved premature and the 'dotcom bubble' burst, the return of big horizontal mergers was evident. Media companies started selling off some of their downstream or upstream units and looking for alliances with companies on the same level of value chain to recoup losses and to strengthen their positions in the fight for the ever more expensive premium content. The merger between News-Corp and Telepiù in Italy, Carlton and Granada in the UK or the acquisition of NTL by UGC in Ireland illustrates this trend. Moreover, the deregulation of the audiovisual sector in most European countries allowed investors from outside the media sector to enter the broadcast market.

Finally, national markets have become saturated and further growth of large media companies is often prevented by national competition rules. Therefore, unhindered by regulatory obstacles, removed by the TVWF Directive, and encouraged by the lack of any regulatory anti-concentration measures at the European level, the integration of media companies more and more often crosses national borders.[62] As noted by Ward, media companies 'have developed an increasingly pan-European strategy'.[63] The examples of Bertelsmann, Vivendi Canal+, RTL Group or BSkyB are the most telling. Bertelsmann, for instance, is a German-based media conglomerate, having twenty-four TV stations and fourteen radio stations in ten countries and holding stakes in content production, new media, music, magazine and book publishing, is the largest European and third largest global media company.[64] And all the above-mentioned companies 'have shown movement towards either closer cooperation with one another or expansion into new markets through mergers and acquisitions'.[65] As noted by former Competition Commissioner, Mario Monti:

> The success of Bertelsmann and Vivendi on the global stage certainly demonstrates rather well that the existence of national markets in Europe is no bar to the creation of an effective global enterprise. In many ways it may be easier for a European company to expand into different

---

61. 'Mega Media Mergers: How Dangerous?', BusinessWeek Online, 23 February 2004.
62. Feintuck, M., Varney, M., *Media Regulation, Public Interest and the Law*, 21.
63. Ward, D., *The European Union Democratic Deficit and the Public Sphere. An Evaluation of EU Media Policy*, 91.
64. Albarran, A.B., Mierzejewska, B.I., 'Media Concentration in the US and European Union: A Comparative Analysis', 6th World Media Economics Conference, 12–15 May 2004.
65. Ward, D., *The European Union Democratic Deficit and the Public Sphere. An Evaluation of EU Media Policy*, 90.

countries, acutely aware of the linguistic and cultural nuances of national markets.[66]

Moreover, apart from the growing number of European media companies investing abroad, more and more US media giants such as News Corporation, have become active in Europe. The media concentration process has thus gained an international dimension.

The current situation in the television broadcasting sector may, therefore, be summarized in one sentence: we live in an era of a digital revolution which is 'transforming media and communications industries world-wide, leading in particular through convergence to a considerable growth of delivery means, without any respect to national borders'.[67]

Digitalization and convergence have not erased the bottlenecks, they just shifted their position in the value chain – from spectrum scarcity to relative content scarcity and technical bottlenecks to access to content, such as conditional access systems. All in all, media industry is becoming more and more concentrated despite the often expressed view that new technologies will lead to a fragmented market structure. In the six-month period ended on 29 March 2012, there were 681 merger or acquisition transactions in the digital media sector in the world, worth USD 36 billion.[68] As the traditional sources of revenue continue to decline and new media companies grow, there may be even more media mergers and acquisitions in the near future. As some authors point out – 'the question isn't if, but who?'.[69] The trend towards concentration, therefore, has not slowed down because technology has changed. Acquiring competitors is still the preferred means of securing more viewers and subscribers, as this will always be far easier than working on better content and innovating new ways to attract audiences.[70] And as noted by Philip Lowe, the former Director General of Directorate General for Competition in the European Commission:

> The *marked trend* towards concentration in the European communications and media sectors during recent years in our view entails two dangers. The first danger is the creation of significant market power of undertakings – or even monopoly – that significantly impedes competition, ultimately to the detriment of consumer welfare. This very often coincides with the second danger, which by the way – as

66. Monti, M., 'Does EC Competition Policy Help or Hinder the European Audiovisual and Telecoms Industries?'.
67. Westphal, D., 'Media Pluralism and European Regulation', (2002) European Business Law Review 5, 459–487; Doyle, G., *Media Ownership* (SAGE Publications, 2002), 1.
68. Generation Equity Advisors, 'Digital Media M&A – Q1 2012 Update', 30 March 2012.
69. '10 Predictions for the News Media in 2011', http://mashable.com/2010/12/20/news-media-predictions/.
70. Hedges, M., 'It Is a Fight to the Death: *Branson v. Murdoch*', http://www.followthemedia.com, 28 March 2007.

> competition authorities – we have no remit to control, namely the possibility for a limited number of media companies to curtail media pluralism, diversity and freedom of information.[71]

All the above trends imply that the main question of this book, that is whether EU-level policy in the public interest is still needed in the television broadcasting industry, is as crucial as ever.[72] Despite the recent trend to proclaim the imminent death of broadcasting as we know it, television in a traditional sense is still the primary source of information for most people in Europe.[73] In addition, viewers expect different standards from broadcasting than from other media, especially the press. As Barendt observes, 'while [the public] expects the print media to be biased or to have selective coverage, it has relied on … television to provide objective news and a comprehensive range of programmes to inform as well as to entertain'.[74] This is why, the need to safeguard pluralism and diversity is much more profound in audiovisual than in any other media source.[75]

As for the regulation of television, digitalization of broadcasting led to a revolution in the regulatory approach in the European Union. The problem of scarcity of frequencies has disappeared undermining the technical rationale for public-service monopolies, which until the late 1980s characterized national broadcasting systems. Suddenly obsolete regulatory policies dissuaded commercial media investment and the proper functioning of the internal market was threatened. The need for pan-European de-regulation meant that the European Union had to get involved. The result was the adoption in 1989 of the TVWF Directive which introduced mutual recognition for trans-frontier broadcasts. The Directive was adopted in the spirit of neo-liberalism which praised broadcasting deregulation as a 'liberation' of television from its historical bonds.[76] The 'fathers' of the Directive believed that the removal of technical and regulatory barriers to market entry would be sufficient for television in Europe to become a medium that would be

---

71. Lowe, P., 'Media Concentration and Convergence: Competition in Communications', Oxford Media Convention, 13 January 2004, emphasis added.
72. Motta, M., Polo, M., 'Concentration and Public Policies in the Broadcasting Industry: The Future of Television', (1997) Economic Policy 12, 295, 296.
73. Open Society Institute, 'Television across Europe: Regulation, Policy and Independence', '4000 Channels in Europe, but What's on TV', Press Release, 11 October 2005; see also Marsden, C., Verhulst, S., 'Convergence: A Framework for Discussion', 2; Tongue, C., 'Culture or Monoculture? The European Audiovisual Challenge', 135; McGonagle, M., *Media Law*, 387.
74. Barendt, E., *Freedom of Speech*, 2nd edn (Oxford University Press, 2005), 448.
75. Hoffman-Riem, W., *Regulating Media. The Licensing and Supervision of Broadcasting in Six Countries*, 267; Feintuck, M., Varney, M., *Media Regulation, Public Interest and the Law*, 79–80.
76. Humphreys, P., 'The Changing Nature of the Broadcast Media in Europe: Some Key Policy Issues', 1995, 1403.

characterized by multiple and diverse products and the rule of 'consumer sovereignty'.[77]

However, the reality proved to be far more difficult. The Directive itself encouraged increasing cooperation and cross-border mergers between the largest European media groups.[78] Moreover, in the growing number of media outlets and almost unlimited stream of information provided by the Internet, television companies embarked on the fight for audience. This inevitably led to the loss in quality of programmes.[79] Only those which attract the biggest numbers of viewers are profitable. This fierce fight for audience is one of the main reasons behind increasing concentration in the television industry. One must not be misled by the increasing number of channels. This trend is not followed by the increasing number of television companies and substantial diversification of the offering.

In December 2007, the TVWF Directive was replaced by the Audiovisual Media Services Directive (AVMS Directive).[80] The change of the name is set to indicate that the legislation should not be limited to 'television' in the traditional sense, but also to the new non-linear audiovisual media. Valcke adds that the Directive:

> advocates a new image of the viewer as the responsible or media-literate consumer ... [and] suggests a corresponding modified regulatory approach that puts more emphasis on the user and makes the role of the user more explicit in achieving certain policy goals (including diversity).[81]

This focus on new media seems to have left little space for the discussion on the issues of pluralism and diversity.[82] Meanwhile, Gibbons observes that 'even if particular features of ownership regulation will be rendered obsolete

77. Humphreys, P., 'The Changing Nature of the Broadcast Media in Europe: Some Key Policy Issues', 1403.
78. Harcourt, A., *The European Union and the Regulation of Media Markets* (Manchester University Press, 2005), 65.
79. Open Society Institute, 'Television across Europe: Regulation, Policy and Independence', '4000 Channels in Europe, but What's on TV'.
80. Directive 2007/65/EC of the European Parliament and of the Council of 11 December 2007 amending Council Directive 89/552/EEC on the coordination of certain provisions laid down by law, regulation or administrative action in Member States concerning the pursuit of television broadcasting activities, OJ (2007) L 332/27.
81. Valcke, P., 'Looking for the User in Media Pluralism Regulation: Unraveling the Traditional Diversity Chain and Recent Trends of User Empowerment in European Media Regulation', 305.
82. Gibbons, T., 'Concentrations of Ownership and Control in a Converging Media Industry', 155.

by convergence, it does not follow that policy choices about media pluralism in general will also disappear'.[83] This is all the more important, because:

> the arrival of new media and in particular the digital convergence of the information and communications industries [is] driving a marked trend towards media concentrations as large, generally internationally-ambitious, private media corporations [seek] to exploit new economies of scale and scope.[84]

Therefore, in modern integrating Europe the aim must be not only to promote the digital agenda, the development of new media and the growth of television companies while protecting effective competition, but also to promote pluralism and diversity in media. Since, as noted by the European Broadcasting Union:

> a free, pluralistic media system which functions properly is essential … not only to national democracies, but also to the democratic foundations of … [Europe] itself. Such a system is also a means of fulfilling the political, cultural and social needs of European citizens and of 'European society' as a whole.[85]

However, the goal to support the growth of media companies often 'clashes' with the goal of maintaining pluralism and diversity, and this is what makes the media sector so very specific, sensitive and resistant to any attempts of pan-European regulation of media concentration.

1.4. NEED TO LEGISLATE FOR PLURALISM?: THE CLASH OF ARGUMENTS

The subject of threats posed by media concentrations has frequently and recurrently been discussed at the European level. In fact, as McQuail and Siune observe, 'the history of [the whole] European media policy can to a certain degree be regarded as a continued debate about the effects, results and consequences of media concentration'.[86] However, the overall result of these

83. Gibbons, T., 'Concentrations of Ownership and Control in a Converging Media Industry', 160.
84. Humphreys, P., 'The EU and Audiovisual Regulation: An Agency for De-regulation', 2005, http://regulation.upf.edu/ecpr-05-papers/phumphreys.pdf, 15–16.
85. European Broadcasting Union, 'EBU Comments on the Charter of Fundamental Rights', 11 May 2000.
86. McQuail, D., Siune, K. (eds), *Media Policy. Convergence, Concentration and Commerce*, 191.

discussions may be summarized in one sentence: 'there has been much concern expressed, but precious little action has been taken'.[87]

The main obstacle to any positive outcome seems to be the impossibility of overcoming the conflict of priorities – Tongue notes that in the recent years, the European debate around the future of broadcasting has polarized.[88] There have been a number of arguments put forward, mainly by the big media companies themselves, against the need for a positive regulatory intervention at EU level aimed at safeguarding media pluralism.

First of all, it has been claimed that *received economic wisdom* suggests that aiming for conglomerate status is the only way for media companies to become successful and internationally competitive.[89] Large media groups may reap economies of scope and scale inherent in the media sector and exacerbated by convergence and technological change. The possession of multiple media outlets provides opportunities for cross-media promotion, allowing the sharing of information, expertise, media products and rights, and the spreading of risk. Investing in new technical systems, whether it be cable, satellite or digital TV, marketing the new services and technologies, setting up conditional access systems for pay-TV, etc., all require substantial capital sums which can only be provided without risk by large media groups.[90] Moreover, the increase in the number of transmission modes, which was not followed by the increase in the amount of available content, meant more competition between broadcasters for scarce valuable media input. This situation has significantly inflated the cost of 'premium content', i.e., the rights to popular sports events, especially football, and recently released movies. The result is that, again, only large media companies with deep pockets can afford them.[91] In summary, therefore, it indeed seems that 'a high level of international and multimedia concentration is virtually a *structural necessity* and goes hand in hand with the media market'.[92] Nowadays, when the ongoing financial crisis and recession cause media

87. Peters, B., 'Corporate Media Trends in Europe', Contribution to the CPBF conference on the 'Communications Revolutions – Who Benefits?', 2001.
88. Tongue, C., 'Culture or Monoculture? The European Audiovisual Challenge', 128; Hoffman-Riem, W., *Regulating Media. The Licensing and Supervision of Broadcasting in Six Countries*, 309.
89. Humphreys, P., 'Regulating for Media Pluralism: Issues in Ownership and Competition', in Andrew, J., Crook, M., Holmes, D., Kolinsky, E. (eds), *Why Europe? Problems of Culture and Identity, Vol. 2: Media, Film, Gender, Youth and Education* (Macmillan, 2000).
90. Humphreys, P., 'Regulating for Media Pluralism: Issues in Ownership and Competition'.
91. Humphreys, P., 'Regulating for Media Pluralism: Issues in Ownership and Competition', 1.
92. Hoffman-Riem, W., *Regulating Media: The Licensing and Supervision of Broadcasting in Six Countries*, emphasis added.

enterprises to 'steer a path trough unprecedented economic upheaval',[93] consolidation seems again to be the answer. National governments, apparently sympathetic to this type of arguments, have in the recent years tended to relax media ownership restrictions. Since the early 1990s, the increasing de-regulatory pressure and the ambition to create 'national champions' compelled countries like Germany, France and the United Kingdom to loosen their grip on the levels of media ownership and restrictions to cross-media mergers.[94]

It has also been claimed that the European Union should support the unhindered growth of media companies as leading to the creation of 'European champions' who would be capable of competing with the omnipresence of American rivals.[95] The expansion of multi-channel distribution possibilities in Europe has not been followed by a boost in programme production capacity. In fact, new commercial broadcasters produce very little of their own programmes, and since they are not subject to any public-service obligations, they have sacrificed the quality of programming and rely heavily on imports from the United States.[96] The result is a constant concern about the spiralling deficit in the balance of audiovisual trade with the United States. Allowing European media companies such as RTL Group, Bertelsmann, Vivendi Canal+ or BSkyB, to concentrate and expand is, therefore, seen as an appropriate remedy.[97] This argument was strengthened by placing the big, strong European media companies at the forefront of the Lisbon Strategy, which was designed, but failed, to make Europe the most competitive, knowledge-based economic area in the world, by 2010.[98] The current Europe 2020 Strategy has Digital Agenda for Europe as one of its flagship initiatives. Again, the emphasis is not on the public interest side of

93. Barnett, S., 'Media Ownership Policy in a Recession: Redefining the Public Interest', (2010) Interactions: Studies in Communication and Culture 1(2).
94. For instance, Germany relaxed restrictions on ownership of broadcasting companies in 1996; France loosened the limitations in the television and radio sectors in 1994; and the UK 1996 Broadcasting Act de-regulated restrictions on broadcasting and cross-media ownership, and the 2003 Communications Act further liberalised the rules; See Doyle, G., 'From "Pluralism" to "Ownership": Europe's Emergent Policy on Media Concentrations Navigates the Doldrums', (1997) The Journal of Information Law and Technology 3; Feintuck, M., Varney, M., *Media Regulation, Public Interest and the Law*, 21.
95. Ward, D., *The European Union Democratic Deficit and the Public Sphere. An Evaluation of EU Media Policy*, 69.
96. Humphreys, P., 'The Changing Nature of the Broadcast Media in Europe: Some Key Policy Issues'.
97. Ward, D., *The European Union Democratic Deficit and the Public Sphere. An Evaluation of EU Media Policy*, 89.
98. See Europa portal glossary at http://europa.eu/scadplus/glossary/lisbon_strategy_en.htm; European Commission 'Growth and Jobs' at http://ec.europa.eu/growthandjobs/index_en.htm.

the media, but more on jobs creation, boosting the economy and reaping the benefits of a digital single market.[99]

Furthermore, there are opinions that single ownership of many media outlets can actually boost pluralism and content diversity, in that the bigger media companies get, the more capable they actually become of 'protecting their independence and autonomy from political, cultural, economic and other vested interest groups in general'.[100] Whereas small, independently owned media firms may only 'pull punches when covering local car dealers, real estate, and industry'[101] only the 'big fish' can 'consistently hold big businesses and big governments accountable'.[102] It seems however, that consolidation of media markets not only fails to foster political accountability but very much to the contrary – 'it poses a very serious threat to democratic pluralism'[103] 'by concentrating control of information, ideas and opinion-forming in the hands of a limited number of media owners'.[104] Large media companies are not immune to political or other forms of pressure. In reality, as the recent 'hacking scandal' in the UK illustrates, politicians often find themselves dependent on big media corporations, and it is in fact much more difficult for those with political or economic power to influence and control larger numbers of smaller media firms.[105] Big media companies can also exercise significant political influence themselves in line with a certain viewpoint. Berlusconi's and Murdoch's media empires serve as the best examples. It has been reported that in large media companies, 'conglomerate journalism' discourages in-depth investigative reporting, and instead of journalistic integrity, it encourages company loyalty.[106]

Finally, the recent key argument against any additional positive regulation for pluralism is that the arrival of new technologies undermines the rationale for specific rules. This seems to be based on the assumption that new technologies per se bring about a significant increase in choice and diversity. According to this reasoning, the arrival of new media renders concerns about excessive media concentration obsolete, as currently there are hundreds of competing channels, and literally anyone and everyone can speak online. This argument was best summarized by James Murdoch, Deputy CEO of News Corporation, who said in 2005 that:

---

99. Europe 2020 is the EU strategy for growth and reviving the EU economy in the period 2010–2020; see http://ec.europa.eu/europe2020/index_en.htm
100. McQuail, D., Siune, K. (eds), *Media Policy. Convergence, Concentration and Commerce*, 44.
101. Kennedy, D., 'Monopoly Money', *Boston Phoenix*, 17 January 2002.
102. Kennedy, D., 'Monopoly Money'.
103. Understood in its 'internal' incarnation.
104. Humphreys, P., 'Regulating for Media Pluralism: Issues in Ownership and Competition'.
105. Humphreys, P., 'Regulating for Media Pluralism: Issues in Ownership and Competition'.
106. Lorimer, R., Scannel, P., *Mass Communications: A Comparative Introduction* (Manchester University Press, 1994); Greenslade, R., 'Their Master's Voice', The Guardian, 17 February 2003.

> The demon of powerful media companies imposing their views on the world belongs to an old James Bond movie. It always was a bit of a myth, but now it is laughable. Nobody can seriously say that there is a problem with plurality when there are hundreds of TV news channels, millions of news websites and weblogs, and the ability for citizens to access information in an unmediated way. Technology and the market are delivering the ultimate pluralism.[107]

This explosion in sources of news and information over the recent years should have 'muted concerns that a single monolithic news source could arise to dominate the media'.[108] The reality nowadays is that 'there has never been so much competition for our eyes and ears, and audiences and advertising [money] have become increasingly fragmented as a result'.[109] The increased merger activity is simply the result of traditional media operators trying to adjust to the new marketplace realities. The conclusion is that consumers face 'a bewildering and unprecedented amount of choice',[110] and the real danger lies elsewhere other than in the imaginary existence of harmful media monopolies. It is in fact the outdated and *unnecessary* restrictions in media companies' growth which limits the ability of media outlets to use resources as effectively as possible with a claimed detriment to consumers. And if the market gets too concentrated to the detriment of *consumers*, there is always competition law to address the problem.[111]

This emphasis on the development and the potential of new media has meant that the issue of ownership controls in the media sector is gradually played down. As Gibbons notes:

> there is a widespread assumption that ownership rules are related to sector structure and that, when that disappears, so does need for regulation. The disappearance of separate media sectors is associated with the development of a full 'electronic publishing' market which will operate on the same principles as the current publishing markets for which regulation is minimal.[112]

However, an increase in the number of channels does not equal an increase of providers or increase in diversity. The European Parliament pointed to this

107. Murdoch, J., 'Net Age Has No Place for Archaic TV Regulation', Financial Times, 22 September 2005.
108. Knee, J.A., 'Should We Fear Media Cross-Ownership?', (2003) Regulation 26(3).
109. Thierer, A., 'A Brief History of Media Merger Hysteria: From AOL-Time Warner to Comcast-NBC', (2009) Progress & Freedom Foundation, Progress on Point 16(25)
110. Knee, J.A., 'Should We Fear Media Cross-Ownership?'.
111. Thierer, A., 'A Brief History of Media Merger Hysteria: From AOL-Time Warner to Comcast-NBC'.
112. Gibbons, T., 'Concentrations of Ownership and Control in a Converging Media Industry', 172.

phenomenon already in 2005 in its Resolution on Television Without Frontiers Directive where it stressed that:

> particular care should be paid, in order to ensure pluralism of opinion and diversity of programme distribution, to preventing, when drafting Community or national regulations on digital switchover, the majority of new digital distribution services from falling under the control or decisive influence of large, capital-rich, multinational media groups – particularly those with interests outside the EU.[113]

The existence of numerous media outlets and multiple channels will not guarantee pluralism and diversity of content if they are owned by a handful of large media companies. This is what Arino calls the 'multi-channel paradox',[114] when the multiplication of channels simply means that 'each owner controls even more formidable communications power'.[115] Without any regulation, 'there is no guarantee that digital interactive television will be democratic and public-interest oriented'.[116] One may even risk suspecting that there is a guarantee that it will not. And James Murdoch's words are particularly telling in the face of the 'hacking scandal' which shook the United Kingdom in 2011 and which once again proved that 'the demon of powerful media companies' does not necessarily belong to an old James Bond movie …

This is why, despite the changing media environment and strong arguments in favour of liberal approach to regulating the evolving sector, there has also been continuous support for positive actions aimed at protection of media pluralism at the European level.

The Council of Europe safeguards the human right of freedom of expression and information, and hence, it has naturally approached the media concentration issue from the human rights perspective and has consistently initiated and supported positive action to protect pluralism and diversity.[117]

113. European Parliament, Resolution on the application of Articles 4 and 5 of Directive 89/552/EEC (Television without Frontiers), as amended by Directive 97/36/EC, for the period 2001–2002, P6_TA(2005)0322.

114. Arino, M., 'Competition Law and Pluralism in European Digital Broadcasting: Addressing the Gaps', (2004) 54 Communications and Strategies, 99.

115. Bagdikian, B., *The Media Monopoly*, 6th edn (Beacon Press, 2000), 223–224.

116. Noveck, B.S., 'Thinking Analogue about Digital Television? Bringing European Content Regulation into the Information Age', 42.

117. See for instance Recommendation No. R (99) 1 of the Committee of Ministers to Member States on Measures to Promote Media Pluralism, 19 January 1999; Recommendation CM/Rec(2007)2 of the Committee of Ministers to Member States on media pluralism and diversity of media content, adopted by the Committee of Ministers on 31 January 2007 at the 985th meeting of the Ministers' Deputies Council of Europe, 'Media Diversity in Europe', report by the AP-MD, Advisory Panel to the Steering Committee on the Mass Media, December 2002; Council of Europe, 'Media Pluralism in the Digital Environment', report by the Steering Committee on the Mass Media, October 2000; Council of Europe, 'Transnational Media Concentrations in Europe', report by the

Within the European Union, however, the views have been divergent.[118] On the one hand, media sector is perceived as vital because of its contribution to technological innovation, economic growth and employment. Indeed, media in general and the audiovisual sector in particular, were to play a substantial role in realizing the Lisbon Strategy which inevitably presupposed allowing European-based media companies to grow into 'European champions.' On the other hand, pluralism and diversity of the media continue to be seen as having fundamental importance for the cornerstone of democracy in Europe – the freedom of expression.[119] In numerous judgments, the European Court of Justice has proclaimed that 'in the light of Article 10 paragraph 2 [of the European Convention on Human Rights], there is a compelling public interest in the maintenance of a pluralistic radio and television system, which justifies restrictions on fundamental freedoms.'[120]

At the institutional level of the European Union, while the European Parliament and the Economic and Social Committee have concurred with the Council of Europe and consistently pressed for a regulation aimed at protection of pluralism and diversity in the European media,[121] within the European Commission, different Directorates General (**DG**) have pursued different objectives.[122] As noted by Sarikakis:

> Culture and media in European policy occupy the two ends of an ostensibly defiant relationship between motives: for the European Parliament, they become the watchdog of integration – for others and, in particular, the technocratic Directorates-General of the Commission, an economic asset.[123]

AP-MD, Advisory Panel to the Steering Committee on the Mass Media, November 2004; Council of Europe, Declaration of the Committee of Ministers on protecting the role of the media in democracy in the context of media concentration, adopted by the Committee of Ministers on 31 January 2007 at the 985th meeting of the Ministers' Deputies;

118. Klimkiewicz, B., 'Is the Clash of Rationalities Leading Nowhere? Media Pluralism in European Regulatory Policies'.
119. European Commission, 'Europe's way to the information society – An action plan', COM(94) 347 final, 19 July 1994, European Commission 'Principles and guidelines for the Community's audiovisual policy in the digital age', n. 1; see also Albarran, A.B., Mierzejewska, B.I., 'Media Concentration in the US and European Union: A Comparative Analysis'.
120. Case C-288/89, *Stichting Collectieve Antennevoorziening Gouda and others v. Commissariaat voor de Media*, ECR [1991] I-4007, para. 22; Case C-353/89, *Commission v. The Netherlands*, ECR [1991] I-4069, para. 29; Case C-148/91, *Veronica Omroep Organisatie v. Commissariaat voor de Media*, ECR [1993] I-487; paras 9 ff. Case C-23/93, *TV 10 SA v. Commissariaat voor de Media*, ECR [1994] I-4795, para. 19; Case C-368/95, *Familiapress*, ECR [1997] I-3689, paras 18 and 26.
121. See Chapter 2 below.
122. Goldberg, D., Prosser, T., Verhulst, S., *EC Media Law and Policy*, 5.
123. Sarikakis, K., 'Defending Communicative Spaces: The Remits and Limits of the European Parliament', in Harrison, J., Wessels, B. (eds), *Mediating Europe. New Media, Mass Communications, and the European Public Sphere* (Berghahn Books, 2009), 255.

Thus, the 'technocratic' DG Information Society has consistently presented a liberal approach. For example, in 1994, in the middle of a discussion on the directive on media ownership restrictions, the Bangemann High-Level Group in the DG Information Society produced a report entitled 'Europe and Information Society', known as the 'Bangemann report.'[124] The paper argued that existing national restrictions impede media companies from taking advantage of new possibilities brought about by technological change.[125] It called for allowing oligopolistic media structures, in order to enable European media companies to effectively compete with non-European (mainly American) rivals. The report is often referred to as 'a credo to guarantee freedom from regulation'[126] to European media companies. It is worth noting that until 1993 the 'father' of the report, Commissioner Bangemann, was responsible for the portfolio on media ownership. After the matter was transferred to DG Internal Market, Bangemann started openly advocating for liberalization.[127] Furthermore, in 1997 – the same year as DG Internal Market presented the second draft directive introducing restrictions to media ownership – DG Information Society again emphasized that the growth in merger activity will be a natural and inevitable consequence of convergence. In the Convergence Green Paper,[128] DG Information Society argued that only big media companies are able to 'straddle the whole value chain within the converged environment, so that the emergence of major players will inevitably rely on partnering to varying degrees'.[129] The discussion on media pluralism was missing from the convergence debate in the mid-1990s. The issue was simply regarded as already being dealt with by 'other Community action'.[130]

---

124. European Commission, High-Level Group on the Information Society, 'Europe and the Global Information Society; Recommendations to the European Council', 26 May 1994.
125. Ward, D., *The European Union Democratic Deficit and the Public Sphere. An Evaluation of EU Media Policy*, 109.
126. McQuail, D., Siune, K. (eds), *Media Policy. Convergence, Concentration and Commerce*, 216.
127. Harcourt, A., 'EU Media Ownership Regulation: Conflict over the Definition of Alternatives', (1998) Journal of Common Market Studies 36(3).
128. European Commission, Convergence of the Telecommunications, media and Information Technology, and the Implications for Regulations, towards an Information Society Approach (Green Paper); for detailed analysis of the Convergence Green Paper see Ward, D., *The European Union Democratic Deficit and the Public Sphere. An Evaluation of EU Media Policy*, 111–120.
129. European Commission, Convergence of the Telecommunications, media and Information Technology, and the Implications for Regulations, towards an Information Society Approach (Green Paper).
130. Humphreys, P., 'Regulating for Pluralism in the Era of Digital Convergence: The Issues of Media Concentration Control and the Future of Public-Service Broadcasting', the ECPR Joint Research Sessions, Mannheim, 26–31 March 1999, Workshop 24: 'Regulating Communications in the Multimedia Age'.

The Convergence Green Paper carried the message that convergence must lead to liberalization in the audiovisual sector. This conclusion was the result of the assumption that *regulatory* convergence is the inevitable outcome of *technological* convergence.[131] Therefore, the Green Paper contributed to framing the debate on media concentration in terms of deregulation 'to a level where only competition law might constrain the new media'.[132] In the end, following the failed attempt to introduce EU-level rules on media concentration, it was this initiative which led to the current policy line in the European Commission; protection of public interests such as pluralism is regarded as only secondary to encouraging convergence and progress of technology, and necessarily, dealt with only at national level.

These liberalization trends of DG Information Society have been inconsistent with DG Culture's pluralistic ideas and DG Internal Market's failure in its reconciliatory attempts to introduce more democratic values through the 'backdoor' of protecting the smooth functioning of the Internal Market has meant that differences of opinion within the Commission have persisted and even deepened over time.

Actors on the media scene are not acting in harmony either. Federations of journalists and industry associations, such as the EBU, support the Council of Europe and the European Parliament in their efforts to introduce additional EU-level rules aimed at safeguarding pluralism, diversity, freedom and journalistic ethics in media.[133] However, commercial media companies understandably advocate for a *laissez-affaire* approach to their constant endeavours to grow, and they have consistently lobbied the European Commission not to introduce any additional rules on concentration and pluralism. Tongue gives the Convergence Green Paper as an example and notes that the document 'was in reality, not drafted to rationalize the future of broadcasting and telecommunications; it was drafted to serve certain narrow commercial interests … The dominance of lobbyist's thinking in the Convergence Green Paper was blatant'.[134]

Failure to reconcile the diverging priorities of different European organizations, institutions and bodies, combined with contradictory lobbying efforts from the industry actors, has resulted in a lack of any form of regulation, despite the attempts to adopt a media concentration directive in the mid-1990s (see Chapter 2). Although, the Council of Europe continuously calls for common standards on media pluralism, this has so far not resulted in the adoption of any binding measures (see Chapter 3). As a result, only market power in the media sector is currently controlled at the European

---

131. Tongue, C., 'Culture or Monoculture? The European Audiovisual Challenge', 132.
132. Gibbons, T., 'Concentrations of Ownership and Control in a Converging Media Industry', 156.
133. Klimkiewicz, B., 'Media Pluralism: European Regulatory Policies and the Case of Central Europe', European University Institute Working Paper, RSCAS No. 2005/19, 7–8.
134. Tongue, C., 'Culture or Monoculture? The European Audiovisual Challenge', 140.

level by the EU competition law, which, 'while strong and intrusive, is limited in scope and is a poor substitute for other regulatory powers and capacities'(see Chapter 4). The AVMS Directive contains very few specific provisions aimed at counteracting growing media concentration in Europe (see Chapter 5). The issues of pluralism and diversity are largely left to be dealt with by the Member States, which often lack necessary powers, or indeed motivation, to address the problems (see Chapter 6).

In effect, the European Union has provided 'little positive integration in the audiovisual field',[135] and its impact on the broadcasting sector has been largely de-regulatory.[136] Positive integration necessitates harmonization of market correcting measures, which requires agreement in the Council of Ministers and the Parliament. Admittedly, in the sensitive field of broadcasting, this is very difficult to achieve.[137] Thus, as Klimkiewicz observes, 'the policy concerning media pluralism has been seen as one of the biggest failures of EU institutions (both the Commission and Parliament)'.[138] Arguably, the European Union still lacks the legal basis to adopt binding measures in the media pluralism field and as the interests and opinions of the Member States continue to diverge in this respect, the introduction of such a legal basis is unlikely in the near future[139] (see Chapter 7).

This book adds to and updates the body of literature discussing the need for action at the EU level specifically addressed at protection of media pluralism. It provides an overview of the current state of the EU law in the area and the social and political forces which have shaped it. The conclusion is that due to the continuing clash of rationales[140] and the lack of legal basis, binding action at the EU level aimed specifically at protection of media pluralism is unlikely in the near future. However, as Gibbons points out:

> that does not mean that pluralism concerns are irrelevant; rather *different techniques* are needed to deal with the control of material received by

135. Humphreys, P., 'The EU and Audiovisual Regulation: An Agency for De-regulation', 15–16.
136. Humphreys, P., 'The EU and Audiovisual Regulation: An Agency for De-regulation', 23, poses a question whether the impact was more de-regulatory or re-regulatory and states that this remains unclear: 'whether or not the EU's impact has been de-regulatory or re-regulatory is a question deserving further … academic research'.
137. Humphreys, P., 'The EU and Audiovisual Regulation: An Agency for De-regulation', 1.
138. Klimkiewicz, B., 'Is the Clash of Rationalities Leading Nowhere? Media Pluralism in European Regulatory Policies', 68.
139. Klimkiewicz, B., 'Is the Clash of Rationalities Leading Nowhere? Media Pluralism in European Regulatory Policies', 68.
140. Klimkiewicz, B., 'Is the Clash of Rationalities Leading Nowhere? Media Pluralism in European Regulatory Policies'.

> the audience, to ensure that a sufficient diversity of material is available.[141]

Therefore, the book ends with the discussion of alternative solutions which, together with the existing, albeit fragmented, legislative measures may provide a comprehensive answer to the continuing need for Europe to defend media pluralism with a united and strong voice (see Chapter 8). Since, as aptly observed by Haraszti in his Discussion Paper on media pluralism prepared for the Council's of Europe Commissioner for Human Rights,:

> the fact this issue is so nuanced ... should not deter anyone from attempting a clear-headed examination of the current problems and the future solutions surrounding media pluralism. Indeed, it makes that lucid analysis even more necessary.[142]

---

141. Gibbons, T., 'Concentrations of Ownership and Control in a Converging Media Industry', 170, 171 (emphasis added).
142. Haraszti, M., 'Media Pluralism and Human Rights'.

Chapter 2

European Approach to Media Concentration Regulation: The Clash of Values*

2.1. LOST BATTLE FOR A MEDIA PLURALISM DIRECTIVE IN THE 1990S

The European Parliament has consistently and strongly advocated for making the protection of pluralism and diversity the main objective of regulatory action.[1] And although it is the Commission which is indicated as the most important actor in EU policy formation, the Parliament's agenda setting role cannot be underestimated – it actually placed the issue of threats to pluralism and diversity posed by media concentrations on the European Union's agenda.[2]

In the 1980s, during the process leading to the adoption of the Television Without Frontiers Directive, the Parliament, on several occasions, requested that the European Commission either introduces limits to media

* Parts of this chapter were published by the author in the article entitled 'European Attempts to Regulate Media Concentrations. Persisting Conflict of Interests', (2004/2005) Hibernian Law Journal 5, 53–82.

1. Goldberg, D., Prosser, T., Verhulst, S., 'Regulating the Changing Media', 146.
2. Harcourt, A., 'The European Commission and Regulation of the Media Industry', (1998) Cardozo Arts & Entertainment Law Journal 16(2), 425–449.

concentration in the text of the directive, or adopts separate media concentration legislation to accompany the main liberalizing instrument. In the 1985 Resolution, the 1986 official request to the European Commission and the 1987 Barzani Report the European Parliament pressed for the legal powers for the Commission to safeguard pluralism within the context of the Television Without Frontiers Directive.[3]

These efforts did not succeed in convincing the Commission that liberalization of the media industry does not automatically lead to greater pluralism and diversity. As a result, while generally admitting in one of the recitals that it was essential for Member States to ensure the prevention of any acts which could lead to restrictions on pluralism, the Television Without Frontiers Directive contained only very limited reference to media concentration (see Chapter 5 for a more detailed discussion on this issue).

Therefore, because the Directive had the effect of liberalizing the European media market, but did not contain any limitations to the level of media concentration, media companies were free to grow and form alliances at the European level. As long as such growth was not stopped by DG Competition on market power grounds, there were no obstacles to European-wide media mergers.

The European Parliament has not, however, given up its quest to introduce harmonising legislation aimed at protection of pluralism and diversity. On the contrary, rapid growth in the number of important media mergers in the early 1990s intensified the Parliament's work and resulted in the adoption of a number of further resolutions and reports calling on the Commission to consider specific media concentration legislation.

In its 1990 Resolution on media takeovers and mergers, the European Parliament expressed its well-known view that restrictions on media concentrations are 'essential in the media sector, not only for economic reasons, but also, and above all, as a means of guaranteeing a variety of sources of information and freedom of press',[4] and stressed that a 'process of unlimited and unchecked concentration in the media threatens the right to information, editorial independence and journalists freedom'.[5] Thus, the European Union must play an active role in defending these core values. The Parliament strongly emphasized that current competition legislation alone, is not sufficient to guarantee diversity of opinion and pluralism. Moreover, in view of the European and worldwide dimension of concentration in the media, the issue cannot be only regulated at national level.[6]

Therefore, the Parliament requested the Commission to submit a proposal for effective measures to combat or restrict concentration in the

3. Harcourt, A., 'The European Commission and Regulatioin of the Media Industry'.
4. European Parliament, Resolution on media takeovers and mergers, OJ (1990) C-68/137.
5. European Parliament, Resolution on media takeovers and mergers, OJ (1990) C-68/137.
6. European Parliament, Resolution on media concentration and diversity of opinions, OJ (1992) C-284/44.

media. It seemed that the Parliament would preferably see these 'effective measures' to take the form of an anti-concentration directive aiming not only at harmonizing national provisions on the concentration of media ownership, but also at guaranteeing diversity of opinion and pluralism where the proposed concentration has a European dimension.

To this end the European Parliament made an interesting suggestion, to establish a European equivalent for national media regulatory bodies – an independent European Media Council. This Council would, among other activities, be responsible for submitting to the European Commission reports and opinions on proposed mergers that have a Community dimension.[7] The argument that mergers that have a Community dimension for competition purposes also have a Community dimension for the sake of pluralism is convincing. The role of such a body could to begin with be simply advisory and its creation, based on the consent of all Member States, would most likely not exceed the European Union's mandate.

In the 1990 Resolution, the Parliament also requested that the Commission ensure that the future legislation: (i) guarantees minimum professional standards; (ii) protects journalistic ethics; and (iii) safeguards freedom of expression for all those working in the media.[8] In addition, those Member States which do not have media ownership rules in place should be forced by the Commission to adopt them.

However, although the Commission responded to the Parliament's calls and embarked on troublesome and lengthy negotiations about the possibility of a directive on media concentration, these proposals were largely ignored. Throughout the process, initiated by the Commission's 1992 Green Paper on pluralism and media concentration in the internal market, the European Parliament continued to press for strict restrictions on European media ownership.[9] However, as will be explained in more detail in section 2.2.1 below, despite two extensive rounds of consultation and two draft directive proposals, no tangible results were produced. The Parliament lost the battle, for the second time.

As mentioned earlier, despite the lobbying against regulation by media companies supported by Member States, growing pressure from the European Parliament in the beginning of the 1990s forced the European Commission to begin analysing the possibilities for regulating media ownership at pan-European level. The history of the arduous drafting of the directive shows that the European Commission was not consistent in this process. As the media ownership portfolio travelled through Directorates

7. European Parliament, Resolution on media concentration and diversity of opinions, 60.
8. European Parliament, Resolution on media takeovers and mergers, 58.
9. European Parliament, Resolution on the European Commission's Green Paper 'Pluralism and media concentration in the internal market, 29 January 1994, OJ C-44/177; European Parliament, Resolution on concentration of the media and pluralism, 2 October 1994, OJ C-323/167.

General, until it finally landed in DG Internal Market, the emphasis and opinions were changing.

The Commission's aim was to attempt to reconcile the opposing interests and concepts of harmonization. DG Culture sought to protect pluralism and the freedom of media in Europe. DG Information Society was the advocate of extreme liberalization and consolidation in the media industry, and DG Competition has always been of a position that competition rules, in the way they are shaped, are sufficient and must remain the only tool for regulating concentrations of power in the media industry. Therefore, the Commission in its endeavour to answer the Parliament's call for media specific regulation found itself not only in between the battle of contradictory rationales for regulation voiced by media companies and Member States on the one hand, and the European Parliament supported by the European Economic and Social Committee and the Council of Europe on the other hand. It also had to face conflict within its own structures. Thus, the task lying ahead of the Commission appeared to be doomed right from the beginning.

The process of a failed attempt to introduce a media ownership directive has been extensively discussed in the existing academic literature.[10] For the purposes of this book, it is useful to recall the decisive battles of the 1990s' 'war for a media concentration directive' in order to understand the realities of the law-making process in the European Union and to realize the obstacles facing any possible future action in this field.

2.1.1. 1992 Green Paper on Media Concentration and Pluralism and Its Follow-Up

Initially, the media ownership portfolio was allocated to DG Information Society, which was at the time, chaired by Commissioner Bangemann.[11] The location influenced the outlook of the first phase of the battle for a media ownership directive and helped to shape the rationale that was chosen.

10. See, *inter alia*, Doyle, G., *Media Ownership*; Doyle, G., 'Regulation of Media Ownership and Pluralism in Europe: Can the European Union Take Us Forward?', (1998) Cardozo Arts & Entertainment Law Journal 16; Harcourt, A., *The European Union and the Regulation of Media Markets*; Harcourt, A., 'EU Media Ownership Regulation: Conflict over the Definition of Alternatives'; Hitchens, L.P., 'Media Ownership and Control: A European Approach', (1994) The Modern Law Review 57; Klimkiewicz, B., 'Is the Clash of Rationalities Leading Nowhere? Media Pluralism in European Regulatory Policies'.
11. Harcourt, A., 'EU Media Ownership Regulation: Conflict over the Definition of Alternatives', 376–377.

In December 1992, the first Green Paper entitled 'Pluralism and media concentration in the Internal Market'[12] was published. This initial response by the Commission to the European Parliament's call for specific media-ownership regulation, designed to protect pluralism, conceded that neither Community antitrust rules, nor its merger control regime were able to address the threats media concentration and multi-media ownership posed for pluralism.[13] In this regard, it seemed to coincide with the Parliament's view.

However, in reality the efforts of Commissioner Bangemann and his DG were, at the time, mainly centred on 'kick-starting' the information society and creating conditions favourable to the growth of media companies into 'European champions.'[14] Therefore, what the Green Paper was in fact concerned with was the *overregulation* of the media industry by the Member States, and hence the conclusion was that there is a need for harmonizing Member States' media ownership rules. The variance of these rules constituted an obstacle for the proper functioning of the Internal Market. This ultimately meant, it was an obstacle to the *growth* of European media companies.

As to the issue of media pluralism, the Green Paper clearly stated that 'protection of pluralism as such, is primarily a matter for the Member States', and hence there is 'no need for action at Community level'. The Community's role in this respect is merely to ensure that its own activities do not adversely affect pluralism. However, the Green Paper was happy to conclude that pluralism would most certainly be achieved through the realization of the internal market, by creating opportunities for media companies.[15] Hence, the promotion of pluralism at EU level was treated by the Green Paper as nothing more than a positive 'side effect' of the realization of the Internal Market.

Having concluded that there might be a need for action at Community level to ensure proper functioning of the Internal Market and competition, which in turn would promote pluralism, the Green Paper suggested three possible courses of action. These ranged from: (i) the proposal of no action at all at the pan-European level; (ii) the light touch of improving levels of transparency to the most radical option; (iii) positive intervention in the form of a regulation or a directive aimed at harmonizing Member States' media ownership rules.

---

12. European Commission, Pluralism and Media Concentration in the Internal market: An Assessment of the Need for Community Action (Green Paper).
13. European Commission, Communication to the Council and Parliament on Audio-visual Policy, COM(90) 78, para. 2.2.3; see Westphal, D., 'Media Pluralism and European Regulation', 463.
14. Harcourt, A., 'EU Media Ownership Regulation: Conflict over the Definition of Alternatives', 376–377.
15. Hitchens, L.P., 'Media Ownership and Control: A European Approach', 591.

The Green Paper seemed to favour the third option, i.e., positive action based on Internal Market principles which were found to be the only possible legal basis for the directive. Thus, the Green Paper stated that the need for a harmonizing directive arose, because the existing patchwork of media ownership rules across Europe caused legal uncertainty, and therefore is an impediment to cross-border investment. Thus, the situation hindered the proper functioning of the Internal Market. However, the Green Paper offered no concrete proposals as to the outlook of the eventual directive.

In general, and in accordance with Commissioner's Bangemann's views, the first Green Paper was clearly designed to pave the way for the liberalization of the industry. In fact, it was aimed at strengthening European media companies in order to allow them to compete globally. Therefore, it was not the Green Paper's intention to propose regulation preventing further concentration of European media markets.[16] This was clearly against the calls of the European Parliament, which indeed had raised the issue as a concern of pluralism.

2.1.2. 1994 'Follow-up' Green Paper

The consultation process which followed the publication of the first Green Paper culminated in a public hearing in 1993, and confirmed the existence of the greatest obstacle to any positive action – the clash of priorities and possible lack of legal basis for the European Union to legislate 'in matters of democratic concern'.[17]

The European Parliament supported by the European Economic and Social Committee, was in favour of action at EU level, but voiced serious concerns about basing it on the Internal Market and industry arguments, and treating the protection of pluralism at the EU level as a mere 'side effect'.[18]

Moreover, the public consultation confirmed the anticipated antagonism among industry actors.[19] The submissions were for the most part predictable. Member States, protecting their own sovereignty in the media sphere, generally favoured no action. Large media corporations campaigned for no change to the current situation, or else only change aimed at further liberalization. For instance, Berlusconi's Fininvest stated that 'before setting limits to ownership or creation of television networks, a positive approach

---

16. Harcourt, A., 'EU Media Ownership Regulation: Conflict over the Definition of Alternatives', 378.
17. Harcourt, A., 'Support for Regulation and Transparency of Media Ownership and Concentration – Russia, Study of European Approaches to Media Ownership', Russia, Department for International Development, 1999.
18. European Parliament, Resolution on Pluralism and Media Concentration, (1995) OJ C-166/133; The Economic and Social and Committee, Opinion on Commission Green Paper, 93/C304/07.
19. Doyle, G., 'Regulation of Media Ownership and Pluralism in Europe: Can the European Union Take Us Forward?', 451–473.

would insist on action to create the greatest possible space for freedom of enterprise and freedom of thought'.[20] BSkyB added that that while the regulation was inappropriate and premature, should it in any event be introduced, it ought to be based on the 'most liberal regime operating amongst the Community Member States'.[21] On the other side of the barricade were public organizations, bodies like the Independent Television Commission, trade union groups, associations of journalists and smaller media companies. They criticized the liberalism of the current national laws and advocated for strict regulation and explicit reference to the need to protect the pluralism of media at European level.[22]

The dispute became even bitterer in 1993 when the media ownership portfolio was moved to its 'permanent home' in DG Internal Market, then chaired by Commissioner d'Archirafi.[23] The portfolio's former 'father', Commissioner Bangemann, withdrew support for the initiative as he considered that any subsequent regulation may weaken European media companies.[24] Open conflict with DG Information Society ensued. In 1994, the aforementioned Bangemann Report revealed this 'clash of priorities' within the structures of the European Commission itself, and provided strong arguments for media companies who were opposing restrictions on media ownership.

The open conflict with DG Information Society meant that the second Green Paper, entitled 'Follow-up to the consultation process'[25] issued in 1994, embarked on an even more difficult task. This was to reconcile pluralism with the Internal Market in order to please the European Parliament, whilst at the same time trying to gain the support of Commissioner Bangemann by inscribing into the proposed harmonizing action the liberalizing arguments based on the concept of 'Information Society.' To this end, the Green Paper 'declared itself to be both a follow-up to the 1992 Green Paper and an initial response to the Bangemann Report'.[26]

Therefore, justification for the need of Community action was supplemented. This time the Green Paper stated that national laws on media

---

20. Fininvest Comunicazioni, 'Considerations on the Advisability of Action at EC Level on Ownership and Control of Concentrations in the Communications Sector', March 1993, quoted in Hitchens, L.P., 'Media Ownership and Control: A European Approach', 596.
21. Hitchens, L.P., 'Media Ownership and Control: A European Approach', 596–597.
22. Hitchens, L.P., 'Media Ownership and Control: A European Approach', 591.
23. Harcourt, A., *The European Union and the Regulation of Media Markets*, 72.
24. Harcourt, A., 'EU Media Ownership Regulation: Conflict over the Definition of Alternatives', 378.
25. European Commission, Communication from the Commission to the Council and the European Parliament, 'Follow-Up to the Consultation Process Relating to the Green Paper on Pluralism and Concentration in the Internal Market – An Assessment of the Need for Community Action', COM(94) 353 final.
26. Harcourt, A., 'EU Media Ownership Regulation: Conflict over the Definition of Alternatives', 73.

ownership must be harmonized, because the current patchwork not only causes lack of legal certainty for the media industry and impedes cross-border investment, but also constricts the growth of the Information Society within the Internal Market.

Second, although the Green Paper was still mainly concerned with enhancing the competitiveness of European media firms, it no longer stressed liberalization as its primary objective. Instead it emphasized the need to harmonize the Member States' media ownership laws, without stating whether it would be following the lesser or greater regulated Member State.[27] This adhered more closely to the Internal Market framework of the DG that was responsible for the portfolio.

At around the same time, it was obvious that leaving pluralism concerns completely aside would result in protests from the European Parliament. This would leave little chance of the Parliament supporting a directive based solely on Internal Market principles. The lack of insistence on harmonization aimed at liberalization of national media ownership rules was most likely aimed at quietening down the worries of the European Parliament and other supporters of the pluralistic framework for regulation. With the increased decision making powers of the European Parliament, conferred on it by the Maastricht Treaty, its support for the initiative became crucial. In particular considering the delay in the adoption of the Voice Telephony directive[28] caused by the Parliament's non-hesitation to use the new powers. The first draft for the Voice Telephony directive was proposed by the Commission in 1992. However, in 1994 the European Parliament used for the first time the veto powers granted to it by the Maastricht Treaty and rejected the proposal for the directive. Only after the Commission presented a revised draft, it was adopted in 1995.[29]

As well as attempting to reconcile all conflicting interests, the 'Follow-up' Green Paper was also more concrete than the 1992 Green Paper, in that it discussed the possible policy instruments and in particular the use of audience share to measure media concentration. This was, in one way or another, a form of bowing down to DG Competition. To this end, the Commission ordered two technical studies on possible policy instruments.

27. Harcourt, A., 'EU Media Ownership Regulation: Conflict over the Definition of Alternatives', 380.

28. Directive 98/10/EC of the European Parliament and of the Council of 26 February 1998 on the application of open network provision (ONP) to voice telephony and on universal service for telecommunications in a competitive environment, now repealed by Directive 2002/21/EC of the European Parliament and of the Council of 7 March 2002 on a common regulatory framework for electronic communications networks and services (Framework Directive).

29. Bekkers, R., *Mobile Telecommunications Standards: UMTS, GSM, TETRA, & ERMES* (Artech House, 2001), 95; See also Sauter, W., 'The Rejection of the ONP Voice Telephony Directive by the European Parliament', (1994) Utilities Law Review 5, 176.

One was on the 'Feasibility of using audience measures to assess pluralism'[30] and the other was on the definition of 'media controller'.[31] The second round of consultation was launched after this, with a questionnaire and both reports circulated to interest groups.

The work on the initiative was, however, difficult. The rejection and withdrawal of the first draft directive from the College of Commissioners led to a surprising decision by Commissioner d'Archirafi not to pursue the idea. Over the next two years, the idea was not completely forgotten, only thanks to the staff of DG Internal Market who carried on the work despite the lack of support from their own Commissioner.[32] Things started looking more encouraging in 1995, when after the induction of the new Commission, Commissioner d'Archirafi was replaced by Commissioner Monti. The staff of DG Internal Market responsible for media ownership portfolio gained an 'outspoken ally'.[33] Monti made the media ownership initiative his priority and launched a third consultation with interest groups.

Understanding the importance of the Parliament's support, DG Internal Market started incorporating 'arguments of the pluralist frame' into the draft directive.[34] The media ownership draft had become much tighter and was ambitiously aimed at reconciling the opposing economic and democratic interests by attempting to 'inscribe the ... quest for pluralism in the logic of the Internal Market'.[35] Monti's objective was to lobby for support from the fiercest promoters of pluralism – the European Parliament's Committee on Culture, Youth, Education and the Media (hereinafter the Culture Committee).[36] On 26 September 1995, Commissioner Monti delivered a speech in which he told the Culture Committee:

> I have to repeat once again that there is no contradiction between the objective of pluralism and that of the internal market. Indeed, the internal market cannot operate smoothly unless an equivalent level of protection of pluralism obtains throughout the Community. In the absence of common rules, Member States will always be free to erect

---

30. Goodhall, Alexander & O'Hare (GAH), Feasibility of Using Audience Measures to Assess Pluralism (1997).
31. European Institute for the Media (EIM), 'Transparency of Media Control'(1994).
32. Harcourt, A., 'EU Media Ownership Regulation: Conflict over the Definition of Alternatives', 380.
33. Harcourt, A., 'EU Media Ownership Regulation: Conflict over the Definition of Alternatives', 382; Harcourt, A., *The European Union and the Regulation of Media Markets*, 76.
34. Harcourt, A., *The European Union and the Regulation of Media Markets*, 81.
35. Beltrame, F., 'Lawmaking in the European Union', paper prepared for the W.G. Hart Legal Workshop, Institute of Advanced Legal Studies, 1996.
36. Harcourt, A., 'The European Commission and Regulation of the Media Industry', 437.

> legal barriers and thus discharge themselves of their responsibility to protect pluralism at Community level.[37]

At that stage, after four years of consultation, Commissioner Monti believed that he had managed to reconcile the quests to level the playing field across the Community, for Information Society and for the protection of pluralism.[38] Therefore, DG Internal Market felt confident that it had support for its harmonizing action from the media industry, the Member States and the European institutions.

2.1.3. THE 1996 DRAFT DIRECTIVE PROPOSAL

In July 1996, the first proposal for a directive on media concentration materialized. With a working title 'Directive on media concentration and pluralism', the act introduced a 25% upper limit of audience share at regional level, 14%–15% at national level and 10% at European level. The percentages of audience share applied both to mono- and cross-media ownership.

The draft directive did not distinguish between markets of different sizes – the same fixed upper limits for media ownership would apply to markets at the local, regional or national level. It thus seemed to have reconciled the diverging priorities. It would introduce a level playing field and legal certainty for media companies and provide 'equality of pluralism for all European consumers'.[39]

However, Commissioner Monti's confidence in support from interested parties proved to be somewhat premature. The draft was resubmitted three times to the College of Commissioners and eventually failed to gain their support. In July, when the first draft was presented, Commissioner Bangemann, not surprisingly, found it too stringent. In September, the resubmitted draft was opposed by the Culture Commissioner Oreja who could not agree with the fact that the directive was not based on the principle of pluralism.[40] In October, the European Parliament's Culture Committee in its Tongue Report severely criticized the draft for the same reasons.[41] Finally, after yet another resubmission in December, both Bangemann and Oreja continued opposing the draft each on different and very much diverging grounds[42] – that it was too stringent and too lenient, respectively. The fate of the 1996 draft had thus been decided.

---

37. Monti, M., 'Pluralism and Media Concentration', speech to the European Parliament's Committee on Culture, Youth, Education and the Media, 26 September 1995.
38. Harcourt, A., 'The European Commission and Regulation of the Media Industry', 437.
39. Doyle, G., 'From "Pluralism" to "Ownership": Europe's Emergent Policy on Media Concentrations Navigates the Doldrums', 6.
40. Harcourt, A., 'The European Commission and Regulation of the Media Industry', 438.
41. Harcourt, A., 'The European Commission and Regulation of the Media Industry', 438.
42. Harcourt, A., *The European Union and the Regulation of Media Markets*, 82.

2.1.4. The 1997 Draft Directive Proposal

Commissioner Monti had no other choice but to embark on the conciliation process with two unconvinced Commissioners. To the surprise of many, he managed to win the support of both, and the fourth draft of the directive, submitted in March 1997, achieved a majority of vote at the College of Commissioners.[43] The victory, however, was bitter-sweet.

Fighting for the support at any price, DG Internal Market had to give up many of its original ambitions. First of all, with the title of the draft directive changed to 'Media ownership in the Internal Market', pluralism seemed to have disappeared from the primary objectives of the harmonizing action. Second, the upper limits for media ownership were also amended. Only the national-level limitations were retained, and they were divided into an upper limit of 30% of audience share for mono-media ownership (for radio and television broadcasters in their own transmission areas) and upper limit of 10% for multi-media ownership (total media ownership in a Member State). The limits of 25% at regional level and 10% on the European level were abandoned. Moreover, Member States were given the right to exclude any broadcaster from the limits, provided that they were not simultaneously infringing the limits in more than one Member State, and that other 'appropriate measures' were taken to secure pluralism. A special opt-out was also introduced for public service broadcasters.

The introduction of a 'flexibility clause' such as this, meant that DG Internal Market's withdrawal from the initial goal, of imposing a fixed minimum level of diversity of ownership for all European markets brought the whole rationale for the legislation into question.[44] While the proposal in theory provided a uniform set of limits to media ownership and prevented Member States from introducing more restrictive rules, the introduction of the 'flexibility clause' in practice resulted in the preservation of status quo. Member States could exclude media companies from the limits and hence keep the previously existing lower restrictions of media ownership. The legal uncertainty remained. In this sense, the 1997 Draft Directive came as a disappointment for the supporters of regulation, as ultimately the initial objectives of harmonization were left unaccomplished. Moreover, the Commission gave up its initial ambitions in order to boost support for the draft, and unfortunately this did not materialized either.

The last act of this heavily politicized play was performed by several large media companies.[45] They targeted the President of the European

43. Harcourt, A., *The European Union and the Regulation of Media Markets*, 82; Harcourt, A., 'EU Media Ownership Regulation: Conflict over the Definition of Alternatives', 386.
44. Doyle, G., 'Regulation of Media Ownership and Pluralism in Europe: Can the European Union Take Us Forward?'.
45. In particular News International, Springer, ITV and CLT; see Harcourt, A., 'The European Commission and Regulation of the Media Industry', 439.

Commission, Jacques Santer, with intense lobbying against the draft directive. In addition, German Chancellor Helmut Kohl, in a letter to President Santer, dated August 1997, expressed 'his resistance to the entire project of common regulation, arguing that it is a matter for national regulation'.[46] Commissioner Monti and his DG Internal Market were ultimately defeated when President Santer officially expressed his objection to the initiative. Thus, it was the high level political considerations which decided the fate of the five-year long saga of harmonizing efforts.

2.1.5. Reasons for the Failure to Adopt the Media Concentrations Directive

DG Internal Market in the mid 1990s proved itself to be a failure in terms of conciliating the two worlds – advocates of even further liberalization and the defenders of structural safeguards for media pluralism. Striving for support for harmonization, DG Internal Market undertook the ambitious task of attempting to reconcile the opposing economic and democratic interests. As economic welfare and pluralism are separate rather than conterminous goals,[47] their reconciliation required making trade-offs which from the beginning seemed very difficult, and eventually proved to be impossible. As noted by Doyle, 'the failure to move forward decisively on one or another of these options may be attributed, in large measure, to the range of conflicting opinions within Europe about the aims and the substance of a collective policy on media ownership'.[48]

Commercial media companies were prepared to support the harmonization of national media ownership rules, but only insofar as it went 'downwards'. They agreed with the aim to level the playing field, but only by relaxing or even abolishing national restrictions. In the first draft of the directive, however, the Commission proposed fixed percentages for permissible levels of media ownership.

Moreover, the introduction of fixed limits regardless of the size of the market was possibly not a prudent thing to do. Different markets can support different levels of diversity of ownership.[49] Smaller countries, for example Finland or Ireland, can only support two broadcasters, and the introduction of a third would be too costly and economically impractical. However, the proposed limits would, in some larger markets, allow even further growth of the media companies than national laws actually permitted. Finally, disregard for the division between national and local markets could result in the

46. Cavallin, J., 'European Policies and Regulations on Media Concentration', 9.
47. Organisation for Economic Co-operation and development (OECD), 'Media Mergers', 9.
48. Doyle, G., 'Regulation of Media Ownership and Pluralism in Europe: Can the European Union Take Us Forward?'.
49. Doyle, G., 'From "Pluralism" to "Ownership": Europe's Emergent Policy on Media Concentrations Navigates the Doldrums', 6.

situation whereby a media supplier with a local ownership of above 30%, but national ownership below that limit would be treated just as severely as a 'media tycoon', with a national level of media ownership above 30%.

The 'flexibility clause', introduced in the 1997 Draft, was an attempt by DG Internal Market to remove these concerns and please the media industry. However, whilst this solved one set of problems, it created another. First of all, the opposition of the European Parliament, which has always pressed for robust limits for media ownership as a guarantee for pluralism, was unavoidable. Second, the 'flexibility clause' brought back the legal uncertainty for the media industry, which the Commission had intended to fight in the first place. Without European legislation potential investors could at least be certain that only national laws would apply.[50] Therefore, if adopted, the directive would have actually worsened the situation.

Nonetheless, one must not forget that the ultimate failure of the harmonizing initiative was due to high level political resistance which emerged during the last stage of the process.[51] The inability of the Commission to reconcile opposing interests certainly fuelled this political opposition, but it is doubtful that it would ever be eliminated, even if the 'golden solution' could be found. Humphreys notes that:

> The EC's 'non-policy making' on the thorny issue of 'pluralism' was ultimately to be explained by the fact that it was unable to override both the determined resistance of influential Member States (notably Germany) and powerful vested interests in the media field (like the European Publishers Council and large media corporations).[52]

Failure to enact a media concentration directive, which exemplifies 'the EU's liberal bias towards negative integration',[53] has exposed the European Union to serious criticism. It has been characterized by Doyle as a 'lost opportunity to provide Community-wide action at a time when a directive in this area appears both necessary and urgent'.[54] The Commission's approach to the issue has often been described as 'fraught with inconsistencies, featuring an endless stop-go-stop modus operandi'.[55] This is claimed to have granted

---

50. Doyle, G., 'From "Pluralism" to "Ownership": Europe's Emergent Policy on Media Concentrations Navigates the Doldrums', 8.
51. Ward, D., *The European Union Democratic Deficit and the Public Sphere. An Evaluation of EU Media Policy*, 77.
52. Humphreys, P., 'The EU and Audiovisual Regulation: An Agency for De-regulation', 16.
53. Humphreys, P., 'The EU and Audiovisual Regulation: An Agency for De-regulation', 16.
54. Doyle, G., 'Towards a Pan-European Directive? From Concentrations and Pluralism to Media Ownership', (1998) Communications Law 3(1), 14; see also Ward, D., *The European Union Democratic Deficit and the Public Sphere. An Evaluation of EU Media Policy*, 77.
55. Kaitatzi-Whitlock, S., 'Pluralism and Media Concentration in Europe: Media Policy as Industrial Policy', (1996) European Journal of Communication 11(4), 477.

strategically precious time to already dominant players, and resulted in irreversible market concentration.[56]

Indeed, many media mergers of the 1990s have allegedly taken place in order to avoid restrictions, which would have been introduced by the directive.[57] Therefore, the Commission has not only failed to prevent future mergers, in addition, the lengthy discussions regarding the introduction of the directive, actually caused the market to concentrate even further without any negative implications for media companies. The result is that the liberalized European market for audiovisual services coupled with the lack of any pan-European instrument counteracting excessive concentration on the supra-national scale, encouraged media companies to concentrate and expand internationally. Apart from the European merger control rules, which are not without boundaries (see Chapter 4 below for detailed analysis), there is currently no EU instrument in place specifically designed to deal with pluralism issues.

Year 2003 marked an episodic come back to the subject during what was much broader consultation on the White Paper on Services of General Interest.[58] The Commission used this opportunity to respond to the European Parliament, which had requested that the Commission return to the issue of media concentration in its 2002 Resolution. Despite admitting that concentration of the media sector was progressing,[59] the White Paper returned the 'no apparent need's' well as the more and more frequent 'no competence's' the answers to media concentration and pluralism concerns. This was despite several interesting submissions in the consultation process which suggested creating a legal basis that would take pluralism issues into account in the application of Community competition rules.

2.2. CURRENT POLICY LINE

2.2.1. European Parliament: Quest Continues

The lost battle for the media ownership directive resulted in the current lack of any provisions in secondary EU legislation that would be aimed specifically at safeguarding pluralism in the media sector. Out of the two opposite policy lines pursued by the Commission in the mid 1990s, the

56. Kaitatzi-Whitlock, S., 'Pluralism and Media Concentration in Europe: Media Policy As Industrial Policy', 477.
57. McQuail, D., Siune, K. (eds), *Media Policy. Convergence, Concentration and Commerce*, 203.
58. European Commission, 'Services of General Interest (White Paper)', COM(2004) 374 final.
59. European Commission, 'Services of General Interest, (Green Paper)', COM(2003) 270 final, 22 and 45.

convergence project prevailed. From the late 1990s onwards, the EU agenda concerning broadcasting regulation was overtaken by a debate about the appropriate methods of stimulating and reaping the benefits of the convergence of broadcasting, telecoms and IT,[60] leaving concerns of pluralism for Member States to address.

Nevertheless, the European Parliament, in accordance with its democratic character and vocation, is not stopping in its efforts to bring the issue of media concentration legislation, back at the European Union's agenda.[61] It regularly calls for the Commission to return to discussions on positive action in this area. In the 2002 Resolution on media concentration,[62] the Parliament noted that the media market had changed considerably since the issue was last discussed at European level, in the mid 1990s. Therefore, it called on the Commission to present an updated Green Paper by the end of 2003. The Parliament also asked the Commission to consider the possibility of a European-level regulatory framework that would safeguard freedom of expression and pluralism in the media industry and to preserve and encourage cultural diversity. Most importantly, however, this time the Parliament insisted on changing the Treaty in order to introduce a clear legal basis for the Commission's action in this field. To this end, the Parliament called on the Commission to submit to the European Convention, which was at the time preparing a draft Constitution for the European Union, an appropriate proposal for a legal basis for the EU action in the area of media freedom and pluralism. The Commission addressed this issue in the Green Paper on Services of General Interest,[63] in which it sought the views of interested parties, as to whether the Commission should re-examine the need for Community action in the area of media concentration. This was actually very good timing for such an initiative. The work on the European Constitution was ongoing, and there was still time to lobby for the introduction of a legal basis for media ownership regulation. However, in the report on public consultation in the Green Paper and then in the subsequent White Paper on Services of General Interest[64] of May 2004, the Commission's response was a brief statement that there is 'little support for a Community initiative on media pluralism' and the issue 'should be left to Member States'.

---

60. Humphreys, P., 'The EU and Audiovisual Regulation: An Agency for De-regulation', 17.
61. See Klimkiewicz, B., 'Is the Clash of Rationalities Leading Nowhere? Media Pluralism in European Regulatory Policies'; Sarikakis, K., 'Defending Communicative Spaces: The Remits and Limits of the European Parliament'
62. European Parliament, Resolution on media concentration, 20 November 2002, OJ (2004) C-25E/205.
63. European Commission, 'Services of General Interest (Green Paper)', 83, 22 and 45.
64. European Commission, 'Services of General Interest (White Paper)', 2.

Notwithstanding this setback, the European Parliament continued its quest. In its Report of 5 April 2004 on the risks of violation, in the EU and especially in Italy, of freedom of expression and information,[65] the Parliament deplored the fact that the protection of pluralism was no longer included in the priorities of the European Commission's strategic communications on the audiovisual sector. The report also disagreed with the fragmentation of EU regulation in the media sector. The Parliament, therefore, put forward a number of very concrete demands aimed at appeasing the situation. Not only, for yet another time, did the Parliament call on the Commission to submit a communication on the state of media pluralism in the EU and a proposal for a directive to safeguard media pluralism in Europe. The Commission was also asked to make the protection of media diversity the priority of EU competition law and to render the mere possession of a dominant position by a media company as harmful to pluralism. The Parliament also endorsed the introduction of a 'pluralism' test to the EC Merger Regulation[66] and proposed lowering the 'European dimension' turnover thresholds for media mergers. The most controversial suggestion however, concerned the proposal to adopt European legislation that would prohibit political figures or political candidates from having major economic interests in the media and would prevent any conflict of interest. The European Commission's only reaction to the report was to once again emphasize the lack of a legal basis for a European legislative measure,[67]

The most recent emanations of the Parliament's continuing quest to keep media pluralism concerns on the EU agenda are (i) the Resolution on concentration and pluralism in the media in the European Union (2008),[68] (ii) the June 2010 Declaration[69] and teaming up with European Alternatives in calling for a European Citizens Initiative (ECI) to protect media pluralism, and (iii) the Resolution on media law in Hungary (2011).[70]

In the 2008 Resolution on concentration and pluralism in the media in the European Union, the Parliament yet again urged the Commission and the Member States to safeguard media pluralism, to ensure that all EU citizens can access free and diversified media in all Member States and to recommend improvements when needed. It also encouraged the disclosure of

65. European Parliament, 'Report on the risks of violation, in the EU and especially in Italy, of freedom of expression and information'.
66. Council Regulation (EC) No. 139/2004 of 20 January 2004 on the control of concentrations between undertakings (EC Merger Regulation), OJ (2004) L24/1.
67. See, for instance, Written Question P-1625/05 by Dimitrios Papadimoulis (GUE/NGL) to the Commission, Subject: Media concentration.
68. European Parliament, Resolution on concentration and pluralism in the media in the European Union, 25 September 2008 (2007/2253).
69. European Parliament, Written Declaration on financing media sector and ensuring the right of information and freedom of expression, 14 June 2010 (033/2009).
70. European Parliament, Resolution on media law in Hungary, 10 March 2011 (2011/0094).

ownership of media outlets to help to understand the aims and background of the media owner.

The 2010 Written Declaration on financing media sector and ensuring the right of information and freedom of expression observed that 'Media pluralism, as a prerequisite for European democracy, is not necessarily ensured by competition and technological progress, and the media sector is facing a historical crisis.' It called for financial support to help the European media sector survive the crisis and urged the Member States to 'support independent journalism free of any political and commercial interference at national level', as well as 'to monitor and ensure full compliance with the principle of media independence by fully enforcing Article 11'of the Charter.

In an interesting move, a group of MEPs teamed up with the civil society group European Alternatives and with the Alliance International de Journalists, in calling for a European Citizens Initiative (ECI) to protect media pluralism.[71] The Citizens' Initiative, as regulated by Article 11 of the Treaty on European Union,[72] is the first transnational instrument of participatory democracy in world history. It allows civil society coalitions to collect one million signatures in at least seven EU Member States to present directly to the European Commission a legislative proposal forming the base of a potential EU Directive.

The media pluralism ECI aims to promote the idea that the EU institutions should do more to safeguard the right to independent and pluralistic information, as stated in Article 11 of the Charter of Fundamental Rights, and to demand a directive for the improvement of anti-concentration regulation at EU level for the media and publicity sectors. The initiative is intended to be launched on 31 May 2012.[73] However, it seems that the media pluralism ECI risks being rejected as inadmissible, since citizens' initiative is possible only in a field where the Commission has the power to propose legislation. The history of the European Commission rejecting the Parliament's proposals for a directive on media pluralism on the grounds of lack of the legal basis is not very promising. Nevertheless, as stated by Niccolo Milanese, Co-President of European Alternatives, and one of the initiators of the media pluralism ECI:

> Given the multiple affronts to the media in recent years, particularly in Italy and Hungary, this ECI is crucial even though we know that it does not come exactly within the European Union's competence. The ECI is

---

71. European Alternatives, 'Launching a European Citizens' Initiative for Media Pluralism', http://www.mdiainitiative.eu/.
72. Consolidated versions of the Treaty on European Union and the Treaty on the Functioning of the European Union, OJ (2010) C-83/1.
73. See http://www.mediainitiative.eu.

> a way of making noise politically and putting pressure on the institutions to listen to the type of Europe that citizens want.[74]

The latest stimulus for the Parliament's quest for the binding EU measures on media pluralism was provided by the controversial media law adopted by Hungary, which entered into force on 1 January 2011, coincidentally on the same day that Hungary assumed the rotating six-month presidency of the Council of the European Union. The new law was intended to transpose the AVMS Directive into Hungarian law, but it seems to have gone beyond this remit. First of all, it created a media control body, called National Media and Infocommunications Authority (NMHH), comprised of members appointed by the ruling party in Parliament. In order to be able to operate in Hungary, all media organizations are required to register with the Authority. The Authority has a power to impose fines of up to EUR 700,000 on media companies for 'imbalanced news coverage', material it considers 'insulting' violating 'public morality'.[75] 'Gross' violations can result in denial of registration. The law also allows Hungarian courts to force journalists to reveal their sources 'in order to protect national security'.

In the Resolution of 10 March 2011, the European Parliament first and foremost called on the Hungarian authorities to restore the independence of media governance and halt state interference with freedom of expression. However, it also used the opportunity to once again call on the Commission to propose a legislative proposal on media freedom, pluralism and independent governance before the end of the year,

> thereby overcoming the inadequacies of the EU's legislative framework on the media, making use of its competences in the fields of the internal market, audiovisual policy, competition, telecommunications, State subsidies, the public-service obligation and the fundamental rights of every person resident on EU territory, with a view to defining at least the minimum essential standards that all Member States must meet and respect in national legislation in order to ensure, guarantee and promote freedom of information and an adequate level of media pluralism and independent media governance.[76]

Predictably, no proposal of a directive on media pluralism materialized before the end of 2011.

---

74. Mertens, E., 'European Citizens' Initiative. Will They Make It? 'EuroPolitics, 2 April 2012.
75. Human Rights Watch, 'Hungary: Media Law Endangers Press Freedom', 7 January 2011.
76. European Parliament, Resolution on media law in Hungary, 10 March 2011 (2011/0094), para. 6.

2.2.2. European Commission: Persistent Reluctance

Notwithstanding the continuing persistence of the European Parliament, the analysis of the Commission's current approach allows certain suspicion that the chances for EU action, aimed at specifically protecting media pluralism, are rather slim.

This is despite the fact that Recital 5 of the codified version of the Audiovisual Media Services Directive[77] states that:

> Audiovisual media services are as much cultural services as they are economic services. Their growing importance for societies, democracy – in particular by ensuring freedom of information, diversity of opinion and media pluralism – education and culture justifies the application of specific rules to these services.

And obviously Article 11 paragraph 2 of the European Charter of Fundamental Rights declares that 'the freedom of information and pluralism shall be respected'.

Therefore, the need for protection of media pluralism at the EU level seems to be acknowledged by the binding instruments of both primary and secondary EU law. However, does this mean that the debate on media pluralism directive could be revived in the near future? To answer this question, it is worth examining the position of the two Directorates General which are at the forefront of the debate on the future of Community action in the area of media concentrations. DG Information Society and Media and DG Competition currently provide the most prominent statements and are the driving forces on the Commission's side in discussions in this area. It is worth noting here that DG Internal Market and DG Culture, which loudly called for a media ownership directive in the 1990s, now seem to have withdrawn their voice in this respect.

2.2.2.1. DG Information Society and Media

Viviane Reding, the former Commissioner for Information Society and Media in the first Barroso Commission, was appointed by the President the 'co-ordinator for relations with the media industry' which in her words was to be 'the first such one-stop-shop for the media industry within the European Commission'.[78] In her role as the Commissioner for Information Society and Media, she spoke on numerous occasions about the approach of her

77. Directive 2010/13/EU of the European Parliament and of the Council of 10 March 2010 on the coordination of certain provisions laid down by law, regulation or administrative action in Member States concerning the provision of audiovisual media services (Audiovisual Media Services Directive) (codified version) OJ (2010) L95/2.

78. Reding, V., 'The European Commission and Media Industry: The Need for a New Partnership', Luxembourg, 5 November 2004, Opening of the European Newspaper Publishers' Association Congress.

Directorate to the issue of regulation of the media in general, and media pluralism in particular.

In one of her earlier speeches delivered on 5 November 2005 at the Congress of the European Newspaper Publishers' Association,[79] she emphasized that media pluralism is a cornerstone of democracy, and the EU and its Member States must take the action necessary to preserve it, each within its own sphere of competence. She stressed however that EU action is not only unnecessary, but also impossible since, and as emphasized by the White Paper on Services of General Interest, under the present Treaties, legislative measures against media concentration fall under the competence of Member States and it is, therefore, difficult to find a legal basis for legislative action on media ownership at EU level. Moreover, Commissioner Reding noted that even if there was a legal basis, there is simply no 'one size fits all' formula for the prevention of media concentration throughout all Member States. Therefore, there is no need and no possibility for action, and all the Commission will do is continue to carefully monitor the situation.

To alleviate the concerns that 'carefully monitor' sounds dangerously like 'do nothing', Commissioner Reding pointed to the 'wide-ranging' possibilities the EU apparently has at its disposal to foster media pluralism in the EU. The most prominent example was, unsurprisingly, the Community competition policy which, as rightly described by the Commissioner, 'plays a pivotal role in preventing the creation of dominant positions and ensuring market access'. Thus, according to Reding, this and 'other possibilities' must and will be conscientiously used to contribute to enhancing media pluralism throughout the EU. Still, one cannot help but wonder – is the prevention of a creation of a dominant position and ensuring market access really enough to guarantee pluralism? In particular, knowing that the Commission has allowed dominant positions that are near monopolies to appear in the European media markets.

Commissioner Reding indicated that with regard to one of her stated political priorities, i.e., to strengthen European content and the European content industry, 'a simple "*no action whatsoever*" approach is not really an option for the years to come'.[80] The Commission will then explore all the possibilities of using 'soft law'. Admittedly, while the use of soft law should be seriously considered not only for the media content but also media concentration issue (see Chapter 8, section 8.2), it should not be 'too soft' or it risks not changing anything, apart from raising awareness and keeping

79. Reding, V., 'The European Commission and Media Industry: The Need for a New Partnership'.

80. Reding, V., 'The European Commission and Media Industry: The Need for a New Partnership'.

matters on the agenda. Then again, perhaps this is all the European Union can and should be doing for the time being.

In general, Commissioner Reding's approach towards the media sector was characterized by three 'leitmotivs': (i) strengthening the European media industry through 'light weight' regulation; (ii) cutting the 'red tape'; and (iii) establishing the right balance between 'light weight' regulation and protection of 'common values'.

First, the ultimate priority was to help unleash all of the economic potential of the media sector.[81] According to the Reding, it had become critical to seize the opportunities offered by convergence in a competitive and global environment for the benefit of all citizens and of the EU economy as a whole. For the Commission, the principal characteristic of the European media industry at the time seemed to be that it made a key contribution to growth and employment in Europe.[82] Therefore, the most important aim for the Commission should be to have a strong European media landscape able to face up to international competition, as was the objective of the Lisbon Agenda.[83]

For that to happen, and this was the second stated priority of Commissioner's Reding, the European policy-makers should endeavour to ensure 'a modern, flexible and open regulatory environment that does not stifle, but instead encourages innovation, investment and competition'. In Commissioner Reding's own words:

> my first policy priority is to use all the means and instruments at my disposal to ensure a modern, market-oriented regulatory framework for the converging digital economy and to stimulate the availability of online content'.[84]

She added that 'this is Europe's best bet for delivering sustained growth and skilled jobs'.[85] The Barroso Commission strives for 'Better Regulation',[86] by which it means less regulation. This implies a roll-back of unnecessary or outdated legislation if it is not in line with competitiveness and jobs goals. In addition, the introduction of new binding legislation should be very carefully considered.

81. Reding, V., 'New Rules for a Convergent Multi-Media World: The Need for a "Light Touch"', IIC and Chatham House 36th Annual Conference, London, 10 October 2005.
82. Reding, V., 'Better Regulation for Europe's Media Industry: The Commission's Approach', Audiovisual Conference – Between Culture and Commerce, Liverpool, 22 September 2005.
83. Reding, V., 'Europe, the Media and European Media Policy', Congress of the Federal Association of German Newspaper Publishers, Berlin, 26 September 2005.
84. Reding, V., 'New Rules for a Convergent Multi-Media World: The Need for a "Light Touch"'.
85. Reding, V., 'New Rules for a Convergent Multi–Media World: The Need for a "Light Touch"'.
86. http://ec.europa.eu/governance/better_regulation/index_en.htm.

Against this background, Commissioner Reding saw the media industry as, first and foremost, the key contributor to growth and employment in Europe.[87] Therefore, to strengthen it even more and to allow it to grow internationally, as was the objective of the former Lisbon strategy and which continues under the current Europe 2020 strategy,[88] the Commission must make sure that media services are regulated to the least extent possible. Hence, there should be no further restrictive regulation for the media industry,[89] and self-regulation should be given preference over regulatory intervention.[90] If there is any new legislation at EU level, it should be there only 'to eliminate rules which are out-of-date, to simplify existing rules and procedures in a clear manner'.[91]

The third leitmotiv of the Commission Reding's mission was finding the best balance between a light burden on industry, aimed at encouraging successful cross-border services, and the protection of common values.[92] However, the Commission's only duty here is to propose a framework under which these shared European values are protected. In general, therefore, media policy in a broader sense should be left to the Member States. In Commissioner Reding's opinion:

> Our most important aim is to have a strong European media landscape *as an expression of media pluralism* and to face up to international competition. Media policy in Europe is in essence a national responsibility, so the European Commission can only lay down a general framework and this must be filled out by the Member States in accordance with their national traditions. Only in the case of obviously cross-border issues does the European Commission itself have a mandate to take political decisions.[93]

Commissioner Reding's Directorate General for Information Society and Media was the one responsible for overseeing the of the Television Without Frontiers Directive. In the 'Frequently Asked Questions' Memo of December 2005 the Commission was asked: 'What does the Directive do in the field of media pluralism?' The answer was that:

> The European Union is committed to protecting media pluralism as well as the right to information and freedom of expression enshrined in Article 11 of the Charter of Fundamental Rights. *Important measures to*

87. Reding, V., 'Europe, the Media and European Media Policy'.
88. Europe 2020, http://ec.europa.eu/europe2020/index_en.htm.
89. Reding, V., 'Europe, the Media and European Media Policy'.
90. Reding, V., 'New Rules for a Convergent Multi-Media World: The Need for a "Light Touch"'.
91. Reding, V., 'Europe, the Media and European Media Policy'.
92. Reding, V., 'Better Regulation for Europe's Media Industry: The Commission's Approach'.
93. Reding, V., 'Europe, the Media and European Media Policy', emphasis added.

> *ensure media pluralism at Community level are included in the Television without Frontiers Directive and are strengthened in this amending directive.*[94]

The measures 'to ensure' media pluralism in the AVMS Directive are those on the country of origin, as well as on the promotion of European and independent productions (see Chapter 5).

It is interesting to note here, that the European Parliament did not share the Commissioner's Reding view that the measures to ensure media pluralism included in the TVWF Directive were strengthened in the AVMS Directive. In the Parliament's reports on the revision of the Directive[95] and subsequent resolutions, the Parliament noted that the proposed revised Directive introduces further liberalization and less regulation, and it still contains no rules for controlling excessive media concentration. Hence, the Parliament has consistently called for measures to at least monitor media concentration at EU level. Furthermore, numerous oral and written questions from the Parliament to the Commission on why the Commission was not including the issue of media pluralism in the discussions on the revision of the directive were answered, in one short sentence by Commissioner Reding: 'under the present Treaties, legislative measures against media concentration fall under the competence of the Member States'.[96] Consequently, the AVMS Directive does mention media pluralism, but safeguards it rather indirectly (see Chapter 5 for more detailed discussion).

The most concrete response of DG Information Society under Commissioner Reding to the Parliament's calls for EU-level action on media pluralism was the so called Three-Step Approach to the issue of media pluralism launched in 2007.[97] The three steps were intended to comprise of: (i) a Commission Staff Working Paper on Media Pluralism; (ii) an independent study on media pluralism; and (iii) a Commission Communication on the indicators for media pluralism in the EU Member States, on which a broad public consultation was to take place. The Staff Working Paper published in 2007,[98] emphasizes in the first sentence that the European Union is committed to protecting media pluralism as an essential pillar of the right to information and freedom of expression enshrined in Article 11 of the Charter of Fundamental Rights, and that since the early nineties the

94. European Commission, 'The Commission Proposal for a Modernisation of the Television without Frontiers Directive: Frequently Asked Questions', 13 December 2005, MEMO/05/475, emphasis added.
95. See European Parliament's reports A6-0202/2005, A5-0251/2003, A5-0286/2001.
96. See, for instance, Written Question P-1625/05 by Dimitrios Papadimoulis (GUE/NGL) to the Commission, Subject: Media concentration.
97. See European Commission, DG Media and Information Society, 'Media Pluralism: The need for transparency, freedom and diversity in Europe's media landscape'.
98. European Commission, 'Media pluralism in the Member States of the European Union (Staff Working Document)'.

discussion on media pluralism has played an important role within the European Union. However, it is very quick to remind that the various consultations held so far, led to the conclusion that at present it would not be appropriate to submit a Community initiative on pluralism. The conclusion of the Working Paper is no different – the result of the 'Three-Step Approach' would be the identification of indicators of media pluralism in the Member States. It did not mention any possibility for a change in the European legislation and showed the Commission's reluctance to positively engage in this area.[99]

The second step – an independent study called 'Indicators for Media Pluralism in the Member States – Towards a Risk-Based Approach' was published in 2009. It was performed by a group of experts from Katholieke Universiteit Leuven, Central European University and Jönköping International Business School, accompanied by Ernst & Young Belgium. Various subcontractors (such as members of the Quality Control Team or so-called Country Correspondents) supported the research team. According to the Commission's website, the objective of the study was to 'develop a monitoring tool for assessing risks for media pluralism in the EU Member States and identifying threats to such pluralism based on a set of indicators, covering pertinent legal, economic and socio-cultural considerations'.[100]

Accordingly, the outcome of this study was a prototype for a Media Pluralism Monitor (MPM), which the Final Report prepared by the research team described as a 'risk-based, holistic, user-friendly and evolving monitoring tool'.[101] As praised by Commissioner Reding:

> The physicist Lord Kelvin said 'To measure is to know'. We need this monitoring tool because of continuing political concern about media pluralism expressed in the European Parliament and in civil society. The restructuring of the media sector under the twin impacts of new technology and economic crisis mans that the problem will grow in future. So doing nothing is not an option.[102]

The MPM uses three types of indicators (legal, socio-demographic and economic) to identify risks for media pluralism across six domains: (i) basic domain, (ii) pluralism and media ownership and control, (iii) pluralism of

---

99. Beunderman, M., 'Brussels Reluctant to Regulate National Media Rules', EUobserver, 17 January 2007; Beunderman, M., 'Brussels Wary of Rules on National Media', BusinessWeek.com, 18 January 2007.
100. Independent Study on Indicators for Media Pluralism in the Member States – Towards a Risk-Based Approach, Final Report, viii.
101. Independent Study on Indicators for Media Pluralism in the Member States – Towards a Risk-Based Approach, Final Report, ix.
102. Reding, V., 'Empowering Citizens – The Magazine Media', FAEP Gala Reception, Speech/ 09/452, 8 October 2009.

media types and genres, (iv) political pluralism in the media, (v) cultural pluralism in the media, and (vi) geographic pluralism in the media.[103]

Legal indicators cover the presence and effective implementation of policies and legal instruments that support media pluralism (such as rules on media concentration, legal safeguards guaranteeing access to media by various political, cultural or minority views or regulatory safeguards for journalistic practice). Importantly, the first legal indicator mentioned in the basic risk domain is the existence and effectiveness of a regulatory framework that guarantees the freedom of expression. As the Report rightly observes:

> an effective protection of free speech is a prerequisite for pluralism and diversity in the media, implying that the public has access to a free media system, which overall, provides balanced, full and varied information'.[104]

As the Report further explains, socio-demographic indicators determine threats to media pluralism related to socio-demographic factors such as geographic location, minority status, age or gender. Finally, the economic indicators measure the range, diversity and economic performance of media on the supply side based primarily on the number of media companies, the level of market concentration and profitability ratios.[105]

Overall, the MPM is to be a diagnostic rather that a prescriptive tool in that it facilitates the collection of information about various risks for media pluralism, but it does not prescribe remedies for the identified risks. Therefore, as the Final Report strongly emphasizes, while the MPM 'urges the application of the same analytical framework in all Member States to ensure comparability of the results obtained, it is not a call for harmonization of policies in this area'.[106] As emphasized by Commissioner Reding:

> We of course do not want a harmonising directive on ownership. The exclusive focus on ownership is in our view inappropriate in a period of structural change. A solid analysis of media pluralism must be broader and also cover combinations of political and media power. (…) I know that nevertheless some stakeholders don't like the indicators and are concerned that monitoring media pluralism will lead to unwanted regulation. They are mistaken. I firmly believe that in order to preserve

103. For a detailed discussion on MPM see Valcke, P., et al., 'The European Media Pluralism Monitor: Bridging Law, Economics and Media Studies as a First Step towards Risk-Based Regulation in Media Markets', (2010) Journal of Media Law 2(1), 85–113.
104. Independent Study on Indicators for Media Pluralism in the Member States – Towards a Risk-Based Approach, Final Report, 29.
105. Independent Study on Indicators for Media Pluralism in the Member States – Towards a Risk-Based Approach, Final Report, viii.
106. Independent Study on Indicators for Media Pluralism in the Member States – Towards a Risk-Based Approach, Final Report, ix.

> our pluralist and free societies, we need the monitoring of freedom of the media and of media pluralism. Only this will demonstrate in a convincing manner that legislation is really not needed at EU level.[107]

The third step – the Commission Communication on indicators for media pluralism in EU Member States was not taken under the Commissioner's Reding term. The initial plan was to hold public consultation following the publication of the Communication and, should the consultation reveal such a need, to commission a second study in order to systematically apply the media pluralism indicators to all EU Member States.

The overall conclusion is that the aim of the Commission's 'Three-step-approach' was to finally respond to the Parliament's decade of calls for positive action. It was no longer possible to ignore the persisting pressure for concrete measures. However, even though the Media Pluralism Monitor may prove a useful tool in monitoring media pluralism in the Member States, there will be no change in EU legislation resulting from the 'Three-step-approach' exercise.

In her 2009 speech, Commissioner Reding commented:

> I know well that Media Pluralism is a perennial favourite for many members of the European Parliament. I personally am rather sceptical about any harmonised 'one size fits all' approach to media governance in the EU. That's why I set out the three step plan for monitoring media pluralism. Note: I said monitoring, not regulating.[108]

With regard to the third step of the plan, in 2009 Commissioner Reding commented that it would be presented by the next Commission.[109] However, it seems that under the new Commissioner Kroes, the third step had been abandoned altogether. Instead, two new advisory bodies have been created: the High Level Group on Media Freedom and Pluralism and a Centre for Media Pluralism and Media Freedom within the Robert Schuman School of the European University Institute.

The first meeting of the High Level Group on Media Freedom and Pluralism, which is to be fully independent from the Commission, was convened by Commissioner Kroes on 11 October 2011.[110] The group's remit is to draw up a report for the Commission with recommendations for the respect, protection, support and promotion of pluralism and freedom of the media in Europe. The findings will be made public. The Commission

107. Reding, V., 'Empowering Citizens – The Magazine Media'.
108. Reding, V., 'Empowering Citizens – The Magazine Media'.
109. Reding, V., 'Empowering Citizens – The Magazine Media'.
110. European Commission, 'High-level group to discuss freedom and pluralism of the media across the EU', Press Release IP/11/1173, 11 October 2011.

indicated that the group should analyse and provide recommendations on six basic issues: (i) limitations to media freedom arising from political interference (state intervention or national legislation); (ii) limitations to media independence arising from private and commercial interference; (iii) the question of the concentration of media ownership and its consequence for media freedom/pluralism and on the independence of journalists; (iv) existing or potential legal threats to the protection of journalists' rights and their profession in Member States; (v) the role and independence of regulatory authorities; (vi) existing or potential measures in favour of quality journalism, ethics and media accountability, within the respective competences of national, EU and international authorities.

The Centre for Media Pluralism and Media Freedom within the Robert Schuman School of the European University Institute was established by the Commission in November 2011 with a EUR 600,000 grant.[111] The aim of the Centre is to develop new ideas on how to ensure a highly diverse and free media, and work to enhance the quality of the reflection on media pluralism in Europe. It will carry out four specific activities: theoretical and applied research (working paper series, policy studies, observatory on media pluralism), debates, education and training activities (academic seminars, summer school) and dissemination of results and outcomes.[112]

The biggest test for Commissioner's Kroes stance on media freedom and pluralism in Europe came in the form of the already mentioned new Hungarian media law which entered into force on 1 January 2011. On 7 January 2011 Commissioner Kroes and President Barroso met with the Hungarian Prime Minister, Viktor Orbán, to seek clarification on the law. The Hungarian government committed to change the Hungarian Media law on four points: (i) obligation of balanced coverage; (ii) country of origin principle; (iii) registration requirements; and (iv) offensive content. The agreed amendments were adopted by the Hungarian Government on 7 March 2011.[113]

However, these changes are still regarded as insufficient and Commissioner Kroes commented in February 2012 that she continues to 'have grave concerns about the current situation'.[114] For the first time, the belief in leaving the matter fully in the competence of the Member States has been put into question. As pointed out by Kroes: 'While there is legally member-state

---

111. European Commission, 'Commission awards €600,000 for new Centre for Media Pluralism and Media Freedom', Press Release IP/11/1307, 7 November 2011.
112. European Commission, 'Commission awards €600,000 for new Centre for Media Pluralism and Media Freedom', Press Release IP/11/1307, 7 November 2011.
113. European Commission, 'Commission awards €600,000 for new Centre for Media Pluralism and Media Freedom', Press Release IP/11/1307, 7 November 2011.
114. 'EU Still Has "Grave Concerns" on Hungary Media Laws, Kroes Says', Bloomberg, 9 February 2012.

discretion in this area, I am worried when that discretion is exercised to the detriment of media pluralism'.[115]

The European Commission has, therefore, indicated that if Hungary does not remove the provisions from the new media law which endanger media freedom and pluralism, the Commission is ready to use its 'nuclear option' – Article 7 of the Treaty on European Union.[116] Article 7 gives the Council a discretionary power to determine that there is a 'serious and persistent breach' or a risk of a breach of fundamental Treaty principles. The ultimate penalty may be the suspension of the guilty Member State's voting rights in the Council.

Commissioner Kroes also informed Hungary that it should ask the Council of Europe for an opinion on the media laws and to implement its recommendations. While the High Commissioner for Human Rights published his opinion on the Hungarian media law (see Chapter 3 section 3.2), according to the Council's of Europe spokesman: 'Hungary has yet to request an opinion from us on media'.[117]

While the stance of Commissioner Kroes towards Hungary seems firm and unapologetic, the situation revealed what the Parliament has stressed on several occasions with regard to Italy – in the instances of Member States choosing to disrespect the principle of media pluralism, the European Union is effectively powerless. Kroes directing Hungary to ask for the Councils of Europe opinion and Hungary disregarding this direction is particularly telling.

2.2.2.2. DG Competition

The belief in the Member States' potential becomes even more apparent with the analysis of DG Competition's position.

Former Competition Commissioner Mario Monti conceded on numerous occasions that competition rules and free markets can only achieve productive and allocative efficiency. Which, in the media sector is 'far from the only public policy objective that we as a society want to pursue', and that 'plurality and diversity – fundamental to the health of an open, democratic society – may not be assured by a simple free market approach'.[118] Nevertheless, Monti believed that pluralism concerns could be *partly* ensured

115. Bloomberg, 'EU Still Has "Grave Concerns" on Hungary Media Laws, Kroes Says', Bloomberg, 9 February 2012.
116. EUObserver, 'Kroes Threatens Nuclear Option against Hungary', 9 February 2012.
117. EUObserver, 'Kroes Threatens Nuclear Option against Hungary', 9 February 2012.
118. Monti, M., 'Does EC Competition Policy Help or Hinder the European Audiovisual and Telecoms Industries?'.

by the competition rules themselves. For instance cases like *RTL/Veronica/ Endemol,*[119] *MSG*[120] or *Bertelsmann/Kirch/Premiere*[121] were sufficiently problematic that the economic concerns about market concentration led to their prohibition. The application of the competition rules, therefore, ensured the maintenance of media plurality.

However, and as admitted by Monti himself, problems start in cases where a concentration triggers legitimate fears about dangers to pluralism, but the market power is less than would trigger competition concerns. Monti's, and thus DG Competition's, answer to this is that Member States are free to implement additional anti-concentration rules. Moreover, where they are seeking to ensure media plurality, Article 21(4) of the Merger Regulation allows them to prevent mergers that would otherwise be approved under the EC competition rules. Indeed, Article 21(4) provides a theoretical mechanism for protection of public interest values not taken into account in the Commission's competition analysis. However, with regard to media pluralism this mechanism has only been used in one case in 1994.[122] Thus, even though there have been instances where it could have been used (see Chapter 4, 4.1 below for a more detailed discussion on Article 21(4)), it seems more like a theoretical mechanism, rarely utilized in practice.

Nevertheless, Monti's approach to the public policy objectives in the media sector was that they are entirely laudable, fully supported by the Commission and consistent with the Community's legal framework. Furthermore, the division of powers between the Commission and the Member States is assumed to work efficiently.

This has been further developed by Herbert Ungerer, the former Head of Unit responsible for media within DG Competition and the most outspoken official from DG Competition on the issue of media pluralism. It is worth noting at the outset, that in his numerous speeches the recurrent theme was that the debate at the European level over the last decade has led to a broad consensus on basic goals for the media sector that are widely shared across the EU. These basic goals are, first of all, a *guarantee* for pluralism,[123] as the basic public interest test for the media sector. According to Ungerer, pluralism is the 'uncontested primary public goal in the media sector'.[124] The second goal is the *maintenance of cultural diversity*, standing for the preservation of national identities. And the final aim is the *widening of choice*, where the task is to give access to new media. In Ungerer's opinion, these goals are in fact achieved at the EU level, in 'a decentralized

119. Case M.553, *RTL/Veronica/Endemol*, 20 September 1995.
120. Case M.469, *MSG Media Service,* 9 November 1994.
121. Case M.993, *Bertelsmann/Kirch/Premiere,* 27 May 1998.
122. Case IV/M.423, *Newspaper Publishing*, 14 March 1994.
123. Ungerer, H., 'Impact of European Competition Policy on Media', IESE Business School & School of Communication of the University of Navarra, Centre for Media Studies, Madrid, 15 February 2005.
124. Ungerer, H., 'Impact of European Competition Policy on Media'.

but *co-ordinated* manner'[125] through a combination of measures and institutions. Thus,[126] apart from just accepting national rules on PSBs and media pluralism, the EU does provide an active contribution to the protection of media pluralism at the European scale. Ungerer listed three main legal foundations on which the current EU action in the media sector is based: (i) the basic freedoms – in particular the freedom to provide services (the legal basis for the AVMS Directive); (ii) the provisions relating to culture and the Protocol on public service broadcasting; and (iii) the EU competition order. This is in fact the best summary of the current approach of the European Commission to the issue of protection of media pluralism at the EU level.

In addition, Ungerer emphasized that, although the European Union lacks competence to regulate media ownership and protect pluralism, the Member States are allowed to put into place their media regulatory framework. In fact, in his opinion not only do the Member States have the right to enact national anti-concentration legislation for the media sector, they also carry a *responsibility* and an obligation to establish such effective controls and to implement them.[127] This statement is interesting given the fact EU legislation imposes no legal obligation on Member States. Admittedly, the European Parliament has in a number of reports and resolutions called for Member States to introduce anti-concentration measures if they did not already have them, but this is not legally binding. The obligation is, therefore, rather moral than legal.

Overall, as could be expected from the representative of DG Competition, Ungerer believed that at EU level competition law plays a pivotal role.[128] He emphasized that 'applying strict competition controls to the sector and the related upstream and downstream markets is a necessary *pre-condition* for achieving effective and sustainable pluralism',[129] and 'only a competitive market structure is a sound basis for sustainable plurality. The underlying, market power structures in the media sector are determining the development of the sector – and ultimately the efficiency and sustainability

125. Ungerer, H., 'Competition Policy and the Issue of Access in Broadcasting Markets: The Commission Perspective', Vision in Business, Broadcasting Competition Law, Brussels, 14–15 January 2003, emphasis added.
126. Ungerer, H., 'Legal Framework to Secure Open Media Markets and the Independence of the Press – The Role of EU Competition Law', Conference on Democracy and Human Rights in the EU, Opole (Poland), 5 June 2004.
127. Ungerer, H., 'Legal Framework to Secure Open Media Markets and the Independence of the Press – The Role of EU Competition Law'.
128. Ungerer, H., 'Legal Framework to Secure Open Media Markets and the Independence of the Press – The Role of EU Competition Law'; Ungerer, H., 'Application of EU Competition Rules to Broadcasting – The Transition from Analogue to Digital'; Ungerer, H., 'Impact of European Competition Policy on Media'.
129. Ungerer, H., 'Legal Framework to Secure Open Media Markets and the Independence of the Press – The Role of EU Competition Law', emphasis added.

of media specific pluralism controls'.[130] In the instances where competition law is indeed not sufficient to provide a desired safeguard for media pluralism – the Member States take over with their PSBs and anti-concentration rules.

It is interesting to note that Neelie Kroes, who succeeded Monti and was the Competition Commissioner in the first Barroso Commission, expressed the view that effective competition is not a pre-condition, but only *one of the keys* to achieving pluralism in the sector.[131] In some situations additional measures will be required to ensure protection of the core values. While admitting that open and efficient markets are the best way to provide consumers with quality products at reasonable prices, sometimes the market alone may not deliver fundamental policy objectives such as cultural diversity or high-quality public services. This is where she sees the role for state aid and public service broadcasting as upholding three essential values in the broadcasting sector: (i) pluralism (mentioned on the first place); (ii) universal access; and (iii) quality of content.

In summary, one could risk a statement that the reasons for the need of anti-concentration directive given by Monti in 1995,[132] have not changed all that much: (i) the risk of the circumvention of national laws is still there, given the fast rise in transfrontier media activities; this renders national laws ineffective and might thus provoke serious conflicts between national authorities; (ii) there is still the need to create a level playing field; and (iii) the fear that Member States had launched projects to modernize/liberalize their national rules on media ownership and media activities is still there and in many instances has materialized. What has changed is the Commission's approach. If one assumes that there are three basic models for ensuring pluralism,[133] then the Commission has now definitely moved from the public policy model to a mix of the new media and market models. As Hoffman-Riem notices, the paradigm in the European broadcasting regulation has shifted in several ways: from the trustee to the marker model, from cultural to economic legitimization of the broadcasting system, from primacy of the communicators and recipients of information to primacy of entrepreneur and

130. Ungerer, H., 'Legal Framework to Secure Open Media Markets and the Independence of the Press – The Role of EU Competition Law'.
131. Kroes, N., 'Strengthening the European Creative Industries in the Light of the i2010 Strategy', Opening address at the Austrian Presidency Expert Seminar: Content for competitiveness, 2 March 2006.
132. European Audiovisual Observatory, Iris Special: 'Television and Media Concentration. Regulatory Models on the National and European Level'.
133. Jakubowicz, K., 'Legislative Guarantees of Plurality of Information Sources', 13, 81–86.

from special culturally based broadcasting regulation to economic regulation *via* competition law.[134]

The focus shifted from 'citizens' to 'consumers' or 'users'. As illustrated by the statement of the former long term Director General of DG Competition, Philip Lowe:

> the emphasis of regulation has shifted away from protection of some broadly defined "public interest" and from public utility management towards opening up markets, ensuring free and fair competition between producers and promoting the interests of *consumers*',[135]

However, competition law and enforcing access alone will not suffice. As noted by Haraszti, 'general competition policy, even a fair market share arrangement, is not conceived for, and is rarely able to, fulfil the function of protecting the diversity which human rights standards demand'.[136] Therefore, these methods *must* be accompanied by additional regulatory measures at the EU level aimed at ensuring pluralism in the media sector. The need to protect public interest by media regulation still exists despite the major transformation of the sector.

The Commission believes, that such additional ground rules for the sector do exist at the European level and are set in a 'decentralized but *co-ordinated* manner'.[137] The next three chapters analyse the existing European tools aimed at or contributing to protection of media pluralism. Chapter 3 analyses the work of the Council of Europe and the case law of the European Court of Human Rights which grants individual protection to persons (including legal persons) affected by the lack of pluralism in national media. Second, selected merger decisions of the European Commission are examined in Chapter 4 with particular emphasis on those in which the Commission managed to 'slip' certain public interest objectives through a backdoor of competition analysis. Finally, Chapter 5 looks at fragmentary legislative measures adopted by the European Union, which contain legally binding provisions contributing to the maintenance of pluralistic media sector in the Member States.

---

134. Hoffman-Riem, W., *Regulating Media. The Licensing and Supervision of Broadcasting in Six Countries*, 340–352.
135. Lowe, P., 'Media Concentration and Convergence: Competition in Communications', emphasis added.
136. Haraszti, M., 'Media Pluralism and Human Rights'.
137. Ungerer, H., 'Competition Policy and the Issue of Access in Broadcasting Markets: The Commission Perspective', emphasis added.

Chapter 3

European Tools I: European Court of Human Rights and the Council of Europe*

3.1. GENERAL OBSERVATIONS

Although the attention of this book centres primarily on the European Union's approach to the issue of protection of media pluralism, it is also necessary to examine, if even briefly, the case law of the European Court of Human Rights and the activities of the Council of Europe in this area, as 'their impact on the [European Union's] policy and lawmaking processes is considerable'.[1]

The Council of Europe was founded in 1949 and its central role is protection and promotion of human rights in Europe. Article 1 of its Statute[2] declares that:

> the aim of the Council of Europe is to achieve a greater unity between its members for the purpose of safeguarding and realizing the ideals and principles which are their common heritage and facilitating their economic and social progress.

---

* An earlier version of this chapter was published by the author in an article entitled 'Is Media Pluralism a Human Right? The European Court of Human Rights, the Council of Europe and the Issue of Media Pluralism', (2009) European Human Rights Law Review 3, 395–414.

1. Westphal, D., 'Media Pluralism and European Regulation', 9.
2. Council of Europe, Statute of the Council of Europe, 5 May 1949.

This aim shall be realised by common actions taking form of conventions and agreements.

The Council has forty-seven Member States[3] and its main institutions are: (i) the Committee of Ministers – the decision-making body, whose conclusions may in appropriate cases take the form of recommendations to the governments of members; the Committee may request the governments of members to inform it of the action taken by them with regard to such recommendations;[4] (ii) the Parliamentary Assembly, consisting of 636 members (318 representatives and 318 substitutes) from the national parliaments; (iii) the Congress of Local and Regional Authorities; and (iv) the secretariat headed by a Secretary General, elected by the Parliamentary Assembly.

This institutional framework prepares and negotiates conventions, which are the main legal instruments of the Council of Europe. Negotiation culminates in a decision of the Committee of Ministers establishing the text of the proposed convention, which is then opened for ratification by Member States. Therefore, conventions of the Council of Europe are non-coercive and are not statutory acts of the Council, since they owe their legal existence to ratification by the Member States.[5]

The European Convention on Human Rights (ECHR)[6] adopted in 1950 forms the legal basis for the operation of the Council of Europe. It sets forth a number of fundamental rights and freedoms,[7] and the Member States have undertaken to secure these rights and freedoms to everyone within their jurisdiction. Most of the Member States have by now incorporated the Convention into their own law, enabling the national courts to take full account of its provisions when deciding cases. The Convention also established international enforcement machinery in the form of the European Court of Human Rights which deals with individual and inter-State petitions. Once domestic judicial remedies have been exhausted, an individual may seek redress in the Court for an alleged breach of the Convention by a Member State. The machinery of the Court is, therefore, 'not a substitute for national courts, but is, in a sense, an extension of them'.[8]

---

3. See the list of the Council of Europe's Member States, available at http://hub.coe.int.
4. Article 15(b) of the Statute of the Council of Europe, London, 5 May 1949, http://conventions.coe.int/Treaty/en/Treaties/Html/001.htm.
5. Council of Europe, About Conventions and Agreements in the Council of Europe Treaty Series (CETS), available at: http://www.conventions.coe.int/?pg=/general/IntroConv_en.asp.
6. Convention for the Protection of Human Rights and Fundamental Freedoms, Rome, 4 November 1950.
7. Right to life, prohibition of torture, prohibition of slavery and forced labour, right to liberty and security, right to a fair trial, no punishment without law, right to respect for private and family life, freedom of thought, conscience and religion, freedom of expression, freedom of assembly and association, right to marry, right to an effective remedy, prohibition of discrimination.
8. Council of Europe, Directorate General of Human Rights and Legal Affairs, Explanatory document on the European Convention on Human Rights.

States, against which a violation of the Convention is found by the Court, are obliged to take all necessary measures to remedy the violation. If there is no appropriate and total remedy in the national law, the European Court of Human Rights may order the Member State to pay financial compensation to the injured party. The execution of judgments of the Court is supervised by the Committee of Ministers. In addition, the effect of the judgments of the Court may extend beyond the actual case when the State is required to modify their legislation and practices for the future.[9] The Secretary General may request the Member States to provide explanations on the manner in which their domestic law ensures the effective implementation of the Convention.[10]

With regard to the case-law of the European Court of Human Rights on the issue of media pluralism, the first question one must ask here is, 'Is media pluralism an individual human right?', and thus can it be protected by the Court? At the outset, there seems to be only one answer – no. Although some authors believe that it achieved the 'status today as an indispensable human right',[11] media pluralism appears to be more of a 'group right' or a 'society right', rather than an individual 'human right'. Hence, media pluralism has always come to agenda of both the Council and the Court as a prerequisite for the unquestionable individual human right of freedom of expression, which is guarded by Article 10 of the European Convention on Human Rights. Obviously, without pluralism, freedom of expression would be non-existent.[12] This chapter argues, however, that in time media pluralism has gained, to a large extent, an independent status in the work of the Council of Europe and in the judgments of the European Court of Human Rights.

The Council of Europe has expressed a belief that Article 10 of the Convention is 'the basic framework for media pluralism on the European scale'.[13] Not only does it confirm the existence of the basic human right to media freedom but also imposes a duty on the Council of Europe's Member States to guarantee pluralism and diversity of the media in order to ensure the freedom of information and functioning democracy.

---

9. Council of Europe, 'The Council of Europe and the protection of human rights', booklet, available at http://book.coe.int/sysmodules/RBS_fichier/admin/download.php?fileid=3055.
10. Council of Europe, 'Convention for the Protection of Human Rights and Fundamental Freedoms-Summary of the Treaty'.
11. Haraszti, M., 'Media Pluralism and Human Rights'.
12. Barendt, M., *Freedom of Speech*, 447.
13. Council of Europe, 'Media Diversity in Europe', December 2002, H/APMD (2003) 1, at 4.

Article 10 paragraph 1 of the Convention codifies the fundamental right to freedom of expression and impartial information. It states that:

> Everyone has the right to freedom of expression. This right shall include freedom to hold opinions and to receive and impart information and ideas without interference by public authority and regardless of frontiers. This Article shall not prevent States from requiring the licensing of broadcasting, television or cinema enterprises.

Paragraph 2 allows Member States to introduce restrictions of freedom of expression, but only provided they are 'prescribed by law', 'are necessary in a democratic society' and 'pursue a legitimate aim',[14] such as national security, territorial integrity or public safety, protection of health or morals, protection of the reputation or rights of others, prevention of the disclosure of information received in confidence, or maintaining the authority and impartiality of the judiciary.

It is clear from the wording of Article 10 that there is no express mention of media pluralism or diversity as individual rights. Therefore, at first sight, one could question the Council of Europe's belief that Article 10 forms 'the basic framework for media pluralism on the European scale'.

However, it was the case-law of the European Court of Human Rights which played a pivotal role in widening the interpretation of Article 10 so as to recognize the need to safeguard media pluralism in Europe. With regard to what this means in terms of the States' obligations, the Court's stance seems to have toughened over time so as to arguably include statements as to the States' duties with regard to excessive media concentration. The Court's judgments have influenced legal systems in the Member States of the Council of Europe, as well as the Council of Europe's policy towards media concentration. The European Court of Human Rights has, therefore, been not only a legal institution of the Council of Europe rigidly applying the law to particular cases, but also a policy actor.

It is obvious that, as observed by Hunt, different stages of the policy making are closely linked. It is a dynamic process which involves interactions between various actors – both legal and political.[15] Therefore, in its judgments, the European Court of Human Rights presents its position alongside the other institutions of the Council of Europe, it both launches and receives ideas.[16] As will be explained below, over the years it has had a significant influence on the Council's of Europe policy towards media

14. Randall, H., 'Commercial Speech under the European Convention on Human Rights: Subordinate or Equal?', (2006) Human Rights Law Review 6, 53.
15. Hunt, J., 'The Court of Justice As a Policy Actor in the Development of the EC Labour Law Regime: The Case of the Acquired Rights Directive', (1998) Legal Studies 18(3), 337.
16. Hunt, J., 'The Court of Justice As a Policy Actor in the Development of the EC Labour Law Regime: The Case of the Acquired Rights Directive', 340.

concentration.[17] Following Hunt's observations with regard to the European Court of Justice, one may say that the role of the European Court of Human Rights in the Council's of Europe policy making process has been one of 'provoking political responses' and 'launching ideas'.[18]

Overall, the Court of Human Rights has been successful in safeguarding internal media pluralism. Cases in the 'internal pluralism' category may be referred to as pure freedom of expression cases – an individual wishes to or has expressed himself/herself in the media and is prevented from doing so by a State. Article 10 protects exactly this type of situation and the Court's use of the word 'pluralism's not necessarily limited to media only – it applies to the need for a pluralistic society as a prerequisite of democracy. Pluralism of ideas presented by media is just a part of this ideal.

It is the case-law involving the protection of structural media pluralism that breaches the boundaries of 'pure' freedom of expression cases. These cases are somewhat paradoxical. On the one hand, structural pluralism is a *prerequisite* for freedom of expression as there is a need for pluralistic media structures to allow multiplicity of ideas being presented. On the other hand, the need to safeguard the pluralism of media providers may sometimes require *restrictions* to freedom of expression for some individuals. Licensing systems and regulations on media concentration may be allowed by Article 10(2) because they serve the aim of pluralism, hence they serve 'the rights of others', even if they restrict freedom of expression. Therefore, structural media pluralism is a prerequisite of freedom of expression and at the same time measures aimed at securing it are capable of restricting this freedom.

The protection of structural pluralism proved more difficult to achieve by means of the Court's case law and prompted the Council of Europe to step in with regulatory proposals.

3.2. EUROPEAN COURT OF HUMAN RIGHTS

3.2.1. Article 10 as a Shield for Internal Media Pluralism

Initially, the mere finding by the Court that Article 10 also entails the need to safeguard pluralism was somewhat revolutionary because, as mentioned earlier, the relationship between pluralism and the freedom of expression is somewhat ambiguous. They are similar only in that the effective realization of both depends on the absence of content-specific censorship. Apart from

17. Hunt, J., 'The Court of Justice As a Policy Actor in the Development of the EC Labour Law Regime: The Case of the Acquired Rights Directive', 336.
18. Alter, K., Meunier-Aitsahalia, S., 'Judicial Politics in the European Community: European Integration and the Path Breaking Cassis de Dijon Decision', (1994) Comparative Political Studies 26, 535.

this however, they differ in their central interest and the purposes they serve. They cannot even be claimed to form 'two sides of a coin' as these two values may contradict one another. The need to ensure media pluralism may result in refusing access to media and thus infringing the freedom of expression. As noted by Craufurd Smith,

> The primary aim of freedom of expression is to protect the right of individuals to express themselves without sanction; a right which may, but need not, lead to the transmission of a variety of ideas and information. The objective underlying media pluralism is, on the other hand, the communication to the public of diverse ideas and information; an objective which is itself likely to benefit from an expansive, individual right to expression, but which may also lead to certain individuals being refused access to the media.[19]

An early 1970s judgment *Handyside v. The United Kingdom*[20] was one of the first cases in which the Court, in express terms, mentioned pluralism in relation to claims of the violation of Article 10 the Convention. The case concerned the prohibition by the United Kingdom of the publication of a book by Mr Handyside's publishing firm. The book entitled 'The Little Red Schoolbook' was intended for school-children aged 12 or over. While it generally dealt with matters such as education and learning, one of the chapters contained information about sex. The UK government believed that some of this information would be harmful for children as young as 12, and on the basis of the Obscene Publications Act, it ordered the seizure of the books that had been published and a prohibition of any further publication. Mr Handyside referred the case to the Court of Human Rights claiming a violation of the freedom of expression, enshrined in Article 10 of the Convention. The Court examined whether a seizure and prohibition of the publication could be a justifiable restriction on the freedom of expression. In paragraph 49 the Court stated:

> Freedom of expression constitutes one of the essential foundations of [a democratic] society, one of the basic conditions for its progress and for the development of every man. Subject to paragraph 2 of Article 10, it is applicable not only to 'information' or 'ideas' that are favourably received or regarded as inoffensive or as a matter of indifference, but also to those that offend, shock or disturb the State or any sector of the population. *Such are the demands of that pluralism, tolerance and broadmindedness without which there is no 'democratic society'.*[21]

19. Craufurd Smith, R., *Broadcasting Law and Fundamental Rights* (Clarendon Press, 1997), 196.
20. *Handyside v. The United Kingdom*, A 24 (1976); (1976) 1 EHRR 737.
21. *Handyside v. The United Kingdom*, A 24 (1976); (1976) 1 EHRR 737 at para. 49, emphasis added.

Therefore, the Court established that pluralism is an indispensable foundation of a democratic society. The need for a democratic society to be truly pluralistic means the need to ensure that all sorts of ideas may be expressed freely and through any medium. Without a variety of voices and opinions the media cannot fulfil their contributory role to democracy. Thus, to guarantee freedom of expression means to contribute to pluralism. However, this is only subject to justifiable restrictions under paragraph 2 of Article 10. In the case at hand, the Court decided that there was no violation of Article 10 of the Convention as the principle of pluralism of ideas was legitimately overridden by the interest of the 'protection of morals' mentioned in paragraph 2 of Article 10.

However, the Court in *Handyside,* and similar cases which followed established a general rule that for the sake of pluralist voices, all opinions and ideas, including those shocking and unpopular, have a right to be presented in the media and the restriction on that right can only be exceptional. This has become an established line of the Court's of Human Rights jurisprudence. Paragraph 49 from *Handyside* has since been quoted by the Court of Human Rights with an introduction 'as the Court has consistently held', 'this is the Court's well-established case-law' or 'the Court reiterates the relevant principles which emerge from its judgments'.[22] Although in *Handyside* itself, the Court did not find pluralism of voices to be the uppermost value, the cited passage has since then been frequently used by the Court to find a violation of Article 10.[23]

For instance in *Lingens v. Austria,*[24] the Court confirmed the role the press and media, in general, play in maintaining political pluralism in a democratic society. In this case, the Court stepped in to protect an Austrian journalist who published articles criticizing the behaviour of prominent Austrian politicians at the time. He was subsequently sued and prosecuted before Austrian courts for defamation and sentenced to a fine, while the issues of a magazine which published the articles were confiscated. The Court repeated word by word paragraph 49 from *Handyside,* and stressed that the principles of 'pluralism, tolerance and broadmindedness' are particularly important for the press, who have an obligation to impart information and ideas on political issues, and furthermore the public has a

22. *Raichinov v. Bulgaria,* 47579/99, Judgment of 10 April 2006; *Malisiewicz-Gąsior v. Poland*, 43797/98, Judgment of 6 April 2006.
23. For instance *Castells v. Spain*, A 236 (1992); (1992) 14 EHRR 445, at para. 42; *Piermont v. France*, A 314 (1995); (1995) 20 EHRR 301, at para. 76; *Oberschlick v. Austria*, A 204 (1995); (1995) 19 EHRR 389, at para. 29, and more recently: *Ukrainian Media Group v. Ukraine*, 72713/01, Judgment of 29 March 2005, at para. 40; *Sokolowski v. Poland*, 75955/01 Judgment of 29 March 2005, at para. 41; *Albert-Engelmann-Gesellschaft Mbh v. Austria*, 46389/00 Judgment of 19 January 2006, at para. 25.
24. *Lingens v. Austria*, A 103 (1986); (1986) 8 EHRR 407.

right to receive them.[25] According to the court, freedom of political debate is at the very core of the concept of a democratic society. In addition, the freedom of the press, and I would add the media generally, 'affords the public one of the best means of discovering and forming an opinion of the ideas and attitudes of political leaders'.[26] Therefore, any restrictions on media dissemination of political views have proven very difficult to justify under Article 10(2).[27]

The *Jersild*[28] judgment praises the role the media play in reflecting the pluralism of voices, opinions and beliefs not only of politicians but of every member of a given society. The Court reiterated that 'freedom of expression constitutes one of the essential foundations of a democratic society and the safeguards to be afforded to [media] are of particular importance'. And while the media must not overstep the boundaries, *inter alia*, in the interest of 'the protection of the reputation or rights of others', it is nevertheless *incumbent* on them to impart information and ideas of public interest. Moreover, not only do the audiovisual media have the task of imparting such information and ideas: the public also has a right to *receive* them.[29] The conclusion from *Jersild* is that, for the sake of safeguarding internal media pluralism, Member States cannot convict journalists for assisting in making known the beliefs of another person, however unpleasant and disturbing these beliefs may be. This would seriously hamper the contribution of the media to discussions on matters of public interest and hence, pluralism of ideas.[30]

Jersild is significant also for other reasons. It was in this case that the Court for the first time emphasized the importance of audiovisual media for functioning, democratic society. The Court ruled that the findings of an earlier case, *Observer and Guardian,* with regard to the press sector must without doubt be extended to audiovisual media.[31] Therefore, by paraphrasing the Court's findings in *Observer and Guardian* and replacing the word 'press' with 'audiovisual media', one can extract the Court's position with regard to the latter: 'since freedom of expression constitutes one of the essential foundations of a democratic society, the safeguards to be afforded

25. *Lingens v. Austria,* A 103 (1986); (1986) 8 EHRR 407, at para. 41.
26. *Lingens v. Austria,* A 103 (1986); (1986) 8 EHRR 407, at para. 42; more recent cases of violation of the freedom of political speech citing *Lingens* include *Malisiewicz-Gąsior v. Poland*, 43797/98 Judgment of 6 April 2006; Wirtschafts-Trend Zeitschriften-Verlags *GmbhH v. Austria*, 58547/00, Judgment of 27 April 2005 or *Sokolowski v. Poland*, 75955/01.
27. Janis, M.W., Kay, R.S., Bradley, A.W., *European Human Rights Law. Text and Materials* (Oxford University Press, 2000), 170.
28. *Jersild v. Denmark,* A 198 (1995) 19 EHRR 1.
29. *Jersild v. Denmark,* A 198 (1995) 19 EHRR 1, at para. 31.
30. Bearing in mind that States, have a generally broader margin of appreciation in cases like *Jersild* than in regulating political speech or debate of questions of public interest; see below for discussion on the *Tierfabriken* judgment.
31. *Jersild v. Denmark,* A 198 (1995) 19 EHRR 1, at para. 31.

to audiovisual media are of particular importance'. The Court then sanctioned the Commission's finding in an admissibility decision in an earlier case[32] that 'audiovisual media have often a much more immediate and powerful effect than the print media… [They] have means of conveying through images meanings which the print media are not able to impart'.[33]

It is worth stressing that while the Court has actively protected the pluralism of voices and beliefs presented in the media, it has never recognized the right of an individual, be it a politician or a private person, of *unlimited access* to media, in particular to broadcasting.[34] Deciding on the admissibility of the case brought by Jörg Haider against Austria, the Commission held that, 'Article 10 of the Convention cannot be taken to include a general and unfettered right for any private citizen or organization to have access to broadcasting time on radio or television in order to forward his opinion.'[35]

Therefore, Article 10 only occasionally protects internal pluralism, that is pluralism of voices and opinions, before they reach the media. However, once ideas have been disseminated by the media, Article 10 makes sure that only exceptional circumstances allow for those ideas to be silenced. In summary, in all the above *Handyside*-type cases, where the Court used the trinity 'pluralism, tolerance and broadmindedness' in relation to media, the Court understood the term pluralism in its internal incarnation. This line of case-law has established that even though there is no general right of access to the media, in principle the media should themselves strive to reflect plurality and diversity of ideas, views and opinions without the interference by a national authority. However, in neither of these cases did the Court mention the need to provide for plurality of media operators, in order that this would be achieved.

3.2.2. Protection of Structural Pluralism as a Legitimate Restriction to Freedom of Expression

The need to maintain structural media pluralism can be implied from the Court's case-law on the licensing of broadcasting. The *Handyside* passage from paragraph 49 of the case has been used by the Court to justify national broadcasting licensing systems and regulations that are aimed at protecting external pluralism. The Court seemed to believe that precisely because Article 10 does not guarantee an unfettered right of access to broadcast media, there is a need to ensure a number of media providers; the more media

32. *Purcell and Others v. Ireland*, 15404/89 [1991] DR 70.
33. *Jersild v. Denmark*, A 198 (1995) 19 EHRR 1, at para. 31.
34. Nicol, A., Millar, G., Sharland, A., *Media Law and Human Rights* (Blackstone Press Limited, 2001), 155.
35. *Haider v. Austria*, 25060/94 [1995] 85 DR 86.

operators the more possible access points. Admittedly, an abundance of media providers does not automatically mean that *everybody* will get a chance to express themselves in the media. However, the chances are that at least the majority of voices and ideas in the society will be represented.

Article 10(1) allows States to license broadcasting, cinema, and television enterprises. Therefore, this subjects broadcasting material to greater regulation than the written publications.[36] There are obvious reasons for allowing more regulation of radio and broadcast television than of print media. The historical justification was scarcity of frequencies[37] – a State decided who could obtain a license and what conditions, including content requirements, would be attached to it. Currently, with the ongoing digital revolution allowing for a multitude of channels, the arguments for broadcasting regulation have shifted from limiting the number of broadcasters to ensuring pluralism, both external and internal. The opinion forming power of broadcasting is much greater than that of the press. Broadcasting is ubiquitous[38] and as a well-known adage goes, 'one picture is worth a thousand words'. Moreover, media consumers expect different standards from broadcasting than from the press. As Barendt observes, 'while [the public] expects the print media to be biased or to have selective coverage, it has relied on radio and television to provide objective news and a comprehensive range of programmes to inform as well as to entertain'.[39]

The fact that the possibility of a broadcasting regulation is expressly mentioned in Article 10(1) could imply that any form of broadcasting licensing or regulation system is automatically exempt from any accusations of an infringement of the right to expression.[40] The Court has, however, decided differently, holding that values protected by a licensing system may only be the 'legitimate aim' for the restriction of freedom of expression.[41] Therefore, every licensing system has to fulfil the conditions of Article 10(2): 'the object and purpose of the third sentence of Article 10(1) and the scope of its application must … be considered in the context of the Article as a whole and in particular in relation to the requirements of paragraph 2'.[42]

This interpretation by the Court makes it clear that 'states cannot simply justify their interference with broadcasters by reference to the licensing

36. Ovey, C., White, R.C.A., *Jacobs and White: 'The European Convention on Human Rights*, 3rd edn (Oxford University Press, 2002), 284.
37. Barendt, E., *Freedom of Speech*, 445.
38. Trager, R., Dickerson, D.I., *Freedom of Expression in the 21st Century* (Pine Forge Press, Inc., 1999), 154.
39. Barendt, E., *Freedom of Speech*, 448.
40. Janis, M.W., Kay, R.S., Bradley, A.W., *European Human Rights Law. Text and Materials*, 206; Van Dijk, P., Van Hoof, G.J.H., *Theory and Practice of the European Convention on Human Rights*, 3rd edn (Kluwer Law International, 1998), 579.
41. Nicol, A., Millar, G., Sharland, A., *Media Law and Human Rights*, 153.
42. *Groppera Radio AG v. Switzerland*, A 173 (1990); (1990) 12 EHRR 321 at para. 61.

power under Article 10(1), they must also show that the particular interference was lawful under Article 10(2)'.[43] Thus, the licensing systems which led to limiting the freedom of expression of some individuals, but are aimed at securing structural media pluralism, have often been justified by the Court as necessary for the 'protection of the rights of others' mentioned in Article 10(2).

In *Groppera*,[44] the Court established that the need to safeguard pluralism by means of a licensing system in a Member State can be an acceptable justification for the limitation on the freedom of expression in the name of the protection of the 'rights of others'. Although the case is somewhat outdated, as it was decided in the era of frequency scarcity,[45] it is nevertheless worthwhile recalling some of the Court's statements which continue to apply in the current era of channel abundance. The Court accepted the Swiss government's submission that restrictions of the right to freedom of expression designed to ensure pluralism can be justified under Article 10(2) of the Convention. The case concerned the Swiss licensing system which resulted in a ban on the retransmission of programmes of Groppera Radio by a cable company, which did not obtain a license for receiving installations. Groppera Radio claimed violation of Article 10 before the Court of Human Rights. The Swiss government responded by saying that even if there was a violation, it was justified under Article 10(2) because its aim was the 'protection of the rights of others'. It was designed 'to ensure pluralism, in particular of information, by allowing a fair allocation of frequencies internationally and nationally'.[46] The Court agreed and stressed that the absence of a licensing system could result in limiting the range of programmes made available to the public in Switzerland, and thus in limiting pluralism in the Swiss media market.[47]

In the ever changing media environment, characterized by progressing digitization which renders scarcity of frequencies a problem of the past, some argue that the need for rigid control of the number of broadcasters in order to protect pluralism will be less relevant. Nevertheless, *Groppera* is significant in that the Court accepted that a national licensing system aimed at protecting structural media pluralism can be a legitimate aim of a restriction of freedom of expression. For instance, in the 2012 document 'Ownership and Control Policy',[48] the Broadcasting Authority of Ireland

43. Mowbray, A., *Cases and Materials on the European Convention on Human Rights* (Butterworths, 2001), at 505.
44. *Groppera Radio AG v. Switzerland*, A 173 (1990); (1990) 12 EHRR 321.
45. Mowbray, A., *Cases and Materials on the European Convention on Human Rights*, 505.
46. *Groppera Radio AG v. Switzerland*, A 173 (1990); (1990) 12 EHRR 321, at para. 69.
47. Craufurd Smith, R., *Broadcasting Law and Fundamental Rights*, 196.
48. Broadcasting Commission of Ireland, 'Ownership and Control Policy', 2012.

specified that in order to counteract excessive concentration in the media sector, no license will be given to a company which holds 25% of the total number of broadcasting services licensed in Ireland. Therefore, if hypothetically, a broadcaster who holds over 25% of broadcasting services in Ireland, applied for a further broadcasting license, he/she would not be granted one. This would, in principle, amount to a restriction of the freedom of expression of this broadcaster. However, it would most certainly be justified under Article 10(2) as such a provision of a broadcasting licensing system is aimed at safeguarding external media pluralism, and thus the 'rights of others', both viewers/listeners and other broadcasters which may wish to enter or expand in the market.

However, arbitrary licensing systems which apply excessively vague criteria for the allocation of broadcasting licenses will not be legitimate under Article 10(2). As was confirmed by the recent judgment of the Court in the *Television A1+* case, 'a licensing procedure whereby the licensing authority gives no reasons for its decisions does not provide adequate protection against arbitrary interferences by a public authority with the fundamental right to freedom of expression'.[49]

3.2.3. Media Monopolies as the Worst Possible Scenario

In *Groppera*, the Court merely *accepted* already existing national measures aimed at safeguarding pluralism in media as justifiable *restrictions* to the primary right to freedom of expression. In subsequent judgments, the Court seems to have taken a step further and established that Member States actually have an obligation to *guarantee* media pluralism in the national media market. This applies in particular to the TV broadcasting sector, given its importance and potential recognized in *Jersild.*

In this regard, the judgment in *Lentia*[50] may be viewed as the most prominent one. It involved several applicants who questioned the legitimacy of Austrian broadcasting monopoly which, as they argued, by its very nature violated Article 10 of the Convention. Austria claimed, first and foremost, that the third sentence of Article 10(1) allows the States to require the licensing of broadcasting or television companies, and this means that States are free to establish whatever broadcasting system they see fit, even one that introduces a broadcasting monopoly. The Court ruled, that even if Member States are indeed free to establish their broadcasting systems, it still must be determined whether such a system satisfies the relevant conditions of paragraph 2 of Article 10. The Austrian government submitted that the maintenance of a broadcasting monopoly in the hands of the Austrian

49. *Meltex Ltd and Mesrop Movsesyan v. Armenia*, Application no. 32283/04, Judgment of 17 June 2008.
50. *Informationsverein Lentia and Others v. Austria*, A 276 (1993); (1993) 17 EHRR 93.

Broadcasting Corporation (ORF) served the purpose of ensuring objectivity and impartiality of reporting, diversity of opinions, balanced programming and the independence of persons and bodies responsible for programmes. As such, it formed a justified restriction on the freedom of expression. The Court could not agree with such a proposition. It reiterated that the preservation of a plural, culturally diverse broadcasting offer was an aim that could justify restrictions to broadcaster's freedoms. The Court specified that the public's *entitlement to receive* diverse information and ideas cannot be successfully accomplished unless it is grounded in the principle of pluralism, of which the State is the *ultimate guarantor*.[51] The Court added that 'this observation is especially valid in relation to audio-visual media, whose programmes are often broadcast very widely'.[52]

In this case, the Court understood pluralism in its structural incarnation as it may be gleaned from the Court's agreement with the applicants that to protect public opinion from manipulation, it is by no means necessary to have a public monopoly in the audio-visual industry. Indeed, on the contrary, true progress towards attaining diversity and objectivity can be achieved only by providing *a variety of stations and programmes*.[53] The Court stated that of all the means of ensuring that the values are respected, a public monopoly is the most restrictive one.

Finally and most importantly, the Court rejected the Austrian government's economic argument that the Austrian market is too small to sustain more than one television company and if liberalized, 'private monopolies' would be created anyway. Invoking examples of other European countries of a comparable size to Austria, the Court stated that 'the coexistence of private and public stations … accompanied by measures preventing the development of private monopolies renders such fears groundless'.[54]

The judgment in *Lentia* is thus of significance for several reasons. First, the Court confirmed that the public is entitled to receive diverse information and ideas. Second, the State is the ultimate *guarantor* of the principle of media pluralism. Furthermore, a monopoly in the broadcasting market, be it public or private, is in its nature harmful to pluralism which, to be accomplished, requires the presence of several actors on the media scene, notwithstanding the fact that they may be regulated by a State by means of licensing. And finally, the Court seemed to point to national anti-concentration rules as an effective means to ensure that private monopolies do not appear in liberalized national media markets.

51. *Informationsverein Lentia and Others v. Austria*, A 276 (1993); (1993) 17 EHRR 93.
52. *Informationsverein Lentia and Others v. Austria*, A 276 (1993); (1993) 17 EHRR 93.
53. *Informationsverein Lentia and Others v. Austria*, A 276 (1993); (1993) 17 EHRR 93, at para. 37.
54. *Informationsverein Lentia and Others v. Austria*, A 276 (1993); (1993) 17 EHRR 93, at para. 42.

All the above read together allow for one to conclude that the Court of Human Rights in *Lentia* found a pluralistic media sector, and broadcasting in particular, to be of great value to democracy and imposed an obligation on Member States to guarantee that several media operators are present in any given national market. The adoption of anti-concentration laws seems to be viewed by the Court as an appropriate means to achieving the above goal.

Some argue that in *Lentia* the Court did not establish such an obligation, and that Member States are under no duty to adopt, or indeed maintain, such regulations once in force.[55] They claim that *Lentia* does not differ much from *Groppera* in that it continues to construe media pluralism only, as a possible justification to restrictions on freedom of expression, and not an essential requirement for its realization. However, it can be argued that even if media pluralism continues to be construed by the Court only as an acceptable restraint to freedom of expression, the way in which the Court treated this principle is different in both cases. While in *Groppera*, it merely accepted the existing laws designed to safeguard pluralism, in *Lentia* it indicated the need to establish such laws that were not present in the country in question at that time. It actually required the *introduction of safeguards of structural pluralism* to the national market. This arguably makes *Lentia* a lot more powerful than *Groppera.*

The liberalization of Austrian broadcasting regulation, which followed the *Lentia* judgment, happened under the watchful eye of the Court and any attempts of the Austrian government to circumvent the findings in *Lentia* were scrupulously punished.[56] Finally, in *Tele I*[57] the Court 'noted with satisfaction'[58] that the new Austrian legislation provides for structural pluralism. The Court found that Austria's solution to give private broadcasters access to cable broadcasting while reserving terrestrial television broadcasting to the ORF was compatible with Article 10 as it provided a solution less restrictive than the former complete broadcasting monopoly of the ORF and in fact introduced pluralism of operators in the media market.[59]

This is what makes the *Lentia* judgment so significant. Not only did the Court say that a monopoly in the media sector is the worst possible scenario, it also influenced a change of law in a Member State so as to allow for multiplicity of media providers.

55. Craufurd Smith, R., *Broadcasting Law and Fundamental Rights*, 180.
56. See *Radio ABC v. Austria,* 1997-VI; (1988) 25 EHRR 185.
57. *Tele I Privatfernsehgesellschaft MBH v. Austria*, (2002) 34 EHRR 181.
58. Mowbray, A., *Cases and Materials on the European Convention on Human Rights*, at 506.
59. *Tele I Privatfernsehgesellschaft MBH v. Austria*, (2002) 34 EHRR 181, at para. 40.

3.2.4. Member States' Positive Obligation to Ensure Pluralistic Media Market

Despite the disappearance of public broadcasting monopolies in the Council of Europe's Member States, there is a growing concern about the current trend of progressing media concentration and creation of 'commercial monopolies'. In this regard, the next step from *Lentia* could only be the Court ruling that the Member States not only cannot justify maintaining public media monopolies, but they also have an *obligation* to actively counteract excessive concentration in the media sector, for instance by introducing and maintaining national anti-concentration laws. Such a requirement has been stated in express terms by the European Commission for Human Rights in two important decisions: *De Geillustreerde Pers NV*[60] and *Verein Alternatives Lokalradio Bern*.[61] The Commission was initially anticipated to have a rather 'instrumental' role in deciding on the admissibility of cases to be judged by the Court. However, throughout its existence right up until 1999, the Commission developed into, what may be called, a 'first instance' Court of Human Rights, which very often issued preliminarily decisions on cases.

In the two mentioned 'preliminary judgments' the Commission expressed firm support for the proposition that under Article 10 Member States have a positive, enforceable obligation to avoid excessive media concentration. The first case, *De Geillustreerde Pers NV*,[62] concerned the refusal by a Dutch national corporation, responsible for co-operation of the broadcasting organizations, to provide complete programme data to the applicant who was the publisher of a general interest magazine. Such complete programme data could only be published by broadcasting organizations to which broadcasting time had been allocated. The applicant complained to the Commission, claiming that such a legally sanctioned absolute monopoly on the part of the broadcasting organizations to publish complete programme data infringes Article 10 of the Convention. The claimant alleged that it violated the applicant's right to freely receive and impart information, as well as the right of the public to be advised about upcoming programmes by impartial publications. Having initially declared the case admissible, the Commission subsequently published a report on the case in which it indicated that there was no violation of Article 10. However, despite that finding, 'between-the lines' the Commission made a potentially groundbreaking suggestion that States have a duty under Article 10 to protect against excessive press concentrations. The Commission noted:

> The protection of the commercial interests of particular newspapers or groups of newspapers is not as such contemplated by the terms of Article 10 of the Convention. These matters might perhaps raise an issue under

60. *De Geillustreerde Pers NV v. Netherlands,* 5178/71 [1976] 8 DR 5.
61. *Verein Alternatives Lokalradio Bern v. Switzerland,* 10746/84 [1986] 49 DR 126.
62. *De Geillustreerde Pers NV v. Netherlands,* 5178/71 [1976] 8 DR 5.

> this provision where a state fails in its *duty* to protect against excessive press concentrations.[63]

From the above passage, one may deduce that the Commission's belief was that Article 10 is not there to protect commercial interests of individual newspapers such as the applicant in the *Geillustreerde Pers* case. However, protection of commercial interests of newspapers by a State by virtue of allowing excessive press concentration may result in Article 10 being applicable so as to defend those companies who cannot enter the thus concentrated market and hence their right to impart information would be hampered.[64]

The second case, *Verein Alternatives Lokalradio Bern*,[65] concerned the allegation by two broadcasting companies that the Swiss government's refusal to grant them a concession for local broadcasting violated Article 10 of the Convention. The companies fulfilled all of their formal conditions for the concession, and it was clear that the additional selection criteria had clear political overtones. So the refusal was as much a political as an administrative act. The Commission held, crucially, that 'a licensing system not respecting the requirements of "pluralism, tolerance and broadmindedness, without which there is no democratic society" would infringe Article 10'.[66] However, in this particular situation, the Commission did not find the application admissible because the additional 'political criteria' were actually there to ensure cultural and linguistic pluralism, balance between lowland and mountain regions and a balanced federalist policy. Therefore, the licensing system respected the requirements of pluralism, even if as a result some entities were refused access to the media. The protection of pluralism came before the individual applicant's right to freedom of expression.

The positive obligation of the Member States to ensure a pluralistic media market has first been confirmed indirectly by the European Court of Human Rights the *Tierfabriken* judgment.[67] The Court was asked to consider whether a refusal to air a controversial television commercial constituted a violation of Article 10 of the Convention. The applicant organization, an animal protection group, reacted to numerous television commercials from the meat industry, by producing its own commercial which concluded with the statement: 'Eat less meat, for the sake of your health, the animals and the

---

63. *De Geillustreerde Pers NV v. Netherlands,* 5178/71 [1976] 8 DR 5, emphasis added.
64. It is worth noting that in the comment on Article 19 of the International Covenant on Civil and Political Rights, the Office of the UN High Commissioner for Human Rights noted that 'little attention has so far been given to the fact that, because of the development of modern mass media, effective measures are necessary to prevent such control of the media as would interfere with the right of everyone to freedom of expression', see http://www1.umn.edu/humanrts/gencomm/hrcom10.htm.
65. *Verein Alternatives Lokalradio Bern v. Switzerland,* 10746/84 [1986] 49 DR 126.
66. *Verein Alternatives Lokalradio Bern v. Switzerland*, 10746/84 [1986] 49 DR 126 at para. 140.
67. *Verein Gegen Tierfabriken v. Switzerland*, 2001-VI; (2002) 34 EHRR 159.

environment.' Wishing the ad to be broadcast on Swiss Radio and Television, the applicant sent a tape to the Commercial Television Company responsible for television broadcasting in Switzerland. Airing the commercial was refused on the grounds of its 'clear political character'. Having reached the Supreme Court in its appeal process, the applicant learned that it had other means of disseminating its political ideals. For example, in foreign programmes which were broadcast in Switzerland, or in the cinema and press (for which political advertising was in fact reserved under Swiss law). The applicant considered this insufficient and complained to the European Court of Human Rights claiming a violation of Article 10 of the Convention.

The Swiss government submitted that the prohibition of political advertising in television was designed to protect public opinion from the pressures of powerful financial groups and from undue commercial influence; to provide for a certain equality of opportunity among the different forces of society; to ensure the independence of broadcasters in editorial matters from powerful sponsors; and to support the press. The Court found this line of reasoning generally acceptable, but not sufficient in the present case to justify the restriction of the applicant's freedom of expression. The Court emphasized that the applicant was not a powerful financial group, and the airing of the commercial was the only way in which the applicant wished to participate in an ongoing political debate on animal protection. The Court's well-known view was stressed again, this time with regard to advertising. The Court said that States have a narrower margin of appreciation in regulating political speech or debate of questions of public interest.[68] Nevertheless, for the purposes of analysing the Court's of Human Rights contribution to media pluralism debate, the Court's general opinion expressed in *Tierfabriken* cannot be overlooked:

> It is true that powerful financial groups can obtain competitive advantages in the area of commercial advertising and may thereby exercise pressure on, and eventually curtail the freedom of expression of [broadcasters]. Such situations undermine the fundamental role of freedom of expression in a democratic society …, in particular where it serves to impart information and ideas of general interest, which the public is moreover entitled to receive. Such an undertaking cannot be successfully accomplished unless it is grounded in the principle of

68. In *Murphy v. Ireland*, 2003-IX; (2004) 38 EHRR 13, the Court decided that the ban on religious advertising was a justified restriction on freedom of expression in Ireland. The Court distinguished the case from *Tierfabriken* by stating in para. 67 that 'a wider margin of appreciation is generally available to the Contracting States when regulating freedom of expression in relation to matters liable to offend intimate personal convictions within the sphere of morals, or, especially, religion'; see also Randall, H., 'Commercial Speech under the European Convention on Human Rights: Subordinate or Equal?', (2006) Human Rights Law Review 6, 53, 64; Barendt, E., *Freedom of Speech*, 445.

> pluralism of which the State is the *ultimate guarantor*. This observation is especially valid in relation to audiovisual media, whose programmes are often broadcast very widely.[69]

Thus, it may be gleaned from the above opinion that the Court believes that one of the ways to safeguard media pluralism is to prevent financial groups that are too large from controlling the advertising sector.[70] And as national governments are the guarantors of media pluralism, they are under an obligation to take appropriate measures to make such a prevention effective. Even broader interpretation of this judgment allows suspicion that the Court could possibly also view the competitive advantage obtained by powerful commercial broadcasters themselves as dangerous for media pluralism, and, thus, freedom of expression.

This has been expressly stated by the Court in a recent judgment in *Manole v. Moldova* and re-affirmed in the recent case *Centro Europa 7*.[71] The Court stressed that:

> A situation whereby a powerful economic or political group in a society is permitted to obtain a position of dominance over the audiovisual media and thereby exercise pressure on broadcasters and eventually curtail their editorial freedom undermines the fundamental role of freedom of expression in a democratic society as enshrined in Article 10 of the Convention, in particular where it serves to impart information and ideas of general interest, which the public is moreover entitled to receive.[72]

Thus, in the Court's opinion, States as ultimate guarantors of pluralism are obliged to take positive action to protect it from all potential dangers, be it state intervention into editorial independence, creation of public media monopolies or excessive concentration in the media sector.

To summarize, in its judgments in *Lentia, Tierfabriken* and especially in *Manole* and *Centro Europa 7,* the European Court of Human Rights did in fact *require* positive action on the part of Member States to promote pluralism in the media. In *Centro Europa* 7 the Court expressly stated that States have 'a positive obligation to put in place an appropriate legislative and administrative framework to guarantee effective pluralism'.[73] This includes the obligation to prevent the formation of excessively large media corporations which may exercise undue pressure on the independence of

69. *Verein Gegen Tierfabriken v. Switzerland*, 2001-VI; (2002) 34 EHRR 159, emphasis added.
70. Jones, C.A., 'Television without Frontiers', in Eeckhout, P., Tridimas, T. (eds), *Yearbook of European Law 1999–2000* (Oxford Clarendon Press, 2000), 306–307.
71. *Manole and Others v. Moldova,* Application no. 13936/02, 17 September 2009.
72. *Manole and Others v. Moldova,* Application no. 13936/02, 17 September 2009, para. 98.
73. *Centro Europa 7 S.r.l and Di Stefano v. Italy,* Application no. 38433/09, 7 June 2012, para. 156.

broadcasters. The Court's approach is that 'rights of broadcasters are limited to the interests of pluralism and it is the *duty* of the legislature to take appropriate steps to secure this end'.[74]

Moreover, this view was confirmed by the Council's of Europe Advisory Panel on Media Diversity. In its 2002 report 'Media Diversity in Europe',[75] having analysed the Court's case-law on media pluralism, the Panel concluded that the Court believes that Article 10:

> not only enshrines an individual right to media freedom, but also entails a *duty to guarantee pluralism* of opinion and cultural diversity of the media in the interest of a functioning democracy and of freedom of information for all. Pluralism is thus a basic general rule of European media policy.[76]

3.2.5. Conclusions on the Role of European Court of Human Rights

Notwithstanding the unquestionable contribution the Court of Human Rights has made over the years to the debate on the need to safeguard pluralism in the media, the individual, *ex post* and case-by-case protection offered by the Court is by no means sufficient to counteract media concentrations at European level. Neither is it sufficient, therefore, to guarantee pluralism in European media.

Although the Court of Human Rights has been braver than any of the EU institutions in formulating the view that the Member States are under *obligation* to safeguard media pluralism,[77] it is still uncertain whether the Court construes the principle of pluralism as a *restriction* upon freedom of expression or an inherent *aspect* of that freedom. Moreover, a judgment made against a Member State is only binding on the Member State in question. Furthermore, the Court will only deal with three types of *individual* cases – first involving restrictions of freedom of expression which at the

---

74. Jones, C.A., 'Television without Frontiers', 306–307.
75. Council of Europe, 'Media Diversity in Europe' (December 2002), 7.
76. Council of Europe, 'Media Diversity in Europe' (December 2002), 7.
77. The European Court of Justice followed the Court's of Human Rights case-law to a certain extent and in several judgments considered, that in the light of Article 10(2) of the Convention, there is a compelling public interest in the maintenance of a pluralistic radio and television system, which justifies restrictions on fundamental freedoms, such as freedom of establishment or freedom to provide services; see for instance Cases C-353/89, *Commission v. Netherlands* [1991] ECR I-04069, at para. 29; C-288/89, *Gouda* [1991] ECR I-04007, at para. 23; C-148/91, *Veronica Omroep* [1993] ECR I-00487, at paras 9, 10; C-368/95, *Familiapress* [1997] ECR I-3689, at para. 18. However, the European Court of Justice only confirmed the *right* of the Member States to regulate for media pluralism; it has never stated that an *obligation* exists.

same time have a negative impact on internal media pluralism (*Handyside, Jersild*). Second, cases where the lack of structural media pluralism constitutes, in itself an impediment to freedom of expression (*Lentia*). And third, cases where national measures aimed at the protection of structural pluralism are a justified (*Groppera*) or unjustified (*Autronic*) restriction to freedom of expression.

Furthermore, the Court has to wait for a complaint to deal with a problem – even if it is aware of this particular problem. It does not pose a concern in instances where there is a lack of internal media pluralism. And he/she who is prosecuted by a State, for expressing his/her views in the media, may complain to the Court of Human Rights. However, in cases of the lack of structural media pluralism, individual viewers and listeners do not seem eligible to bring complaints before the Court. For instance, the Commission has considered that they do not have sufficient standing to call for the correction of misleading information which does not affect them directly. In the case *X v. Sweden*,[78] the complainant alleged that Swedish television had given a misleading impression of a company in Liberia. The Commission held that the claimant was not a victim because he was not affected *personally* by the report. This suggests that individuals concerned with not being sufficiently and impartially informed as a result of excessive media concentration are not entitled to seek protection by the Court of their right to *receive* diverse information, unless they can prove a *direct concern*. Therefore, it seems that as far as structural media pluralism is concerned, the only category of applicants with a realistic chance to succeed before the Court are broadcasters affected by excessive media concentration which in turn restricts their right to freedom of expression. If the Court then recognizes such a plea, the pluralist structure of the market may, as a result, be restored with a positive effect for viewers or listeners.

Ultimately, that the main weakness is that the protection of media pluralism offered by the Court is individual and incidental. Thus, there is a need for organised and structured *ex ante* action on media concentration at the European level. As noted by the European Broadcasting Union:

> Freedom of expression and information as a right for individuals cannot offer its full benefits for a democratic society unless there is a *framework* which ensures that the media system functions properly, and unless there are safeguards for media pluralism (and media conglomerates are prevented from becoming dominant and controlling public opinion), as well as safeguards for cultural identity and diversity (so that they are not brushed aside by market forces and globalisation).[79]

78. *X v. Sweden*, 3071/67 [1968] DR 71.
79. European Broadcasting Union, 'EBU comments on the Charter of Fundamental Rights', 11 May 2000.

This is why the Council of Europe has stepped in to fill in the gap left by the individual, incidental and *ex post* protection of media pluralism thus far, offered by the Court. However, it was the Court's role of a policy actor that stimulated the Council's actions.

3.3. COUNCIL OF EUROPE: AN ADVOCATE FOR POSITIVE ACTION AT THE EUROPEAN LEVEL

The Council of Europe associates the need for diversity and pluralism in the media with the fundamental human right to freedom of expression and information. It believes that Article 10[80] of the European Convention on Human Rights is 'the basic framework for media pluralism on the European scale'.[81] It therefore imposes a duty on the Council of Europe's Member States to guarantee pluralism and diversity in the media in order to ensure freedom of information and a properly functioning democracy.

The Council of Europe has since 1989 worked towards creating common regulatory initiatives aimed at guaranteeing the *ex ante* protection of media pluralism and diversity. Numerous bodies and committees established over the last decade have produced even more detailed and rigid reports. Many of these reports have resulted in recommendations that have been adopted by the Council of Europe's Committee of Ministers. Having started with 'shy' suggestions of information exchange in the beginning of the 1990s, the Council of Europe's stance evolved towards suggesting in 2004, the need for a convention on media diversity in Europe. The table at the end of this chapter lists the instruments adopted by the Council of Europe in the field of media pluralism and summarises their main findings. All of this has been aimed at assisting the Member States in the realization of the 'obligation' imposed by the European Court of Human Rights to provide for adequate measures aimed at safeguarding media pluralism.[82]

Thus, to start a more detailed analysis of the Council of Europe's work in this area, one must first mention the Committee of Experts on Media

80. Article 10 (1) of the ECHR: 'Everyone has the right to freedom of expression. This rights shall include freedom to hold opinions and to receive and impart information and ideas without interference by public authority and regardless of frontiers'; Article 10(2) allows Member States to introduce restrictions of freedom of expression, but only provided they are 'prescribed by law', 'are necessary in a democratic society' and pursue a legitimate aim in the interest of national security or public safety, for the prevention of disorder or crime, for the protection of health or morals or for the protection of the rights and freedoms of others.
81. Council of Europe, 'Media Diversity in Europe', report by the AP-MD, Advisory Panel to the Steering Committee on the Mass Media, December 2002.
82. Van Loon, A., 'Media Freedom versus Access Rights in a European Context', in Marsden, C., Higgott, R. (eds), *Regulating the Global Information Society*, Routledge Globalisation Series (Routledge, 2000), 287.

Concentrations and Pluralism (hereinafter MM-CM[83]), established in 1991 and tasked with conducting an in-depth examination of the impact of media concentrations on pluralism. The Committee introduced a procedure for periodic exchanges of information between Member States aimed at establishing the degree of media concentration and national measures taken to control it. The exchange of information was intended, first of all, to provide Member States with points of reference when introducing or reforming media ownership laws, and second, to help the Council of Europe in determining whether there is a need for the introduction of harmonized measures at European level.

The MM-CM prepared a Recommendation on measures to promote media pluralism, which was adopted and presented to Member States by the Committee of Ministers of the Council of Europe, on 19 January 1999.[84] The Recommendation identified a range of possible measures to guarantee media pluralism and also recommended that Member States should consider the inclusion of these in their domestic laws on media ownership. One of the main measures recommended was the setting of thresholds for admissible levels of media ownership, based on either audience share, revenue / turnover or capital share. Companies exceeding these thresholds would not be awarded additional broadcasting licenses. Moreover, Member States were encouraged to introduce specific media authorities empowered to act against media concentrations threatening pluralism and diversity. However, if the Member States did not consider this appropriate, the Recommendation stressed that, general competition authorities should take pluralism and diversity considerations into account in their assessment of media mergers. Finally, it was recommended that Member States should encourage media companies to strengthen editorial and journalistic independence, voluntarily, through self-regulation.

The work and efforts of MM-CM have also led to the introduction of the provision of pluralism to the Council of Europe's main legislative instrument in the media sector is the Convention on Transfrontier Television. In 1998 the Amending Protocol to the Convention added Article 10(a). This amendment provided that Member States, 'in the spirit of co-operation and mutual assistance which underlies this Convention, shall endeavour to avoid that programme services transmitted or retransmitted by a broadcaster or any other legal or natural persons within their jurisdiction ... endanger media pluralism'. Although laudable, the words 'shall endeavour' create nothing more than a 'please do your best' obligation for Member States. With no sanctions, this Convention was even weaker than the EU Television Without Frontiers Directive adopted in the same year. Although the Directive only mentioned pluralism in recitals, at least it admitted that it was 'essential for

83. The official abbreviation applied by the Council of Europe.

84. Council of Europe, Recommendation No. R (99) 1 of the Committee of Ministers to Member States on Measures to Promote Media Pluralism, 19 January 1999.

the Member States to *ensure* the prevention of any acts which may promote the creation of dominant positions which would lead to restrictions on pluralism'.[85]

In 1999, the MM-CM was succeeded by another body set up to examine if and how media pluralism is influenced by new technologies and convergence. The work of the Group of Specialists on Media Pluralism (hereinafter MM-S-PL[86]) resulted in the publication in 2000 of a report on media pluralism in a digital environment.[87] While acknowledging that digital television is able to offer more channels and more services, the MM-S-PL was concerned whether this would coincide with increased pluralism of content. The Group expressed doubts that this would actually be the case.

The report observed that technological convergence and emergence of new delivery systems naturally pushes companies to strive for control over both content production and its transmission and delivery. This growing vertical integration of media companies, which renders access of independent content providers to major platforms more difficult, was described as one of the biggest obstacles for effective pluralism in digital television. The report, therefore, recommended introducing different types of *ex ante* control rules aimed at 'unbundling' vertically integrated companies. The MM-S-PL admitted that on several occasions EC merger control was successful in preventing the emergence of dominant vertically integrated conglomerates.[88] It nevertheless rightly pointed to mechanisms such as must-carry obligations for dominant players, technical regulations to open gateways or cross-ownership restrictions as necessary to ensure access to platforms and protect pluralism. This was particularly the case where competition authorities would allow mergers viewed as beneficial to the development or introduction of new technologies, as was for example in the *Newscorp/Telepiù*[89] decision. In this case, the European Commission allowed a merger to near monopoly and justified it by the difficult economic situation of the two merging platforms and the interest in growing a digital platform and to provide continued digital service to users.[90]

After the sixth Ministerial Conference on mass media policy held in Cracow, Poland, in June 2000, yet another body was established to assist the

---

85. Council Directive 89/552/EEC of 3 October 1989 on the coordination of certain provisions laid down by Law, Regulation or Administrative Action in Member States concerning the pursuit of television broadcasting activities, OJ (1989) L331/51, emphasis added.
86. The official abbreviation applied by the Council of Europe.
87. Council of Europe, 'Media Pluralism in the Digital Environment', report by the Steering Committee on the Mass Media, October 2000.
88. See, for instance, Case IV/M.469, *MSG Media Service* where the European Commission forbid a joint venture between Bertelsmann, Kirch and Deutsche Telekom.
89. Case COMP/M.2876, *Newscorp/Telepiu.*
90. Ungerer, H., 'Application of Competition Law to Media – Some Recent Issues', Nera Conference, Brussels, 22 June 2004.

Council of Europe's Steering Committee on Mass Media. The Advisory Panel on Media Concentrations, Pluralism and Diversity Questions (hereinafter AP-MD[91]) produced two extensive reports outlining the recommendations on the ways in which to protect pluralism and diversity in the increasingly consolidated European media sector. Both reports mark the toughening of the Council's stance and the transition from general observations and statements, to more concrete proposals.

Thus, the 2002 Report on media diversity in Europe[92] contained much more detailed and stringent recommendations than the 1999 Recommendation on measures to promote media pluralism. First, not only did it emphasize the need for pluralism in the ownership structure of media companies, but for the first time, it also clearly stressed that the Council of Europe's opinion should be, that in order to secure genuinely diversified and pluralistic media content many, and indeed competing, sources of information are necessary. The current situation, whereby media companies become more and more reliant on the supply of content by a few existing news agencies renders even fierce competition between television stations or newspapers absolutely meaningless in terms of providing for pluralism and diversity. Second, the report went on to point out the shortcomings of competition law in the protection of pluralism and diversity in the media sector. It confirmed that from a media pluralism perspective, competition legislation deals only with a minority of relevant cases, and thus it cannot ensure satisfactory protection against media concentrations that are unquestioned from the competition point of view, but at the same time are harmful to pluralism. The conclusion, therefore, was that there is definitely a need for sector-specific regulation of media concentrations. Acknowledging the existence of various national laws in this area, the report recommended the audience share approach as the best way of measuring the level of ownership in the media sector.

Nevertheless, despite outlining fairly detailed rules for preferable models of control of media concentrations the authors of the report were at that point in time, very wary of directly suggesting taking action at European level. The observation was made that the European media markets differ in culture, size and characteristics. There are also different legal and administrative traditions among the European countries and therefore, no common or single regulatory model will be suitable for all European countries.

The second report prepared by AP-MD in November 2004 entitled 'Transnational media concentrations in Europe'[93] went even further in its recommendations. Expressing serious concerns about the impact the growing number of transnational media concentrations has on media pluralism and

91. The official abbreviation applied by the Council of Europe.
92. Council of Europe, 'Media Diversity in Europe', December 2002, H/APMD (2003) 1, at 4.
93. Council of Europe, 'Transnational Media Concentrations in Europe', report by the AP-MD, Advisory Panel to the Steering Committee on the Mass Media, November 2004.

the inability of individual countries to counteract the negative effects of this trend, the report emphasized the need for action at European level. It recommended the Council of Europe not only to initiate the ongoing monitoring of transnational media concentrations, but also to 'urgently study the appropriate means, including a convention, to prevent the negative impact that this phenomenon may have on freedom of expression, pluralism and diversity'.

The great set-back for the authors of the report was the rejection by the Parliamentary Assembly of the Council of Europe of the recommendation to join forces with the European Union to confront the crisis of media concentration in Europe. This caused dismay in journalists' circles, which criticized the 'missed opportunity' and 'making noise' without the suggestions of concrete action.[94]

In 2003, the Council of Europe took a stance on the effects of digitalization and the resulting multiplication of channels on pluralism and diversity. In the Recommendation on measures to promote the democratic and social contribution of digital broadcasting,[95] the Committee of Ministers noted that despite multiplication of channels, trends toward concentration continue. Therefore, transition to digital broadcasting should be accompanied by positive measures to fight concentration trends and preserve plurality of services and quality and diversity of programmes.

In 2005, the Council of Europe produced a Resolution on cultural diversity and media pluralism in times of globalization. This was accompanied by an Action Plan, adopted during the seventh European Ministerial Conference on Mass Media Policy that was held in March 2005 in Kyiv (Ukraine).[96] In the resolution the Ministers noted, as they had on numerous occasions, the increasing trend towards concentration in the media sector, both in Europe and worldwide. They stressed that to prevent a potentially harmful impact of media concentrations on pluralism, the adoption of sector specific rules designed to safeguard plurality and diversity in the media, is vitally important. The Ministers also emphasized the need for the transparency of media ownership, the importance of monitoring media concentrations and the need for a single European voice in international discussions on media concentrations. Interestingly, the Ministers pointed to the Council of Europe as an appropriate framework for the exchange of information and experience on these issues. They also recommended that the Council should

94. European Federation of Journalists, 'Media power in Europe: the big picture of ownership', 'EFJ expresses dismay over Council of Europe "Missed Opportunity" to conform media concentration crisis', 29 June 2004, http://www.ifj.org.

95. Council of Europe, Recommendation Rec(2003)9 of the Committee of Ministers to member states on measures to promote the democratic and social contribution of digital broadcasting, 28 May 2003.

96. Council of Europe, 7th Ministerial Conference on Mass Media Policy, Kyiv (Ukraine), 10–11 March 2005, 'Integration and Diversity: the new frontiers of European media and communications policy', adopted texts, MCM(2005)005.

address the transnational aspects of media concentrations in Europe. Consequently, in the Action Plan the Council of Europe undertook to continue to monitor the development of media concentrations in Europe as a political priority and, where appropriate, suggest legal or other initiatives which it may consider necessary in order to preserve media pluralism.

To ensure these promises were met, in January 2007 the Committee of Ministers of the Council of Europe adopted a declaration aimed at protecting the role of the media in democracy, in the context of media concentration.[97] This was accompanied by two Recommendations – one on Media pluralism and diversity of media content,[98] and the other on the remit of public service media in the information society.[99] In the declaration, the Ministers alerted the Member States to the risk of misusing the power of the media in a situation of strong concentration. They also drew attention to the usefulness of regulatory measures that guarantee full transparency of media ownership and counteracting excessive media concentration. In the Recommendation on media pluralism, the Council of Europe yet again stressed the need for Member States to introduce measures to safeguard structural pluralism as well as content diversity in the media. The Ministers recommended the adoption and maintenance of sector specific rules aimed at ownership regulation by introducing thresholds, access regulation and content regulation. It is probably one of the most strongly worded recommendations so far issued by the Committee of Ministers.

The second Recommendation produced in 2007 – on the remit of public service media in the information society[100] – confirmed that the Council of Europe is also a vocal advocate of public service broadcasting as a 'counterweight' for concentrating commercial media and supporting pluralism and diversity. In this regard, the earlier recommendation of the Council of Europe's Parliamentary Assembly on Public Service Broadcasting[101] is highly significant. The Recommendation notes that public service broadcasting which is a vital element of democracy in Europe is challenged by 'political and economic interests, by increasing competition from commercial media [and] by media concentrations'. It therefore recommended that the

97. Declaration of the Committee of Ministers on protecting the role of the media in democracy in the context of media concentration, adopted by the Committee of Ministers on 31 January 2007 at the 985th meeting of the Ministers' Deputies.
98. Recommendation CM/Rec(2007)2 of the Committee of Ministers to Member States on media pluralism and diversity of media content, adopted by the Committee of Ministers on 31 January 2007 at the 985th meeting of the Ministers' Deputies.
99. Recommendation CM/Rec(2007)3 of the Committee of Ministers to Member States on the remit of public service media in the information society, adopted by the Committee of Ministers on 31 January 2007 at the 985th meeting of the Ministers' Deputies.
100. Recommendation CM/Rec(2007)3 of the Committee of Ministers to Member States on the remit of public service media in the information society, adopted by the Committee of Ministers on 31 January 2007 at the 985th meeting of the Ministers' Deputies.
101. Recommendation 1641 (2004) of the Parliamentary Assembly on Public Service Broadcasting, 27 January 2004.

Committee of Ministers should adopt a new major policy document on public service broadcasting and called on the Member States to 'reaffirm their commitment to maintaining a strong and vibrant independent public broadcasting service, whilst adapting it to the requirements of the digital age'.

The Recommendation also explains the Council's understanding of the remit of public service broadcasting as consisting of five elements: (i) a reference point for all members of the public, offering universal access; (ii) a factor of social cohesion and integration for all individuals, groups and communities; (iii) a source of impartial and independent information and comment, and of innovatory and varied content which complies with high ethical and quality standards; (iv) a forum for pluralistic public discussion and a means of promoting broader democratic participation for individuals; and (v) an active contributor to audiovisual creation and production, and greater appreciation and dissemination of the diversity of national and European cultural heritage.

The Council's position on the importance of public service broadcasting was once again stressed in 2012 in a Declaration[102] and Recommendation[103] on public service media governance, adopted on the same day. The Committee of Ministers stressed that media in general are the most important tool for freedom of expression in the public sphere, enabling people to exercise the right to seek and receive information. Public service media in particular play a specific role with regard to the respect of this right and the provision of a varied and high-quality content, contributing to the reinforcement of democracy and social cohesion, and promoting intercultural dialogue and mutual understanding. The Committee alerted to the risks to pluralism and diversity in the media and, in consequence, to democratic debate and commitment, if public service media are not preserved. In consequence, the Committee of Ministers recommended that Member States to further strengthen and enhance the appropriate legal and financial environment for public service media organizations, thereby guaranteeing their independence and sustainable development and 'empowering them to take up the challenges of technological progress and editorial competition'.

Finally, it is worth noting that the most recent of the expert reports – Report on methodology for monitoring media concentration and media content diversity (2008) – observed that very few Member States are effectively monitoring media concentration, pluralism and diversity and recommended that Member States start regular collection of basic data showing their media market structure, including data on owners. It suggested that the secretariat of the CoE should prepare an online READER in media

102. Council of Europe, Declaration of the Committee of Ministers on Public Service Media Governance, 15 February 2012.
103. Council of Europe, Recommendation Rec(2012)1 of the Committee of Ministers to member States on public service media governance, 15 February 2012.

concentration, pluralism and diversity which will contain all of the CoE's standards and reports on the matter adopted so far.

The latest challenge for the principles established by the Council of Europe in the field of media pluralism and diversity came in the form of the already discussed Hungarian media law which came into force on 1 January 2011. In February 2011 the Council's Commissioner for Human Rights issued an Opinion on the law in light of the Council of Europe standards on freedom of the media[104] and concluded that the wide range of problematic provisions in Hungary's media legislation, as identified in this Opinion, is sufficient to warrant a wholesale review of the law by Hungary. The Commissioner pointed out that the best guide for the Hungarian authorities in their wholesale review is the body of Council of Europe standards that have been developed in Court judgments, recommendations and resolutions over the past six decades. In March 2012, the Council of Europe issued its own expert report on the Hungarian media law and again observed that the unclear definitions and provisions on the protection of journalists' sources run counter the Council's standards on freedom of expression and pluralism.[105] However, the report noted that it takes into account the judgment of the Hungarian Constitutional Court's of December 2011[106] declaring the media law partially unconstitutional. Thus, the Council's analysis will be finalized and made public when the amendments to the law adopted in compliance with the judgment are submitted to the Council of Europe.

In summary, the Council of Europe and its permanent judiciary body – the European Court of Human Rights – are the only consistent and resilient pan-European advocates of the need to safeguard media pluralism, both internal and external, in the European media. The European Court of Human Rights provides the forum for individual media consumers and media providers in Europe to complain of breaches of the right to freedom of expression and information caused by lack of pluralistic media structures. This is probably the only existing pan-European mechanism able to effectively enforce the principle of media pluralism. In the numerous judgments, the Court managed to prove that it has a great potential to defend media pluralism in its 'internal' incarnation, i.e., to protect pluralism of ideas and diversity of opinions presented in the media. Ensuring structural pluralism in media, i.e., numerous and diverse media providers, proved a more difficult task. With the exception of *Lentia*, the Court has never intervened nor expressly stated that in order for freedom of expression to

104. Opinion of the Commissioner for Human Rights on Hungary's media legislation in light of Council of Europe standards on freedom of the media, CommDH(2011)10, 25 February 2011.
105. 'Council of Europe report says Hungary media law lacks guarantees for independence', 22 March 2012.
106. 'Hungary Court Rules Media, Criminal Law Violate Basic Rights', 19 December 2011.

flourish there is a need for a number of media providers, and the Member States must ensure that structural pluralism is safeguarded on their territories.

This is where the Council of Europe steps in and fills the gap with initiatives aimed at encouraging organized and *ex ante* protection of structural media pluralism. Indeed, the outline of the history of the Council's of Europe regulatory efforts leaves the impression that the Council would like to see itself as 'a vehicle for European harmonization of legislation'[107] in the media concentrations area. The European Commission also directly pointed to the Council of Europe as 'the only organization at pan-European level dealing with the human and democratic dimension of communication'.[108] Commissioner Kroes has recently directed Hungary to seek and apply the Council's recommendations on the new controversial media law.[109] However, given the non-coercive nature of the Council's various declarations, recommendations and other policy documents, it may be difficult for the Council to be a vehicle for European harmonization in the media pluralism area. Nevertheless, the effect of the Council's declarations and recommendations, as well as of its constant awareness-raising through its numerous reports, and conferences[110] should not be underestimated.

In this regard, it would be interesting to see the materialization of the convention on transnational media concentrations as suggested by the 2004 report entitled 'Transnational media concentrations in Europe.'[111] In fact, the European Commission pointed out to the possibility, if not desirability, of the Council of Europe adopting an instrument with the human rights side of the media, which would undoubtedly include media pluralism.[112] This suggestion materialized during a dispute between the Council of Europe and the European Commission on the revision of the Convention on Transfrontier Television.[113] The European Union claimed exclusive competence in the area regulated by the AVMS Directive and practically prevented its Member States from signing the revised Convention, rendering the Councils of Europe instrument virtually defunct. This leaves the Council free to adopt a

107. Cavallin, J., 'European Policies and Regulations on Media Concentration', 1.
108. European Commission, 'Media Pluralism – What Should Be the European Union's Role?', Issues Paper for the Liverpool Audiovisual Conference, July 2005.
109. 'EU Still Has "Grave Concerns" on Hungary Media Laws, Kroes Says', Bloomberg, 9 February 2012.
110. For instance, a conference on 'Concentration of media ownership and its impact on media freedom and pluralism', held in Bled, Slovenia in 2004.
111. Council of Europe, 'Transnational Media Concentrations in Europe', report by the AP-MD, Advisory Panel to the Steering Committee on the Mass Media, November 2004.
112. See 45th meeting of the Standing Committee on Transfrontier Television, 1–2 July 2010, TT (2010) 2.
113. For a complete discussion of the issue, see Mac Síthigh, D., 'Death of a Convention: Competition between the Council of Europe and European Union in the Regulation of Broadcasting', paper presented at SLS Annual Conference, Cambridge, September 2012 (unpublished).

new convention dealing with public interest aspects of the media and consolidating case law of the European Court of Human Rights and the work of the Council in the area of media freedom, pluralism and diversity. Mac Síthigh asks, 'even if such an instrument is agreed, how significant will it be?'.[114] The answer could lie in the fact that such a 'Media Pluralism Convention' would apply to all forty-seven Member States of the Council of Europe and therefore to all twenty-seven Member States of the European Union. Although not as powerful a tool as an EU Directive, since it would owe its legal force to the Member States' decision to ratify it, such an instrument could potentially stimulate and encourage the decision-making process in the European Union. If it were possible for Member States to reach agreement over a Council of Europe's convention, agreement over a more rigid EU instrument could possibly be the next step.

Thus, although the efforts of the Council of Europe and the judgments of the Court of Human Rights are by no means sufficient to guarantee media pluralism on the European scale, they are nevertheless vital for awareness raising and debate-stimulating. While binding action at the European level is without a doubt a task for the European Union, the Council of Europe may be the body which provides enough stimulus for that to happen.

114. Mac Síthigh, D., 'Death of a Convention: Competition between the Council of Europe and European Union in the Regulation of Broadcasting'.

Table 3.1 Main Instruments Adopted by the Council of Europe in the Field of Media Pluralism

Conventions	*1989*	*Convention on Transfrontier Television*	*Article 10a (added in 1998): 'Member States, in the spirit of co-operation and mutual assistance which underlies this Convention, shall endeavour to avoid that programme services transmitted or retransmitted by a broadcaster or any other legal or natural persons within their jurisdiction … endanger media pluralism.'*
Resolutions	2005	Resolution the Committee of Ministers on Cultural Diversity and Media Pluralism in Times of Globalization, accompanied by an Action Plan	– Need for transparency of media ownership, the importance of monitoring media concentrations and the need for a European voice in international forums discussing media concentrations; – Action Plan: to monitor the development of media concentrations in Europe as a political priority and, where appropriate, suggest legal or other initiatives which it may consider necessary in order to preserve media pluralism.
Recommendations	1994	Recommendation No R(94) 13 of the Committee of Ministers to Member States on Measures to promote media transparency	5 Guidelines: (1) Access by the public to information on the media, (2) Exchange of information on media transparency between national authorities, (3) Disclosure of information when granting broadcasting licenses to broadcasting services, (4) Disclosure of information following the grant of broadcasting licenses to broadcasting services, (5) Exercise of the functions of the service or authorities responsible for ensuring transparency in the running of broadcasting services.
	1999	Recommendation No. R (99) 1 of the Committee of Ministers to Member States on Measures to Promote Media Pluralism	– Recommendation to introduce thresholds for the admissible level of media ownership, based on either audience share, revenue/turnover or capital share.

			– Encouragement to introduce specific media authorities empowered to act against media concentrations threatening pluralism and diversity. – General competition authorities should take pluralism and diversity considerations into account in their assessment of media mergers. – Member States recommended to encourage media companies to strengthen editorial and journalistic independence voluntarily through self-regulation.
	2003	Recommendation Rec(2003)9 of the Committee of Ministers to Member States on Measures to Promote the Democratic and Social Contribution of Digital Broadcasting	– Despite multiplication of channels, trends toward concentration continue. – Transition to digital broadcasting should be accompanied by positive measures to fight concentration trends and preserve plurality of services and quality and diversity of programmes.
	2004	Recommendation 1641 (2004) of the Parliamentary Assembly on Public Service Broadcasting	Call on the Member States to 'reaffirm their commitment to maintaining a strong and vibrant independent public broadcasting service, whilst adapting it to the requirements of the digital age'.
	2007	Recommendation CM/Rec(2007)2 of the Committee of Ministers to Member States on media pluralism and diversity of media content	Recommendation of the adoption and maintenance of sector specific rules aimed at ownership regulation by introducing thresholds, access regulation and content regulation.

	2007	Recommendation CM/Rec(2007)3 of the Committee of Ministers to Member States on the remit of public service media in the information society	Explanation of the Council's understanding of the remit of PSBs as consisting of five elements: (i) a reference point for all members of the public, offering universal access; (ii) a factor of social cohesion and integration for all individuals, groups and communities; (iii) a source of impartial and independent information and comment, and of innovatory and varied content which complies with high ethical and quality standards; (iv) a forum for pluralistic public discussion; and (v) an active contributor to audiovisual creation.
	2012	Recommendation Rec (2012)1 of the Committee of Ministers to Member States on public service media governance	– Public service media play a specific role with regard to the provision of a varied and high-quality content, contributing to the reinforcement of democracy and social cohesion, and promoting intercultural dialogue and mutual understanding. – If public service media are not preserved, there is a high risk to pluralism and diversity in the media. – Recommendation to Member States to further strengthen and enhance the appropriate legal and financial environment for public service media organizations.
Declarations	2007	Declaration of the Committee of Ministers on protecting the role of the media in democracy in the context of media concentration	Member states alerted to the risk of power misuse of the media in a situation of strong concentration and their attention drew to the usefulness of regulatory measures guaranteeing full transparency of media ownership and counteracting excessive media concentration.
	2012	Declaration of the Committee of Ministers on Public Service Media Governance	As in the 2012 Recommendation Rec(2012)1 above.

Chapter 4

European Tools II: European Competition Law

4.1. MERGERS: POLICY EVOLUTION

Article 3 of the Treaty on the Functioning of the European Union (*TFEU*) provides that the European Union has exclusive competence to establish the competition rules necessary for the functioning of the internal market. The rules thus established consist of rules prohibiting anti-competitive agreements between undertakings (Article 101), rules prohibiting abuse of a dominant position (Article 102) and rules regulating State involvement is business practices (Articles 106 and 107). Since 1990, the EC has also had the power to regulate mergers (EU Merger Regulation[1]). Consumer welfare is the main objective of the EU competition law, accompanied by other objectives such as market integration and development of healthy European industry. Therefore, the EU competition policy complements the internal market rules 'by preventing businesses from partitioning the internal market and by encouraging competition across borders'.[2]

Competition law is currently the only tool for active and direct EU action and regulation in the field of media concentration. Therefore, not

---

1. Council Regulation (EEC) No. 4064/89 of 21 December 1989 on the control of concentrations between undertakings amended in 1997 and recently replaced by Council Regulation (EEC) 139/2004 of 20 January 2004 on the control of concentrations between undertakings (the EC Merger Regulation).
2. Chalmers, D., et al., *European Union Law: Text and Materials* (Cambridge University Press, 2006), 928.

surprisingly, the contribution of competition law, both its merger control and antitrust branches, to the maintenance of pluralism has been recurrently and frequently discussed in academic literature.[3] One of the most interesting approaches was offered by Arino, who analysed the impact of both EU competition law and legislation on pluralism across the value chain (content-network-platform).[4] I, however, propose yet another angle. In the analysis of salient mergers and antitrust decisions in the broadcasting sector, I consider their impact on structural and internal pluralism alongside examining the policy developments in DG Competition under the rule of four Commissioners – from Van Miert, through to Monti and Kroes and finally through to, Almunia. This policy development has mirrored the changing approach in the European Union as a whole, to the issue of media concentration. This shows that competition law can be stretched if necessary and if there is a political will.

4.1.1. 'Smuggling' Public Interest to Merger Analysis under Van Miert

The European Commission has had specific merger control powers since 1989 when the first Merger Regulation[5] was adopted. The Commission becomes solely responsible for the assessment of a concentration (a merger, an acquisition or a joint-venture) if the latter has a 'Community dimension'. That is where certain, high turnover thresholds are exceeded.[6] The Commissions merger decisions are subject to review in the first instance by the

3. See, for instance, Arino, M., 'Pluralism in Digital Broadcasting: Myths, Realities and the Boundaries of European Intervention', in Preissl, B., Muller, J. (eds), *Governance of Communications Networks. Connecting Societies and Markets with IT* (Physica-Verlag, 2006); Arino, M., 'Competition Law and Pluralism in European Digital Broadcasting: Addressing the Gaps'; Doyle, G., *Media Ownership*; Harcourt, A., *The European Union and the Regulation of Media Markets*; Nitsche, I., *Broadcasting in the European Union: The Role of Public Interest in Competition Analysis* (T.M.C. Asser Press, 2001); Wheeler, M., 'Supranational Regulation: The EU Competition Directorate and the European Audio-Visual Marketplace', in Harrison, J., Wessels, B. (eds), *Mediating Europe. New Media, Mass Communications, and the European Public Sphere* (Berghahn Books, 2009).
4. Arino, M., 'Pluralism in Digital Broadcasting: Myths, Realities and the Boundaries of European Intervention'.
5. Council Regulation (EEC) No. 4064/89 of 21 December 1989 on the control of concentrations between undertakings.
6. Article 1 of the Merger Regulation states that in general a concentration has a Community dimension where (i) the combined aggregate worldwide turnover of all the undertakings concerned is more than EUR 5 billion; and (ii) the aggregate Community-wide turnover of each of at least two of the undertakings concerned is more that EUR 250 million, unless each of the undertakings concerned achieves more than two-thirds of its aggregate Community-wide turnover within one and the same Member State. There are more detailed rules for establishing a Community dimension even if a concentration does not meet the two general thresholds.

General Court and then on appeal by the European Court of Justice (ECJ). Neither the Council of Ministers nor the European Parliament's consent is necessary.

The test applied by the Commission when deciding whether to allow or prohibit a merger is the 'substantial impediment of effective competition-'(SIEC) test introduced by the Merger Regulation 139/2004 in place of the dominance test applied before the 2004 amendment. Thus, Article 3 of the current Merger Regulation, provides that the Commission will prohibit, that is declare incompatible with the common market, a concentration 'which would significantly impede effective competition, in the common market or in a substantial part of it, *in particular* as a result of the creation or strengthening of a dominant position'.[7] The change from a narrower dominance test to a wider SIEC test was motivated by the Commission's realization that mergers may have anti-competitive effects even when they do not lead to creation of a dominant position.[8]

There are generally speaking three types of mergers that the Commission deals with: horizontal, vertical and conglomerate. Accordingly, the Commission published Horizontal and Non-horizontal Merger Guidelines explaining the differing treatment of the three types of mergers.[9] The vast majority of cases before the European Commission have concerned horizontal concentrations, that is concentrations between undertakings on the same level of trade (for instance two providers of the same type of goods).[10] The Horizontal Merger Guidelines explain that in analysis of this type of cases the Commission will first establish relevant markets in which the merging undertakings operate. Then, the parties' market shares are calculated, the power of customers and suppliers checked and entry barriers reviewed, in order to establish whether the merger would lead to substantial impediment

---

7. Article 3 of the Council Regulation (EEC) 139/2004 of 20 January 2004 on the control of concentrations between undertakings (the EC Merger Regulation).
8. Chalmers, D., et al., *European Union Law: Text and Materials*, 1090.
9. For the European Commission's position on the assessment of horizontal mergers see Guidelines on the assessment of horizontal mergers under the Council Regulation on the control of concentrations between undertakings, OJ (2004) C-31/5; For the European Commission's position on the assessment of vertical mergers see Guidelines on the assessment of non-horizontal mergers under the Council Regulation on the control of concentrations between undertakings OJ (2008) C-265; For the European Commission's position on the assessment of conglomerate mergers, see Guidelines on the assessment of non-horizontal mergers under the Council Regulation on the control of concentrations between undertakings, paras 91–121.
10. Chalmers, D., et al., *European Union Law: Text and Materials*, 1090.

of effective competition in the relevant markets identified.[11] Vertical mergers take place between companies operating on different levels of trade, for instance a merger between a raw material manufacturer (e.g., fabric) and an undertaking using this raw material to produce a finished product (e.g., clothes). In deciding whether to allow a merger of this type the Commission is looking to prevent a foreclosure effect, that is elimination or weakening of competitors in downstream or upstream markets due to the merged entity dominance. Finally, conglomerate mergers, that is mergers between undertakings present on different markets, may be anti-competitive if they lead to portfolio effects or leveraging.[12] Portfolio effects arise when a merged entity gains competitive advantage by being able to offer a wide portfolio of products.[13] Leveraging occurs when the merged entity sells bundles of products cheaper than competitors who sell the products separately, in order to bind the customers, eliminate competitors and then raise prices. The European Courts provided further guidance in its seminal judgments on conglomerate mergers.[14] The Court emphasized that proving anti-competitive risks of portfolio effects and leveraging must be done with great care[15] and even if those risks are indeed proven, the Commission is obliged to consider any behavioural commitments offered by the parties.[16] There have been fears expressed that after *Tetra Laval/Sidel* and *GE/Honeywell* judgments, the standard of proof imposed by the Courts on the Commission is now so high that it is doubtful whether the Commission will attempt to prohibit a merger on grounds of conglomerate effects in the near future.[17] This may have wide ranging implications for media mergers which very often involve companies operating in different but related markets (e.g., broadcasting and newspaper publishing or pay-TV and free-TV operation).

There is no media-specific merger review at the EU level. However, the Merger Regulation contains one specific provision – Article 21(4) – which is known as the 'legitimate interest' exception.[18] It allows Member States to take 'appropriate measures' to protect legitimate interests other than those taken into consideration by the Merger Regulation. Public security, plurality

11. Chalmers, D., et al., *European Union Law: Text and Materials*, 1090.
12. Chalmers, D., et al., *European Union Law: Text and Materials*, 1104.
13. See for instance Case IV/M.938, *Guiness/Grand Metropolitan*, OJ 1998 L228/24; Case IV/M.794, *Coca-Cola Enterprises/Amalgamated beverages*, OJ 1997 L218/15.
14. Cases C-12/03, P *Commission v. Tetra Laval* [2005] 4 CMLR 8; T-210/01, *General Electric v. Commission* [2005] ECR II-5527
15. There is now a presumption of legality of conglomerate mergers, unless the Commission can prove that they are anti-competitive.
16. Case C-12/03 P, *Commission v. Tetra Laval* [2005] 4 CMLR 8, para. 85
17. Practical Law Company, 'Tetra Laval Decision: Good News for Business?', 31 March 2005.
18. Ritter, L., Braun, W.D., Rawlinson, F., *European Competition Law: A Practitioner's Guide* (Kluwer Law International, 2000), 435.

of the media and prudential rules are expressly mentioned as such legitimate interests. This means that for the sake of protecting the legitimate interest of media pluralism, Member States may *prevent or attach additional conditions* to media mergers that may be detrimental to media pluralism, even if they were approved by the Commission on competition grounds.[19] However, the Commission has explained that Article 21(4) does not give the Member States any power to *authorise* concentrations which the Commission may have prohibited under this regulation.[20]

The Commission cooperates with the Member State concerned when examining concentrations which may involve any of the legitimate interests mentioned in Article 21(4). In fact, it has been argued that the Commission has itself carefully considered the legitimate interest of maintaining media pluralism when prohibiting mergers in the media sector.[21]

Other public interests must be communicated to the Commission by the Member State concerned and may only be relied on after they have been accepted by the Commission as compatible with the general principles and other provisions of Community law. The Commission and the European Court of Justice have clarified the scope of the application of this exception in the 2004 case *Secil/Holderbank/Cimpor.*,[22] which involved a takeover bid for cement company Cimpor Cimentos de Portugal SGPS (which was in the process of privatization) by the Portuguese company Secil and the Swiss company Holderbank. Portugal blocked the transaction explaining its decision by the need to protect the development of shareholding structures in companies undergoing privatization with a view to reinforcing the corporate capacity and the efficiency of the national production apparatus. The Commission was not informed about this potential legitimate interest, and thus it has not accepted it on the basis of Article 21(4) (then Article 21(3)). The Commission decided that even if it was informed, its conclusion would have been that the reasons for blocking the merger could not have been accepted as a legitimate interest under Article 21(4).[23] The Commission also emphasized that Member States are obliged to notify to the Commission any measures that they intend to adopt on the basis of the 'legitimate interests' exception, if those interests are not expressly mentioned by Article 21(4)

19. See European Commission, *Notes on Council Regulation (EEC) 4064/89,* published in 'Merger control law in the European Union', European Commission, Brussels-Luxembourg, 1998.
20. See European Commission, *Notes on Council Regulation (EEC) 4064/89,* published in 'Merger control law in the European Union', European Commission, Brussels-Luxembourg, 1998.
21. For instance, Case M.469, *MSG Media Service*, OJ (1994) L364/1 or Case M.993, *Bertelsmann/Kirch/Premiere,* OJ (1999) L53/1.
22. Case COMP/M.2054, *Secil/Holderbank/Cimpor*, Commission decision of 22 November 2000, upheld by the European Court of Justice in Case C-42/01, *Portugal v. Commission* [2004] ECR I-6079.
23. Case C-42/01, *Portugal v. Commission* [2004] ECR I-6079, paras 26–40.

ECMR or even if they are mentioned, but there is some doubt as to whether the interests pursued are really covered by one of the exceptions listed in that article. This basically means the requirement to inform the Commission of any intended national action with regard to a merger allowed by the Commission. This may have a significant impact on the Member States' willingness to intervene in media mergers on the grounds of media pluralism. In fact, there has been only one such intervention to date, and it was in fact to a large extent 'suggested' by the European Commission in its decision approving the merger.

Besides the 'legitimate interests' exception, competition law in general and merger control rules in particular apply to the television as they do to any other sector of the economy. However, this was only made clear in the 1970s by the ECJ in the *Sacchi*[24] judgment, in which the Court expressed its seminal view that:

> In the absence of express provision to the contrary in the Treaty, a television signal must, by reason of its nature, be regarded a provision of services'[25] and 'trade in material, sound recordings, films, apparatus and other products used for the diffusion of television signals are subject to the rules relating to freedom of movement for goods.[26]

This and a later judgment in *Debauve*,[27] paved the way for the adoption of the Television Without Frontiers Directive in 1989. In its interpretation of the Directive, the ECJ adopted a very liberal line, defending vigorously the liberalization of European market as the 'basic aim' of the Directive and, consequently, often sacrificing the public interests (such as protection of minors) which the Directive tries to protect.[28] One would expect that DG Competition, realizing the limitations of its competence, would be more than happy to follow this track and advocate liberalization of the markets while ignoring public interest considerations. This is why, the hardline attitude of DG Competition towards media mergers in the early 1990s came as a bit of a surprise.

Following the adoption of the *Television Without Frontiers* Directive in 1989, there had been a significant increase in European-wide media mergers.[29] Anticipating the growth in media-related competition decisions,

---

24. Case C-155/73, *Sacchi*, [1974] ECR 409.
25. Case C-155/73, *Sacchi*, [1974] ECR 409, para. 6.
26. Case C-155/73, *Sacchi*, [1974] ECR 409, para. 7.
27. Case C-52/79, *Procureur du Roi v, Debauve*, [1980] ECR 833.
28. See for instance Case C-56/96, *VT4 Ltd v. Vlaamse Gemeenschap,* [1997] ECR I-3143; Case C-14/96, *Criminal proceedings against Denuit*, [1997] ECR I-2785; Case C-34/95 *Konsumentombudsmannen v. De Agostini and TV-Shop*, [1997] ECR I-3843.
29. Lang, M., 'Entering the Digital Age. The Promise of Pluralism and the Danger of Monopoly Control', article presented at the ECPR-Workshop on *New Media and Political Communication* in Bern, 27 February 1997; Harcourt, A., *The European Union and the Regulation of Media Markets*, 41

the European Commission's Directorate General for Competition decided to clarify its policy towards the sector. In the Communication to the Council and European Parliament on audio-visual policy,[30] adopted in February 1990, the Commission emphasized that the media industry differs significantly from other sectors due to a number of 'specific economic and cultural considerations'. In this respect, the Communication clarified that although competition law will continue to apply to the media sector, specific features of the industry will be taken into account when taking media-specific competition decisions. In addition, in 1990, a special unit specifically devoted to media sector was created within DG Competition (Unit C-2 - Media).

This official position determined the way media mergers, in particular those in the broadcasting sector, were treated by the European Commission under the rule of the then Competition Commissioner Karel Van Miert (1993–1999). Under Van Miert's leadership in DG Competition, there were many compromises made between the economic and non-economic objectives in media mergers.[31] In fact, the policy can be described as 'smuggling' public interest considerations through the backdoor of competition analysis. Out of the total number of twenty-two transactions prohibited to date, six, i.e., almost one-third, have been media mergers concerning broadcasting markets. Furthermore, all six negative decisions were taken when Van Miert was in charge of the Competition portfolio. The burning need for the EU level regulation of media concentration made DG Comp under Van Miert's rule the guardian of pluralism with the sword of competition law.[32] As noted by a C-2 Unit official during Van Miert's term in office:

> While the competition rules are of general application, they must take account of each sector's special characteristics. In the case of television, there are many such characteristics ... One quite specific ... should be stressed here, namely the dangers inherent in the creation or strengthening of dominant positions for media plurality. The goal of media plurality must, therefore, *always* be kept in mind.[33]

This policy continued in a similar way under Van Miert's successor, Mario Monti (1999–2004) when important decisions with 'conditions and obligations' were made. However, the next Commissioner Neelie Kroes applied a more liberal approach to media mergers, consistent with the current Commission's policy line towards the media industry.

30. European Commission, 'Communication to the Council and European Parliament on audio-visual policy', COM(90) 78, Brussels, 21 February 1990.
31. Chalmers, D., et al., *European Union Law: Text and Materials*, 937.
32. Whiddington, C., 'European Union', in De Avillez Pereira, M. (eds), *Antitrust and New Media* (Kluwer Law International, 2000), 199.
33. McCallum, L., 'EC Competition Law and Digital Pay Television', 1999 Competition Policy Newsletter 1, 6.

Under Van Miert's rule and according to his own words 'strict application of the competition rules [was also able to] contribute to maintaining plurality in this sensitive sector'.[34] He had six negative media merger decisions under his belt to prove that and, remarkably, all six involved the television sector. This goes to show the importance attached to this medium and proves the point that excessive concentration in the television sector is seen as far more dangerous than in any other area of the media.[35]

The first of the negative decisions was the *Media Service GmbH (MSG)*[36] decision taken in 1994 which concerned a proposed digital pay-TV joint venture on the German market between Bertelsmann, Kirch and Deutsche Telekom. Bertelsmann is a parent company of a leading German (and now international) media group. Kirch was, at the time, the leading German supplier of feature films and television programming and was also active in commercial television. Deutsche Telekom was the public telecommunications operator, which at that time held a monopoly on the German telephone network and covering over 90% of the German cable television market.

The proposed joint venture, called Media Service GmbH (MSG), intended to offer technical, business and administrative handling of pay-TV, as well as to provide the necessary technical infrastructure for the supply of such services and all related business. MSG would offer decoder, conditional access and subscriber management from a single body.

At the time of the decision, the only supplier of pay-TV in Germany was Premiere, jointly controlled by Bertelsmann, Kirch and Canal Plus. Premiere itself provided the necessary technical services and the subscription management. Similar services as MSG's were offered only by Selco, a JV between Pro 7, a German private television company and News Corporation. German Telecom operated a cable network that was predominant on the German market.

After discussions between the Commission and more than 100 companies and industrial bodies, the Commission concluded that the JV would adversely affect competition on all four identified relevant product markets. First of all, on the market for administrative and technical services for pay-TV (defined for the first time in this case), the Commission observed that MSG would to begin with hold a monopoly given that it would be the first

34. Harcourt, A., *The European Union and the Regulation of Media Markets*, 51.
35. Garzaniti, L., *Telecommunications, Broadcasting and the Internet* (Thomson, Sweet & Maxwell, 2003), 532.
36. Case M.469, *MSG Media Service,* OJ (1994) L364/1.

supplier of such technical and administrative services and as such, it would enjoy a first-mover advantage.[37]

The Commission stated that normally a monopoly on the 'future markets' is not questionable if it is temporary. However, in this case the Commission believed that the market had already been sealed off in the development phase.[38] This was due to the fact that the creation of MSG would, from the start, exclude all likely competition for these services in the form of Premiere (with a strong subscriber base and preferential access to programme software) on the one hand, and Deutsche Telekom with its cable network covering over 90% cabled households in Germany, on the other hand.[39] The Commission saw new entry to such a market virtually impossible, given the fact that an alternative supply of services would have to impose itself against such combined competitive advantages of Deutsche Telekom and Premiere, owned by Bertelsmann and Kirsch respectively.[40]

As to actual competition, the Commission noted that the only company at the time of the decision which offered, in Germany, similar services to those to be offered by MSG was Selco – a joint venture between the private television broadcaster Pro 7 and News Corporation, which belonged to the Murdoch group. However, the Commission established that, first of all, Selco operated a niche market with a limited subscriber base, as its business object is confined to the marketing of foreign-language programmes in Germany. Second, and more importantly, the Commission observed that 47.7% of the shares in Pro 7 were held by Thomas Kirch, the son of the owner of the Kirch group. It appeared furthermore that Pro 7 to a large extent purchased Kirch-group program software for use in its programmes. In the Commission's opinion 'Pro 7 therefore should probably be included *at least in the sphere of influence* of Kirch group.'[41] Against this background, the Commission concluded that it is hardly to be expected that Selco would enter into active competition against MSG.

The second relevant market was the one for pay-TV, which is downstream of the first defined market for technical and administrative services for pay-TV on which MSG would have been active. The Commission found that the fact that MSG would be dominant on the upstream market would considerably strengthen the position of Bertelsmann/Kirch.[42] Given that Bertelsmann and Kirch enjoyed preferential access to the software that is attractive for pay-TV, had widespread activities in free-access commercial

37. Nitsche, I., *Broadcasting in the European Union: The Role of Public Interest in Competition Analysis*, 116.
38. Case M.469, *MSG Media Service,* OJ (1994) L364/1, para. 55.
39. Case M.469, *MSG Media Service,* OJ (1994) L364/1, para. 56.
40. Case M.469, *MSG Media Service,* OJ (1994) L364/1, para. 60; see also Whiddington, C., 'European Union', 188.
41. Case M.469, *MSG Media Service,* OJ (1994) L364/1, para. 65, emphasis added.
42. Case M.469, *MSG Media Service,* OJ (1994) L364/1, para. 74.

television as well as in print media, they already had an extraordinarily strong position on the pay-TV market.[43] The creation of MSG would do nothing else but solidify this position as all potential other pay-TV suppliers would be forced to procure the technical services underlying pay-TV from a company which would not only on a lasting basis hold a monopoly position as an operator of a digital infrastructure for pay-TV, but would also be controlled by the pay-TV suppliers that were already in a leading position.[44]

In such a situation, Bertelsmann and Kirch via MSG could significantly influence competition from future pay-TV suppliers and to a large extent shape it as they wished.[45] First, they could ensure that MSG's terms and conditions, and in particular the price structure, were arranged in such a way that it was advantageous to their own programmes and disadvantageous to those of their competitors.[46] Second, through MSG, Bertelsmann and Kirch would have control over the electronic programme guide (EPG) necessary to find one's way in the 'programme jungle'. The EPG is contained in the decoder box and hence operated by whoever installs the decoder, in this case MSG. Such control would give Bertelsmann and Kirch the possibility to influence the location of their potential competitors' programmes. This would place them at positions in the programme menu which would make them less attractive.[47] MSG would also allow Bertelsmann and Kirch to acquire substantial informational advantages over their competitors, in relation to the customer structure and viewer behaviour of the subscribers handled by its subscriber management system. For example, information on the age structure of the viewers of particular programmes.[48]

In the third identified relevant market for cable networks, Deutsche Telekom had a monopoly at the time of the decision. However, as observed by the Commission this could soon come to an end following the deregulation of the market which would open the market up to competition. Therefore, the Commission concluded that in the same way as Bertelsmann/Kirch removed Deutsche Telekom as a potential competitor in the market for technical and administrative pay-TV services, Deutsche Telekom, through the proposed joint venture, prevents Bertelsmann and Kirch from being available as potential partners for other future cable operators.[49]

In conclusion, the Commission prohibited the proposed concentration after first rejecting the undertakings offered by the parties as insufficient to remedy the danger of creating or strengthening dominant positions.

---

43. Case M.469, *MSG Media Service,* OJ (1994) L364/1.
44. Case M.469, *MSG Media Service,* OJ (1994) L364/1, para. 82.
45. Case M.469, *MSG Media Service,* OJ (1994) L364/1, para. 84.
46. Case M.469, *MSG Media Service,* OJ (1994) L364/1, para. 84.
47. Case M.469, *MSG Media Service,* OJ (1994) L364/1, para. 87.
48. Case M.469, *MSG Media Service,* OJ (1994) L364/1, para. 89; see also Garzaniti, L., *Telecommunications, Broadcasting and the Internet*, 454.
49. Case M.469, *MSG Media Service,* OJ (1994) L364/1, para. 92.

The *MSG* decision is a fine example of DG Competition, under Commissioner Van Miert's direction, 'smuggling' public interest considerations into what should be a pure market efficiency analysis. Particularly interesting here is the Commission's assessment of the market for technical and administrative services for pay-TV and the potential competition in the form of Selco. As explained above, the Commission found that one of the parents of Selco, Pro 7, should be included *at least in the sphere of influence* of the Kirch group, given the fact that Thomas Kirch, the son of the owner of the Kirch group, held almost 50% of the shares in Pro 7. In terms of competition, such an argument is quite weak as family bonds are not something that pure economic analysis of market efficiency takes into account. Indeed, the vague notion of 'sphere of influence' is not frequently used by competition authorities. Moreover, some authors[50] argue that this finding of the Commission is contestable in the light of the definition of control in the Merger Regulation, which requires the 'possibility of exercising decisive influence'(Article 3(1)(b)). Therefore, Thomas Kirch did not *control* Pro 7 and hence did not influence the actions of Selco, which means that Selco could be taken into account as a potential competitor. However, this just proves the point that in *MSG* the Commission's reasoning went well beyond pure competition law principles and exclusively economic arguments. First of all, it seems that the Commission deliberately said nothing about control. It just mentioned the relatively high percentage of shares held by Thomas Kirch in Pro 7. The Commission intentionally and very clearly invoked a careful notion of 'at least in the sphere of influence' just because there was a family bond between Kirch Group and Pro 7, regardless of how big a portion of shares Thomas Kirch held in Pro 7. The Commission, in my opinion correctly, assumed that holding almost 50% of shares allowed Thomas Kirch to have quite a significant influence over Pro 7. Therefore, what mattered for the Commission here was that due to this family connection, Thomas Kirch would be trying to steer Selco's activities away from competition with MSG. Eventually, the approach of the Commission proved to be justified given the subsequent integration of Pro 7 into the Kirch group.[51]

Therefore, the Commission excluded the possibility of competition between MSG and Selco on the market for technical and administrative services for pay-TV, not only on the purely economic grounds but also because it decided that father and son will not want to compete with each other. The latter is an assumption based on life experience and psychological, rather than economic arguments.

50. Nitsche, I., *Broadcasting in the European Union: The Role of Public Interest in Competition Analysis*, 117.
51. Nitsche, I., *Broadcasting in the European Union: The Role of Public Interest in Competition Analysis*, 117.

Moreover, the Commission's assessment of the market for pay-TV also allows one to draw a conclusion that there was something more than pure economic reasoning behind the prohibition of the joint venture. In this market, the Commission concluded that the fact that MSG would have had a fairly permanent monopoly on the upstream market for services would have solidified the dominant positions of Kirch and Bertelsmann on the downstream market for pay-TV. Via MSG, the two large media companies could shape the competition by influencing prices, the position of competitors' programmes on the electronic programme guide and obtaining informational advantages. As observed by Harcourt, 'even though these were economic rationales for preventing the joint venture, it is plain to see that such a JV could have presented serious implications for cultural (and political) pluralism in Germany'.[52]

Clearly, this would have happened with Bertelsmann and Kirch's ability to control the pay-TV content not only by having preferential access to attractive software but also by influencing the positions on which their competitors' programmes appeared in the electronic programme guide. The result would inevitably be an overwhelming majority of Bertelsmann/Kirch content on pay-TV with both companies able to popularize whatever political or cultural messages they saw fit and silence those they regarded as useless, harmful or otherwise not worthy of being shown. This makes the *MSG* decision an exemplary case of DG Competition applying competition law reasoning to achieve aims that proved politically impossible to achieve by the means of legislation.

The negative decision in the *MSG* case also had wider implications in that it indirectly prompted the Commission to adopt the Television Standards Directive[53] in 1995. Following the prohibition of the MSG joint venture, Kirch and Bertelsmann set up two separate digital platforms using different technologies for set-top boxes. Failed attempts of the Commission to convince Bertelsmann to use Kirch's technology and the accompanying debate on standards in the transmission of television signals provided momentum for suggesting the adoption of a Directive.[54] However, the Directive did not go as far as imposing standards. It only made suggestions which would preferably be taken on board by the television companies. This liberal approach of the Directive was to have a serious impact on the result of a later case *Cablevision/Telefonica/Sogecable* in Spain (see below).

---

52. Harcourt, A., *The European Union and the Regulation of Media Markets*, 50.
53. Directive 95/47/EC of the European Parliament and of the Council of 24 October 1995 on the use of standards for the transmission of television signals, OJ (1995) L281/51, now revoked and replaced by the Directive 2002/19/EC of the European Parliament and of the Council of 7 March 2002 on access to, and interconnection of, electronic telecommunications networks and associated facilities ('Access Directive'), OJ (2002) L108/7.
54. Harcourt, A., *The European Union and the Regulation of Media Markets*, 51.

The second prohibition decision in the media merger case taken under Van Miert's rule as a Competition Commissioner was *Nordic Satellite Distribution*[55] in 1995. The case concerned the creation of a joint venture under the name Nordic Satellite Distribution (NSD) by Norsk Telekom, Tele Danmark and Kinnevik. Norsk Telekom was a Norwegian company controlled by Telenor which provided telephone services in Norway and owned or leased transponder capacity[56] from the satellites Thor, Intelsat and TV-Sat, situated at one degree West. It also owned a large cable network in Norway. Tele Danmark is the Danish telecom operator which provided voice-telephony services, broadband and cable networks. Swedish company Kinnevik's media activities included satellite television broadcasting of commercial (TV3) and pay-TV (TV 1000) channels, the distribution of satellite television (via Viasat), managing conditional access systems and radio broadcasting.

The joint venture's aim was to provide transponder capacity and the transmission and distribution of satellite TV channels in the Nordic market.[57] In this regard, NSD was to establish an attractive or even leading satellite position for the transmission of TV signals to the Nordic countries, named by the parties as the Nordic 'Hot Bird'(orbital positions 1 degree West or 5 degrees East).[58] The transponder capacity and satellite network service provided by NSD would be subleased from *inter alia* Telenor. In addition, NSD was to provide satellite TV channels to cable TV operators and direct-to-home households.[59] The distribution of the channels would take place via the parents' distribution companies Viasat (Kinnevik) and Telenor CTV (Norsk Telekom) and through the parents'(Norsk Telekom and Tele Danmark) cable TV operators. NSD would use open encryption system in which smart-cards of Viasat, Telenor or others could be interchanged by consumers in one and the same decoder.

The Commission identified three relevant markets affected by the concentration[60] and concluded that each of them would be, in one way or another, threatened by the proposed transaction.

To begin with, as a result of the links with Kinnevik, NSD would acquire a dominant position on the market in the provision of satellite TV transponder capacity suitable for Nordic viewers.[61] As a result of the transaction, Astra and Eutelsat satellites would cease to play any role in the

55. Case M.490, *Nordic Satellite Distribution*, OJ (1996) L53/20.
56. Transponder is an element of a satellite used to receive and transmit TV signals. Each satellite contains several transponders.
57. Case M.490, *Nordic Satellite Distribution*, OJ (1996) L53/20, para. 8.
58. Case M.490, *Nordic Satellite Distribution*, OJ (1996) L53/20, para. 31.
59. TV signal from a satellite may be received by a privately owned small satellite dishes (direct-to-home system) or by one or two larger dishes owned by cable TV operators and then distributed to homes (cable TV system).
60. Case M.490, *Nordic Satellite Distribution*, OJ (1996) L53/20, para. 74.
61. Garzaniti, L., *Telecommunications, Broadcasting and the Internet*, 456.

Nordic region and hence, contrary to the parties' arguments, would not constitute even a shadow of competition to NSD. At the time of the decision, approximately 70% of the Nordic direct-to-home households, as well as almost all Nordic cable networks, had dishes directed to Astra and Eutelsat.[62] However, the Commission concluded that after the creation of NSD, most dishes in the region would be turned towards satellites controlled by NSD. There would be three main reasons for this. First of all, NSD would offer the most popular Nordic TV channels, Kinnevik's TV3 channels, on an exclusive basis.[63] Second, as opposed to Astra and Eutelsat, NSD's satellites have footprints aimed at the Nordic regions; hence, NSD would be able to reach *all* Nordic viewers.[64] Third, notwithstanding the parties' statements to the contrary, customers would not be willing to invest in additional equipment, be it additional dishes or motorized dishes, just to be able to continue receiving signals from Astra and Eutelsat. Not only would there have been aesthetic, planning and financial constraints, but also the customers would just have no interest in the channels offered by Astra and Eutelsat.[65] They would get everything they want, in terms of television, from NSD.

On the second relevant market for the operation of cable TV networks, it was Tele Danmark's dominant position in Denmark which would have been strengthened by the creation of NSD.[66] As NSD's package of programmes would be *a must* for cable operators, several cable operators would compete to obtain exclusivity arrangements. This would put NSD in a position to price-discriminate or impose unfavourable terms on cable TV operators other than one of its parents – Tele Danmark, which even without that advantage already had an exceptionally strong position in the Danish market.[67] Moreover, those independent cable operators wishing to carry NSD channels on an exclusive basis would have to negotiate with, Tele Danmark, as one of the parents of NSD![68] This clearly would have made the situation even more distorted.

On the final relevant market for distribution of satellite pay-TV channels to direct-to-home households, the operation would create a dominant position for Kinnevik's Viasat.[69]

The Commission rejected as insufficient the undertakings proposed by the parties describing them as having only a minor short-term effect, too limited in scope, too vague, ambiguous and difficult to enforce.[70] Therefore,

62. Case M.490, *Nordic Satellite Distribution*, OJ (1996) L53/20, para. 78.
63. Case M.490, *Nordic Satellite Distribution*, OJ (1996) L53/20, para. 79.
64. Case M.490, *Nordic Satellite Distribution*, OJ (1996) L53/20, para. 79.
65. Case M.490, *Nordic Satellite Distribution*, OJ (1996) L53/20, para. 90.
66. Case M.490, *Nordic Satellite Distribution*, OJ (1996) L53/20, para. 132.
67. Case M.490, *Nordic Satellite Distribution*, OJ (1996) L53/20, para. 128.
68. Case M.490, *Nordic Satellite Distribution*, OJ (1996) L53/20, para. 132.
69. Case M.490, *Nordic Satellite Distribution*, OJ (1996) L53/20, para. 136.
70. Case M.490, *Nordic Satellite Distribution*, OJ (1996) L53/20, paras 154–158.

the inability to remedy the situation in which the vertical integration of NSD would cause the positions of the joint venture and its parents to reinforce each-other on various markets,[71] led the Commission to prohibit the transaction.

The *NSD* decision stimulates two important observations. First, it indicated the Commission's attitude to similar cases: (i) the coming together of ex-monopolists (like Tele Danmark, Norsk Telekom) in the telecommunications sector and a strong broadcasting content provider (like Kinnevik) will not meet with a favourable assessment; and (ii) the Commission will prevent any attempt to replace dominant positions enjoyed by former 'legal monopolists' with dominant positions held by private companies.[72]

The second observation is that like in *MSG*, the Commission in *NSD* seemed to have in mind more than just economic concerns relating to market foreclosure. This time, however, it even expressly talked about public interest considerations in the decision. Analysing the possible economic and technical progress resulting from the transaction, the Commission observed: 'it is likely that the operation will lead to less variety in the offer to Nordic TV households in the future'.[73] Therefore, hidden in the array of purely economic considerations was the vital concern about the decrease in diversity and plurality of television offerings in the Nordic countries. This renders the *NSD* decision another interesting example of DG Competition chaired by Van Miert, subtly smuggling public interest considerations to competition analysis.

The precedents established by the *MSG* and *NSD* decisions meant that when two years later Bertelsmann and Kirch submitted to the Commission their 'second-try MSG'[74] proposal, the fate of the transaction was decided almost from the start. Indeed, in 1998 the Commission prohibited the proposal to change shareholdings in the German pay-TV operator Premiere, which would involve Canal Plus relinquishing its share and Kirch and CLT-UFA – Bertelsmann's joint venture with Audiofina – raising theirs.[75] The outcome of this shift would be Bertelsmann (via CLT-UFA) and Kirch holding 50% each in Premiere and Kirch closing down its pay-TV channel DF1.[76]

The Commission again established that the transaction would impede effective competition on both identified relevant markets: for pay-TV and for technical services for pay-TV. On the market for pay-TV, the Commission concluded that Premiere would achieve a permanent dominant position

71. Case M.490, *Nordic Satellite Distribution*, OJ (1996) L53/20, para. 164.
72. Nitsche, I., *Broadcasting in the European Union: The Role of Public Interest in Competition Analysis*, 114.
73. Case M.490, *Nordic Satellite Distribution*, OJ (1996) L53/20, para. 151.
74. Nitsche, I., *Broadcasting in the European Union: The Role of Public Interest in Competition Analysis*, 118.
75. Case M.993, *Bertelsmann/Kirch/Premiere,* OJ (1999) L53/1.
76. Case M.993, *Bertelsmann/Kirch/Premiere,* OJ (1999) L53/1, para. 8.

which, despite the parties' arguments, would not be off-set by the position of public television suppliers. This long-term dominant position of Premiere would arise out of a combination of factors. First of all, following the closing down of DF1 Premiere would be the only provider of pay-TV in Germany, having indeed a monopoly position. Second, Premiere would have access to programme resources unparalleled in Germany, thanks to its parents'– Bertelsmann's and Kirch's – extremely strong positions on the upstream market for the acquisition of programme rights.[77] Although the output deals for premium films and sports held by Kirch and Bertelsmann were not unlimited, they ran for different terms and thus potential competitors would have to embark on a several-year long quest for taking these rights away from Premiere, before they could offer an equally attractive pay-TV bouquet.[78] However, even after termination of the output deals, Bertelsmann and Kirch, given their financial strength, would probably still be most likely to acquire those rights for another term. Furthermore, given the fact that the Premiere's d-box decoder worked with a proprietary conditional access system (Beta system) potential new entrant to the pay-TV market would either have to establish its own decoder infrastructure, alternative to the d-box, or obtain a license to use Beta access technology. Since households are not usually prepared to procure another decoder,[79] establishing a new decoder infrastructure would not be an option for potential competitors of Premiere. Therefore, by way of licensing the Beta access technology, Bertelsmann and Kirch would gain absolute control over decoder infrastructure in Germany. This would give them, just as the Commission already pointed out in *MSG,* considerable information advantages, the opportunity to shape terms for the use of a Beta system which would be advantageous to Premiere and disadvantageous to its competitors, as well as the ability to influence the positioning of their competitors' programmes on the electronic programming guide.

The parties tried to argue that even if Premiere did in fact have a long-term monopoly for the provision of pay-TV in Germany, this would not be so detrimental overall as in fact pay-TV subscribers devote only 10% of their viewing time to pay-TV, with 90% going to free TV. The Commission was, however, not convinced and stated, very importantly, that:

> if pay-TV subscribers are prepared, in addition to the existing broadcasting fees … , to pay an extra [fee] for a pay-TV subscription, although they use this for only 10% of their viewing consumption, this shows that the economic success of pay-TV is not exactly dependent on the audience share.[80]

77. Case M.993, *Bertelsmann/Kirch/Premiere,* OJ (1999) L53/1, para. 35.
78. Case M.993, *Bertelsmann/Kirch/Premiere,* OJ (1999) L53/1, para. 50.
79. Case M.993, *Bertelsmann/Kirch/Premiere,* OJ (1999) L53/1, para. 56.
80. Case M.993, *Bertelsmann/Kirch/Premiere,* OJ (1999) L53/1, para. 44.

The parties also failed to convince the Commission about their 'failing company defence'[81] argument. They claimed that DF1's limited success thus far meant that if it was not acquired by Premiere it would close down. The Commission responded that first of all, the withdrawal of DF1 from the market would not automatically follow Kirch's decision to close it down. Furthermore, even if it was finally withdrawn, Kirch could easily develop a new marketing platform and operate pay-TV given its extensive programme resources.

On the market for technical services for pay-TV, the dominant position of Premiere on the market for pay-TV would result in creating a dominant position for BetaDigital (which would be 50/50 owned by Bertelsmann and Kirch) in technical services for satellites.

The fact that by establishing a digital infrastructure and jointly offering an attractive programme, the parties could be successful in securing the general acceptance of digital television, did not convince the Commission that the transaction led to promoting technical and economic progress. Finally, the undertakings proposed by the parties were rejected as insufficient to remedy such an extensive monopoly situation. Therefore, the Commission prohibited the merger. In fact, considering its previous negative decisions, and in particular the *NSD*, which had been blocked despite the fact that the parties planned to use open conditional access technology, the Commission had no other choice but to block the merger between Bertelsmann and Kirch.

In parallel to the Bertelsmann/Kirch/Premiere joint venture, the Commission investigated a closely linked case involving joint control by Bertelsmann, Kirch and Deutsche Telekom over BetaResearch.[82] Before the transaction this was Kirch's wholly owned subsidiary holding licenses for Beta technology used for the encryption of programmes on the basis of the d-box decoder. The Commission prohibited both joint ventures on the same day and on similar grounds. It concluded that, just like BetaDigital would have dominant position in technical services for satellites, Deutsche Telekom would have a monopoly of the provision of such services for the transmission of pay-TV over cable networks.

These two parallel investigations of the European Commission into concentration on the German pay-TV market are significant also because they caused a major political stir. The Commission upheld its stance against the highest level of lobbying from Germany – one of the most powerful EU Member States. The Commission initially put informal pressure upon Germany to investigate the joint ventures at national level.[83] Only when the German government decided to approve them, did the DG Competition open the investigation. It was instantly faced with intense lobbying by the German

81. Developed by the European Commission in Case M.308, *Kali and Salz/MdK/Treuhand*, OJ (1994) L186/38.
82. Case M.1027, *Deutsche Telekom/BetaResearch*, OJ (1999) L53/31.
83. Harcourt, A., *The European Union and the Regulation of Media Markets*, 52.

government which claimed that despite the fact that the joint ventures were approved in Germany on competition grounds, German national rules against media concentration were adequate to counteract any negative non-competition related consequences.[84] Interestingly, Commissioner Van Miert had not only Kohl's administration against him. Indeed, within the Commission itself, Commissioners for Culture, Education and Information Society supported German demands for approving the concentration.[85] German industry and government, as well as the three Commissioners were 'infuriated' by the situation in which the Commission's investigation temporarily suspended the expansion of digital TV in Germany, which meant that American, and not European, companies were 'stealing a lead' in this area.[86] Nevertheless, DG Competition held out its stance against the strong political pressures. This showed that it 'had acquired a considerable degree of legitimacy in arbitrating media markets'.[87]

Following the prohibition by DG Competition of any of their attempts to join forces, Bertelsmann, Kirch and Deutsche Telekom lamented that the inevitable consequence would be the abandonment of digital television in Germany.[88] This has not materialized despite the whirlwinds on the market that followed the prohibition decision. In 1999, Bertelsmann sold its share in Premiere to Kirch which resulted in the merger of Kirch's pay-TV activities in DF1 and Premiere into KirchPayTV. Bertelsmann's CLT-UFA became RTL Group which is still a strong pan-European broadcasting and production company while in 2002 the Kirch group collapsed. Nevertheless, digital TV in Germany very much does exist, even if it lags behind its UK or French counterparts. Public broadcasters, ARD and ZDF, as well as Bertelsmann's RTL Group offer digital television packages in free TV and pay-TV respectively. In 2003 Premiere was bought and revitalized by the German private equity house Permira, and it also provides digital TV. Therefore, even if digital television in Germany developed slower than it would had the merger between Kirch and Bertelsmann been allowed, it surely developed in a more competitive, and also a more pluralist environment.

The Commission's two remaining negative decisions in the broadcasting sector, *HMG* and *Telefonica/Sogecable/Cablevision*, concerned Dutch and Spanish television markets respectively.

---

84. The Guardian, 'Brussels Risks War with Kohl', 2 February 1998.
85. Harcourt, A., *The European Union and the Regulation of Media Markets*, 52.
86. Humphreys, P., 'Regulating for Pluralism in the Era of Digital Convergence: The Issues of Media Concentration Control and the Future of Public-Service Broadcasting'.
87. Harcourt, A., *The European Union and the Regulation of Media Markets*, 52.
88. McCallum, L., 'EC Competition Law and Digital Pay Television', (1999) Competition Policy Newsletter 1, 5.

In *RTL/Veronica/Endemol (Holland Media Groep – HMG)*,[89] following the request from the Dutch government,[90] the Commission analysed a proposed joint venture called Holland Media Groep (HMG) between two commercial television companies operating in the Netherlands (RTL 4 and Veronica) and a producer of Dutch-language television programmes, Endemol. Because there is no suspension effect for concentrations without a Community dimension analysed by the Commission at the request of a Member State concerned, the joint venture had already been implemented and was operative by the time the Commission started the investigation. This has probably to a large extent influenced the final outcome of the case.

The Commission identified three relevant markets: for TV broadcasting, for TV advertising and for independently produced Dutch TV programmes, i.e., TV productions excluding in-house productions of the broadcasters.

Delineating the first relevant market, the Commission argued that all TV broadcasters compete against each other for *audience shares* and therefore, the impact on the transaction has to be analysed against the market for TV broadcasting.[91] Moreover, the Commission decided to conduct its analysis on the broadcasting market even though, as the Commission itself admitted, was not so much a market in a strict economic sense of the notion,[92] but rather a term 'in common use by all concerned'.[93] This can be seen as a hint that the *HMG* decision provides something much more than just a purely economic analysis of the effects of the proposed joint venture.

On such a defined broadcasting market, the Commission found HMG to have a very strong position due to a combination of the three popular channels (RTL 4, RTL 5 and Veronica) strengthened by the structural link with Endemol, which was the largest Dutch independent producer of television programmes.[94] RTL was, at that time, the only commercial broadcaster offering full programme service and Veronica was generally acknowledged as the most popular public broadcaster. In 1995, Veronica was to become a fully fledged commercial broadcaster, and without HMG it would have been the strongest competitor to RTL. Instead, the programmes of the two companies had been coordinated and in place of fierce competition, HMG was peacefully enjoying the position of the strongest broadcaster in the Netherlands. This position could by no means be equalled or off-set by public broadcasters which could not coordinate programming on their channels so as to provide complementary programme schedules. The Commission rejected the parties' arguments that income from license fees places public broadcasters in an advantageous competitive position.

---

89. Case M.553, *RTL/Veronica/Endemol*, OJ (1996) L134/32.
90. Pursuant to Article 22 of Council Regulation (EC) No. 4064/89 (Merger Regulation).
91. Case M.553, *RTL/Veronica/Endemol*, para. 17.
92. Since there is no direct trade relationship between free TV suppliers and their viewers.
93. Case M.553, *RTL/Veronica/Endemol*, para. 17.
94. Case M.553, *RTL/Veronica/Endemol.*, paras 43, 45.

HMG's dominant position on the TV broadcasting market was reflected on the market for TV advertising. The Commission concluded that HMG would be the clear market leader which will allow it to counteract all existing competition and make new entry very difficult.[95] In fact, a number of advertisers expressed their concerns to the Commission about the creation of HMG. Finally, the Commission decided that the creation of HMG would strengthen the already dominant position of Endemol on the market for independent Dutch television production.[96]

Given the fact that HMG already operated on the Dutch television market, ordering its dissolution by the Commission's negative decision would have had profound financial consequences. Therefore, the Commission did not order the parties to immediately abandon cooperation within HMG, but offered them three months to come back with proposals to restore effective competition in the relevant markets. This resulted in the eventual approval of the joint venture a year later following the withdrawal of Endemol from the project. The final outcome was therefore the authorization of HMG despite strong reservations. Had it been a normal case with a Community dimension, the Commission would most probably have not allowed such a combination at all. However, had the Dutch government not referred the case to the Commission, HMG could be allowed by national authorities without any changes. The truth is that HMG was bad in itself, but with Endemol involved, it was unbearable. Therefore, the Commission's involvement at least resulted in choosing a 'lesser evil'.

Moreover, as observed by Harcourt, 'clearly, as this [was] a purely national case and a venture with a comparatively low turnover, the Commission's concern overstepped those of ensuring a competitive market'.[97] The comment on the case by Commissioner Van Miert himself serves best as a confirmation of this statement:

> Today's decision is a further example of the Commission's commitment to protect competitive market structures in media sector. It is also worth mentioning that the strict application of the competition rules can also contribute to maintaining plurality in this sensitive sector.[98]

DG Competition under Van Miert also intervened in the British television broadcasting market and prevented the creation of a dominant position in digital terrestrial pay-TV. In 1997 Carlton, Granada and BSkyB entered into a joint venture called British Digital Broadcasting (BDB). Carlton and Granada operated commercial television channels and also had interests in

95. Case M.553, *RTL/Veronica/Endemol*, para. 87.
96. Case M.553, *RTL/Veronica/Endemol*, para. 104; see also Garzaniti, L., *Telecommunications, Broadcasting and the Internet*, 457.
97. Harcourt, A., *The European Union and the Regulation of Media Markets*, 51; see also Whiddington, C., 'European Union'.
98. Harcourt, A., *The European Union and the Regulation of Media Markets*, 51.

pay-TV. BSkyB is a satellite pay-TV operator and a major programming supplier. Granada had a share in BSkyB, and both companies operated a pay-TV joint venture company.[99] The joint venture was approved by the UK Department of Trade and Industry. However, informal discussions between DG Competition and the UK regulators resulted in the UK Independent Television Commission (ITC) informing the parties that it would grant a broadcasting license to BDB only if BSkyB withdrew from the joint venture while honouring the long-term programme supply agreement.[100] Without BSkyB as a shareholder, DG Competition granted a comfort letter for BDB in May 1998. The letter attached further conditions aimed at avoiding cooperation between BDB and BSkyB to the greatest possible extent. The conditions also included a reduction of the duration of the programme supply agreement, the deletion of clauses from the supply agreement which would have acted as a deterrent to BDB competing itself for premium programme content, and finally, changes to the joint venture agreement that were aimed at excluding the possibility of Granada becoming a shareholder in BSkyB which would have prevented competition between BDB and BSkyB.[101]

After the amendments and elimination of BSkyB, the Commission was satisfied that BDB would provide the necessary competition in the market for pay-TV, which was at that time dominated by BSkyB.[102] Indeed, at the beginning of October 1998, BSkyB launched its own digital satellite platform called Sky Digital and 'the prospect of competition from [BDB] has led BSkyB not only to reduce its prices for digital pay television, but also to offer consumers a wider choice of services'.[103] BDB started broadcasting in November 1998. It was later renamed ON Digital. Unfortunately, without BSkyB's technical expertise and customer-service infrastructure, BDB struggled[104] and ultimately generated substantial debt. Rebranding to ITV Digital did not help and in 2002, operations terminated. Currently BSkyB is a dominant pay-TV supplier in the UK. Other pay-TV suppliers are cable

99. Pons, J.F., 'The Application of Competition and Anti-trust Policy in Media and Telecommunications in the European Union', speech at International Bar Association, 14 September 1998, Vancouver, Speech 1998/41.
100. Smith, P., 'The Politics of UK Television Policy: The Introduction of Digital Television', paper presented at Workshop 24, Regulating Communications in the 'Multimedia Age', European Consortium of Political Research, 27th Joint Sessions of workshops, University of Mannheim, Germany, 26–31 March 1999.
101. Pons, J.F., 'The Application of Competition and Anti-trust Policy in Media and Telecommunications in the European Union'.
102. Pons, J.F., 'The Application of Competition and Anti-trust Policy in Media and Telecommunications in the European Union', speech at International Bar Association, 14 September 1998, Vancouver, Speech 1998/41.
103. McCallum, L., 'EC Competition Law and Digital Pay Television', (1999) Competition Policy Newsletter 1, 5.
104. 'ITV Digital Seeks Cooperation', http://www.advanced-television.com, 1–8 October 2001.

operators NTL and Telewest, which merged in 2005. However, as they produce only marginal amounts of their own programming content, they are more customers than competitors of BSkyB. This shows that although competition intervention is able to counteract the creation of a monopoly as a result of a merger, it cannot intervene in the situation of a broadcaster becoming dominant as a consequence of its competitors disappearing from the market. This is where additional media concentration laws should complement competition control. Notwithstanding the later developments, DG Competition's intervention in the BDB joint venture managed to secure competitive and pluralist pay-TV market in the UK, at least for four years.

Other interesting example of DG Competition, under Commissioner Van Miert, going beyond a purely economic analysis of the effects of media mergers, is the 1994 *Newspaper Publishing*[105] case. This was the only case, thus far, in which the Commission expressly mentioned the possibility of using Article 21(4) (then Article 21(3)) of the Merger Regulation. The case concerned the notification by PRISA, Espresso and Mirror Group Newspapers of a public bid for the acquisition of joint control of Newspaper Publishing, a UK company which produced *The Independent* and *The Independent on Sunday*. PRISA is a Spanish media holding with interest in publishing, media relations and pay-TV. Espresso's interests included newspaper publishing and radio broadcasting, and Mirror Group Newspapers was a UK newspaper publishing company. The Commission concluded that there was no overlap between Newspaper Publishing's quality newspapers and Mirror Group Newspapers' tabloids. News International, publisher of *The Times and The Sun*, was a much larger player on the UK market at that time. Ultimately, it was found that there was no overlap between Newspaper Publishing on the one hand and PRISA and Espresso on the other hand, as all three operated in three different geographic markets. For these reasons, the Commission decided not to oppose the transaction as it did not affect competition on any of the markets.[106]

However, in paragraph 22 of the Decision, the Commission made a very interesting and important remark. It recalled Article 21(4) of the Merger Regulation and stated that 'the proposed transaction involves issues such as the accurate presentation of news and free expression of opinion'. Therefore, the UK Secretary of State's formal consent under the UK Fair Trading Act was required, and the Commission demanded to be kept informed of any conditions which the UK authorities might deem appropriate to attach to the transaction. This clearly indicated that the Commission believed that some conditions, aimed at protection of pluralism, *must* be attached to the decision. As it was itself not empowered to do so, it went as far as it could by suggesting to the Member State that it must make use of Article 21(4). The transaction was eventually prohibited by the UK due to media pluralism

105. Case M.423, *Newspaper Publishing*, OJ (1994) C-85/5.
106. Case M.423, *Newspaper Publishing*, OJ (1994) C-85/5, paras 18–20.

concerns, without the Commission raising any objections against this decision.

If the Commission had not expressly mentioned Article 21(4), which meant the actual legitimization of the UK's prohibition of the concentration, it cannot be excluded that the UK would not have had the courage to go counter the Commission's decision, approving the concentration. It could be argued that the Commission realized this fact, and thus its recourse to Article 21(4) was more than simple drawing it to the Member State's attention. The way the Commission structured its analysis allows suspicion that the Commission had examined the transaction from a pluralist perspective and considered it dangerous. However, as it could not act itself, it pointed to Article 21(4). It is, therefore, possible to see this seemingly innocent 'attention drawing' statement by the Commission as in fact a veiled *obligation* imposed on the UK to act against media concentration due to pluralism concerns.

Despite this, and all the other positive developments mentioned above, DG Competition under Commissioner's Van Miert rule failed to remain consistent, and it did not manage to avoid some costly mistakes. The final negative merger decision in relation to broadcasting sector taken under Van Miert can be treated as the first symptom of competition policy's inadequacy to protect pluralism. The *Telefonica/Sogecable/Cablevision*[107] case concerned the Spanish television market and, just like *HMG*, resulted in a major political clash between DG Competition and the Member State involved.

The case concerned the plans of a telecommunications company, Telefonica de Espana and a subsidiary of Canal Plus Spain, Sogecable to merge their activities relating to the supply of services to cable operators and pay-TV providers into a joint venture, called Cablevision. Initially, the Commission had not been notified as the parties regarded their concentration to be of a purely national dimension. Following the authorization granted by the Spanish government, the parties completed the transaction and Cablevision started operating.[108] However, the European Commission considered that the finding of a purely national dimension of the transaction was incorrect, as the turnover of Canal Plus Spain rather than Sogecable should only be taken into account. This intervention obviously caused a serious political clash within the Spanish government. DG Competition, again, bravely went above the Member State's head in its attempts to defend competitive media markets in Europe.

The statement of objections was sent to Telefonica and Canal Plus Spain requesting the notification of the concentration to DG Competition. Against all odds, the Commission decided to prohibit the concentration. It concluded that the creation of Cablevision would lead to foreclosure effects by preventing new entry into the market for technical services for pay-TV

---

107. Case M.709, *Telefonica/Sogecable/Cablevision*, OJ (1996) C-167/3.
108. XXVI Annual Report on Competition Policy 1996, Part Two, 5.

providers and cable operators in Spain.[109] Three days after the Commission's decision, the parties decided to withdraw from the strategic alliance. Cablevision was de-merged and went under the sole control of Sogecable.

The effect of the Commission's negative decision was that Canal Plus Spain and Telefonica each created their own satellite platform – Canal Satélite Digital and Via Digital respectively – which used different encryption technologies. Realizing the potential of Canal Plus, which had acquired valuable soccer rights, the Spanish government tried to defend 'national' Via Digital. Hence, two laws were adopted in 1997. One mandated the use of an encryption technology (multicrypt), and the other imposed mandatory sharing of soccer rights between the pay-TV operators.[110] The law on standard encryption technology, 'sought to protect the consumer's right to receive information and to guarantee pluralistic offer of services. Multicrypt was a synonym of pluralism; it was more open than the simulcrypt technology which requires a prior agreement between operators'.[111]

Notwithstanding the apparently vital interests of pluralism and diversity which were at the heart of the Spanish government's intervention, DG Competition, inspired by Canal Plus, opposed the laws and initiated formal proceedings against Spain. In the reasoned opinion, the Commission requested the removal of the provisions which were allegedly contrary to the free movement of goods and services. Faced with the possibility of being taken to the European Court of Justice, Spain succumbed to the Commission's demands and amended the laws removing the obligation on pay-TV providers to use the same encryption standard. The Commission's reaction in this case was astonishing and troubling for several reasons.

First, the Commission went against its own recommendations in the Television Standards Directive.[112] The rationale for the Directive was to recommend the use of uniform standards. If the Commission felt that it was not entitled to mandate such standards, then it would be logical to allow any steps taken by the Member States to make it happen. Admittedly, the Directive did not expressly allow the Member States to mandate encryption standards. However, it also did not expressly *prohibit* them from doing so. The Commission failed to use this unique opportunity to interpret the Directive as permitting the Member States to *impose* a common standard on market operators.[113] Thus, the Spanish government's action was not obviously incompatible with Community law. The Commission simply chose not

109. XXVI Annual Report on Competition Policy 1996, Part Two, 6.
110. Llorens-Maluquer, C., 'European Responses to Bottlenecks in Digital Pay-TV: Impacts on Pluralism and Competition Policy', (1998) Cardozo Arts & Entertainment Law Journal 16(2–3), 580.
111. Llorens-Maluquer, C., 'European Responses to Bottlenecks in Digital Pay-TV: Impacts on Pluralism and Competition Policy'.
112. Harcourt, A., *The European Union and the Regulation of Media Markets*, 54.
113. Harcourt, A., *The European Union and the Regulation of Media Markets*, 54.

to interpret the Community law in such a way so as to *make* this action lawful.

Second, it may also be argued that by intervening in the Spanish government's decision, the Commission did not respect the provisions of Article 21(4) of the Merger Regulation. The Article allows Member States to take appropriate measures to protect legitimate interests, other than those taken into consideration by the Merger Regulation, provided these measures are compatible with the general principles and other provisions of Community law. Plurality of the media, which was one of the rationales behind the Spanish government's intervention, is expressly mentioned as such a legitimate interest. Consequently, if simple prohibition of the Cablevision venture by the Commission was not enough to secure pluralism on the Spanish pay-TV market, Spain should be free to implement the competition ruling by any 'appropriate measures'. By aggressively preventing it from doing so, DG Competition threw the rationale for Article 21(4) into question. It signalled to Member States that it may be empowered to challenge any of the pluralism-oriented measures they introduce at national level by simply interpreting the Community law in such a way so as to make the national rules incompatible. This is regrettable, especially that the same DG Competition two years earlier pointed to Article 21(4) in the *Newspaper Publishing* decision. This could have been taken forward in the *Cablevision* case. Instead, the Commission decided to take a step backwards.

Third, the long-term implications of the *Telefonica/Sogecable/Cablevision* decision devalued the initial prohibition of the Cablevision joint venture against the will of the Spanish government. Following the withdrawal of the obligation to use one encryption standard, Canal Satélite Digital opted for simulcrypt and Via Digital for multicrypt technology. This meant that each one required a different set-top box which locked customers into their respective systems. The competition on the content level decreased, 'neither operator was able to generate enough profit to overcome the high costs of technology and sports rights'.[114] Finally in 2002, the two platforms merged creating a near monopoly on the Spanish pay-TV market.[115] Therefore, the end result was as if the Commission did not intervene in the Cablevision venture at all.

Some argue that this was not a coincidence, and the whole saga had an ulterior motive. Perhaps the Commission was actually doing everything to defend a 'European champion'(Canal Plus) against a national champion (Telefonica).[116] However, if this was the case, then why prohibit Cablevision in the first place, if it would actually strengthen Canal Plus?

---

114. Harcourt, A., *The European Union and the Regulation of Media Markets*, 54.
115. Case M.2845, *Sogecable/Canal Satélite Digital/Via Digital*, approved by the Spanish government following the referral from the European Commission.
116. Harcourt, A., *The European Union and the Regulation of Media Markets*, 61.

All six prohibition decisions taken by DG Competition under Commissioner's Van Miert rule concerned transactions involving some degree of vertical integration and affecting national markets. The Commission seems to believe that it contributed to the protection of pluralism by defining narrow relevant markets, both product and horizontal in the media merger cases. While this policy has resulted in prohibiting national vertical mergers, it also meant approving pan-European horizontal concentrations. For instance in *Kirch/Richemont/Telepiù*[117] and in *Bertelsmann/News International/Vox*,[118] the Commission allowed pan-European expansion of the biggest media conglomerates in Europe. In *Kirch/Richemont/Telepiù*, a media giant of that time, the Kirch Group, was allowed to expand into Italian markets by means of acquiring joint control over Telepiù – an Italian pay-TV company. Similarly, in *Bertelsmann/News International/Vox*, not only did News Corporation expand into the German market but also, the two European media conglomerates, Bertelsmann and News Corporation, entered into a close joint venture.

In these, as well as in all the other cases involving broadcasting, the Commission defined the geographic market as national and, admittedly, at the national level the transactions were not objectionable from a competition perspective. The reasons the Commission has provided for defining national geographic markets around linguistic and cultural barriers[119] is that language differences influence the purchase of programme rights and varying programme mixes on the basis of cultural interests of a national or regional audience.[120] This is all despite the Commission acknowledging the growing internationalization of broadcasting, whereby satellite and digital television renders national borders increasingly irrelevant.

Therefore, under the current Commission approach and in the current state of law, if a merger does not affect a national market, it will be permitted, even if it leads to further expansion of media conglomerates at European level. The Commission seems to believe that as long as competition is not affected at the national level, broadcasting may be provided by a handful pan-European companies. This fitted into the Commission's flawed belief in the continuing need to promote 'European champions' in the media sector. Commissioner Monti's words are meaningful in this respect:

> Imagine there is a problem with a particular [media] company on a national market in Europe. We would be doing a great disservice to the citizens of that country if we were to put the globalisation interests of the company ahead of the more local interests of the citizens. The

117. Case M.410, *Kirch/Richemont/Telepiu*, OJ (1994) C-225/4.
118. Case M.489, *Bertelsmann/News International/Vox*, OJ (1994) C-274/6.
119. European Audiovisual Observatory, Iris Special: 'Television and Media Concentration. Regulatory Models on the National and European Level', Strasbourg 2001.
120. Case M.410, *Kirch/Richemont/Telepiu*, n. 521, para. 17; Case M.489, *Bertelsmann/News International/Vox*, n. 522, para. 20.

> competition rules will intervene wherever there is a problem be it national, as in Kirch/Bertelsmann, or global, as in AOL/TimeWarner and Vivendi/Universal.[121]

The truth is however, that the Commission *is* in fact putting globalization or Europeanization interests of media companies at the forefront by being concerned with national markets only.

There is currently no remedy for pan-European pluralism concerns. The first draft of the unsuccessful Media Concentration Directive suggested a 10% ceiling for audience share at the European level, which would have addressed the problem to some extent. However, this threshold disappeared in only the second draft. One would still believe that serious pluralism concerns with the current Commission approach would be alleviated, at least at the national level, by the use of Article 21(4) of the Merger Regulation. However, with the replacement of Van Miert by Monti in the chair of Competition Commissioner, which also coincided with the dawn of the 'convergence tend', the Commission went even further. It started accepting media mergers, even those competitively affecting national markets. At least some of these mergers should trigger the use of Article 21(4) by a Member State concerned. Unfortunately, *Newspaper Publishing* remains the only case when this procedure was used.

4.1.2. 'Convergence Trend' and Regulated Monopolies under Monti and Kroes

Under Monti DG Competition's stance towards media mergers in the broadcasting industry, especially those with vertical aspects, was substantially relaxed. In several controversial cases, instead of smuggling public interest considerations into competition analysis in order to prohibit anti-competitive media mergers, the Commission decided to allow them, but impose extensive sets of conditions and obligations and this way the concentrated market would be 'regulated'. The result of the change in policy was a series of vertical mega-mergers and two horizontal near-monopoly cases.

The U-turn with regard to the approach to vertical integration can be seen as a result of the 'convergence trend' which characterized the Commission's work in the early years of the twenty-first century. The Commission saw progress of convergence and facilitating the advance of technology and new media as higher values than preserving pluralistic media structures. The case in the television broadcasting sector which illustrates this trend is

121. Monti, M., 'Does EC Competition Policy Help or Hinder the European Audiovisual and Telecoms Industries?'.

Vivendi/Seagram.[122] Vivendi is the ultimate parent company of a group active in France and internationally. Its television activities at the time of the case included equity interests in two pay-TV operators: Canal+ (49%) and BSkyB (25%). The Canadian-based company Seagram was active in the media industry, especially through its subsidiary Universal – one of the six major Hollywood film studios. The case involved the acquisition of sole control of Seagram by Vivendi. The Commission was concerned with the strong position of Canal+ on the pay-TV market and the transaction's effect on the market for premium film rights. The merged Vivendi/Seagram entity would have the world's second largest film library and the second largest library of TV programming in the European Economic Area.[123] Canal+ was already dominant in France, Spain, Italy, Belgium and the Netherlands and had a strong position in the Nordic countries. The Commission concluded that following the merger, Canal+ would be in an even better position both to renew its existing contracts with Universal, as well as to enter into new output deals with the other major Hollywood studios, which have certain structural links and specific arrangements with Universal.[124] Therefore, the Commission feared that *post-merger*, Canal+'s bargaining power vis-à-vis the US studios would be increased, which in turn would strengthen its position on the premium film rights market and would further foreclose the pay-TV market.[125]

In order to eliminate the serious concerns raised by the Commission, Vivendi proposed a package of commitments. With regard to pay-TV markets, Vivendi undertook not to grant to Canal+ the first-window rights[126] covering more than 50% of Universal production and co-production, unless there should not be competing offers at fair market value. However, this undertaking was limited to only five years from the expiry of the current output deals because, according to the Commission, during this period competitors apparently 'will in all likelihood be in a position to adapt themselves to the new structure of the market'.[127] Moreover, Vivendi undertook to divest its entire stake in BskyB, which would eliminate links with both Fox, as a film supplier, and BSkyB as a potential competitor for Canal+, in the pay-TV market.

---

122. Case M.2050, *Vivendi/Seagram/Canal Plus*, OJ (2000) C-311/3; significant examples of the trend in other sectors include Case M.1845, *AOL/Time Warner*, OJ (2000) C-130/06, Case M.1943, *Telefonica/Endemol,* OJ (2000) C-170/5.
123. Mendes Pereira, M., 'Vertical and Horizontal Integration in the Media Sector and EU Competition Law'.
124. Case M.2050, *Vivendi/Seagram/Canal Plus*, OJ (2000) C-311/3, para. 44.
125. Case M.2050, *Vivendi/Seagram/Canal Plus*, OJ (2000) C-311/3, para. 50; see also Garzaniti, L., *Telecommunications, Broadcasting and the Internet*, 443.
126. First window rights cover television rights to films available on pay-TV shortly after cinema screenings and video rental.
127. Case M.2050, *Vivendi/Seagram/Canal Plus*, OJ (2000) C-311/3, para. 74.

This way, after the approval of medium to harsh and some temporary commitments, the creation of the world's second biggest media group at the time after Time Warner was sanctioned by the European Commission. One of the factors here was, without a doubt, the merged group's plan to establish an internet portal Vizzavi and engage into a then-nascent practice of online music delivery. The case raised a worrying suspicion that if media companies manage to dazzle the Commission with the promise of creating something technologically new and exciting, they were almost guaranteed to jump any competition hurdles.

This however, was not the end of the saga. Apart from adopting a far more lenient approach to vertical mega-mergers than its predecessor, DG Competition under Monti, left a legacy of two horizontal near-monopolies in the pay-TV sector.

In *BSkyB/Kirch Pay-TV* , the Commission allowed the acquisition of 24% of KirchPayTV by BSkyB, leading to joint control of KirchPayTV by Kirch and BSkyB. At the time of the case KirchPayTV, through Premiere, had virtually a monopoly in the provision of pay-TV services in Germany. The Commission raised concerns that as a result of the transaction a dominant position of KirchPayTV on the pay-TV market in Germany will be strengthened, and a brand new dominant player will be created on the market for digital interactive television services. KirchPayTV would be the only pay-TV operator in Germany offering, through one decoder, the d-box, pay-TV in combination with digital interactive television services. The result would be the d-box becoming the standard decoder in Germany for both interactive services and pay-TV.[128] The main danger of the d-box becoming the standard decoder stems from the fact that the d-box operates with a proprietary encoding technology developed by BetaResearch.[129] Therefore, possible new entrants wishing to reach customers using the d-box would have to obtain a license from BetaResearch. Moreover, together with the license application, they would need to submit their plans in advance to BetaResearch to ensure their compatibility with the system. The result would be that BetaResearch, KirchPayTV's sister company, would first of all have no interest in granting licenses, and second, it would have access to commercially sensitive information on the potential competitors of KirchPayTV.[130]

Again, instead of prohibiting the merger, as was the practice under Van Miert's DG Competition, DG Competition under Monti imposed a set of conditions on the merging parties. Apart from the somewhat standard requirements of offering licenses for the d-box network on a reasonable and non-discriminatory basis, together with all necessary technical services enabling the interested third parties' digitally transmitted services to be

128. Case JV.37, *BSkyB/KirchPayTV*, OJ (2000) C-45/3, para. 78.
129. See Case M.993, *Bertelsmann/Kirch/Premiere*.
130. Case JV.37, *BSkyB/KirchPayTV*, para. 79.

received by viewers,[131] the Commission went beyond behavioural commitments and made the rather 'unorthodox use of competition law for standardization purposes'.[132] The Commission mandated Kirch to implement an open application programming interface (API),[133] as standardized by the Digital Video Broadcasting Group (DVB)[134] into the d-box or any of its successors.[135] Moreover, the Commission required that Kirch enter into Simulcrypt[136] arrangements (including the provision of the necessary coding information) with all interested digital conditional access providers in the German speaking territories.[137]

The story of the 'convergence trend' and technological optimism of the Monti era would not be complete without mentioning *Newscorp/Telepiù*[138] – the milestone case marking the change of the Commission's policy towards mega-mergers in the media sector, and arguably one of the most controversial media merger cases ever decided by the Commission. The case involved an acquisition of the only two Italian pay-TV operators Stream and Telepiù by News Corporation and their subsequent merger into one digital satellite pay-TV platform, to be named Sky Italia.

As the merger would lead to nothing less than a monopoly in the Italian pay-TV market, the Commission raised a series of concerns. The Commission noted that prior to the merger, Telepiù already held a dominant position in the Italian pay-TV market so there would be virtually no competition left in the pay-TV market in Italy after the merger (competition from cable operators was negligible). First of all, the Commission considered that because News Corporation was present in the upstream market for encryption technologies for Conditional Access Systems (CAS) for pay-TV, the merger would lead to a precarious situation whereby a pay-TV monopolist would own a proprietary CAS. The Commission viewed this factor as in

131. Case JV.37, *BSkyB/KirchPayTV*, paras 1 and 8 of Annex I.
132. Arino, M., 'Pluralism in Digital Broadcasting: Myths, Realities and the Boundaries of European Intervention'.
133. Application Programming Interface (API) is an interface to a decoder's operating system – it defines how different programmes and applications interact with the operating system. If it is closed/proprietary other operators have to obtain a license to provide their services through the network.
134. As per DVB's website http://www.dvb.org – the Digital Video Broadcasting Project (DVB) is an industry-led consortium of over 260 broadcasters, manufacturers, network operators, software developers, regulatory bodies and others in over 35 countries committed to designing global standards for the global delivery of digital television and data services.
135. Case JV.37, *BSkyB/KirchPayTV*, n. 532, para. 5 of Annex I.
136. Simulcrypt technology allows different decoders to decode different bouquets of channels from different service providers if the appropriate smartcard is present. Other technology – Multicrypt – allows a decoder to decode different encryption systems without the necessity of inserting appropriate smartcards.
137. Case JV.37, *BSkyB/KirchPayTV*, n. 532, para. 5 of Annex I; see also Garzaniti, L., *Telecommunications, Broadcasting and the Internet*, n. 503, 465.
138. Case M.2876, *Newscorp/Telepiù*, OJ (2004) L110/73.

itself increasing barriers to entry into the downstream pay-TV market in Italy.[139] Moreover, by controlling the only digital satellite pay-TV platform in Italy, News Corporation would have the incentive and the ability to refuse access or raise barriers to the consolidation of channels (e.g., by systematically changing their position in the EPG). Furthermore, they could impose unfair or discriminatory conditions to digital satellite channels.[140] This would give News Corporation the possibility and the incentive to set the standard for the accepted level of intra-platform competition.

The second type of concerns involved the possibility of creating or strengthening the dominant position in the market for the acquisition of content rights, in particular rights to premium films and football content. Before the merger, Telepiù already held a dominant position in the market for the acquisition of exclusive rights for premium films and Stream had had exclusive broadcasting rights for the Serie A and Serie B Italian football league. Therefore, the Commission concluded that the acquisition of Telepiù by Stream, would lead to a quasi-monopolistic situation in the acquisition of exclusive rights for films and to a quasi-monopsonistic situation of the new entity for the acquisition of exclusive rights for regular football events.[141] Thus, because potential pay-TV competitors would be prevented from having access to premium content on pay-TV for a number of years, the Commission's finding was that no other undertaking would have the essential content to establish an alternative pay-TV platform. The possibility to create inter-platform competition would therefore have been minimal.[142]

Considering the seriousness of the concerns and the fact that the result of the concentration was nothing less than a monopoly, it is rather surprising that the Commission was easily convinced by a package of commitments offered by the parties. Therefore, a set of safeguards was imposed on the merged entity. To ensure future inter-platform competition, the Commission required the parties to provide access to premium input (sports and film rights). The exclusivity of key content contracts for Sky Italia was shortened (two years for top football league A-series contracts and three years for premium film content). Concerns for the lack of intra-platform competition were alleviated by the parties' undertaking to grant third-party operators access to the Sky Italia's satellite platform, in order to allow such operators to offer channels that compete with the combined platform's retail offer.[143] To give full effect to this commitment, the Commission required that in addition to granting access to platform, the parties also supply the third parties in fair, transparent, non-discriminatory and cost-oriented conditions, with the technical services that are necessary and instrumental to the offering

139. Case M.2876, *Newscorp/Telepiù,* OJ (2004) L110/73, 133.
140. Case M.2876, *Newscorp/Telepiù,* OJ (2004) L110/73, 138.
141. Case M.2876, *Newscorp/Telepiù,* OJ (2004) L110/73, paras 150 and 162.
142. Case M.2876, *Newscorp/Telepiù,* OJ (2004) L110/73, para. 183.
143. Case M.2876, *Newscorp/Telepiù,* OJ (2004) L110/73, para. 11.1 of Annex I.

of TV channels in Italy. Moreover, Sky Italia was compelled not to re-organize the listing of channels in its electronic programme guide, without objective justification.

This way, the most dangerous and the worst possible situation in the media sector – a complete monopoly – was sanctioned by the European Commission for the first time.[144] On the first reading, the commitments are indeed tough. However, they are arguably not only inconsistent, but also behavioural, which means that, as admitted by the Commission itself, their effectiveness depends largely on '*faithful and goodwill* interpretation by the parties'.[145] The inconsistency arises from the fact that on the one hand the Commission regards the Italian pay-TV market as almost a natural monopoly with no room for two players, and at the same time it imposes a set of strict remedies centred on granting access, so as to facilitate new entry. The question arises as to what the Commission actually believed? Was there a possibility of two players on the Italian pay-TV market or not? If there was, as the imposition of strict access remedies indicates – why then allow a monopoly in the sensitive media sector?

Another aspect is that, despite rejecting the News Corporation's failing company defence, the Commission took the 'difficult economic situation' of Stream into account as one of deciding factors for authorizing the merger.[146] The conclusion was that authorization of the monopoly subject to appropriate conditions would be more beneficial to consumers than a disruption caused by the potential bankruptcy of Stream.[147] This inevitably raises questions with regard to the *mirror* case in the Spanish market. In this case, the creation of a digital pay-TV platform, Digital+, by means of a merger of Sogecable, the dominant pay TV operator in Spain, with Vía Digital, the second pay TV operator in Spain, was allowed by the Spanish Competition Authority after referral from the Commission.[148] Both companies were economically viable; there was no risk of a monopoly regardless of whether the transaction was authorized or not. And yet the monopoly was sanctioned, again.

There may only be one conclusion. There is a bigger interest in facilitating the development of a digital satellite pay-TV platform than prohibiting a media monopoly.[149] This in a nutshell, is the Commission's current philosophy towards the media sector. Both cases mark a change in the Commission's policy – from discouraging mergers and favouring a new

144. Garzaniti, L., *Telecommunications, Broadcasting and the Internet*, 490.
145. Ungerer, H., 'Impact of European Competition Policy on Media'.
146. Garzaniti, L., *Telecommunications, Broadcasting and the Internet*, 490.
147. Case M.2876, *Newscorp/Telepiù*, n. 545, para. 221.
148. Case M.2845, *Sogecable/Canalsatélite Digital /Vía Digital*, OJ (2002) C-166/6.
149. Feintuck, M., Varney, M., *Media Regulation, Public Interest and the Law*, 93.

entry, to accepting monitored monopolies in order to facilitate the development and progress of new technologies. In the Commission's eyes, intra-platform competition seems to prevail over inter-platform competition or going even further – internal pluralism currently wins over structural. And, as noted by Arino, the 'Spanish and Italian concentrations may merely constitute the beginning of a wider consolidation trend across Europe.'[150]

4.1.3. Approval of Newscorp's Acquisition of BskyB under Almunia

News Corp's latest merger activity in the UK involved its bid to acquire the remaining 61% of BSkyB it does not yet own. In December 2010, the takeover bid was approved by the European Commission under the EU competition rules.[151] The Commission concluded that News Corp and BSkyB are mainly active on different relevant markets in the UK and Ireland and compete with each other only to a limited extent, in the wholesale supply of basic pay-TV channels and in the supply of online and TV advertising space. In addition, the Commission found that the parties have a small combined market share in the market for online and TV advertising and, finally, the proposed transaction would only lead to a small increase in BSkyB's existing share of the market for the supply of basic pay-TV channels in the UK and Ireland. Thus, the Commission concluded that the merger did not raise any horizontal competition concerns.[152]

The analysis, therefore, focused on three types of possible anticompetitive effects in the vertically linked or neighbouring sectors: audiovisual, newspaper publishing and advertising.

With regard to the audiovisual sector, the Commission was concerned about the existence of BSkyB's exclusive deals for premium movies with all six Hollywood majors However, according to the Commission, News Corp lacked sufficient market power in the market for the licensing of broadcasting rights for premium movies, and that BSkyB's competitors would retain several alternative suppliers with equally attractive content. In addition, the transaction would not materially worsen the existing market situation.

The concerns in the newspaper publishing sector cantered on conglomerate effects. The Commission examined the possibility of the merged entity to foreclose competing newspaper publishers by offering mixed bundles of subscriptions to Sky and News Corp's print, online or tablet-based newspapers and 'leverage' a dominant position of BSkyB in the UK pay-TV market

---

150. Arino, M., 'Competition Law and Pluralism in European Digital Broadcasting: Addressing the Gaps', 97.
151. Case COMP/M.5932, *News Corp/BSkyB*.
152. European Commission, 'Commission clears News Corp's proposed acquisition of BSkyB under EU merger rules', IP/10/1767.

to gain advantage on the newspaper publishing market.[153] However, as mentioned earlier, following the ECJ decisions in *Tetra Laval/Sidel*[154] and *GE/Honeywell,*[155] proving anti-competitive risks of portfolio effects and leveraging must be done with great care.[156]

Thus, the Commission must establish that a transaction would 'in all likelihood' lead to such leveraging 'in the relatively near future'.[157] Thus, in the case at hand the Commission concluded that no competition concerns in the newspaper publishing sector would arise from the transaction for four main reasons: (i) price is only one, and not the main factor determining readers' choice of and loyalty to a newspaper; (ii) no such bundling has been attempted before; (iii) subscription model currently does not appeal to a majority of readers; and finally (iv) the vast majority of newspapers' online editions as well as other news sources are currently free of charge, and there is no evidence that this will dramatically change in the foreseeable future.[158]

Finally, the Commission investigated whether the merged entity could either refuse advertising by BSkyB's competitors in News Corp's newspaper titles or charge a competitive premium. Such concerns were dismissed by the Commission since the finding of the investigation was that there were sufficient alternative opportunities to advertise with other print media.

In summary, therefore, the Commission was confident that the merger would not weaken competition in the UK. However, as emphasized by Commissioner Almunia, 'the effects on media plurality are a matter for the UK authorities'.[159]

Obviously, the European Commission's competence is limited to the assessment of the competition aspects of the proposed transaction. Article 21(4) of the EU Merger Regulation allows the Member States to take appropriate measures, including prohibiting proposed transactions, to protect legitimate interests, such as the plurality of the media. Accordingly, on 4 November 2010 the UK Secretary of State for Business Innovation and Skills issued a European intervention notice which required the relevant UK authorities to investigate and report by the end of 2010 on whether the proposed transaction is or may be expected to operate against the public interest in sufficiency of plurality of persons with control of media enterprises. On 31 December 2010, in a report presented to the Department for

---

153. Moonen, S., 'News Corp/BSkyB and the Boundaries of Merger Review', (2011) Journal of Competition Law and Practice 2(4), 351
154. Case C-12/03, *Commission v. Tetra Laval*, [2005] 4 CMLR 8, para. 85
155. Case T-210/01, *General Electric v. Commission*, [2005] ECR II-5575.
156. There is now a presumption of legality of conglomerate mergers, unless the Commission can prove that they are anti-competitive
157. Case C-12/03, *Commission v. Tetra Laval*, [2005] 4 CMLR 8.
158. European Commission, 'Commission clears News Corp's proposed acquisition of BSkyB under EU merger rules', IP/10/1767.
159. European Commission, 'Commission clears News Corp's proposed acquisition of BSkyB under EU merger rules', IP/10/1767.

Culture Media and Sport, OFCOM recommended that the acquisition should be referred to the Competition Commission. There were reports that News Corp offered to divest Sky News to alleviate any media pluralism concerns, and it seemed that the transaction was set to be cleared by the UK authorities.[160]

However, in July 2011 a so-called Hackergate scandal shook the UK media and political scene. It was discovered that the *News of the World* newspaper owned by News International – a subsidiary of News Corp – used illegal phone hacking techniques to gain access to private information about various people, including the missing teenager Milly Dowler, who was later found murdered. Police questioned the newspaper's senior editors; five people resigned from their positions following the eruption of the scandal;[161] and News Corp's Rupert and James Murdoch were questioned by the House of Commons' Select Committee for Culture, Media and Sport. On 7 July 2011, News International announced the closure of the *News of the World*, which was published since 1843. The scandal shed a different light on the power exercised by News Corp on the UK media market, and questions started to be asked about the relationship between Rupert Murdoch and the UK government. The leader of the opposition party called for News Corp to drop the bid for BSkyB.[162] On 11 July 2011, News Corp announced that it had withdrawn the offer to divest Sky News which left the Secretary for Culture Media and Sport no other choice than to refer the transaction to the Competition Commission. The move by News Corp was seen as a delaying tactic – the Competition Commission's assessment would have taken approximately six months, by which time the phone hacking scandal would not be the front page news anymore. It would have also taken the deal off the hands of the government which was being called by the opposition to check whether News Corp should own any shares at all in BSkyB.[163] However, just two days after the transaction was referred to the Competition Commission, the pressure surrounding the scandal caused News Corp to drop the bid altogether.[164]

160. BBC News, 'BSkyB News Corp bid: Ofcom calls for Competition review', 13 January 2011.
161. They are: Andy Coulson, Prime Minister's director of communications; Rebekah Brooks, News International chief executive; Les Hinton, CEO of Dow Jones & Company; Sir Paul Stephenson, Metropolitan police commissioner; and John Yates, Metropolitan police assistant commissioner.
162. Bloomberg, 'Murdoch Should Drop BSkyB Takeover, U.K. Opposition Leader Milib and Says', 10 July 2011.
163. The Guardian, 'News Corp's BSkyB bid referred by Hunt to Competition Commission', 11 July 2011.
164. Reuters, 'Instant view: News Corp withdraws bid for BSkyB', 13 July 2011.

4.2. ANTITRUST: ACCESS TO PREMIUM CONTENT AS A CONDUIT FOR PLURALISM?

It is often argued[165] that, under Commissioners Monti and Kroes, DG Competition also tackled the pluralism issue by enforcing access to premium content in a series of Article 101 cases.[166] Premium content is essentially the rights to Hollywood films and prestigious football tournaments.[167] As rightly noted by the former long-term Director General of DG Competition Philip Lowe:

> The restricted access to premium content contributes to media concentration, limits output and opens the risk of higher prices and less choice for consumers as well as less innovation in the sector.[168]

It is therefore interesting to have a closer look at two more recent cases concerning the sale of media rights to prominent football events: the pan-European Champions League and the national Premier League in the United Kingdom. Both cases were considered before the modernisation of competition rules by Regulation 1/2003.[169] Therefore, they both involved requests for an exemption under Article 81(3) of joint-selling of media rights from ordinary competition rules and the Commission's subsequent intervention into those arrangements. However, the final outcome of the Premier League case was reached under new rules.

Article 101 TFEU prohibits anti-competitive agreements and concerted practices between competitors. The modernisation of EU competition law took place in 2004 with the entry into force of Regulation 1/2003 which replaced the previous Regulation 17/62.[170] While the reform did not change the substance of Articles 101 and 102, the procedures for enforcement changed radically.[171] Under the previous regime, every agreement between competitors had to be formally notified to the Commission, and the Commission was the only body which could 'exempt' the agreement from

---

165. See, for instance, Arino, M., 'Competition Law and Pluralism in European Digital Broadcasting: Addressing the Gaps', n. 97; Arino, M., 'Pluralism in Digital Broadcasting: Myths, Realities and the Boundaries of European Intervention'.
166. Case IV/32.150, *EBU/Eurovision System*, OJ (1993) L179/23; Case COMP/37.398, *UEFA Champions League,* OJ (2003) L291/25; Case COMP/38.453, *FA Premier League*, OJ (2004) C-115/3.
167. Geradin, D., 'Competition Law Problems Raised by the Entry of Incumbent Telecommunications Operators in the Media Content Delivery Market', University of Zurich, 7 September 2005.
168. Lowe, P., 'Media Concentration and Convergence: Competition in Communications'.
169. Council Regulation (EC) No. 1/2003 of 16 December 2002 on the implementation of the rules on competition laid down in Articles 81 and 82 of the Treaty, OJ (2003) L1/1.
170. Council Regulation No. 17: First Regulation implementing Articles 85 and 86 of the Treaty, OJ (1962) 13/204.
171. McCarthy, A., Power, V., *Irish Competition Law. The Competition Act, 2002* (LexisNexis, 2003), 96

the competition rules on the basis of Article 101(3), that is declare it compatible with the common market. The notification system became too burdensome both on the Commission and on the businesses once the European Union expanded to twenty-five Member States. Decision was thus made to abolish the notification regime, make Article 101(3) directly applicable and decentralize the EC competition law enforcement. Therefore, under Regulation 1/2003, it is now a matter for undertakings to assess whether their agreement fulfils the efficiencies mentioned in Article 101(3). If this assessment proves wrong and the agreement is suspected of being anti-competitive, both the Commission and the Member States may investigate (there is a case-allocation system in place to decide which authority or authorities are 'best placed' to deal with a particular case).[172] National competition authorities and courts may now also declare the agreement compatible with the common market on the basis of Article 101(3), or incompatible – and impose sanctions.[173] If the Commission is declared as 'best placed' it may accept commitments from the undertakings concerned and make them legally binding.[174]

Turning now to the Commission's Article 101 media cases, it is worth to kick off the analysis with the *Champions League* case. Champions League tournament is essentially a football competition that is organized annually by a body known as the Union of European Football Associations (UEFA). The competitors in the tournament are those football teams who finish in the top tier of their respective national leagues each season. At present, it consists of three stages: three qualifying rounds, the group stages and the knockout rounds. Media rights to qualifying rounds are sold by national football associations, and the demand for these rights is generally local and does not tend to be high. It is the group stage and knockout phases that attract the great interest and, therefore, media rights to those stages are sold centrally by UEFA. The original arrangement notified by UEFA to the Commission involved central selling of both pay-TV and free-TV rights by UEFA on an exclusive basis, in a single bundle to a single TV broadcaster per national territory for periods of up to four years. Whilst the Commission generally accepted the need for consistent brand presentation of the tournament as the main justification for joint-selling, the Commission raised a series of competition concerns and demanded significant amendments to the joint-selling arrangement. The Commission believed that the benefit of single-branding did not outweigh a series of anti-competitive effects derived from

172. Commission Notice on cooperation within the Network of Competition Authorities, OJ (2004) C-101/43.
173. In order to aid uniform application of EC competition law throughout the Community, the Commission published Guidelines on the application of Article 81(3) (OJ (2004) C-101/97). However, decentralization of application of Article 81(3) may potentially give rise to increased number of requests for a preliminary ruling on the basis of Article 234 of the EC Treaty.
174. Article 9 of Regulation 1/2003.

central selling. The breadth of exclusivity offered to winning broadcasters meant that significant numbers of rights were effectively unexploited. Moreover, clubs were not able to sell any of the group and knock-out phase rights independently of UEFA, and there was no utilization of new media rights, as the winning broadcaster was not interested in cannibalizing its viewing ratings, and thus the income, by granting licenses to ISPs and mobile operators.

Given the seriously anti-competitive effect of the joint-selling arrangement, the Commission granted the requested exemption of the joint-selling arrangements under several stringent conditions.[175] First, the single rights package was unbundled and split into several packages ensuring that more than one broadcaster would be able to obtain the rights. In order to prevent all of the most interesting matches being crammed into one package, the Commission requested that the main rights be split into Gold and Silver Packages. Second, the Commission required that media rights contracts with winning bidders be concluded for a period not exceeding three UEFA Champions League seasons. Further, UEFA's exclusivity was reduced by allowing clubs to sell some of the media rights relating to matches in which they are participating. And finally, new media rights were made available for the first time.

Following the Commission's intervention, Silver and Gold packages of rights to UEFA live matches did not go to one and the same broadcaster in any of the national markets.[176] This clearly shows that the UEFA Champions League was undoubtedly a success in utilizing EU competition law to disarm, if only just a little, national media giants. It also unquestionably paved the way for a positive result of the second case, involving the joint selling of media rights to a prestigious football event – this time a national football tournament with European appeal – the English Premier League.

The history of the battle between the Commission and the Football Association Premier League (FAPL) stretches over a period of five years. The first major development was a Statement of Objections issued by the Commission in December 2002,[177] in response to the notification by FAPL of a joint-selling arrangement of four packages of media rights to the Premier League football tournament. The Commission's concerns, centred on the combination of horizontal and vertical anti-competitive effects of the notified arrangement, which led to a very strong market foreclosure. Horizontal anti-competitiveness resulted from pulling the rights from the clubs to a central joint-selling agency. The effect was limited coverage of Premier League matches (only about 25% were covered); there was no right for the

175. Case COMP/C.2-37.398, *UEFA Champions League*, OJ (2003) L291/25.

176. European Commission, 'Background Note: The UEFA Champions League', 24 July 2003, MEMO/03/156.

177. See European Commission press release, 'Commission opens proceedings into joint selling of media rights to the English Premier League', 20 December 2002, IP/02/1951.

clubs to sell independently and no new media rights. The vertical effect became vividly apparent when, in the middle of the proceedings, FAPL held a public auction for the rights to the 2004–2007 Premier League seasons. All four packages were won by BSkyB which paid a premium to secure the deal. It was clear that the arrangement in its notified form could, and in fact has, lead to a long-term monopoly over media rights to this prestigious and highly popular regularly held event. This intensified the Commission's work and accelerated the settlement discussions with FAPL, which resulted in substantial revisions to the FAPL joint selling arrangement, codified in the Commission's decision of March 2006, which made FAPL's commitments legally binding on the basis of Article 9 of Regulation 1/2003.[178]

The revised arrangement which has been operable as of the 2007 season onwards, provides for six balanced packages of live television rights as well as near-live and new media rights[179] sold in an open bidding process monitored by a Commission-appointed trustee. Importantly, following the BSkyB experience, there is a 'no single buyer' rule. Hence, every single package of rights is subject to a separate bidding procedure, and no one bidder is allowed to purchase all six packages. The commitments are legally binding until 2013. The effects of the revision were evident very quickly when in April 2006, BSkyB won only four of the rights packages with the Irish company Setanta winning the remaining two and breaking up Sky's Premiership monopoly for the first time in almost fifteen years. In 2009, Setanta ran into financial difficulties and could not meet its contractual agreements with Premier League leading to termination of the license agreement.[180] The package of forty-six UK live matches for the 2009/10 season, which had previously been held by Setanta, was subsequently auctioned and won by ESPN.[181] ESPN was also awarded a contract for the 2010–2013 seasons with a single package of twenty-three matches a year. The latest auction for the Premier League television rights will was held in June 2012. BSkyB and BT won the rights to show 154 matches starting in the 2013-14 season, with ESPN losing the bid.[182] The sale of the seven packages amounted to GBP 3.02 billion, which is double the amount of the current price of GBP 1.77 billion. Even though BSkyB will show the majority of the matches (116), BT won the right to show 38 attractive and competitive games.

---

178. Case COMP/38.453, *FA Premier League*, OJ (2004) C-115/3; See Commission's press release 'Commission makes commitments from FA Premier League legally binding', 22 March 2006, IP/06/356.
179. The packages encompass: live rights; near live rights; free-to-air highlights rights; mobile clips rights and web-based clips rights.
180. '*Setanta loses Premier TV rights*', BBC News, 19 June 2009.
181. '*ESPN snaps up Premier League TV packages*', ESPN Soccernet, 22 June 2009.
182. '*BSkyB, BT Win Rights To Premier League For Record Amount*', Bloomberg, 14 June 2012.

It seems, therefore, that by ordering open tenders, unbundling of rights packages and limiting the exclusivity of central sales agencies as well as the length of contracts, the Commission was able to 'improve the prospects of competition in providing services to consumers'.[183] It has also broken up the monopolies of the likes of BSkyB, if only with regard to one type of media rights and thus contributed to a reinforcement of structural pluralism in many European media markets.

However, enforcing access to *the same* premium content by a number of broadcasters only has a very limited beneficial effect when viewed from the perspective of the two 'faces' of pluralism – as an abundance of operators, providing an abundance of content. Admittedly, exclusive rights to Premier League matches contributed to strengthening the position of BSkyB by increasing its audience share. This in turn reinforced the company's media power and made it a potential influence on viewers' minds. From this perspective, by creating the conditions for other operators to enter the market, the Commission contributed to a potential increase in structural pluralism in the UK broadcasting market. Moreover, gaining access to some of the Premier League matches would increase the audience share of smaller operators or make entry of the new ones possible. This could potentially provide those operators with additional financial resources which they could spend to produce fresh content they would not otherwise produce, therefore adding to the increase in internal pluralism. The latter link is however fairly tenuous and has not materialized as the other buyers of the Premier League media rights apart from BSkyB were exclusive sports broadcasters.

The Commission's intervention in the above antitrust cases has been to a large extent *ex post*. BSkyB had already managed to build its position in the UK market based on its fourteen-year monopoly over Premier League matches, before the Commission gathered enough clout to break it up. Therefore, albeit noble and appreciable, the introduction of competition in the form of Setanta and latyer ESPN was 'too little too late' and produced limited results. With the commitments coming to an end in 2013, it will be interesting to see how the situation develops. However, with Al-Jazeera expected to successfully bid against BSkyB, the return of the BSkyB's monopoly is unlikely.

However, the *FAPL/BSkyB* case illustrates that despite the Commission's *ex post* reversal of an anti-competitive agreement leading to a monopoly, the media powerhouse in the form of BSkyB has already been established. And once a strong position on the media market has been secured, it is very difficult to reverse it.[184] This is why, in the media sector, what is of utmost importance is the *prevention* of monopolies or significant

183. European Commission, 'Commission makes commitments from FA Premier League legally binding'.

184. Hoffman-Riem, W., *Regulating Media. The Licensing and Supervision of Broadcasting in Six Countries*, 308.

market powers from ever being built. Whether is be by mergers or 'natural growth', by means of acquiring premium content. Competition law is simply unable to achieve this aim.

4.3. LIMITS OF COMPETITION LAW IN ADDRESSING THE ISSUE OF MEDIA PLURALISM

The analysis of the history of DG Competition's involvement in the media sector allows the conclusion that, most notably under Commissioner Van Miert, competition law has significantly 'expanded the European Union's scope for media regulation'.[185] Furthermore, competition law 'had more of an impact in Europe's broadcasting industry than any of the European regulation specifically targeted at the sector'.[186] There have even been opinions expressed that DG Competition takes the complexity of the media sector into account and is actually more vigilant in media cases than in other sectors.[187] Indeed one-third of all prohibition decisions in merger cases, relate to mergers in the media sector.[188] And the Commission prides itself on its very narrow definitions of the relevant market in media cases – both product and geographical. Thus, as noted by Arino,[189] in several cases merger control contributed to alleviating the dangers of media concentration by enforcing access to platforms and networks. In addition, in a series of antitrust decisions the Commission managed to deprive premium content deals of their exclusivity clauses. Therefore, competition law does provide a useful tool with which to prevent the creation of barriers of *access* to content and distribution channels.[190] Moreover, as praised by economists Motta and Polo:

> Unlike regulation, competition policy can be adapted more smoothly to the complex strategic conditions of the industry. It does not require continuous intervention and it reduces the risk of market distortion which would be especially harmful in a period of technological change.[191]

---

185. Humphreys, P., 'The EU and Audiovisual Regulation: An Agency for De-regulation', 11.
186. Levy, D., *Europe's Digital Revolution. Broadcasting Regulation, the EU and the Nation State* (Routledge, 1999), 81.
187. Arino, M., 'Competition Law and Pluralism in European Digital Broadcasting: Addressing the Gaps', 109.
188. European Commission, 'European Merger Control – Council Regulation 139/2004 – Statistics, http://ec.Europa.eu/comm/competition/mergers/statistics.pdf.
189. Arino, M., 'Pluralism in Digital Broadcasting: Myths, Realities and the Boundaries of European Intervention'.
190. Fastweb, 'Comments on "Media Pluralism – What Should Be the European Union's Role?", Issues Paper' 2005.
191. Motta, M., Polo, M., 'Concentration and Public Policies in the Broadcasting Industry: The Future of Television', 326, 327.

The same authors even claim that 'in the presence of competition laws or regulations which place strict limits on the market share of a firm, limits on shares owned by a single investor tend to be superfluous'.[192]

Undeniably, when utilized, competition law not only can contribute but indeed has contributed to preventing the creation of monopolies or breaking up the existing ones, thus maintaining or even introducing structural pluralism onto European media markets.[193] Therefore, competition law does have its role, however 'indirect' or 'limited',[194] in the process of protecting pluralism at the EU level.

However, notwithstanding the unquestionable positive role competition law plays in safeguarding pluralism in Europe, there has been a dangerous tendency in the European Union recently, to believe that the accomplishment of digitalization and convergence allows media pluralism to be secured solely through normal market mechanisms and competition regulation. This belief, initiated by the Commission's Convergence Green Paper, stems from the conviction that in the digital and converged media world the only concern is access to key 'gateways', which are the conditional access systems, subscriber management systems and electronic programme guides.[195] And indeed, those concerns can and have been addressed by competition law in cases such as *MSG* or *Nordic Satellite Distribution.*

DG Competition has often emphasised that it takes particular care when dealing with media markets.[196] As noted above, there are allegedly two indications of this 'intensive care': narrow market definitions (both product and geographic) and more negative and conditional competition decisions in media cases, than in any other sector.

The policy of defining narrow broadcasting markets means that mergers on the same market, for instance, two pay-TV stations in one country, are less likely to be approved than mergers across markets, for instance pay-TV buying free TV as in *Bertelsmann/News International/Vox*, or pay-TV from one country buying pay-TV in another country as in *Kirch/Richemont/Telepiù.* If the only free-TV in any one country decided to buy the only pay-TV in the same country, this would probably be approved, given the currently prevailing market definition. Some argue that there is nothing wrong with this approach.[197] Certainly, if there is no harm in a small product

192. Motta, M., Polo, M., 'Concentration and Public Policies in the Broadcasting Industry: The Future of Television', 326.
193. Feintuck, M., Varney, M., *Media Regulation, Public Interest and the Law*, 94, 99.
194. Arino, M., 'Pluralism in Digital Broadcasting: Myths, Realities and the Boundaries of European Intervention'.
195. Humphreys, P., 'Regulating for Pluralism in the Era of Digital Convergence: The Issues of Media Concentration Control and the Future of Public-Service Broadcasting'.
196. Monti, M., 'Does EC Competition Policy Help or Hinder the European Audiovisual and Telecoms Industries?'.
197. Gibbons, T., 'Concentrations of Ownership and Control in a Converging Media Industry', 168.

market, there will most probably be even less harm in a larger one, so cross-media ownership is not necessarily dangerous.[198] However, even if by imposing a package of commitments, the Commission is able to prevent the risk of leveraging economic power from one service market (e.g., free-TV) to another (e.g., pay-TV), this only solves competition concerns. Accumulation of ownership in many media markets by a single conglomerate, even if fenced by a number of competition safeguards, still seriously increases the prospect that the audience will be subjected to similar content in different media outlets[199] and thus raises significant pluralism concerns. Therefore, 'it is the impact of cross-ownership on the audience that is significant, not necessarily the fact of cross-ownership in itself'.[200]

Therefore, narrow definitions of product and geographic markets only serve to protect national markets from being controlled by too few operators of the same type (i.e., pay-TV or free-TV).[201] In line with the need for a competitive European media market, and the desire to create the mythical 'European champions',[202] the current approach of DG Competition leaves the European market open to conquest by media moguls with cross-media and cross-border operations.[203] As Ward explains:

> Regulatory ground [established by the European Commission's approach to mergers and joint ventures] was favourable to companies looking to strengthen the audiovisual market by building up company portfolios and expanding the size of production by exploiting cross border strategies within the common market zone.[204]

Moreover, in the example of free-TV buying pay-TV, even if there were more than one pay-TV in the country and the merger would not result in one company controlling the entire broadcasting market in that country, this could quickly change. For instance, the other pay-TVs could go bankrupt (as Kirch in Germany). The result would be one company controlling both free- and pay-TV in the Member State. Competition analysis at the time of the merger cannot predict such developments and given the 'once off' approval

---

198. Gibbons, T., 'Concentrations of Ownership and Control in a Converging Media Industry', 169.
199. Gibbons, T., 'Concentrations of Ownership and Control in a Converging Media Industry', 169.
200. Gibbons, T., 'Concentrations of Ownership and Control in a Converging Media Industry', 168.
201. Garzaniti, L., *Telecommunications, Broadcasting and the Internet*, 532
202. Humphreys, P., 'The EU and Audiovisual Regulation: An Agency for De-regulation', 91, 94.
203. The best example is the continuing expansion of Murdoch's News Corporation in Europe. After UK (where it recently bought a 17.9% stake in ITV, see 'ITV rejects merger move from NTL', BBC News, 21 November 2006. Ireland and Italy, it sought to conquer the Polish and Baltic states' markets.
204. Ward, D., 'Media Concentration and Pluralism: Regulation, Realties and the Council of Europe's Standards in the Television Sector'.

of a merger it is not possible to unwind it later on. The exception to this would be unless the parties do not fulfil conditions and obligations imposed as a condition for approval. As noted by Harcourt:

> The EC's reliance on competition policy to govern media markets has been problematic. Media markets are highly volatile. Therefore, the market status quo at the time of a decision could alter itself dramatically in a relatively short period of time. It would aid both market investor and public interest regulators if clear rules on media ownership could be agreed at the European level, rather than having to rely on case-by-case analyses.[205]

The second alleged indicator of the intensive care taken by the Commission in media cases is greater vigilance in case-analysis. Some authors rightly point out that there are generally more cases involving the media than other sectors and one-third of all prohibition decisions in merger cases relate to mergers in the media sector.[206] However, as already argued above, all of the negative decisions have taken place under the particularly vigilant Competition Commissioner Van Miert. His successor, Monti, not only allowed several mergers which Van Miert would most likely have prohibited, but also expressly rebutted the suspicion of any special care being offered to media markets, expressed in a greater number of media cases:

> There is a perception that competition rules intervene in media and telecoms cases more often than in other sectors. This is, I believe, false. There have certainly been a number of important media and telecoms cases having competition law problems. But there have also been – quite simply – a large number of media and telecoms cases.[207]

Indeed, as a direct result of the TVWF Directive, there has been a dramatic increase in the number of media mergers and joint ventures at the European level.[208] Therefore, the undeniably substantial involvement of DG Competition in the media market is not the result of some special care, but simply the reflection of the underlying problem – the consolidation trend in the media industry.

In any event, notwithstanding the above criticism of the Commission's 'intensive care' claim, and even if it were actually true that the Commission, especially under Commissioner Van Miert, did in fact exercise more vigilance in media cases, competition law *by definition* cannot be used to guarantee media pluralism. This is so not only because media pluralism and diversity depend on more factors than access to key 'gateways', but mainly

205. Harcourt, A., *The European Union and the Regulation of Media Markets*, 50.
206. Arino, M., 'Competition Law and Pluralism in European Digital Broadcasting: Addressing the Gaps', 109.
207. Monti, M., 'Does EC Competition Policy Help or Hinder the European Audiovisual and Telecoms Industries?'.
208. Humphreys, P., 'The EU and Audiovisual Regulation: An Agency for De-regulation', 11.

because competition law and media concentration rules have fundamentally different focuses.[209]

As noted by the Commission itself 'competition rules alone may not be sufficient to ensure cultural diversity and media pluralism',[210] because fighting 'dominant market position' on a relevant market differs from counteracting the development of the 'dominant power of opinion' in the media sector.[211]

These different focuses result in a number of problems with the application of competition law to media merger cases. First, some media mergers which are harmless for competition will raise serious pluralism concerns.[212] As already mentioned, the Commission's tendency to define narrow relevant markets may and indeed already has, led to regulatory approval for pay-TV/free-TV mono-media mergers or a newspaper/TV cross-media merger.[213] The merging companies were able to persuade the Commission that the merger actually leads to an improvement in competition on the relevant, narrowly defined markets (newspapers, pay-TV or free-TV).[214] While this may be the case, the plurality and diversity of the overall media industry, encompassing all viewers, listeners and readers may suffer as a result of a decreased number of content providers. Those media specific objectives are not taken into account in the competition analysis. They may be subject to national scrutiny as allowed by Article 21(4) of the EU Merger Regulation, however, as already discussed, Member States have not made extensive use of the possibilities offered by this Article.

Second, the EU Merger Regulation only deals with a concentration in the media market taking place by means of a merger, an acquisition or a joint venture. Natural growth of media companies, for instance, by adding new channels or programmes, is outside the scope of the Regulation's application. Dominant positions, held by a media company, are unquestionable from the

209. Scheuer, A., Strothmann, P., 'Media Supervision on the Threshold of the 21st Century. What Are the Requirements of Broadcasting, Telecommunications and Concentration Regulation?', Iris Plus, Legal Observations of the European Audiovisual Observatory, Issue 2002-2.
210. European Commission, 'Pluralism and Media Concentration in the Internal Market: An Assessment of the Need for Community Action (Green Paper)', Directive 2002/19/EC of the European Parliament and of the Council of 7 March 2002 on access to, and interconnection of, electronic communications networks and associated facilities (Access Directive), Rec. 10.
211. Scheuer, A., Strothmann, P., 'Media Supervision on the Threshold of the 21st Century. What Are the Requirements of Broadcasting, Telecommunications and Concentration Regulation?'.
212. Hitchens, L.P., 'Media Ownership and Control: A European Approach'.
213. Hitchens, L.P., 'Media Ownership and Control: A European Approach'.
214. Scheuer, A., Strothmann, P., 'Media Supervision on the Threshold of the 21st Century. What Are the Requirements of Broadcasting, Telecommunications and Concentration Regulation?'.

EC competition point of view. Only the abuse of that position, in the economic sense of 'abuse', will be prosecuted on the basis of Article 102 TFEU.[215] Media power, however, may be abused by the mere existence of a single or a few large media firms.[216] Dominance or oligopoly on the media market achieved by natural growth will be unproblematic from a competition law perspective, but it will eliminate structural media pluralism, which in turn will almost certainly reduce the diversity of content and 'the likelihood of the audience experiencing other views of the world'.[217] Therefore, because the abuse of power in the media sector may have more than just economic implications and the formation of dominant opinion is, in itself dangerous. It follows that the need to control media concentrations must be more of a 'risk assessment' than a retrospective and narrower fight with the actual abuse of market power with the weapon of competition.[218] As pointed out by Scheuer and Strothmann, development of a dominant opinion in the media must be prevented 'for constitutional reasons'.[219] This certainly cannot be achieved by means of competition law, and there is as a consequence a need for an additional media specific regulation 'separate from that which governs other parts of the national and global economy'.[220]

Essentially therefore, the main argument against the exclusive reliance on competition law to foster media pluralism comes down to what seems like a trivial statement, that media power and market power are two different things. The Commission's current belief in the potential of competition law to boost media pluralism rests on assumptions.[221] The first is that, if competitive conditions are provided 'a multiplicity of operators will follow'.[222] However, this has not happened – the competition for markets has resulted in concentration in the media sector.[223] Second, diversity of sourceor

215. Scheuer, A., Strothmann, P., 'Media Supervision on the Threshold of the 21st Century. What Are the Requirements of Broadcasting, Telecommunications and Concentration Regulation?'.
216. The Campaign for Press and Broadcasting Freedom, 'Comments on "Media Pluralism – What Should Be the European Union's Role?", Issues Paper', 2005.
217. Gibbons, T., 'Concentrations of Ownership and Control in a Converging Media Industry', 168.
218. Komorek, E., 'European Attempts to Regulate Media Concentration. Persisting Conflict of Interests', (2004/2005) Hibernian Law Journal 1, 76; see also Cavallin, J., 'European Policies and Regulations on Media Concentration', 1; European Audiovisual Observatory, 'Iris Special: Television and Media Concentration. Regulatory Models on the National and European Level'.
219. Scheuer, A., Strothmann, P., 'Media Supervision on the Threshold of the 21st Century. What Are the Requirements of Broadcasting, Telecommunications and Concentration Regulation?', 2005.
220. The Campaign for Press and Broadcasting Freedom, 'Response to the Commission's consultation on the revision of the TVWF directive, Issues Paper 6 (Media Pluralism)', 70.
221. Hitchens, L.P., 'Media Ownership and Control: A European Approach', 64.
222. Hitchens, L.P., 'Media Ownership and Control: A European Approach', 64.
223. Barendt, E., *Broadcasting Law. A Comparative Study* (Clarendon Press, 1993), 122; see also Hitchens, L.P., 'Media Ownership and Control: A European Approach', 64.

structural pluralism, which may be provided by competition analysis, does not automatically lead to diversity of content (internal pluralism). So far, there has even been a tendency to the contrary with 'competitors targeting the same, large audiences with similar products'.[224] Therefore, protection of pluralism can at best only be a positive 'side effect' of competition analysis. However, it is not a primary aim and there remains a strong case for retaining, or indeed introducing, media-specific anti-concentration restrictions.[225]

Even the greatest advocates of the potential of competition law in the changing media environment acknowledge the need to accompany it with media specific anti-concentration rules.[226] The Commission itself admits that 'competition rules alone may not be sufficient to ensure cultural diversity and media pluralism'.[227] Even economists, such as Motta and Polo, who otherwise praise the potential of competition law in the changing media environment and generally advocate for a 'hands-off' approach, admit that competition law is unable to deal with a very important market failure or an externality, namely the impact of the media industry on the formation of public opinion.[228] Therefore, competition policy should be 'complemented by regulations which guarantee that no single firm has enough market power to jeopardize the pluralism of opinions in society ... even if such measures are in contradiction to economic efficiency objectives'.[229]

The question, therefore, is not whether there is a need for additional media-concentration rules to accompany EU competition law, as this assertion appears to be conclusive.[230] The question should rather be whether there is a need for *EU media-specific rules*. In this regard, despite the forecastthat 'EU competition policy will continue to be the dominant mode of European-level intervention in the ... TV market for some time to

224. Gibbons, T., 'Concentrations of Ownership and Control in a Converging Media Industry', 168.
225. Humphreys, P., 'Regulating for Pluralism in the Era of Digital Convergence: The Issues of Media Concentration Control and the Future of Public-Service Broadcasting'; see also Goldberg, D., Prosser, T., Verhulst, S., *EC Media Law and Policy*, 90.
226. Scheuer, A., Strothmann, P., 'Media Supervision on the Threshold of the 21st Century. What Are the Requirements of Broadcasting, Telecommunications and Concentration Regulation?'.
227. European Commission, 'Pluralism and Media Concentration in the Internal Market: An Assessment of the Need for Community Action (Green Paper)'; Directive 2002/19/EC of the European Parliament and of the Council of 7 March 2002 on access to, and interconnection of, electronic communications networks and associated facilities (Access Directive), Rec. 10.
228. Motta, M., Polo, M., 'Concentration and Public Policies in the Broadcasting Industry: The Future of Television', 313.
229. Motta, M., Polo, M., 'Concentration and Public Policies in the Broadcasting Industry: The Future of Television', 327.
230. Garzaniti, L., *Telecommunications, Broadcasting and the Internet*, 543.

come',[231] the words of the former Competition Commissioner Karel van Miert still resonate this day:

> I am convinced of a need for European legislation on media concentration. From a democratic point of view, it is necessary. (…) We cannot use competition rules to govern democratic issues.[232]

231. Levy, D., *Europe's Digital Revolution. Broadcasting Regulation, the EU and the Nation State*, 81.
232. Cited in Harcourt, A., 'The European Commission and Regulation of Media Industry'.

Chapter 5

European Tools III: Fragmentary EU Legislative Measures

The current political line in the European Union is that the combination of national legislation, EU competition law and EU legislative instruments provides a balanced solution for the protection of both structural and internal media pluralism in Europe. It is, therefore, important to complete the discussion of the European Union's engagement in the protection of media pluralism with the analysis of existing legislative tools, directly or indirectly offsetting negative consequences of growing media concentration in Europe.

The passion and enthusiasm characterising the European Parliament's engagement in the fight for media pluralism is well known and has already been discussed in Chapter 5 above. It is the European Commission and the Council who have proven resistant to the Parliament's calls for positive legislative action in this field. Admittedly, in general statements and policy declarations, both the Commission and the Council recognise that there are more aspects to broadcasting than sheer contribution to the economy and job creation ability. In the 1999 Communication 'Principles and guidelines for the Community's audiovisual policy in the digital age',[1] the Commission admitted that audiovisual media plays a central role in the functioning of modern democratic societies. And it is the social and cultural role of the audiovisual media that should form the point of departure for policy making and social impact of broadcasting should be central to any regulation.[2] Crucially, the Commission emphasised that:

---

1. European Commission, 'Principles and guidelines for the community's audiovisual policy in the digital age (Communication)'.
2. European Commission, 'Principles and guidelines for the community's audiovisual policy in the digital age (Communication)'.

> The audiovisual is … not an industry like any other and does not simply produce goods to be sold on the market like other goods. It is in fact a cultural industry *par excellence*. It has a major influence on what citizens know, believe and feel and plays a crucial role in the transmission, development and even construction of cultural identities.[3]

It follows that broadcasting should be subject to specific regulation based on values such as freedom of expression, pluralism and promotion of cultural and linguistic diversity. The Commission also asserts that the 'audiovisual policy of the European Community has incorporated these principles and common objectives' in development of its own regulation of media industry according to the EU's competence, which covers the freedom to provide services and support for the industry.

Similarly, the unique status of the audiovisual sector is underlined in the Council of Ministers' Resolution, of 21 January 2002, on culture and the knowledge society.[4] This resolution emphasises the need to regulate the sector so as to incorporate its cultural, competitive and industrial dimensions at the same time. It also invites the Commission to continue to make a more effective contribution to the development of the audiovisual sector based on the approach that integrates the cultural, competitive and industrial dimensions of the industry.

However, a year after the Council's Resolution, there was a noticeable change in the Commission's position. The Commission issued a Communication on 'The future of European regulatory audiovisual policy'[5] in which the most important value seems to be 'a clear and predictable policy environment' allowing media companies to plan investment and develop their business strategies. The Commission continues to admit that Community policy in the audiovisual sector supports the paramount objectives of general interest. However, unlike the 1999 Communication, the 2003 Communication does not name media pluralism as one of such objectives[6] and does not perceive the social and cultural role of the audiovisual media as the point of departure for policy making. Instead, this time the Commission asserts that Community policy in the audiovisual sector is mainly aimed at promoting the development of the audiovisual sector in the EU, *through the completion of the Internal Market.*[7] With regard to media pluralism, the Communication admits that at present, secondary Community legislation

---

3. European Commission, 'Principles and guidelines for the community's audiovisual policy in the digital age (Communication)'.
4. Council of the European Union, 'Culture and the knowledge society (Resolution)', 2002/C-32/01.
5. European Commission, 'The future of European regulatory audiovisual policy (Communication)', COM(2003) 784 final.
6. The values mentioned are: cultural and linguistic diversity, the protection of minors and human dignity and consumer protection.
7. European Commission, 'The future of European regulatory audiovisual policy (Communication)', 21, 3.

does not contain any provisions specifically aimed at safeguarding the pluralism of the media. However, it is quick to point out that the protection of media pluralism is primarily a task for the Member States,[8] and Community law *allows* the application of national measures to secure this aim. Moreover, EU competition law and certain provisions of the TVWF Directive contribute to the safeguarding of media pluralism. The 2003 Communication is therefore the best summary of the current policy of the European Commission towards negative effects of excessive media concentration: national measures accompanied by EU competition law and selected EU legislation provide a complete and sufficient legal framework for the protection of media pluralism in Europe.

The following analysis of the existing legislative measures which, according to the Commission's claims, contribute to safeguarding media pluralism at the European level, remains unchanged by the recent policy developments – the introduction in 2009 of the Media Policy Monitor (MPM) which resulted from the DG Information Society's 'Three-Step-Approach' to media pluralism as well as the creation of two advisory bodies in 2011: the High Level Group on Media Freedom and Pluralism and a Centre for Media Pluralism and Media Freedom within the Robert Schuman School of the European University Institute. Although all three are laudable and mark the formal re-introduction of media pluralism as one of the pillars of the Commission's work in the audiovisual and media sectors, they bring little change to the EU legislative framework.

The aforementioned 1999 Commission Communication 'Principles and guidelines for the Community's audiovisual policy in the digital age'[9] set out principles for the regulation of the audiovisual sector in the era of digitalization. The Commission declares that it will observe the following six rules when regulating the 'new' audiovisual sector: (i) proportionality; (ii) separation of transport and content regulation; (iii) the realization of general interest objectives, including pluralism and diversity; (iv) recognition of the role of public service broadcasting and the need for transparency in its financing; (v) the complementary role of self-regulation; and (vi) the independence of regulatory authorities.

The principle of the separation of transport and content regulation was realized in the European Union by the adoption of two separate legal frameworks for the audiovisual sector. The Audiovisual Media Services Directive (AVMS)[10] deals with selected content issues and the 2003

8. As observed in the European Commission's Green Paper on services of general interest.
9. European Commission, 'Principles and guidelines for the community's audiovisual policy in the digital age (Communication)'.
10. Directive 2010/13/EU of the European Parliament and of the Council of 10 March 2010 on the coordination of certain provisions laid down by law, regulation or administrative action in Member States concerning the provision of audiovisual media services (Audiovisual Media Services Directive), OJ (2010) L95/1.

regulatory framework for Electronic Communications and Services (E-Communications framework)[11] regulates transmission through networks. According to the Issues Paper for the Liverpool Audiovisual Conference[12] prepared by Directorate General for the Information Society and Media, both of these instruments contain measures aimed at the active protection of pluralism, both in its structural and internal incarnation.

Table 5.3 at the end of this chapter summarises and illustrates the current EU-level legislative tools which contribute to support of media pluralism.

5.1. LEGISLATIVE SUPPORT FOR STRUCTURAL PLURALISM

With the failure to adopt a media concentration Directive in the mid 1990s, the winners in the 'war of priorities' were those advocating for the liberalisation of the broadcasting sector by means of applying the 'country of origin principle' and subjecting it to *ex post* regulation by means of competition law.

The result of the victory of the European Commission's propensity for convergence is the 2003 E-Communications Framework, recently amended in 2009.[13] This framework consists of five directives: Framework Directive, Authorization Directive, Access Directive, Universal Service Directive and Privacy Directive.[14] The E-Communications Framework covers all electronic communications networks, regardless of the kind of services carried over them ('horizontal' approach) and aims at establishing a harmonized regulatory framework for all electronic communications networks and

11. The 2003 Regulatory Framework consists of the following directives: Directive 2002/21/EC on a common regulatory framework for electronic communications networks and services (Framework Directive); Directive 2002/19/EC on access to, and interconnection of, electronic communications networks and associated facilities (Access Directive); Directive 2002/20/EC on the authorization of electronic communications networks and services (Authorization Directive); Directive 2002/22/EC on universal service and users' rights relating to electronic communications networks and services (Universal Service Directive); Directive 2002/58/EC concerning the processing of personal data and the protection of privacy in the electronic communications sector (Directive on privacy and electronic communications)
12. European Commission, 'Media Pluralism – what should be the European Union's role?', Issues Paper, 2005.
13. Directive 2009/140/EC of the European Parliament and of the Council of 25 November 2009 amending Directives 2002/21/EC on a common regulatory framework for electronic communications networks and services, 2002/19/EC on access to, and interconnection of, electronic communications networks and associated facilities, and 2002/20/EC on the authorization of electronic communications networks and services, OJ (2009) L337/37.
14. See n. 11.

services, across the European Union.[15] This harmonization is to be achieved in particular by the roll-back of individual licensing for the provision of electronic communications networks, and its replacement by the general authorization regime provided in the Authorization Directive. The Framework is, therefore, deregulatory as it 'abolishes the burdensome old telecoms licensing system, replacing it with a much lighter weight authorization regime for all networks and services providing electronic communications *carriage*, including those (e.g., terrestrial, satellite, cable etc.) providing broadcasting content'.[16]

In accordance with the principle of the separation of regulation of content and transmission, the Framework does not deal with regulation of content broadcast over electronic communications networks. Therefore, broadcasting content continues 'to be regulated "vertically" according to Member States' preferred socio-cultural models'.[17] This means that Member States can retain content requirements attached to broadcasting licenses. However, in various general policy statements[18] and also in the recitals of the Directives, the Commission claims that the Directives do *take account* of the links between transmission and content regulation, in particular in order to promote media pluralism. Recital 5 of the overarching Framework Directive states that the separation of regulation of content and transmission 'does not prejudice the taking into account of the links existing between them, in particular in order to guarantee media pluralism, cultural diversity and consumer protection'. Several aspects of the Directives show that the Commission at least made an attempt to stand by this statement and introduce provisions aimed at safeguarding public interests, other than effective competition in the e-communications sector. The regulation of must-carry rules in the Universal Service Directive does possibly foster internal media pluralism,[19] and the rules on access and interoperability in the Access Directive are aimed not only at enhancing competition, but also at securing structural media pluralism.

15. European Commission, 'The 2003 regulatory framework for electronic communications – Implications for broadcasting (Working Document)', Brussels, 14 June 2002, 3.
16. Humphreys, P., 'The EU and Audiovisual Regulation: An Agency for De-regulation', 19.
17. Humphreys, P., 'The EU and Audiovisual Regulation: An Agency for De-regulation', 19.
18. European Commission, 'The 2003 regulatory framework for electronic communications – Implications for broadcasting (Working Document)', 2.
19. See section 5.2 below for detailed discussion on must-carry rules.

5.1.1. Access Remedies In the E-Communications Framework

One of the main ideals underlying the E-Communications Framework is that *ex ante* regulation of e-communications networks is gradually rolled back, with the exception of operators who have a significant market power (SMP) in a relevant market.[20] The designation of operators with SMP is carried out by national regulatory authorities (NRAs) following market analysis and in accordance with market dominance tests established in EU competition law.[21] The consequence of designating an operator with SMP, is that a national regulator may burden that operator with certain obligations, as set out in the Access and Universal Service Directives. An obligation that is particularly valid from the structural pluralism angle is that of access rights.

The Access Directive establishes a regime on providing access to electronic communications networks. Operators with SMP may be obliged to meet reasonable requests for access to, and use of, networks. Associated obligations may include transparency, non-discrimination, accounting separation or price control. The principle, however, is that regulators should only intervene when commercial negotiations fail. In addition, the Access Directive makes an effort to address the issue of bottlenecks created by the existence of conditional access systems (CAS) in the era of digital television.[22] The digital revolution has led to a shift in the location of bottlenecks in the supply chain.[23] In the days of analogue, there was an abundance of content spread out over scarce outlets. Today, outlets are multiplying and content is becoming scarce. Moreover, the existence of CAS resulted in market power moving down the supply chain to the level of household receiving equipment. CAS allows operators to deliver broadcasting services only to consumers that have paid for it.[24] In order to receive digital programmes safeguarded by CAS, a viewer must be equipped with special

20. The European Commission issued Guidelines aimed at setting out the principles for use by national regulatory authorities in the analysis of markets and effective competition under the new regulatory framework for electronic communications networks and services; see European Commission, 'Guidelines on market analysis and the assessment of significant market power under the Community regulatory framework for electronic communications networks and services', OJ (2002) C-165/6.
21. Article 14(2) of the Framework Directive: 'An undertaking shall be deemed to have significant market power if, either individually or jointly with others, it enjoys a position equivalent to dominance, that is to say a position of economic strength affording it the power to behave to an appreciable extent independently of competitors, customers and ultimately consumers'.
22. For a detailed analysis of challenges posed by the existence of bottlenecks see Helberger, N., *Controlling Access to Content: Regulating Conditional Access in Digital Broadcasting* (Kluwer Law International, 2005).
23. Cowie, C., Marsden, C.T., 'Convergence, Competition and Regulation', (1998) International Journal of Communications Law and Policy 1.
24. Varney, E., 'Regulating the Digital Television Infrastructure in the EU. Room for Citizenship Interests?', (2006) SCRIPT-ed 3(3), 226.

receiver technology in the form of a set-top-box (STB). A STB comprises a software called Application Programming Interface (API) and an Electronic Programme Guide (EPG) which allows viewers to navigate between different channels. The positioning of channels is determined by the owner of the EPG, and any bias in listings may seriously influence viewing patterns.[25]

It is, therefore, obvious that vertically integrated operators who own CAS and associated facilities such as APIs and EPGs exercise significant market power and may limit the access of these facilities to newcomers, thus, restricting competition and also limiting structural media pluralism. For instance, BSkyB in the UK owns a proprietary CAS and controls its own API and EPG. The Access Directive addresses the issue by requiring *all* CAS operators, whether designated with SMP or not, to provide services to other broadcasters on 'fair, reasonable and non-discriminatory terms'. The Directive also insists that trans-control between CAS providers and other network operators must be possible. This allows, for example, cable operators to directly manage CAS services offered to their own customers.[26] NRAs may also impose obligations on CAS operators to provide access to associated facilities such as APIs and EPGs to the extent that it is necessary to ensure accessibility for end-users to digital radio and television broadcasting services. What the Directive does not regulate is content and presentational issues related to CAS and associated facilities. For instance, rules on the prominence of channels on EPGs are left to the Member States to provide, only if they so wish.

Thus, the access regime has several limitations. First, access remedies will only be imposed on operators designated with SMP, which in the current regime equals market dominance. Second, market negotiations between an SMP provider and a newcomer have to take place and subsequently fail, before there is any regulatory intervention. Finally, rules on access to CAS are not complete, as there is a lack of EU regulation on presentational aspects on EPGs and lack of obligatory rules on interoperability.

5.1.2. Interoperability Rules in the E-Communications Framework

With different proprietary CAS and no standardisation of APIs and EPGs, the problems posed by bottlenecks in digital interactive television will persist notwithstanding the possibility of imposing access obligations. The EU's legislative efforts in this area are not promising. The now repealed 1995 Advanced Television Standards Directive[27] specified that CAS providers

25. Cowie, C., Marsden, C.T., 'Convergence, Competition and Regulation', 41.
26. European Commission, 'The 2003 regulatory framework for electronic communications – Implications for broadcasting (Working Document)', 13.
27. Directive 95/47/EC of the European Parliament and of the Council of 24 October 1995 on the use of standards for the transmission of television signals, OJ (1995) L281/51.

should supply third-party access to their conditional access services on 'fair, reasonable and non-discriminatory' terms. It also obliged national regulatory authorities to ensure that CAS operators do not prohibit set-top-box manufacturers from including a common interface allowing connection with other access systems. However, Humphreys notes that this 'was a far cry from mandating the inclusion of a common interface against the wishes of their customers'.[28] In addition, the Directive was 'so vague as to leave national officials unclear as to what the provisions meant, and as to which needed to be written into national law. The result was that national implementation varied hugely'.[29]

Unfortunately, the E-Communications Framework, which replaced the 1995 Advanced Television Standards Directive, does not entirely solve the problem of the lack of standardisation, resulting in the lack of interoperability. The Access Directive obliges CAS operators to provide access to CAS, as well as to APIs and EPGs on 'fair, reasonable and non-discriminatory terms'. With regard to standards, the Framework Directive is very articulate and promising in Recital 31, which states that:

> interoperability of digital interactive television services and enhanced digital television equipment, at the level of the consumer, should be encouraged in order to ensure the free flow of information, *media pluralism and cultural diversity*'.

The recital continues that it is therefore 'desirable for consumers to have the capability of receiving all digital interactive television services', regardless of the transmission mode. This is possible only through promoting open APIs which 'facilitate interoperability, i.e., the portability of interactive content between delivery mechanisms, and full functionality of this content on enhanced digital television equipment'. As a necessary consequence, open APIs are a must.

The Framework Directive, however, does not go as far as to mandate open APIs and common standards. Recital 31 ends with a vague statement that 'digital interactive television platform operators should *strive* to implement an API which conforms to standards or specifications adopted by a European standards organization' and that 'migration from existing APIs to new open APIs should be *encouraged* and organized, for example by Memoranda of Understanding between all relevant market players'. This is further developed in Article 18 of the Framework Directive which requires Member States to *encourage* the use of open APIs. In accordance with Article 17 of the Framework Directive, the Commission has published a list

28. Humphreys, P., 'The EU and Audiovisual Regulation: An Agency for De-regulation', 21, 22.
29. Levy, D., *Europe's Digital Revolution. Broadcasting Regulation, the EU and the Nation State*, 73.

of standards for electronic communications networks, services and associated facilities,[30] listing Digital Video Broadcasting (DVB) Multimedia Home Platform (MHP) as only a *recommended* standard for API. The Commission did not avail of the possibility to make the standards mandatory. Therefore, again, Member States are required only to *encourage* the use of listed standards. With regard to the commonly used proprietary CAS, paragraph 2 of Article 18 requires Member States to encourage the proprietors of such systems to disclose, against appropriate remuneration, all necessary information enabling other providers of digital TV services to provide all services supported by the API in a fully functional form.

Before it was amended in 2009, the Framework Directive contained Article 18(3) which required the Commission to examine its effects and, if interoperability has not been achieved, to consider mandating the use of listed standards. The last assessment of the interoperability of digital interactive television services was summarized in the Commission's Communication of 2 February 2006.[31] The Commission applauded Italy for the most extensive deployment of interactive set-top-boxes using the MHP standard. The Italian success was basically due to a combination of two factors: the voluntary agreement of Italian broadcasters to use MHP, and the state subsidy scheme for interactive decoders. In other countries, however, the take up of interactive decoders is slow if not non-existent, and there is apparently no will on the Commission's side to accelerate the process. On the contrary, the conclusions of the Communication were that there is still 'no clear case' for mandating open standards, and that at this point of market development mandating EU-wide standards could even have significant negative effects. The way forward is therefore to continue to promote open standards and interoperability. Exactly how this is to be done is, unfortunately, not explained … In the 2009 amendment, paragraph 3 of Article 18 was deleted from the Access Directive. Instead, a new point (ab) was inserted to Article 5 which deals with the powers and responsibilities of the national regulatory authorities with regard to access and interconnection. National regulatory authorities will now be able to impose, in justified cases, and to the extent that is necessary, obligations on undertakings that control access to end users to make their services interoperable. The responsibility was, therefore, shifted from the Commission to the Member States. The results of the change remain to be seen.

30. European Commission, 'List of standards and/or specifications for electronic communications networks, services and associated facilities and services, replacing all previous versions (Decision)', COM(2006) 6364 final.

31. European Commission, 'Reviewing the interoperability of digital interactive television services pursuant to Communication COM(2004) 541 of 30 July 2004 (Communication), COM(2006) 37 final.

The EBU noted that there may be only one level of interoperability that counts in this case, and that is, the 'citizen' level.[32] Interoperability in this respect is achieved when viewers can access the full range of available broadcasting services without technological constraint. From this standpoint, it is obvious that there is no interoperability in Europe. As emphasized by EBU, equipment made in one country cannot be used to receive services in other countries. In many Member States there are several proprietary systems in use which make access to competitive services, in practical terms, impossible. All of this leads to the situation of European television with technological frontiers.[33]

The Commission's approach to the issue is somewhat unfortunate. The EBU rightly suggests that only mandating the use of open APIs, for instance as of the date of digital switchover in 2012, can remedy the problem. The accompanying measures could involve the requirement on labelling decoders equipped with open API and EU-level financial support for interactive decoders. Active promotion of open APIs is the effective way to foster structural media pluralism, as it gives access to broadcasting services offered by many providers, not constraining the viewers to the selection of channels offered by one platform provider.[34] However, with the deletion of Article 18(3), the hope for EU-mandated standards seems to have disappeared.

5.1.3. 'Country of Origin Principle' in the AVMS Directive

Discussion on the measures allegedly contributing to fostering structural pluralism in the European Union would not be complete without mentioning the 'country of origin principle' introduced by the TVWF Directive. The principle has from the beginning been the cornerstone of the Directive, and it remained unchanged, if not strengthened, in the new AVMS Directive.

Article 3(1) of the AVMS Directives provides that 'Member States shall ensure freedom of reception and shall not restrict retransmissions on their territory of television broadcasts from other Member States for reasons which fall within the fields coordinated by this Directive.' This leaves only one EU Member State with a jurisdiction over any given broadcaster in Europe. As defined in Article 2, broadcasters find themselves under the jurisdiction of a particular Member State if they are *established* there, or if they use a frequency granted by, satellite capacity appertaining to or they use a satellite up-link situated, in that Member State. This gives broadcasters the

32. European Broadcasting Union, 'Comments on the Commission Staff Working Paper on the Interoperability of Digital Interactive Television Services', 20 April 2004 .
33. European Broadcasting Union, 'Comments on the Commission Staff Working Paper on the Interoperability of Digital Interactive Television Services', 2.
34. European Broadcasting Union, 'Comments on the Commission Staff Working Paper on the Interoperability of Digital Interactive Television Services', 4.

legal certainty that they have to comply with only one national legal system. The AVMS Directive extended the benefits of the 'country of origin' principle to new non-linear (on-demand) audiovisual services (in particular video on demand).

Importantly, The AVMS Directive reverses the order of the criteria used to determine which Member State has jurisdiction over non-EU satellite television channels which are not established in the EU but which are either uplinked from a Member State or use satellite capacity controlled by a body within the jurisdiction of a Member State. Previously it was the Member State responsible for the satellite capacity that had jurisdiction over any non-EU channels transmitted via that satellite. Satellite uplink was the secondary criterion. The AVMS Directive reversed the order of the jurisdiction criteria. It is now the Member State from which the channels are uplinked to the satellite, that has jurisdiction over those channels. Only if the channels are not uplinked from within the EU do they fall within the jurisdiction of the Member State responsible for the satellite capacity.

The change was dictated by the need to provide 'a more equitable division of responsibility between the Member States and a more effective control of third country programmes'.[35] Under the previous regime, most third country programmes fell under jurisdiction of two Member States only: Luxembourg and France, since the majority of programmes broadcast in Europe use satellite capacities of two satellites under the jurisdiction of these two countries: Astra and Eutelsat respectively. And in fact it is the uplink-operators, not satellite operators who have direct contracts with broadcasters and are in a better position than satellite operators to close down a specific channel. Satellite operators would have to shut down the entire multiplex.[36]

All of the above means that broadcasters have the freedom to choose the Member State in which they wish to establish themselves. For instance, according to the 2009 data, out of 7200 TV channels established in Europe (twenty-seven Member States + two candidate countries, Croatia and Turkey), 1033 have been established in the United Kingdom. Almost half of the channels established in the UK are broadcasting to other European countries.[37] The European Commission believes that the 'country of origin' principle contributes not only to the establishment of a competitive Internal Market in audiovisual services in the European Union, but also 'should enhance media pluralism and diversity, by opening up national markets to

---

35. Katsirea, I., *Public Broadcasting and European Law: A Comparative Examination of Public Service Obligations in Six Member States* (Kluwer Law International, 2008), 216.
36. This difficulty was particularly apparent during the 2004 and 2006 experiences with the Al Manar and Sahar 1 channels which were prohibited by the French authorities for inciting racial hatred; See Katsirea, I., *Public Broadcasting and European Law: A Comparative Examination of Public Service Obligations in Six Member States*, 216.
37. 'Growth of the number of television channels and multi-channel platforms in Europe continues despite the crisis', http://www.digitaltvnews.net, 13 January 2010.

more competition from other EU countries'.[38] This is confirmed by recital 34 of the AVMS Directive which states that:

> In order to promote a strong, competitive and integrated European audiovisual industry and *enhance media pluralism* throughout the Union, only one Member State should have jurisdiction over an audiovisual media service provider and pluralism of information should be a fundamental principle of the Union.[39]

5.2. LEGISLATIVE SUPPORT FOR INTERNAL PLURALISM

While the EU support for structural pluralism is, to say the least, limited, there are admittedly some harmonized provisions on content requirements that contribute to fostering internal pluralism in European media. They include must-carry rules regulated by the E-Communications Framework, and several provisions in the AVMS Directive (production quotas, list of events and short reporting).

5.2.1. Must-Carry Rules in the E-Communications Framework

The ongoing digital revolution has led to a proliferation of the delivery networks and increased bandwidth on those networks. This development should, in theory, lead to increased pluralism and diversity in content, as there is more capacity for more providers to express various voices and ideas in the media.[40] However, as E. Varney observes, just as every revolution, the digital one also has its victims.[41] As discussed earlier, liberalisation and deregulation of the e-communications networks in Europe has led to the private ownership of the means of content transmission. Concentration

38. European Commission, 'The Commission Proposal for a Modernisation of the Television without Frontiers Directive: Frequently Asked Questions', 13 December 2005, MEMO/05/475.
39. Directive 2010/13/EU of the European Parliament and of the Council of 10 March 2010 on the coordination of certain provisions laid down by law, regulation or administrative action in Member States concerning the provision of audiovisual media services (Audiovisual Media Services Directive), OJ (2010) L95/1, Recital 34, emphasis added.
40. Valcke, P., 'The Future of Must Carry. From Must-Carry to a Concept of Universal Service in the Info-Communications Sector', in European Audiovisual Observatory, Iris Special: *To Have or Not to Have – Must Carry Rules*, 2005, 31; Varney, M., 'Must-Carry Provisions and Digital Broadcasting: An Effective Means of Protecting Pluralism and Diversity in Media Output?', paper presented at SLS Annual Conference in Keele, September 2006 (unpublished), 1.
41. Varney, E., 'Regulating the Digital Television Infrastructure in the EU. Room for Citizenship Interests?', 222.

tendencies of recent years have resulted in the numerous networks with theoretically unlimited capacity, being owned not only by private but also *very few* large media corporations.[42] What follows is the private control of access to networks on market terms, which runs a risk of smaller operators or public service broadcasters not gaining access due to the lack of financial leverage.[43] As analysed above, the dangers this state of affairs creates for structural pluralism, have been to some extent, addressed by the E-Communications Framework which allows Member States to impose access obligations on network operators designated with significant market power.

Equally important, however, is the threat the concentrated ownership of transmission networks poses for internal pluralism. The proliferation of transmission networks means that viewers benefit from a choice of platforms. However once they have chosen a platform, they tend to become locked-in and very rarely change provider. This has led to the fragmentation of universal coverage of certain contents, 'which is a basic tenet of the public service element of pluralism'.[44] It follows, therefore, that even if digitalization and the resulting increase in capacity means that the market is indeed able to make diverse content *available*, this does not automatically mean that this content will be universally *accessible*.[45] The remedy to this concern applied by some Member States was to require mainly cable operators to carry certain 'public interest' channels 'supplying an unencrypted diversity of opinion over the cable bouquet'.[46] This method has been transferred by the European Union to the E-Communications Framework. Article 31 of the Universal Service Directive allows Member States to impose must-carry rules in favour of certain public interest channels on certain network providers. Interestingly, although Article 31 deals only with the carriage of certain 'public interest' channels and does not impose any specific requirements on content offered by those channels,[47] the regulation of must-carry is necessarily some intervention into content provision, which the E-Communications Framework declares not to do. However, as noted by EBU, the Framework:

---

42. Varney, M., 'Must-Carry Provisions and Digital Broadcasting: An Effective Means of Protecting Pluralism and Diversity in Media Output?', 4; see also in general Harcourt, A., *The European Union and the Regulation of Media Markets*; Doyle, G., *Media Ownership*.
43. Varney, M., 'Must-Carry Provisions and Digital Broadcasting: An Effective Means of Protecting Pluralism and Diversity in Media Output?', 4.
44. Marsden, C.T., 'Pluralism in the Multi-channel Market – Suggestions for Regulatory Scrutiny', (1999/2000) International Journal of Communications, Law and Policy 4, 23.
45. Varney, M., 'Must-Carry Provisions and Digital Broadcasting: An Effective Means of Protecting Pluralism and Diversity in Media Output?', 10.
46. Marsden, C.T., 'Pluralism in the Multi-channel Market – Suggestions for Regulatory Scrutiny', 23.
47. European Broadcasting Union, 'Comments on the Eurostrategies Report regarding Must Carry', 26 June 2003.

> cannot ignore the links which exist between infrastructure and content, particularly in terms of guaranteeing the pursuit of legitimate general interest objectives such as media pluralism, cultural diversity and consumer protection in the transmission of audiovisual content.[48]

Moreover, an important public interest goal in broadcasting, associated with internal pluralism, is 'connectivity'. That is, the need to ensure that citizens have universal access to certain information and certain public interest contents.[49] This is particularly vital these days when 'the commercial sphere becomes the ultimate arbiter of who is connected in a … global economy'.[50] Furthermore, public service broadcasters, as well as other operators of channels with a public interest potential, have to negotiate access with numerous powerful network operators.[51] Imposing must-carry rules offers an obvious solution to the 'universal coverage' issue as they have 'the potential to lead to a diverse range of material being available to viewers on all broadcasting networks'.[52] Overall therefore, must-carry obligations seem 'a logical and necessary measure in the *transmission* layer in order to achieve [all the] public policy goals set at the *content* level'.[53]

Having established the rationale behind the must-carry rules, it is interesting to have a closer look at how the E-Communication Framework regulates this matter. As mentioned above, the rules on must-carry are laid down by the Universal Service Directive. Article 31 develops general policy statement on the rationale of must-carry provided by Recital 43[54] and declares that:

---

48. European Broadcasting Union, 'Comments on the Eurostrategies Report regarding Must Carry', 5.
49. Collins, R., 'Realising Social Goals in Connectivity and Content', in Marsden, C.T. (ed.), *Regulating the Information Society* (Routledge, 2000), 108; see also Varney, E., 'Regulating the Digital Television Infrastructure in the EU. Room for Citizenship Interests?', 231.
50. Rifkin, J., *The Age of Access* (Penguin Putnam, 2001), 230.
51. Varney, E., 'Regulating the Digital Television Infrastructure in the EU. Room for Citizenship Interests?', 231.
52. Varney, M., 'Must-Carry Obligations in the New European Regulatory Framework for Communications: A True Guardian of Pluralism and Diversity?', (2004/2005) Utilities Law Review 14, 113.
53. Valcke, P., 'The Future of Must Carry. From Must-Carry to a Concept of Universal Service in the Info-Communications Sector', 32.
54. Recital 43 of the Universal Service Directive: 'Currently, Member States impose certain "must carry" obligations on networks for the distribution of radio or television broadcasts to the public. Member States should be able to lay down proportionate obligations on undertakings under their jurisdiction, in the interest of legitimate public policy considerations, but such obligations should only be imposed where they are necessary to meet general interest objectives clearly defined by Member States in conformity with Community law and should be proportionate, transparent and subject to

> Member States may impose reasonable 'must carry' obligations, for the transmission of specified radio and television broadcast channels and services, on undertakings under their jurisdiction providing electronic communications networks used for the distribution of radio or television broadcasts to the public where a significant number of end-users of such networks use them as their principal means to receive radio and television broadcasts. Such obligations shall only be imposed where they are necessary to meet clearly defined general interest objectives and shall be proportionate and transparent.

Consequently, must-carry obligations must first and foremost be reasonable, that is to say, they must be proportionate and transparent 'in the light of clearly defined public interest objectives'.[55] Therefore, as interpreted by the European Commission in two Working Documents,[56] before any must-carry obligation can be imposed and accepted as 'reasonable', a range of complex requirements must be fulfilled.[57] These are with regard to (i) undertakings burdened with must-carry, (ii) channels benefiting from must-carry, and (iii) transparency and proportionality of the imposition of the must-carry obligation.

5.2.1.1. Which Undertakings Can Be Burdened?

A broadcasting value chain consists generally speaking of three levels: content providers, service providers (or 'packagers') and network providers.[58] These days, the three roles may be provided by two or three separate undertakings, but also more and more often by one vertically integrated company. For instance, BSkyB has its own Sky channels and is a service provider – a packager of channels, but it does not control the satellite network that carries Sky channels as this is operated by the Astra satellite. However, the no longer operating Irish cable company Chorus used to fulfil

---

periodical review. "Must carry" obligations imposed by Member States should be reasonable, that is they should be proportionate and transparent in the light of clearly defined general interest objectives, and could, where appropriate, entail a provision for proportionate remuneration. Such "must carry" obligations may include the transmission of services specifically designed to enable appropriate access by disabled users.'

55. Roukens, T., 'What Are We Carrying across the EU These Days? Comments on the Interpretation and Practical Implementation of Article 31 of the Universal Service Directive', in European Audiovisual Observatory, Iris Special: *To Have or Not to Have – Must Carry Rules*, 2005, 10.
56. European Commission 'The 2003 regulatory framework for electronic communications – Implications for broadcasting (Working Document)'; European Commission, '"Must-carry" obligations under the 2003 regulatory framework for electronic communications networks and services (Working Document)', Brussels, 22 July 2003.
57. Varney, M., 'Must-Carry Obligations in the New European Regulatory Framework for Communications: A True Guardian of Pluralism and Diversity?', 114.
58. Valcke, P., 'The Future of Must Carry. From Must-Carry to a Concept of Universal Service in the Info-Communications Sector', 36.

all three functions: it had its own channel, Chorus Sports;[59] it packaged and offered bouquets of channels and owned its own cable network.

Article 31 makes it clear that must-carry obligations may be imposed on operators located at only one level of the broadcasting value chain: *network operators*. Recital 44 of the Directive explains that networks include cable, satellite and terrestrial broadcasting as well as other networks, such as DSL, 'to the extent that a significant number of end-users use such networks as their principal means to receive radio and television broadcasts'. As clarified by Recital 45, must-carry obligations should not be imposed on service providers.[60] Moreover, not all network providers may be subject to a must-carry obligation. First of all, Member States may impose must-carry obligations only on network operators under their jurisdiction. And second, only on operators of those networks which are used by a significant number of end-users as their principal means to receive radio and television broadcasts.

In addition, as explained by the European Commission,[61] Article 31 of the Universal Service Directive does not give broadcast content providers access to associated facilities, such CAS, API or EPG. As explained above, access to such facilities is regulated by the Access Directive which requires *all* CAS operators, whether designated with SMP or not, to provide these services on 'fair, reasonable and non-discriminatory terms to any requesting broadcaster, including the one benefiting from a must-carry regime'. Therefore, even though network operators might be obliged to carry certain channels, 'if the channels require access to CAS, API and EPG, they must still negotiate for access to these facilities under market conditions'[62] and pay for the access, which represents a significant cost for broadcasters who are granted must-carry status.[63] Admittedly, currently must-carry channels tend to appear on first positions on the EPG, because they are usually the popular public service channels generating a significant audience. However, the popularity of those channels is not guaranteed and is not time-resistant. To

59. The channel was closed in January 2007.
60. Recital 45 of the Universal Service Directive: 'Services providing content such as the offer for sale of a package of sound or television broadcasting content are not covered by the common regulatory framework for electronic communications networks and services. Providers of such services should not be subject to universal service obligations in respect of these activities. This Directive is without prejudice to measures taken at national level, in compliance with Community law, in respect of such services.'
61. European Commission, 'The 2003 regulatory framework for electronic communications – Implications for broadcasting (Working Document)'; European Commission, '"Must-carry" obligations under the 2003 regulatory framework for electronic communications networks and services (Working Document)'.
62. Varney, M., 'Must-Carry Obligations in the New European Regulatory Framework for Communications: A True Guardian of Pluralism and Diversity?', 121.
63. Varney, M., 'Must-Carry Provisions and Digital Broadcasting: An Effective Means of Protecting Pluralism and Diversity in Media Output?', 7.

leave the issue unregulated means possibly jeopardizing the favoured EPG positioning of must-carry channels in the future.

5.2.1.2. Which Channels Benefit?

Article 31 of the Universal Service Directive allows Member States to impose must-carry obligations, for the transmission of *specified*, i.e., clearly identified in advance, radio and television broadcasts channels and services.[64] Moreover, the channels benefiting from must-carry must meet certain, clearly defined *general interest* objectives. Recital 43 explicitly states that one of the public interest motives behind the imposition of 'must-carry' obligations may be the transmission of services designed to enable appropriate access by disabled users. Other than that, the Directive does not specify what exactly it means that a channel pursues a general interest. It is the analysis of the Commission's approach to must-carry rules that is actually imposed by the Member States on the basis of Article 31 that allows certain conclusions to be drawn.

Neither the Directive itself nor the accompanying, Working Documents and Notices require that only public service broadcasters may benefit from must-carry status. The Working Document on must-carry obligations explains only that the general interest objectives pursued by beneficiary channels should be '*clearly defined*', and they will '*normally include considerations linked to pluralism or cultural diversity*'.[65] The Working Paper goes as far as to say that these considerations are not, per se, limited to radio and television broadcasts of public service broadcasters. Nevertheless, it is obvious, and it has been confirmed by the ECJ's case-law, that the support of public service broadcasters will generally be considered to be in the general interest.[66] In fact, most of the Member States have imposed must-carry obligations in favour of the core *public service* channels.[67] For instance, in Ireland the must-carry television channels on cable are RTE1, Network 2, TV3 and TG4. In the UK, the must-carry channels on both analogue and digital cable are BBC, ITV and Channel 4.[68] All of these channels are either public service broadcasters (RTE, Network 2, TG4, BBC) or with some PSB obligations (TV3, ITV, Channel 4).

64. European Commission, 'The 2003 regulatory framework for electronic communications – Implications for broadcasting (Working Document)'.
65. European Commission, 'Must-carry' obligations under the 2003 regulatory framework for electronic communications networks and services (Working Document)', section 1.2.2.1.
66. See for instance state aid cases Case NN88/89, *BBC News,* Case NN 631/01, *BBC Licence Fee;* see also Varney, M., 'Must-Carry Obligations in the New European Regulatory Framework for Communications: A True Guardian of Pluralism and Diversity?', 119.
67. Varney, M., 'Must-Carry Obligations in the New European Regulatory Framework for Communications: A True Guardian of Pluralism and Diversity?', 114.
68. Article 64 of the Communications Act, 2003.

However, although the Commission has expressly vowed that it would not limit the must-carry status to public service channels, the reality proved somewhat different. Some Member States have encountered opposition from the European Commission to the imposition of must-carry status in favour of channels without any explicit public interest obligations. The Commission used the well-known ECJ statement that 'economic considerations would not be considered general interest obligations'[69] to oppose certain Dutch and Belgian must-carry channels as incompatible with the public interest requirement enshrined in Article 31.[70] Both countries have imposed extensive must-carry obligations in favour of, not only public service broadcasters, but also commercial channels, without any specifically assigned public service remit. The Belgian government justified the imposition of must-carry obligations in favour of some non-PSB channels with the need to 'reflect the linguistic and cultural diversity of Belgian society' and the 'retention, pursuant to the cultural policy of the state, of the pluralist character of the television programmes available in the territory'.[71] The Commission seemed to acknowledge these reasons,[72] and in the 2007 judgment the European Court of Justice confirmed that Member States may in principle impose must-carry obligations on cable operators providing services on the relevant territory of that State to broadcast television programmes transmitted by *private broadcasters*, provided that the must-carry obligations pursue an aim in the general interest, and are not disproportionate.[73]

Nevertheless, in 2009 the European Commission decided to take Belgium to the European Court of Justice for breach of the EU law, alleging that there was no transparent procedure for designating 'must-carry' channels, and that individual channels should be designated as 'must-carry' and not entire broadcasting companies.[74] In 2011 the European Court of Justice decided against Belgium, and held that even though the need to maintain media pluralism is a legitimate public interest justifying the imposition of must-carry obligations, the Belgian must-carry rules in question did not fulfil the requirement of proportionality as they were based on the mere statement of a general policy objective, which was not accompanied by 'any additional

69. European Commission, 'Must-carry' obligations under the 2003 regulatory framework for electronic communications networks and services (Working Document)', section 1.2.2.1; see Case C-211/91, *Commission v. Belgium* [1992], ECR I-6757.
70. European Commission, 'New round of infringement proceedings in electronic communications: What are the issues?', MEMO/06/371, 12 October 2006.
71. Varney, M., 'Must-Carry Provisions and Digital Broadcasting: An Effective Means of Protecting Pluralism and Diversity in Media Output?', 14.
72. European Commission, Annex to the 11th Report on the European Electronic Communications Regulation and Markets, 2005, SEC(2006)193, 85.
73. Judgment of the Court of justice of the European Communities, *United Pan-Europe Communications Belgium and Others*, 13 December 2007, C-250/06
74. European Commission press release, 'Legal action against Germany, the Netherlands and Sweden closed while Belgian must-carry rules case goes to Court', 8 October 2009, IP/09/1491.

factor capable of enabling operators to determine in advance the nature and effect of the precise conditions and obligations to be fulfilled if they apply for the award of must-carry status'.[75] In addition, the Court decided that must-carry status should not be awarded to a broadcaster covering all its channels, but must be strictly limited to *specified channels* whose content contributes to the public interest objective.

It seems, therefore, that both the European Commission and the European Court of Justice lean towards a very narrow definition of 'public interest' in relation to channels which may possibly benefit from the must-carry status.[76]

5.2.1.3. Transparency and Proportionality

Article 31 allows Member States to impose *reasonable* and *proportionate* must-carry rules in a *transparent* fashion. The transparency requirement is closely related to the condition that must-carry rules must be *specified.* It is relatively easy to fulfil by simply publishing the networks that are burdened by and the channels benefiting from the must-carry obligations in a legislative act[77] or on the regulator's website.[78] It must, however, be borne in mind that mentioning broadcasting organizations and not specific channels, or leaving it to the ad hoc decision of a regulator to grant a must-carry status, would most probably not pass the transparency test.[79]

It is the requirement of reasonability and proportionality that poses more difficulty. The Commission's Working Documents highlight that the principle of proportionality is well-established in Community law and that:

> in order to establish that a proposed measure is compatible with the principle of proportionality, the action to be taken must pursue a legitimate aim, and the means employed to achieve the aim must be both necessary and the least burdensome, i.e., it must be the minimum necessary to achieve the aim ...[80]

The Commission further explains that the disproportionality of the imposition of must-carry rules may derive from the nature of networks burdened, too high a number of benefiting channels and the lack of remuneration.

---

75. Case C134/10, *Commission v. Belgium*, 3 March 2011, para. 54.
76. Varney, M., 'Must-Carry Provisions andDdigital Broadcasting: An Effective Means of Protecting Pluralism and Diversity in Media Output?', 15.
77. For instance Article 63 of the Communications Act 2003 in the United Kingdom.
78. See for instance the website of the Irish telecommunications regulator – Commission for Communications Regulation http://www.comreg.ie.
79. Roukens, T., 'What Are We Carrying across the EU These Days? Comments on the Interpretation and Practical Implementation of Article 31 of the Universal Service Directive', 14.
80. European Commission, 'Must-carry' obligations under the 2003 regulatory framework for electronic communications networks and services (Working Document)', section 1.2.2.2.

To begin with, the Commission noted that the imposition of must-carry rules on other networks other than cable, satellite and terrestrial (e.g., 3G mobile networks or DSL) would be disproportionate at the present stage of technological and market development. This is primarily because the vast majority of viewers are expected to use traditional networks for reception of broadcasting for some time to come.[81] The imposition of must-carry obligations on those 'new' networks will only be legitimate once a significant number of viewers begin using them as the principal means to receive radio and television broadcasts.

Second, the Commission explained that the situation in which the number of channels and services benefiting from must-carry status actually constrained the capacity of a burdened network, this would most probably be regarded as disproportionate.[82]

Finally, and rather controversially, the Commission notes that remuneration can be one means of ensuring that the universal access to specified channels and services guaranteed by must-carry is secured in an economically efficient way, and therefore would be proportionate.[83] As M. Varney notes, 'must-carry is the area where the interplay between two vital constitutional issues is at stake: on the one hand lies freedom of expression and media pluralism, while on the other lies broadcaster's right to private property'.[84] The European Commission's original plan was to allow Member States to impose must-carry obligations, but only and where necessary and with a compensation obligation attached. However, the remuneration requirement was removed during the consultation period for the Universal Service Directive.[85]

There is therefore no *obligation* on Member States to require remuneration for network operators in return for must carry obligations. However, as noted by the Commission, Article 31 may be read as *implying* that 'under specific circumstances some form of remuneration should be provided in order for the must-carry obligation to be considered proportionate or reasonable'.[86]

---

81. European Commission, 'The 2003 regulatory framework for electronic communications – Implications for broadcasting' (Working Document), 11.
82. European Commission, 'Must-carry' obligations under the 2003 regulatory framework for electronic communications networks and services (Working Document)', section 1.2.2.2.
83. European Commission, 'Must-carry' obligations under the 2003 regulatory framework for electronic communications networks and services (Working Document)', section 1.2.2.2.
84. Varney, M., 'Must-Carry Obligations in the New European Regulatory Framework for Communications: A True Guardian of Pluralism and Diversity?', 114.
85. Humphreys, P., 'The EU and Audiovisual Regulation: An Agency for De-regulation', 19.
86. European Commission, '"Must-carry" obligations under the 2003 regulatory framework for electronic communications networks and services (Working Document)', section 1.2.2.2

This argument has been strengthened by the report prepared by Eurostrategies for the Commission, which asserts that it is *logical* for must-carry broadcasters to pay for the benefit they receive for cable carriage.[87] This is because commercial negotiations between cable operators and must-carry broadcasters are generally biased in the broadcasters' favour. The report suggests that the Commission should issue guidelines for the remuneration of the carriage service. Some argue that the Report is the Commission's attempt to encourage Member States to provide for the remuneration of must-carry in every instance, despite the wording of Article 31 to the contrary.[88]

Many reject the Eurostrategies line of reasoning.[89] The argument is that cable is a local monopoly wherever it exists in Europe, and there is little competition between platforms at end-user level due to the lock-in effect. Moreover, through market consolidation most markets in Europe are left with two digital platform operators (one satellite and one cable, with cable holding dominant position). This means that, especially when mirrored with must-offer, commercial negotiations between the cable operator and must-carry broadcasters, is biased in the *cable operators' favour*. The truth is that cable operators do not really need the money for transport of must-carry channel, and government's support for cable may come in other ways such as reduced VAT rates.[90] But for channels burdened with must-carry, any money they have to pay cable companies for carrying their channels will no longer be available for investment in diverse and quality programmes.[91]

Finally to ensure that the existing must-carry rules *remain* reasonable and proportionate, Article 31 requires Member States to subject their must-carry rules to *periodic* review. In the Working Document on must-carry, the Commission states:

> The obligation to review must-carry regime on a regular basis should encourage Member States to re-evaluate the need for and scope of must-carry rules and, in particular, regularly assess, taking into account technology and market developments and the views of interested parties,

87. Eurostrategies, 'Assessment of Member States Measures aimed at fulfilling certain general interest objectives linked to broadcasting, imposed on providers of electronic communications networks and services in the context of the new regulatory framework (Report)', March 2003, emphasis added.
88. Roukens, T., 'What Are We Carrying across the EU These Days? Comments on the Interpretation and Practical Implementation of Article 31 of the Universal Service Directive', 15.
89. European Broadcasting Union, 'Comments on the Eurostrategies Report regarding Must Carry'.
90. European Broadcasting Union, 'Comments on the Eurostrategies Report regarding Must Carry', 12.
91. European Broadcasting Union, 'Comments on the Eurostrategies Report regarding Must Carry', 2.

whether such rules still match the necessity and proportionality requirements.[92]

The implication is that Member States will gradually phase out the must-carry obligations which the Commission seems to view as an anomaly in the digital era.[93]

Table 5.1 below, illustrates the EU must-carry regime as regulated by the Universal Service Directive.

Table 5.1 EU Rules on Must-carry In the Broadcasting Value Chain

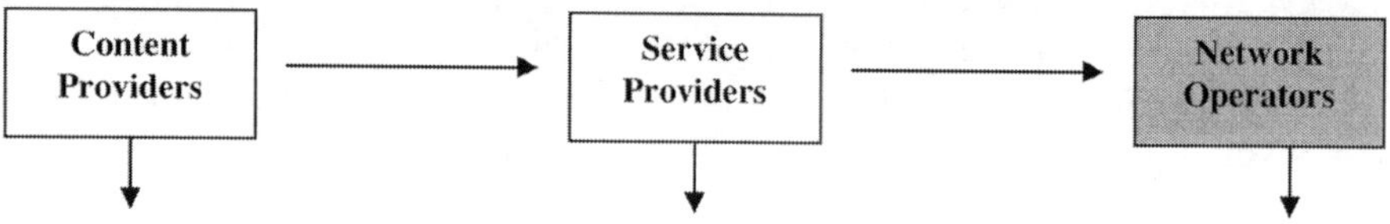

NO	*NO*	*YES*
		(Article 31 Universal Service Directive)
should be must-offer	*should be must-distribute*	– under jurisdiction of a MS; – used by *significant* number of end-users of such networks as their principal means to receive radio and TV broadcasts; – in favour of *specified* channels meeting narrowly defined *general interest* objectives (in practice only PSB); – proportionate=>remuneration; – transparent =>published; – subject to periodic review; – no access to 'associated facilities' (CAS, API, EPG) on preferential terms.

Note: Based on P. Valcke, 'The Future of Must Carry. From Must-Carry to a Concept of Universal Service in the Info-Communications Sector', 36.[94]

92. European Commission, '"Must-carry" obligations under the 2003 regulatory framework for electronic communications networks and services (Working Document)', 72, section 1.2.2.
93. Arino, M., Valcke, P., 'The Future (or Non-future) of Must-Carry', OfcomWatch, 11 April 2005; Roukens, T., 'What Are We Carrying across the EU These Days? Comments on the Interpretation and Practical Implementation of Article 31 of the Universal Service Directive', 14.
94. Valcke, P., 'The Future of Must Carry. From Must-Carry to a Concept of Universal Service in the Info-Communications Sector'.

5.2.1.4. Weaknesses in the EU Must-Carry System

It must be observed at the outset, that contrary to some claims, must-carry rules will not become obsolete in the digital broadcasting era, since in the jungle of hundreds of channels there will still be a requirement to ensure the universal coverage of general interest content. However, what the dawn of the digital broadcasting era does bring is the need for reform. Must-carry rules must be changed and adjusted, but not abandoned. The three areas which require particular attention in this regard are: (i) a too narrow definition of 'public interest' currently applied by the Commission; (ii) no preferential access for must-carry broadcasters to 'associated facilities'; and (iii) the need to complement the must-carry system with must-offer and must-distribute rules.

5.2.1.4.1. A Too Narrow Definition of 'Public Interest'

First of all, as has already been discussed above, the European Commission seems to lean towards a very narrow definition of 'public interest' in relation to channels which may possibly benefit from must-carry status.[95] Although, it has officially vowed not to limit the must-carry status to public service broadcasters, the reality, however, proved much different. The result is that while many public service channels benefit from must-carry status even though they would be carried by cable operators anyway. Furthermore, new commercial channels under current regime are denied the benefit of must-carry status, even though they could just as easily as PSBs, contribute to the promotion and development of local culture and language, but often encounter problems in gaining access to the cable.[96] A must-carry regime which endorses only PSB channels or channels with some public service remit are necessarily very shallow and limited, no matter how good the public service broadcasters' channels actually are.[97] Therefore, M. Varney warns that 'if such a narrow interpretation of Article 31 is reached, then it seems likely that the must-carry regime in Europe is destined to be a very limited one that will be ineffective in delivering enhanced pluralism and diversity'.[98]

95. Varney, M., 'Must-Carry Provisions and Digital Broadcasting: An Effective Means of Protecting Pluralism and Diversity in Media Output?', 15.
96. Valcke, P., 'The Future of Must Carry. From Must-Carry to a Concept of Universal Service in the Info-Communications Sector', 33.
97. Varney, M., 'Must-Carry Provisions and Digital Broadcasting: An Effective Means of Protecting Pluralism and Diversity in Media Output?', 14.
98. Varney, M., 'Must-Carry Provisions and Digital Broadcasting: An Effective Means of Protecting Pluralism and Diversity in Media Output?', 14.

5.2.1.4.2. *No Preferential Access to Associated Facilities*

As explained above, the current EU system of must-carry does not guarantee the must-carry beneficiaries any preferential access to 'associated facilities' in digital broadcasting such as CAS, API or EPG. It is regulated by a 'normal' regime based on access on a 'fair, reasonable and non-discriminatory' basis. This solution is a serious oversight, as negotiations merely on the basis of fair, reasonable and non-discriminatory access rules run the serious risk of being unsuccessful.[99] And it is very likely that at some point all broadcasters will need access to the technical facilities in order to facilitate digital broadcasting.[100] Therefore, the fact that currently the EU must-carry regime does not envisage an obligation on the network provider to provide must-carry beneficiaries, with access to associated facilities on preferential terms (without charge, or for a heavily reduced fee), 'reduces the effectiveness of the must carry obligations'.[101] The EBU has suggested remedying the situation by amending the first sentence of Article 31(1) of the Universal Service Directive so as to allow Member States to impose must-carry obligations on either network providers, or providers of conditional access and other associated facilities.[102]

The problem of the lack of preferential access to associated facilities for must-carry channels is particularly relevant in countries which impose must-offer obligations on certain broadcasters without mirroring them with must-carry benefits. Must-offer 'sits on the opposite side to must-carry' as it requires particular channels, usually the public service ones, to offer their services on *all* delivery platforms.[103] The upside of must-offer is universal coverage of public service channels regardless of the delivery mode chosen by a viewer. The downside, however, is that channels burdened with must-offer conditions that are not mirrored with must-carry, have to negotiate for access to the technical facilities on market terms, placing the network operator in an advantageous position.[104] The recent Eurostrategies report ordered by the Commission argues that '... must offer may distort negotiations between network operators and broadcasters, to the benefit of

99. European Broadcasting Union, 'Proposed EU Regulatory Framework for Electronic Communications. EBU comments for the European Parliament's second reading'.
100. Varney, M., 'Must-Carry Obligations in the New European Regulatory Framework for Communications: A True Guardian of Pluralism and Diversity?', 121.
101. Varney, M., 'Must-Carry Provisions and Digital Broadcasting: An Effective Means of Protecting Pluralism and Diversity in Media Output?', 8.
102. European Broadcasting Union, 'Proposed EU Regulatory Framework for Electronic Communications. EBU comments for the European Parliament's second reading'.
103. Varney, M., 'Must-Carry Obligations in the New European Regulatory Framework for Communications: A True Guardian of Pluralism and Diversity?', 122.
104. Varney, M., 'Must-Carry Obligations in the New European Regulatory Framework for Communications: A True Guardian of Pluralism and Diversity?', 122.

network operators'.[105] Since Articles 5 and 6 of the Access Directive clearly provide that access to associated facilities must be *negotiated*, Member States cannot mandate access to these facilities at a rate below the market rate. Even if commercial negotiations fail, regulators may only intervene in order to allow access on 'fair, reasonable and non-discriminatory terms'.[106] M. Varney observes that operators of associated facilities are unlikely to 'make endeavours to facilitate access for channels which may not have the same ability or willingness to pay as mainstream commercial competitors'.[107]

The United Kingdom is one of the Member States which imposes a must-offer on public service broadcasters without mirroring it with a must-carry on every platform.[108] Public service broadcasters are obliged to provide their services on BSkyB's satellite platform, but BSkyB is not burdened with must-carry obligations.[109] BSkyB levies charges for access to its platform, and in particular it charges the public service broadcasters for use of a proprietary CAS, as if they were pay channels using it to collect subscriptions, rather than being obliged to purchase conditional access primarily to meet their obligations to provide regional services.[110] This obviously creates an unequal negotiating position between the broadcasters and BSkyB. During the drafting of the current Communications Act 2003, public service broadcasters lobbied for matching 'must offer' with 'must carry' on BSkyB, that is, to require it not only to carry the PSB channels, but also to make available on preferential terms all facilities required to ensure that audiences receive them.[111] This has not materialised and BSkyB gets paid for carrying channels it currently needs anyway.[112] While this is still the case it shows some reason in calculating the fees, even though it could

105. Eurostrategies, 'Assessment of Member States Measures aimed at fulfilling certain general interest objectives linked to broadcasting, imposed on providers of electronic communications networks and services in the context of the new regulatory framework (Report)', 75.
106. Varney, M., 'Must-Carry Obligations in the New European Regulatory Framework for Communications: A True Guardian of Pluralism and Diversity?', 122.
107. Varney, M., 'Must-Carry Obligations in the New European Regulatory Framework for Communications: A True Guardian of Pluralism and Diversity?', 123.
108. It is worth noting that the UK is one of relatively few EU Member States not singled out in the most recent Commission report on implementation as being investigated for a potential breach of Article 31, see Varney, M., 'Must-Carry Provisions and Digital Broadcasting: An Effective Means of Protecting Pluralism and Diversity in Media Output?', 19.
109. Compare section 64 of the Communications Act 2003, which regulates must-carry on *network operators* with section 273 of the Communications Act 2003, which regulates must-offer on *network operators* and *satellite television services*.
110. BBC, 'Memorandum to the Joint Committee on The Draft Communications Bill', 2002.
111. BBC, 'Memorandum to the Joint Committee on The Draft Communications Bill'.
112. In Ireland Sky offers 'Bonus Mix' package with every purchase, which includes *inter alia* RTE One, RTE Two, TV3, TG4, BBC One, BBC Two and Channel 4; see http://www.sky.com/portal/site/ireland.

probably go higher, given the fact that PSBs are under statutory obligation to have their channels present on Sky. Still, in the future when channels multiply and BSkyB will not be in a desperate need to carry the PSB channels, failure to mirror must-offer with must-carry could result in a significant increase in fees.

However, the greatest difficulty with the idea of mirroring must-offer with must-carry on Sky is that the must-carry regime applies to *network operators*. And while BSkyB is a service provider, Astra is the satellite operator – which is a network provider. And because its satellite uplink and the ownership of the relevant satellite capacity is situated in Luxembourg,[113] the network is outside the jurisdiction of the UK. This is vital as Article 31 of the Universal Service Directive allows Member States to impose must-carry obligations upon:

> undertakings *under their jurisdiction*[114] providing electronic communications networks used for the distribution of radio or television broadcasts to the public where a significant number of end-users of such networks use them as their principal means to receive radio and television broadcasts.

This means that the largest digital broadcaster in the UK is not caught by the must-carry provisions. This is one of the major weaknesses of the current must-carry regime and has been extensively criticized.[115]

5.2.1.4.3. The Need to Complement Must-carry with Must-offer and Must-distribute

The solution to the problem with the likes of BSkyB who escape the must-carry regime is to apply a 'layered approach' suggested by Valcke.[116] She believes that there should be a switch-in approach to the must-carry regime. Rather than being treated as an issue involving only PSBs and cable operators, must-carry rules should be made part of a global concept of

113. Barendt, E.M., Hitchens, L.P., *Media Law: Text, Cases and Materials* (Longman, 2000), 97; Humprheys, P., *Mass Media and Media Policy in Western Europe* (Manchester University Press, 1996), 168–169; for a perspective on the private law issues see Robertson, G., Nicol, A., *Media Law*, 4th edn (Penguin Books, 2002), 837–840.

114. Jurisdiction is determined by Article 2 of the AVMS Directive. The activities of British Sky Broadcasting are covered by both paras 3 and 4 of Article 2, rendering jurisdiction in Luxembourg's hands.

115. See for instance, Cowling, J., 'Winner Takes All', *Media World*, 1 January 2004; Gibson, O., 'Davies Hits Out over Satellite Coverage', The Guardian, 25 November 2002; Didizian, M., Romer, J., 'The Communications Bill – The Place of the BBC', (2003) Computer and Telecommunications Law Review 9(4), 95, 98; Valcke, P., 'The Future of Must Carry. From Must-Carry to a Concept of Universal Service in the Info-Communications Sector', 31–40.

116. Valcke, P., 'The Future of Must Carry. From Must-Carry to a Concept of Universal Service in the Info-Communications Sector', 36.

'universal service obligations with regard to content'.[117] Therefore, Valcke recommends that safeguards should be built in at every level of the broadcasting value chain. Certain content providers should be burdened with must-offer obligations, which should be mirrored by must-distribute obligations on service providers (such as BSkyB) and must-carry obligations on network operators. This would solve the jurisdiction issues with the must-carry regime and would offer a comprehensive safeguard for universal coverage of content serving the 'public interest'.

5.2.1.5. Overall Conclusions on Must-Carry

In summary, as noted by M. Varney that 'an examination of the operation of the provisions in Article 31 reveals what is a relatively weak protection for pluralism and diversity'.[118] In fact, the narrow interpretation of 'public interest', coupled with no preferential access to associated facilities and the Commission's insistence on remuneration as a guarantee of proportionality allow the conclusion that, despite being social in concept, the EU must-carry rules do not offer much more than the economic rights of access.[119] The narrow approach adopted by the European Commission towards the must-carry rules prevents the Member States from expanding the lists of must-carry channels beyond the obvious public service broadcasters. The result of the outright exclusion of smaller commercial channels with obvious quality but with no public service remit may be, that viewers will have access to a basic package of public service channels on whatever platform they choose, but there will be little value added to pluralism and diversity.

Obviously, must-carry rules are only one of the weapons available in the armoury of the defenders of pluralism and diversity of media.[120] However, if the weapon is not constructed properly it will not fire properly, and it will be ineffective in the battle for media pluralism and diversity. Therefore, due to the many flaws of the current EU system of must-carry, there are some doubts as to the Commission's claim that the rules are one of the mechanisms of *actively* safeguarding pluralism.

---

117. Valcke, P., 'The Future of Must Carry. From Must-Carry to a Concept of Universal Service in the Info-Communications Sector', 36.
118. Varney, M., 'Must-Carry Obligations in the New European Regulatory Framework for Communications: A True Guardian of Pluralism and Diversity?', 123.
119. Varney, M., 'Must-Carry Obligations in the New European Regulatory Framework for Communications: A True Guardian of Pluralism and Diversity?', 123; Feintuck, M., Varney, M., *Media Regulation, Public Interest and the Law*, 228, 229.
120. Varney, M., 'Must-Carry Provisions and Digital Broadcasting: An Effective Means of Protecting Pluralism and Diversity in Media Output?', 23.

5.2.2. Measures Supporting Internal Pluralism in the AVMS Directive

In several statements, the European Commission has declared that because the European Union is committed to protecting media pluralism as well as the right to information and freedom of expression, the Television Without Frontiers Directive already contained several measures which *actively* promote internal media pluralis,[121] and these were significantly strengthened by the revised AVMS Directive.[122] In the preparatory stages of the AVMS Directive, the Commission claimed that the Directive reaffirms the pillars of Europe's audiovisual model, which are, *inter alia,* cultural diversity and media pluralism, and that it enhances media pluralism in the twenty-seven EU Member States by 'opening up national media markets to more competition from other EU countries and by facilitating a diversified offer of TV- and audiovisual on-demand content from all over Europe'.[123]

The importance of media pluralism is emphasized very early in the Directive – in Recitals 5 and 8 of the codified version:

> (5) Audiovisual media services are as much cultural services as they are economic services. Their growing importance for societies, democracy – in particular by ensuring freedom of information, diversity of opinion and media pluralism – education and culture justifies the application of specific rules to these services.
>
> (8) It is essential for the Member States to ensure the prevention of any acts which may prove detrimental to freedom of movement and trade in television programmes or which may promote the creation of dominant positions which would lead to restrictions on pluralism and freedom of televised information and of the information sector as a whole.

These general declarations from the Recitals are, according to the Commission's statements,[124] given concrete meaning in the substantive part of the Directive in the form of regulation of (i) broadcasting of events of major

121. European Commission, 'Media Pluralism – what should be the European Union's role?', Issues Paper, 2005; European Commission, 'Why and how Europe seeks pluralism in audiovisual media', DG Information Society and the Media (2005).
122. European Commission, 'The Commission Proposal for a Modernisation of the Television Without Frontiers Directive: Frequently Asked Questions', MEMO/06/28.
123. European Commission, 'Boosting the Diversity of European TV and On-Demand services: Commission paves the way for the new Directive 'Audiovisual without Frontiers"', Press Release IP/07/311.
124. See European Commission, 'Media Pluralism – what should be the European Union's role?', Issues Paper, 2005; European Commission, 'Why and how Europe seeks pluralism in audiovisual media'35; European Commission, 'The Commission Proposal for a Modernisation of the Television Without Frontiers Directive: Frequently Asked Questions', MEMO/06/28.

importance and short reporting, and (ii) independent and European production quotas.

5.2.2.1. Broadcasting of Events of Major Importance and Short Reporting

In the era of digitalization and conditional access, the acquisition of exclusive rights to popular events became the standard practice of pay-TV broadcasters. The acquisition of exclusive rights to the Premier League football tournament by BSkyB serves as the prime example. The risk that this carries is the 'information divide' or a 'digital divide'– 'splitting society into groups with different levels of access to information'.[125] Also, as emphasized by the AVMS Directive itself in Recital 48:

> Television broadcasting rights for events of high interest to the public may be acquired by broadcasters on an exclusive basis. However, it is essential to promote pluralism through the diversity of news production and programming across the Union and to respect the principles recognised by Article 11 of the Charter of Fundamental Rights of the European Union.

The EU legislation tries to tackle this problem by regulating must-carry rules (as discussed above) and by introducing the possibility of Member States to draw up a list of events which have to be shown on widely accessible free-TV. It must be noted that the list may only include organized events and not films or documentaries which are subject to copyright law.[126] The solution was first introduced in the 1997 version of the TVWF Directive,[127] following an extended pressure from the European Parliament.[128] The Parliament's initial ambitious proposal was to introduce a binding EU list of basic events which should be accessible to all European viewers with an option for Member States to extend the list if they so wished. Not surprisingly, the suggestion did not materialize due to claims of breaches of

125. Schoental, M., 'Major Events and Reporting Rights', IRIS-plus, 2006-04.
126. Helberger, N., 'The "Right to Information" and Digital Broadcasting: About Monsters, Invisible Men and the Future of European Broadcasting Regulation', (2006) Entertainment Law Review 2, 70–80.
127. Directive 97/36/EC of the European Parliament and of the Council of 30 June 1997 amending Council Directive 89/552/EEC on the coordination of certain provisions laid down by law, regulation or administrative action in Member States concerning the pursuit of television broadcasting activities OJ (1997) L202/60.
128. European Parliament, Resolution of 22 May 1996 on the broadcasting of sports events, OJ (1996) C-166; European Parliament, Committee on Culture, Youth, Education and the Media (Rapporteur: Galeote Quecedo, G.), Recommendation for second reading on the common position established by the Council with a view to the adoption of a European Parliament and Council Directive amending Directive 89/552/EEC, A4-0346/96; see also Schoental, M., 'Major Events and Reporting Rights'.

the principles proportionality and subsidiarity.[129] Member States are the only subjects responsible for drafting the lists, and they have full discretion whether to prepare such a list or not. The Commission's role is limited to approving the lists and ordering their publication in the Official Journal.

The result of the compromise was the introduction of Article 3a to the text of the TVWF Directive. In the AVMS Directive, it is Article 14 which states that:

> Each Member State may take measures in accordance with Union law to ensure that broadcasters under its jurisdiction do not broadcast on an exclusive basis events which are regarded by that Member State as being of major importance for society in such a way as to deprive a substantial proportion of the public in that Member State of the possibility of following such events via live coverage or deferred coverage on free television. If it does so, the Member State concerned shall draw up a list of designated events, national or non-national, which it considers to be of major importance for society …

Despite the extended discussions and major political heat surrounding the introduction of this article, only eight Member States, out of twenty-seven, have notified their lists so far.[130] Most, but not all, of the listed events relate to sport. As noted by Commissioner Reding:

> all of the lists notified contain the Olympic Games – though in Ireland only the Summer Olympics – and a variety of football events. For other Member States, the lists take into account national interests like the Giro d'Italia in Italy, the Derby in the UK or skiing events in Austria.[131]

Table 5.2 below illustrates the events of major importance listed by Member States pursuant to Article 14.

In paragraph 3, the Article introduces the concept of the 'mutual recognition of the lists of events of major importance' by requiring Member States to:

> … ensure … that broadcasters under their jurisdiction do not exercise the exclusive rights purchased by those broadcasters … in such a way that a substantial proportion of the public in another Member State is deprived of the possibility of following events which are designated by that other Member State.

For instance, if hypothetically BSkyB, which is under the jurisdiction of the United Kingdom, purchased the exclusive rights to broadcast the All-Ireland

---

129. Schoental, M., 'Major Events and Reporting Rights'.
130. Denmark was the ninth Member State, but it has withdrawn its list; See European Commission, http://ec.Europa.eu/comm/avpolicy/reg/tvwf/implementation/events_list/index_en.htm.
131. Reding, V., 'Sport and Television: Ready to Face New Challenges?', Sportel Monaco, 11 October 2004, Speech/04/448.

Senior Inter-County Football and Hurling Finals, which is an event listed by Ireland, it is up to United Kingdom to ensure that BSkyB allows the finals to be shown on free TV in Ireland. The concrete example of the functioning of the 'mutual recognition' principle comes in the form of the House of Lords judgment *R. v. Independent Television Commission,* Ex Parte *TV Danmark 1 Ltd.*[132] The case was decided before Denmark withdrew its notification of the list of events of major importance. One of the events included in Denmark's list were all football matches involving the Danish men's football team. TV Danmark 1, a pay-TV operator broadcasting via cable and satellite in Denmark, but registered in the UK, acquired exclusive rights to broadcast Denmark's Football World Cup qualifying matches and intended to show the matches in an encrypted form. The United Kingdom objected on the basis of paragraph 3 of the then Article 3a (now Article 14). This is despite the fact that TV Danmark 1 was regarded as a free-TV operator in Denmark due to its 60% coverage. The UK's regulator, however, believed that in order for Article 3a (now Article 14) to be observed, at least 90% of the public needs access to the listed events. The decision of the regulator was upheld by the House of Lords and not objected to by the European Commission.[133] The judgment provides a valuable example not only of the application of Article 14(3), but also sheds a light on what is to be understood under the notion of the *substantial proportion of the public.*

Overall, Article 14 may be said to have introduced a 'new category of universal service', as the basic concept behind the article is 'to limit the exclusive exploitation of transmission rights for the sake of a general public interest in the wide accessibility of certain content'.[134] Moreover, the existence of lists may indirectly lead to increased internal pluralism in free-to-air television. As noted by Schoental, major events, and in particular sports events, 'guarantee high viewing figures, which in turn mean substantial advertising revenue and good publicity for the broadcaster. This also leads to larger audiences for other programmers that are advertised during the sports broadcasts'.[135] This in turn may mean that free-to-air broadcasters will have more financial resources to invest in other innovative quality programming such as documentaries and films, and as a result audiences have free access to diverse content. All these arguments, led Commissioner Reding to believe that 'Article 3a *(now Article 14)* of the Directive is useful, necessary, effective and proportionate'[136] and that is why it is undoubtedly a tool that actively promotes pluralism at EU level.

132. *R. v. Independent Television Commission, Ex Parte TV Danmark 1 Ltd,* [2001] UKHL 42.
133. Schoental, M., 'Major Events and Reporting Rights'.
134. Helberger, N., 'The "Right to Information" and Digital Broadcasting: About Monsters, Invisible Men and the Future of European Broadcasting Regulation'.
135. Schoental, M., 'Major Events and Reporting Rights'.
136. Reding, V., 'Sport and Television: Ready to Face New Challenges?'.

It is worth mentioning that the idea of a pan-European list of events of major importance for European society returned during discussions on the revision of the Television Without Frontiers Directive.[137] The idea of such a list was suggested by some public service broadcasters, who were concerned with the necessity of marketing certain rights on a territorial basis. However, there was no consensus as to how to define at European level the notion of 'a substantial proportion of the public' and by and large, the proposal 'met with widespread scepticism'.[138] The regulation, therefore, remained unchanged because the overall conclusion of the Commission was that 'the concept of a European list would have no value added as the present concept of the Directive leaves it to the Member States to designate events of major importance owing to national and regional cultural and societal specifities'.[139] It is probably still too early to expect the Commission to acknowledge, even to a limited extent, the existence of a 'European society'.

Table 5.2 Events of Major Importance Listed by the Member States Pursuant to Article 14 of the AVMS Directive[140]

Country	*Event*
Austria	Summer and Winter Olympic Games; FIFA World Cup football matches (for men) if the Austrian national team is involved, as well as the opening match, the semi-finals and the final of the football World Cup (for men); European Championship football matches (for men) if the Austrian national team is involved, as well as the opening match, the semi-finals and the final of the football European Championship (for men); The final of the Austrian Football Cup; FIS World Alpine skiing championships; World Nordic skiing championships; The Vienna Philharmonic Orchestra's New Year Concert; The Vienna Opera Ball

137. European Commission, 'The future of European regulatory audiovisual policy (Communication)'.
138. European Commission, 'The future of European regulatory audiovisual policy (Communication)'.
139. European Commission, 'The future of European regulatory audiovisual policy (Communication)'.
140. *Source*: European Commission, http://ec.europa.eu/avpolicy/reg/tvwf/implementation/events_list/index_en.htm.

Country	*Event*
Belgium	Summer and Winter Olympic Games; Belgian Football Cup Final (men), live and in full; All matches involving the Belgian men's football team; Football World Cup Finals (men); European Football Championship, final round (men); Champion's League, matches involving Belgian clubs; UEFA Cup, matches involving Belgian clubs; Tour de France, men, professional; Liège-Bastogne-Liège; Amstel Gold Race; Tour of Flanders; Paris-Roubaix; Milan-San Remo; Belgian Road Cycling Championships, professional (men); World Road Cycling Championships, professional (men); Ivo Van Damme Memorial; Belgian Formula 1 Grand Prix; The following Grand Slam tennis tournaments: Roland Garros and Wimbledon, quarter finals, semi finals and finals involving a Belgian player;
	The Davis Cup and the Fed Cup, quarter finals, semi finals and finals involving the Belgian team; Queen Elisabeth Music Competition, the final; La Flèche wallonne; World Athletics Championships, where Belgian athletes are taking part
Finland	Summer and winter Olympic Games, the opening match, quarter-finals, semi-finals and final of the World Cup as well as the matches of the Finnish team in that tournament, men's Ice Hockey World Championships, organized by the International Ice Hockey Federation (IIHF), Nordic World Ski Championships (cross-country skiing, ski jumping and Nordic combined), organized by the International Ski Federation (FIS), World Championships in Athletics, organized by the International Association of Athletics Federations (IAAF), and the European Athletics Championships, organized by the European Athletics Association (EAA)
France	Summer and winter Olympic Games, the opening match, semi-finals and final of the football World Cup as well as the semi-finals and final of the European Football Championship, the official matches of the French national football team in the FIFA calendar, the final of the UEFA Cup, where a French club involved in one of the French championships is playing, the French football Cup final and the final of the football Champions' League, The French Rugby Championship final, the European Rugby Cup final where a French club involved in one of the French championships is playing, the Six Nations rugby tournament, and the semi-finals and final of the Rugby World Cup
Germany	Summer and Winter Olympic Games, All European Championship and World Cup matches involving the German National Football Team, as well as the opening match, the Semi-finals and Finals The Semi-finals and Final of the German FA Cup; The German National Football Team's home and away matches; The Final of any European Football club competition (Champions League, UEFA Cup) involving a German club

Country	*Event*
Ireland	***Live broadcasting:*** The Summer Olympics; The All-Ireland Senior Inter-County Football and Hurling Finals*;* Ireland's home and away qualifying games in the European Football Championship and the FIFA World Cup Tournaments; Ireland's games in the European Football Championship Finals Tournament and the FIFA World Cup Finals Tournament*;* The opening games, the Semi-finals and Final of the European Football Championship Finals and the FIFA World Cup Finals Tournament; Ireland's games in the Rugby World Cup Finals Tournament; The Irish Grand National and the Irish Derby; The Nations Cup at the Dublin Horse Show***; Coverage on a deferred basis:*** Each of Ireland's games in the Six Nations Rugby Football Championship
Italy	Olympic Games (summer and winter games); The Football World Cup Final and all matches involving the Italian national team; The European Football Championship Final and all matches involving the Italian national team; All matches involving the Italian National Football Team, at home and away, in official competitions; The Final and the Semi-finals of the Champions' League and the UEFA Cup where an Italian team is involved; The Tour of Italy (Giro d'Italia) cycling competition; The Formula One Italian Grand Prix; The San Remo Italian music festival
United Kingdom	***Group A (full live coverage):*** Olympic Games (summer and winter games); The FA World Cup Finals Tournament; The European Football Championship Finals Tournament; The FA Cup Final; The Scottish FA Cup Final (in Scotland); The Grand National Steeplechase; The Derby; The Wimbledon Tennis Finals; The Rugby League Challenge Cup Final; The Rugby World Cup Final; ***Group B (adequate secondary coverage):*** Cricket test matches played in England; Non-Finals played in the Wimbledon Tournament; All other matches in the Rugby World Cup Finals Tournament; Six Nations Rugby Tournament matches involving the United Kingdom's National Teams (England, Scotland, Wales, Northern Ireland); The Commonwealth Games; The World Athletics Championship; The Cricket World Cup – the Finals, Semi-finals and matches involving the United Kingdom's National Teams (England, Scotland, Wales, Northern Ireland); The Ryder Cup; The Open Golf Championship;

While the model of the lists of events of major importance is well embedded in EU law, the access of 'secondary' broadcasters to short extracts from newsworthy events has not been regulated at the EU level, until recently. That is, however, not to say that there was no European regulation whatsoever on this issue. Article 9 of the Council of Europe's Convention on

Transfrontier Television[141] has paved the way for 'short reporting' rights in Europe. The Article urges Member States of the Council of Europe to:

> where necessary, take legal measures such as introducing the right to short reporting on events of high interest for the public to avoid the right of the public to information being undermined due to the exercise by a broadcaster within its jurisdiction of exclusive rights for the transmission or retransmission.

This led many Member States to introduce 'short reporting' rights into their national legislation, which in turn presented a case for harmonization at EU level. This is just one of the examples of the Council of Europe's ability to influence legislation in the European Union. The AVMS Directive added Article 15, which requires Member States to ensure that for the purposes of short news reports, any broadcaster established in the EU must have access on a fair, reasonable and non-discriminatory basis, to the extract from broadcasts of events of *high interest* to the public, which are transmitted on an exclusive basis by a broadcaster under their jurisdiction. Examples of events to which access is guaranteed by Article 15 include less important sports and cultural events, as well as 'newsworthy events such as a report about an accident, a natural disaster, or an armed conflict'.[142] Recital 55 clarifies further that short extracts should not exceed ninety seconds and should be transmitted before the event concludes, or for sports events before the end of a single day's play – whichever is the sooner. The Article does not mention whether short reporting rights may also include access to the site of event, and a negative interpretation dictates that there is no such right provided by the AVMS Directive. The Council of Europe is, however, deliberating whether Article 9 of the Convention on Transfrontier Television should be complemented, so as to encompass the right of secondary broadcasters to enter the site of event.[143] However, this is now unlikely to happen since, as explained in Chapter 3, the Convention is currently practically defunct.

It is notable, that whereas the lists of events only apply to events of 'major importance' to society, it is sufficient that the event is of 'high interest to the public' for the short reporting rights to be applicable.[144] Listed events require a stricter test, since they are to be accessible *in full* on free TV. Moreover, Helberger observes, that unlike the lists concept, short reporting

141. European Convention on Transfrontier Television, Strasbourg 5 May 1989, European Treaty Series No. 132.
142. Helberger, N., 'The "Right to Information" and Digital Broadcasting: About Monsters, Invisible Men and the Future of European Broadcasting Regulation'.
143. Council of Europe, Report of the group of specialists on the democratic and social implications of digital broadcasting (MM-S-DB), 8th meeting, 6–8 October 2003.
144. Helberger, N., 'The "Right to Information" and Digital Broadcasting: About Monsters, Invisible Men and the Future of European Broadcasting Regulation'.

rights do not remove the exclusivity of the transmission rights.[145] Instead, the effect of Article 15 is similar to an exception to copyright law – the exercise of exclusive transmission rights is subject to limitations created by the right to short reporting.

Before the introduction of Article 15, some authors[146] expressed concerns that even with the time limit the 'short reporting' rules may be liberally interpreted and may lead to abuses. The example of Austria was given, where hour long sports programmes were created based entirely on broadcasting a number of 'short extracts' followed by a studio discussion.[147] The answer to those concerns seems to be the requirement in Article 15 of the AVMS Directive that the short extracts may 'be used exclusively for general news programmes'. The rights of 'primary' broadcasters are further protected by the right to compensation for the costs incurred.

Overall, the idea of 'lists of events of major importance' and short reporting rights is valuable and worth keeping in mind. However, it has some critical weaknesses. Not all Member States assumed it was necessary to draft and submit a list. And it is difficult to believe that only in eight European societies there are events of such importance that they should be available on free TV. Moreover, because viewers are not involved in the list-making process,[148] it is the State which decides whether a list ought to be drafted at all, and if it did, which events should be included. Had the viewers been consulted, the end result could have been quite different. In this regard, Helberger observes that the right to short reporting is more flexible than the concept of a list of important events, and there are potentially more events that can be subject to a right to short reporting as they are not restricted to a predefined list.[149] Nevertheless, the biggest problem is that contrary to the Commission's claims, neither the lists of events nor the short reporting rights are tools *actively* promoting internal media pluralism at the EU level. Both concepts are mainly concerned with guaranteeing everybody equal access to information, and therefore they only, to a very limited extent, contribute to internal media pluralism.

5.2.2.2. Independent and European Production Quotas

While Articles 14 and 15 of the AVMS Directive are concerned mainly with the right to information and have, at best, only indirect effect on internal media pluralism. Articles 16 and 17 deal with European and independent

145. Helberger, N., 'The "Right to Information" and Digital Broadcasting: About Monsters, Invisible Men and the Future of European Broadcasting Regulation'.
146. Schoental, M., 'Major Events and Reporting Rights'.
147. Schoental, M., 'Major Events and Reporting Rights'.
148. Helberger, N., 'The "Right to Information" and Digital Broadcasting: About Monsters, Invisible Men and the Future of European Broadcasting Regulation'.
149. Helberger, N., 'The "Right to Information" and Digital Broadcasting: About Monsters, Invisible Men and the Future of European Broadcasting Regulation'.

production quotas respectively, and are specifically designed to protect cultural values, for example media pluralism and diversity.

Article 16 requires Member States:

> to ensure where practicable and by appropriate means, that broadcasters reserve for European works … *a majority* proportion of their transmission time, excluding the time appointed to news, sports events, games, advertising, teletext services and teleshopping.

European works are defined in Article 1(n) as: (i) works originating from Member States; (ii) works originating from European third States party to the European Convention on Transfrontier Television; and (iii) works co-produced in the framework of agreements between the European Community and third countries, and which fulfil the conditions defined in each of these agreements. The European works quota has been introduced primarily as one of the remedies against swamping European television with cheap American imports.[150] Article 17 however, obliges Member States, again where practicable and by appropriate means, to ensure that broadcasters reserve *at least 10%* of their transmission time or, this time alternatively also programming budget, excluding the time appointed to news, sports events, games, advertising, teletext services and teleshopping for European works created *recently* by producers who are independent of broadcasters. While recent works are defined as those, less than five years old, the notion of 'independent producer's' not defined in the Directive and is left to the discretion of the Member States. Recital 71 of the AVMS Directive gives only a general indication that when defining the term 'independent producer', Member States should take account of the ownership of the production company, the amount of programmes supplied to the same broadcaster and the ownership of secondary rights.

Member States are required to provide the Commission with a bi-annual report on the application of Articles 16 and 17, including statistics on the achievement of the quotas, the reasons for the failure to attain the quotas and the measures adopted or envisaged in order to achieve them. On the basis of the country reports, the Commission prepares its own summary report. The latest, which is the ninth report by the Commission on the application of Articles 16 and 17, dates from September 2010 and covers the period from 2007 to 2008.[151] The report highlights that the total number of reported channels covered by Articles 16 and 17 increased from 1,107 in 2006 to 1,590 in 2007 and 1,679 in 2008. The EU-average transmission time reserved for European works was 62.64% in 2007 and 63.21% in 2008. The

150. McGonagle, M., *Media Law*.

151. Communication from the Commission to the Council, the European Parliament, the European Economic and Social Committee and the Committee of the regions, Ninth Communication on the application of Articles 4 and 5 of Directive 89/552/EEC, as amended by Directive 97/36/EC and Directive 2007/65/EC for the period 2007–2008 (Promotion of European and independent audiovisual works), COM(2010) 0450 final

EU-average proportion reserved for European works by independent producers was approximately 35% in both referenced years. Both indicators suggest that Member States went significantly over the minimum quotas provided for in Articles 4 and 5. Therefore, on the face of it, it looked like both measures would provide a powerful tool in the EU quest to be the campaigner for internal media pluralism in the European media industry.

Nevertheless, the quota system has many enemies. Their arguments centre on the questioning of the two main reasons for independent production quotas, that is: (i) the tendency of independent producers to select projects that have a higher innovative content than those promoted by big networks; and (ii) the reduction of the risk of vertical integration and the risk of market foreclosure.[152] Opponents of the quota system reject the first reason on the grounds that:

> the production of programmes is a very risky activity and a TV group may be in a better position than small producers to promote innovative projects, since it may be able to spread its risk over many different projects ... [and] it may also have a clearer idea about what projects the market will accept.[153]

The second 'sectoral' aim of the quota system can be just as effectively achieved by competition law which is 'less distortionary than making use of quotas'.[154]

Bearing this in mind, the Commission considered the need to revise Articles 16 and 17 during the preparatory stages of the AVMS Directive. Issues Paper No 3 for the Liverpool Audiovisual Conference in September 2005, dealt with cultural diversity and the promotion of European and independent audiovisual production.[155] The starting point of the Issues Paper was the conclusion that the quotas provided for in Articles 16 and 17 (then Articles 4 and 5), 'appear still to be valid in substance' since, as evidenced by the latest Commission report on the application of Articles 16 and 17 (then Articles 4 and 5), transmissions of European works have grown consistently, which proves that the two Articles have achieved cultural objectives and contributed to strengthening of the European audiovisual industry. This seems to rebut the claims of the opponents to the system that quotas constitute a 'disproportionate restriction on broadcasters' scheduling

152. Motta, M., Polo, M., 'Concentration and Public Policies in the Broadcasting Industry: The Future of Television', 325.
153. Motta, M., Polo, M., 'Concentration and Public Policies in the Broadcasting Industry: The Future of Television', 325.
154. Motta, M., Polo, M., 'Concentration and Public Policies in the Broadcasting Industry: The Future of Television', 325.
155. European Commission, 'Media Pluralism – what should be the European Union's role?', Issues Paper, 2005.

freedom'[156] and that 'European consumer demand will in any case ensure a high level of original content on screen.'[157]

The Commission provided stakeholders with several issues regarding Articles 16 and 17 (then Articles 4 and 5), which may require adapting or reforming in the new media environment. They included: (i) extension of the quota system to non-linear services; (ii) the strengthening of monitoring of the application of Articles 4 and 5; (iii) the encouragement for broadcasting of non-national European works; and (iv) an EU level definition of an 'independent producer'.[158]

With regard to the extension of the quota system to non-linear services, the Commission considered that there should be a signal sent by the European Union that new non-linear services will be expected to contribute to the promotion of European works.[159] In the end, however, the draft AVMS Directive only mentions the European works quota for non-linear services in one of the recitals. Recital 69 declares that non-linear audiovisual media services have the potential to partially replace linear services, and therefore, they should promote the production and distribution of European works and actively contribute to the promotion of cultural diversity. Accordingly, Article 13 requires the Member States to ensure that 'on-demand audiovisual media services provided by media service providers under their jurisdiction promote, where practicable and by appropriate means, the production of and access to European works'. Both Recital 69 and Article 13 further clarify that such promotion could relate, *inter alia*, to a minimum share of European works proportionate to economic performance, a minimum share of European works in video-on-demand catalogues, or the attractive presentation of European works in electronic programme guides. The caveat is that this promotion and contribution should only take place 'where practicable'. The first report from the Commission to the European Parliament and the Council under the AVMS Directive on the application of Articles 16 and 17, which for the first time will cover both broadcasting services and on-demand services, is due mid-2012.[160] It will be interesting to see how on-demand services providers approach the European and independent production quotas issue.

---

156. Association of Commercial Television in Europe, 'Response to Issues Paper 3 for the Liverpool Audiovisual Conference 2005 on 'Cultural Diversity and Promotion of European and Audiovisual Production'.
157. Association of Commercial Television in Europe, 'Response to Issues Paper 3 for the Liverpool Audiovisual Conference 2005 on 'Cultural Diversity and Promotion of European and Audiovisual Production'.
158. European Commission, 'Cultural Diversity and Promotion of European and Audiovisual Production', Issues Paper for the Liverpool Audiovisual Conference, July 2005.
159. European Commission, 'Cultural Diversity and Promotion of European and Audiovisual Production', Issues Paper for the Liverpool Audiovisual Conference, July 2005, 2.
160. See European Commission, Audiovisual and Media Policies, http://ec.europa.eu/avpolicy/reg/tvwf/implementation/promotion/index_en.htm.

Further, the reason the Commission considered strengthening the monitoring of the application of Articles 16 and 17 was that there are often significant differences between Member States as regards the nature and intensity of checks.[161] Moreover, in previous consultations many broadcasters and producers expressed concerns that national monitoring and enforcement of the EU production quota requirements is relatively relaxed.[162] The adherence to the quotas is not systematically monitored, many of the regulatory authorities do not apply sanctions against channels that fail to meet the quotas, and there are often inconsistencies between the data submitted by Member States and the data collected independently.[163] In addition, due to the non-binding wording of Articles 16 and 17 (where practicable) the application and monitoring of the quota system is only as effective as a Member State wishes it to be. Some Member States continue to exempt a large number of channels from the quota requirements for very unclear reasons. Examples include Italy exempting satellite channels and the United Kingdom, where only PSBs are burdened with quotas, leaving other providers, such as BSkyB, free from the quota obligations. This means, that the European Union is not going far enough in the enforcement of the quota system.

In the Issues Paper No 3, the Commission proposed to address the problems associated with monitoring, by revising the 'Suggested guidelines for the monitoring of the implementation of Articles 4 and 5 (*now Articles 16 and 17*)'of 11 June 1999.[164] The suggested revision was to include inserting an obligation for an independent audit of Member States' statistical statements before their submission to the European Commission. In addition, there would be a requirement for efficient sanctioning of cases of non-compliance or non-reporting. However, the 'Revised Guidelines for Monitoring the Application of Articles 16 and 17 of the AVMS Directive'[165] adopted in July 2011 are silent on the issues of independent audit and sanctions.

In addition, some stakeholders[166] suggested that the overall effectiveness of the quotas is questioned not only by poor monitoring and sanctioning, but more generally, by the non-binding nature of the system caused by the

161. European Commission, 'Seventh communication on the application of Articles 4 and 5 of Directive 89/552/EEC 'Television without Frontiers', as amended by Directive 97/36/EC, for the period 2003–2004, 14 August 2006', COM(2006) 0459 final.
162. European Commission, 'Cultural Diversity and Promotion of European and Audiovisual Production', Issues Paper, 2005, 3.
163. Feintuck, M., Varney, M., *Media Regulation, Public Interest and the Law*, 216.
164. European Commission, 'Suggested guidelines for the monitoring of the implementation of Articles 4 and 5', 11 June 1999.
165. European Commission, Revised Guidelines for Monitoring the Application of Articles 16 and 17 of the AVMS Directive, Doc CC AVMSD (2011) 2, July 2011.
166. Endemol, International Federation of Actors (FIA), European Coordination of Independent Producers (CEPI).

existence of the 'where practicable' clause. Some broadcasters used the clause to find a 'loophole' in the Directive. As explained by Tongue:

> BSkyB has been allowed to use a loophole [created by the 'where practicable' clause] placed in the TVWF Directive by Margaret Thatcher ... In the past, BSkyB has claimed that adherence to EU quotas was impracticable because the satellite channel was still not profitable. This is clearly no longer the case. [Still] BSkyB relies heavily on imported programming and commissions little work from local independent producers. It makes about 14,000 first-run hours, mostly in sport and news production – none of which counts as far as the TVWF quota is concerned.[167]

The suggestion was therefore, not only to strengthen monitoring, but also to remove the words 'where practicable' from the text of Articles 16 and 17 (then Articles 4 and 5). However, so far, the 'where practicable' clause is still firmly in place.

Further, the Commission was concerned with limited trade in non-national European works:

> Article 4 (*Now Article* 16) may have reinforced national objectives to protect and encourage the domestic content sector rather than fostering a truly European market in programming and encouraging the exchange/circulation of European TV programmes within Europe.[168]

The suggestions to remedy this scenario included creating incentives for the increased distribution of European co-productions as well as encouraging the circulation of European works of non-domestic origin. Again, as with almost all previous suggestions for reform, the issue was addressed in the AVMS Directive in one of the recitals only. Recital 70 only recommends that Member States should make provision for broadcasters to include an adequate share of co-produced European works or of European works of non-domestic origin. One of the reasons for this cautious approach, could have been a concern that any positive encouragement of the circulation of non-domestic European works could run counter Article 18 of the Treaty on the Functioning of the European Union, which prohibits any discrimination on grounds of nationality.[169]

A final, although probably most important, suggestion for a reform presented by the Commission during consultation process, was the need to have a European-level definition of an 'independent producer'. The Commission pondered whether the clarification of the concept of 'independent

167. Tongue, C., 'Culture or Monoculture? The European Audiovisual Challenge', 120.
168. European Commission, 'Cultural Diversity and Promotion of European and Audiovisual Production', Issues Paper, 2005, 4.
169. European Commission, 'Cultural Diversity and Promotion of European and Audiovisual Production', Issues Paper, 2005, 5.

producer' would lead to a more uniform application of Article 17 (then Article 5).

Despite the extended consultation, the AVMS Directive does not include a binding EU-level definition of an 'independent producer'. As has already been mentioned, Recital 71 provides Member States only with limited guidance, recommending that in defining the term 'independent producer', Member States should take account of the ownership of the production company, the amount of programmes supplied to the same broadcaster and the ownership of secondary rights. During the consultation process, the Commission suggested moving the definition of 'independent producer' to the body of the Directive (Article 1) and changing the wording so as to include a phrase '*at least* the following three criteria'.[170] This has not materialized, definition is still in the recitals and the wording remains similar. In the Revised Guidelines for Monitoring the Application of Articles 16 and 17 of the AVMS Directive, the Commission clarifies that the concept of *independence* should be understood in the light of Recital 71 and the three criteria mentioned there are indicative and not exhaustive.[171]

Overall, therefore, despite significant support from a number of stakeholders,[172] the new AVMS Directive, only to a limited extent, addresses the issues concerning the quota system that was discussed during the revision process. The Commission apparently followed the advice of the stakeholders, who opposed any changes or even advocating for gradual weakening of the quota requirements.[173]

Moreover, some stakeholders[174] raised one other issue which requires attention and which was conspicuously missing in the Commission's consultation process of the adoption of the AVMS Directive. The issue is the actual percentage of the quotas, especially the independent production quota. It was argued that some Member States introduced 25% quota of independent production,[175] and in the UK this was actually lowered from the initial proposal of 40%.[176] The argument was that there is no reason that other Member States cannot follow this example and, therefore, there is a need to raise the European independent production quota to 25% of *programming*

170. European Commission, 'Cultural Diversity and Promotion of European and Audiovisual Production', Issues Paper, 2005, emphasis added.
171. European Commission, Revised Guidelines for Monitoring the Application of Articles 16 and 17 of the AVMS Directive, Doc CC AVMSD (2011) 2, July 2011, points 7.1 and 7.2.
172. See written contributions to the Public Consultation for the review of the Television without Frontiers Directive, e.g. Endemol, FIA, UK Film Council, European Film Companies Alliance (EFCA), CEPI.
173. Examples include Association of Commercial Television in Europe (ACT) or Fox.
174. Endemol, CEPI, EFCA.
175. The United Kingdom, Ireland, Denmark, The Netherlands, Austria.
176. European Coordination of Independent Producers (CEPI), 'Contribution to the 2003 public consultation on the review of the Television Without Frontiers Directive'.

budget. This has not only failed to materialize, but has not even been discussed.

In summary, therefore, while in theory the quota system has probably the greatest potential to be a tool actively fostering internal media pluralism in European media, it has a range of weaknesses which prevent it from being such a tool in practice. The percentages should be higher; non-binding wording should be abandoned; independent producers should be defined; monitoring and enforcement should be strengthened; and non-domestic circulation of European works promoted. And as neither of these suggestions materialised in the AVMS Directive, the Commission's claims that the quotas *actively* promote pluralism at the EU level, are a little overstated.

5.2.3. Subsidising European Audiovisual Production: MEDIA Programme

A necessary response to requiring broadcasters to adhere to independent production quotas must be to subsidize the European audiovisual production. It is all the more important in the digital era. The development of digital television in Europe has led to a multiplication of channels, but it has not been accompanied by the abundance of new European audiovisual content. The newly created broadcasting capacity has been filled mainly with cheap American imports. The result is that currently, as defined by Jacques Delors, European television is for the most part 'a [European] viewer watching an American programme on a Japanese television set'.[177] There is a multiplicity of distribution channels, but there is no diversity on offer. Therefore, one of the techniques suggested by Gibbons as possible alternatives to media ownership regulation was 'to target programme production and supply in order to guarantee diversity of output', in order to ensure that the supply of content 'does not fall into too few hands'.[178]

In addition, Tongue warned that unless the EU invests more in the production of diverse content, 'the digital age will be a failure for all, except the Hollywood studios'.[179] And instead of passing a flourishing European culture to the next generations, we will pass nothing on but a monoculture.[180] She argued that the current digital age has actually reduced diversity, instead of creating it and that '... developments over the last decade have proved that technological progress cannot be translated into *real* progress without more investment in TV programmes'.[181]

---

177. Fraser, M.W., 'Television', in Kassim, H., Menon, A. (eds), *The European Union and National Industrial Policy* (Routledge, 1996), 204.
178. Gibbons, T., 'Concentrations of Ownership and Control in a Converging Media Industry', 171.
179. Tongue, C., 'Culture or Monoculture? The European Audiovisual Challenge', 101.
180. Tongue, C., 'Culture or Monoculture? The European Audiovisual Challenge', 106.
181. Tongue, C., 'Culture or Monoculture? The European Audiovisual Challenge', 101.

The fight against diminishing internal pluralism in European television caused by the invasion of cheap American imports is, therefore, a fight for pluralism and diversity on the one hand and for the heart and soul of Europe on the other hand:

> in Europe, we have less to learn from the American social model, and more to learn from our European partners. It is time that we started getting to know them, and we can begin by watching more of their programmes and less American TV.[182]

Tongue believed that the European deficit in trade in television broadcasting programmes with the United States and the resulting diminished diversity is a clear example of market failure.[183] Culture is a positive merit, and it needs to be defended against market forces. It, therefore, calls for a regulatory intervention.

The Commission's response was to launch the so-called MEDIA[184] programme to finance the development of the European audiovisual industry. The first programme was initiated in January 1991 and since then there have been four multiannual programmes: MEDIA I (1991–1995), MEDIA II (1996–2000), MEDIA Plus (2001–2006) and MEDIA 2007 (2007–2013). The current MEDIA 2007 programme has a budget of EUR 755 million, an increase from EUR 453 million in the previous MEDIA Plus.[185] There are three main objectives of the current programme: (i) to strive for a stronger European audiovisual sector, reflecting and respecting Europe's cultural identity and heritage; (ii) to increase the circulation of European audiovisual works inside and outside the European Union; and (iii) to strengthen the competitiveness of the European audiovisual sector by facilitating access to financing. MEDIA 2007 provides support in five main areas: professional training (in screenwriting, business and new technologies), project development, distribution and promotion of European audiovisual works and pilot projects. Interested parties, that is producers of film, television, animation, new media companies, distribution and sales companies training bodies or film schools and promotional events or festival organizers,[186] may apply for financing to a MEDIA office in one of the Member States. In the cinema sector, the programme seems to be achieving some success. The German film 'The Lives of Others'('Das Leben der Anderen') by Florian Henckel von Donnersmarck, which benefited from the MEDIA initiative won an Oscar for

---

182. Tongue, C., 'Culture or Monoculture? The European Audiovisual Challenge', 127.
183. Tongue, C., 'Culture or Monoculture? The European Audiovisual Challenge', 125.
184. MEDIA: Mesures pour Encourager le Development de l'Industrie Audiovisuelle (Measures to Encourage the Development of the Audiovisual Industry); see http://ec.Europa.eu/information_society/media/index_en.htm.
185. Decision No. 1718/2006/EC of the European Parliament and of the Council of 15 November 2006 concerning the implementation of a programme of support for the European audiovisual sector (MEDIA 2007), OJ (2006) L327/12.
186. MEDIA Desk Ireland, http://www.mediadeskireland.ie.

the best foreign language film at the 2007 Academy Awards ceremony. The EUR 500,000 of EU funding helped to boost the distribution of the film in cinemas and on DVDs outside Germany.[187]

With regard to the television broadcasting sector, MEDIA 2007 offers support for the production stage of fiction, documentary, and animated films involving the co-operation of broadcasters from two or more Member States that belong to different language zones.[188] Half of the production budget financed by European sources must be in place before application is made for MEDIA support. The MEDIA 2007 programme assistance will only cover up to 12.5% of the production budget for fiction and animated films and 20% of the production budget for documentary films, with the maximum financial contribution awarded not exceeding EUR 500,000 for each work.[189]

Some believe that subsidising the broadcasting production may be a better way to achieve diversity than regulating media ownership or audience share. For instance, Hitchens notes that:

> the use of grants and subsidies to enable independent alternative or community media groups to operate might be much more likely to encourage diversity than the encouragement of a competitive environment which will do little that enable yet another profit motivated company to enter the media field.[190]

However, the MEDIA programme is still rather modestly financed,[191] and it does not have a significant impact on diversity of content available on European television. The European Film Companies Alliance (EFCA) has noted that while, at theatrical level, the MEDIA programme provides a valuable contribution to the cross-border distribution of European works, it had very little effect on television: 'the quantity of non-national European programmes available to viewers across the EU is incredibly low and the situation seems to be getting worse'.[192]

5.3. OVERALL CONCLUSIONS ON LEGISLATIVE EU MEASURES SUPPORTING MEDIA PLURALISM

The comments on the EU legislative measures directly or indirectly contributing to safeguarding media pluralism may be summarized in one

187. 'EU claims a bit of Oscars glamour', EU Business, 26 February 2007.
188. MEDIA Desk Ireland.
189. MEDIA Desk Ireland..
190. Hitchens, L.P., 'Media Ownership and Control: A European Approach'.
191. Humphreys, P., 'The EU and Audiovisual Regulation: An Agency for De-regulation'.
192. European Film Companies Alliance (EFCA), 'Contribution to the public consultation on the revision of the 'Television without frontiers' Directive launched by the European Commission ahead of the Liverpool Audiovisual Conference'.

sentence: there are some measures present, however they are fragmented and imperfect.

This applies in particular to safeguards for structural media pluralism. The rules contributing to a larger or lesser extent to structural media pluralism are economic in focus and have only a passing effect on media pluralism. Access rights regulated in the Access Directive apply only in situations where an operator is designated with significant market power. Therefore, they are effective only in situations of dominance, and they have an inevitable *ex post* effect, which in for media pluralism, is far from ideal. The E-Communications framework also fails to take action in terms of securing interoperability, as there are no binding EU standards on CAS and APIs. As noted by Humphreys:

> The European Commission abdicated from the responsibility to regulate for either common standards on access terms for digital TV networks and instead chose to defer to the decisions of an industry grouping – the Digital Video Broadcasting (DVB) project. This group reached agreement only over a common European digital transmission standard, but provided no common standard for conditional access systems. This allowed the market players to develop their own proprietary systems and resulted in the emergence of a fragmented European digital TV market, characterised by incompatible conditional access systems in different national or linguistic areas.[193]

Finally, the country of origin principle which is the cornerstone of the AVMS Directive, can indeed contribute to structural pluralism. However, it can also lead to situations where operators purposefully locate themselves in countries with liberal regulatory regimes and thus avoid more strict regulations in countries to which they actually intend to broadcast. The example of BSkyB licensed in the UK and broadcasting to Ireland is one of the most prominent examples. Similar practices have caused serious concerns among the defenders of media pluralism in Europe. The result is the introduction of an infringement procedure in the AVMS Directive.

Article 4 clarifies that Member States are free to require media service providers under their jurisdiction to comply with more detailed, or stricter rules *in the areas covered by this Directive.* Article 4(2) envisages a situation where a Member State has exercised adopted more detailed or stricter rules of general public interest, and it is concerned that a broadcaster under the jurisdiction of another Member State provides a television broadcast which is wholly or mostly directed towards its territory infringes these stricter rules. The procedure is that the Member State may contact the Member State having jurisdiction with a view to achieving a mutually satisfactory solution. On receipt of a substantiated request by the first Member State, the Member State having jurisdiction shall request the broadcaster to comply with the

193. Humphreys, P., 'The EU and Audiovisual Regulation: An Agency for De-regulation', 20.

rules of general public interest in question, and it shall inform the first Member State of the results obtained following this request within two months. When the Member State which adopted the stricter rules, assesses that the results notified are not satisfactory, and that the broadcaster in question has established itself in the Member State having jurisdiction in order to circumvent the stricter rules, it may adopt appropriate measures against the broadcaster. Before adopting the measures, it must notify the Member State with the jurisdiction and the European Commission, and the Commission has to decide that the measures are compatible with Union law.

This procedure will, however, not be applicable to the cases, where stricter media ownership rules are circumvented, as this is not covered by the Directive. Moreover, the European Court of Justice openly allowed for the circumvention of media ownership rules by relocating to countries with more liberal regimes. For instance, all the rules, set by the Broadcasting Commission of Ireland apply to media operators under Irish jurisdiction. Therefore, even if, for example, BSkyB gains a substantive market and audience share in Ireland, the BCI will not be able to take any corrective steps because it is not the regulator which licensed BSkyB.

Turning now to measures supporting internal media pluralism, these are admittedly more numerous and with a more specific public interest focus. Still, the picture arising is that internal media pluralism is safeguarded at the EU level by rules assembled in a fairly random way. The weaknesses of must-carry, as already explained, centre on too narrow definition of public interest, no preferential access to associated facilities, and the fact that they should be implemented with must-offer and must-distribute rules on other levels of the broadcasting value chain. Lists of events and short reporting rights focus on citizens' right of information, and only in an indirect manner contribute to media pluralism. Finally, the production quotas have probably the greatest potential, but they too have their shortcomings in that they are non-binding (the 'where practicable' clause); some argue they are too modest (if the UK can have 25% independent production quota, why can't the others?) and they are poorly monitored, executed and sanctioned. With regard to the MEDIA programme, it is laudable, but still rather modestly financed and it has, in practice, had little impact on increasing the diversity of content available in European television.

In general, all EU level measures aimed at supporting pluralism are based on voluntary action by Member States. Everything is about being 'allowed'(must-carry, list of events) or 'where practicable'(quotas). As a result, if Member States suddenly decided to abolish all national media pluralism rules and if they got rid of public service broadcasting, there is little the EU could do. In summary, therefore, as summarised by Goldberg, Prosser and Verhulst, 'the [EU's] media and communications policy is certainly not the product of a single and unified [EU] vision of the sector'.[194]

194. Goldberg, D., Prosser, T., Verhulst, S., 'Regulating the 'Changing Media', 146.

Table 5.3 Current EU Legislative Tools Contributing to the Protection of Media Pluralism

		Tool	EU level	Weakness	National level	Weakness
STRUCTURAL PLURALISM	Public Interest Focus (direct impact)	Legislative measures aimed at prevention of media concentration	**NO**	Lack of it	**Yes**	Dispersed, varied. not in every Member State; liberalisation trends
	Economic focus (indirect impact)	Competition law	**Yes** Art.101, 102 TFEU +Merger Regulation	*Ex post* protection, different focuses	**Yes**	*Ex post* protection, different focuses, no use of Art.21(4) Merger Regulation
		Access to SMPs'infrastructure, including access to CAS	**Yes** Art,5.5 Access Directive	*Ex post* protection	**Yes** (implementing EU rules)	*Ex post* protection; no public interest focus in regulation of access
		Standardisation of CAS, APIs and EPGs	**NO** Only encouragement in Art.17 and 18 Framework Directive	Only 'encouragement' to use open APIs	**NO**	Voluntary, industry-driven=not standardised
		Country of origin principle	**Yes** Article 2 of the AVMS directive	Open to abuse. Infringement procedure imperfect	**Yes** (implementing EU rules)	MS cannot impose their national media ownership thresholds to broadcasters outside their jurisdiction
INTERNAL PLURALISM	Public Interest Focus (direct impact)	Must-carry*	**Yes** Art.31 Universal Service Directive	Not obligatory, no obligation on CAS providers	**Yes** (implementing EU rules)	Not all Member States; CAS, API and EPG not covered; not every level of broadcasting value chain
		Production quotas*	**Yes** Art.16,17 AVMS directive	Ceiling not floor; not obligatory ('where practicanle')	**Yes** (implementing EU rules)	Not all Member States
		List of events of major importance + short reporting rights*	**Yes** Art.14,15 AVMS directive	Indirect impact only; rather 'right to information'	**Yes** (implementing EU rules)	Indirect impact; not all Member States
		Subsidising*	**Yes** MEDIA programme	Modestly financed; support mainly for cinema, less impact on television	**Yes** (various instruments)	Do not achieve the desired effect; television production often openly excluded from financing schemes
		Public Service Broadcasting*	**Yes/No** Protocol to the Treaty of Amsterdam	Support not strong enough; just permission	**Yes**	Shrinking licence fees; retreat from tradition of Public Service Broadcasting tradit
	Economic focus (indirect impact)	—	—	—	—	—

* According to the European Commission, these are the measures which *actively* promote media pluralism at the EU level (see Issues Paper on Media Pluralism for the Liverpool Audiovisual Conference, July 2005)

Chapter 6

National Tools: Media Concentration Laws in Four Member States

As already mentioned in previous chapters, the current political line in the European Union is that the combination of national legislation, EU competition law and EU legislative instruments provides a balanced solution for the protection of both structural and internal media pluralism in Europe.[1] As a result, the Audiovisual Media Services (AVMS) Directive contains very few specific provisions aimed at counteracting growing media concentration in Europe. The concerns of pluralism and diversity are primarily left to the Member States.

Meanwhile, media laws and, consequently, the levels of protection for media pluralism vary hugely within the twenty-seven EU Member States. Twenty-one Member States do not have any special rules for media mergers.[2] Six[3] have no specific media concentration rules whatsoever, and three[4] have very limited media concentration rules. Ten Member States[5] have no

1. European Commission, 'Media Pluralism – what should be the European Union's role?', (Issues Paper for the Liverpool Audiovisual Conference) July 2005, European Commission, European Commission, 'Services of general interest (White Paper)', COM(2004) 374 final.
2. Media specific competition law applies only in the United Kingdom, Ireland, Germany and Austria.
3. Denmark, Finland, Estonia, Lithuania, Poland, Portugal.
4. Sweden, Latvia, Luxembourg.
5. Spain, Poland, Portugal, Czech Republic, Belgium, Sweden, Denmark, Finland, Lithuania, Latvia, Luxembourg.

cross-media ownership rules,[6] i.e., rules prohibiting for instance owners of national television stations from holding interests in national newspapers. Crucially, in many Member States the rules, even if they are in place, are not being observed (Italy is a prime example).

Hallin and Mancini, in their book *Comparing Media Systems*, identify three basic models of media regulation in Europe: (i) the Mediterranean or 'Polarized Pluralist' model present in countries like France, Greece, Italy, Portugal and Spain; (ii) the Northern/Central European or 'Democratic Corporatist' model in Austria, Belgium, Denmark, Finland, Germany, the Netherlands and Sweden; and (iii) the North Atlantic or 'Liberal' model in the United Kingdom and Ireland.[7] Hallin and Mancini's book left post-Communist countries out of consideration, but there have been opinions suggesting that these countries' media systems are closest to the polarized-pluralist (Mediterranean) model.[8]

Having the above taxonomy in mind, this chapter briefly analyses media concentration laws in four selected EU Member States, which are most interesting from this books' point of view. The first two analysed Member States belong to the North Atlantic 'Liberal' model: United Kingdom as one of the biggest, most influential, but also one of the most liberal media markets in Europe; and Ireland as an example of a smaller Member State heavily influenced by its bigger neighbour. Then, two countries from the polarized-pluralist model are examined: Italy as an arena of the most spectacular abuses of media pluralism in recent years, and Poland as a representative of new Member States from Central and Eastern Europe and the one where plans to introduce cross-media ownership restrictions resulted in major political scandal and the resignation of the government. Examples of the application of the rules in practice are also provided with some comments and conclusions regarding sufficiency of national legislation to prevent growing cross-border media concentration in Europe.

6.1. UNITED KINGDOM

6.1.1. STRUCTURE OF THE TELEVISION MARKET

The United Kingdom has one of the largest media markets in Europe, and its television sector has undergone a significant change over the last fifteen

6. Kevin, 'Media Ownership and Pluralism: Regulatory Trends and Challenges in the European Union Member States', presentation at the 20th EPRA meeting, Istanbul 2004.
7. Hallin, D., Mancini, P., *Comparing Media Systems* (Cambridge University Press, 2004).
8. See for instance Conference on Comparing Media Systems. West meets East, 23–25 April 2007, Wroclaw, Poland; Jakubowicz, 'PSB in Post-communist Countries: Finding the Right Place on the Map', the 2007 Spry Memorial Lecture, Montreal, 27 November 2007.

years. However, what remained unchanged and unique about British television broadcasting is that all terrestrial broadcasters have some form of public service obligations.[9] Initially there were only three terrestrial channels: BBC1 and BBC2 provided by the BBC and Channel 3 provided by the companies that comprised the ITV network. The BBC, with an audience share of almost 38%, now has two national channels and a range of free digital channels (a youth channel BBC3, BBC 4, BBC News 24, BBC Parliament, and two children's channels—CBBC and CBeebies).[10] With no advertising revenue, the BBC still manages to earn additional income through its wholly owned commercial subsidiary BBC Worldwide, which distributes television programmes, sells videos, publishes books and magazines (*e.g.*, Radio Times), organizes exhibitions, live events and English language teaching. The ITV network, with an audience share of almost 55%, consists of fifteen regional licenses and one breakfast television license.[11] One company, ITV Plc, formed after the merger of Carlton and Granada in 2003, now owns twelve of ITV's licenses. As will be explained below, the merger was made possible by the liberalization of media ownership laws.[12]

The fourth channel, Channel 4, was established in 1982 as 'a non-profit public corporation with a unique remit to innovate and cater to the programme areas and groups that were neglected by the established broadcasters'.[13] In addition, its original programming was to be commissioned from the independent production sector. Channel 5 is the final terrestrial broadcaster. It was licensed in 1995. In 2000, RTL Group bought a 66.6% majority share in FIVE from Pearson—an international media company. Since 2010 it has be owned by Norther & Shell.

The public service nature of British terrestrial television is unique and has been praised by Tongue:

> Britain can boast the finest broadcasting ecology in the world. If the UK urges one institution upon its partners as a model, it should be the BBC.[14]

---

9. Open Society Institute, 'Television across Europe: Regulation, Policy and Independence', (Monitoring Report) 11 October 2005, 1605.
10. European Institute for the Media, Final report of the study on 'The information of the citizen in the EU: obligations for the media and the Institutions concerning the citizen's right to be fully and objectively informed', 206.
11. European Institute for the Media, Final report of the study on 'The information of the citizen in the EU: obligations for the media and the Institutions concerning the citizen's right to be fully and objectively informed', 206
12. European Institute for the Media, Final report of the study on 'The information of the citizen in the EU: obligations for the media and the Institutions concerning the citizen's right to be fully and objectively informed', Düsseldorf, 31 August 2004, 206; Ward, D., Fueg, O.C., D'Armo, A., 'A Mapping Study of Media Concentration and Ownership in Ten European Countries', published by the Commissariaat voor de Media, 2004.
13. Open Society Institute, 'Television across Europe: Regulation, Policy and Independence', 1607.
14. Tongue, 'Culture or Monoculture? The European Audiovisual Challenge', 100.

Multichannel, pay-television in the UK is provided by BSkyB via satellite and Virgin Media via cable. It is fair to say that satellite dominates cable in terms of both subscribers and revenue share.[15] BSkyB, with News Corporation as its largest shareholder, has a monopoly in the satellite industry. In fact, many claim that any real competition in the satellite market in the foreseeable future is highly unlikely.[16] With regard to cable, there used to be two operators NTL and Telewest. In 2006, they merged with Virgin Mobile under the Virgin Media brand. However, rather than being BSkyB's competitor, Virgin Media is its main customer – it broadcasts the main Sky channels as one of its principal selling points.

6.1.2. Media Pluralism Legislation

The Broadcasting Act, 1990 was the first major piece of legislation in the UK to affect the terrestrial broadcasters. This is because it changed the way that licenses for the ITV franchises were allocated. There was the introduction of an auction plus a quality threshold, and a 25% independent production quota for all UK terrestrial broadcasters was established.[17] The first rules on media concentration and ownership based on audience share were introduced in the UK by the Broadcasting Act, 1996.

Nevertheless, the Broadcasting Act, 1996 began the liberalization process of the UK media ownership rules. The Act introduced different regulatory regimes for terrestrial and satellite broadcasters. While terrestrial broadcasters are subject to a set of ownership and content restrictions, satellite broadcasters (such as BSkyB) are virtually regulation-free. As a result, a great number of satellite broadcasters in Europe have either chosen the UK as the location for their headquarters or have relocated to the UK; examples include Time Warner and Al Jazeera. This means that they are effectively subject to no ownership or content restrictions in any country.

Further liberalization brought by the Communications Act, 2003 created one of the most liberal media ownership regimes in the European Union. The policy document which accompanied the draft Communications Bill, openly stated that: 'across the economy, deregulation brings benefits for consumers and businesses … unnecessary regulations need to be removed

15. Ward, D., Fueg, O.C., D'Armo, A., 'A Mapping Study of Media Concentration and Ownership in Ten European Countries', 203.
16. Ward, D., Fueg, O.C., D'Armo, A., 'A Mapping Study of Media Concentration and Ownership in Ten European Countries', 207.
17. Open Society Institute, 'Television across Europe: Regulation, Policy and Independence', 1607.

wherever possible'.[18] The same document declared that the existing ownership rules must necessarily be liberalized as 'they are not flexible enough to respond to the rapid change we have seen in media markets' and that they appear 'directed at particular media interests'.[19] Therefore, deregulation is a must in order to allow the UK media companies 'to grow, to find new opportunities to reduce costs and attract new investment, if they are to bring better products to consumers'.[20] The competition, innovation and consumer terminology have replaced the main focus on culture, public interest, pluralism, common knowledge and citizens.

One of the main changes brought about by the Communications Act, 2003 was to merge the powers and functions of the five previous regulatory authorities into one 'converged' regulator—the Office of Communications (OFCOM). Before that, three regulatory bodies dealt with content issues (the Independent Television Commission (ITC), the Radio Authority (RA) and the Broadcasting Standards Commission (BSC)). The Radio Communications Agency was responsible for spectrum management, and OFTEL was the telecommunications regulator.[21] OFCOM, therefore, regulates both structural (market and technical) and content issues involving the media.[22] In addition, the relevant government departments involved in the regulation of the media are the Department for Business, Innovation and Skills (formerly known as Department for Business, Enterprise and Regulatory Reform—BERR) and the Department of Culture, Media and Sport (DCMS). Mergers and acquisitions in the media sector are assessed by the Competition Commission, which is an independent body established by the Competition Act, 1998. The Competition Commission conducts in-depth inquiries into mergers, markets and the regulation of the major regulated industries, at the request of the Office of Fair Trading (OFT) or other authorities such as the Secretary of State for Culture, Media and Sport, or by the regulators relating to other industries.[23]

The Communications Act, 2003 created the most liberal media ownership regime in Europe and led to a consolidation in the UK television

18. Department of Trade and Industry/Department for Culture, Media and Sport (2002a), The Draft Communications Bill – The Policy, London, HMSO.
19. Department of Trade and Industry/Department for Culture, Media and Sport (2002a), The Draft Communications Bill – The Policy, London, HMSO.
20. Petley, 'The Re-regulation of Broadcasting, or the Mill Owners' Triumph', (2002) Journal of Media Practice.
21. European Federation of Journalists, 'Media power in Europe: the big picture of ownership', 154.
22. European Institute for the Media, Final report of the study on 'The information of the citizen in the EU: obligations for the media and the Institutions concerning the citizen's right to be fully and objectively informed', 204.
23. European Institute for the Media, Final report of the study on 'The information of the citizen in the EU: obligations for the media and the Institutions concerning the citizen's right to be fully and objectively informed', 204.

market.[24] As noted by Doyle, the impetus for the liberalization was provided by the 'arguments submitted by ... large UK media firms ... and the Government's receptiveness to these arguments'.[25] The leading argument was that there is a need to establish 'a framework which would strengthen the economic performance of the UK media industry'.[26] The main changes brought about by the 2003 Act are as follows:[27].

(i) A 15% Market Share Limit – removed

The 2003 Act removed the previous basic threshold for interests in the broadcasting sector which was set at 15% of the total market share, measured in terms of audience share.

(ii) No Joint Ownership of Two ITV London Franchises – removed

The rule introduced by the 1996 Act preventing the joint ownership of the two ITV (Channel 3) London franchises was removed by the 2003 Act. This has allowed for the merger of Carlton and Granada in 2003 – the two main owners of the ITV franchises, and the creation of a single ITV company, ITV plc., in February 2004. ITV plc. owns all, but three ITV franchises.[28] The Department of Trade and Industry claimed that the reason behind allowing the merger was that 'a stronger ITV will be better able to invest in and provide programming of high quality, including regional programmes. Broadcasting as a whole will benefit'.[29]

(iii) No Joint Ownership of An ITV Company and Channel 5 – removed

The rule preventing ownership of both an ITV company (a franchise from the network) and Channel 5 was removed by the Communications Act, 2003.

(iv) Newspaper Owner with A Market Share of over 20% Cannot Hold National Terrestrial Channel 5 Licenses – removed (Upheld in Relation to ITV Licenses)

The provisions on cross media ownership in the Broadcasting Act, 1996 preventing a newspaper owner with a market share of 20% from holding national terrestrial licenses of Channel 3 or FIVE, were meant to limit the cross-media expansion of media

24. European Federation of Journalists, 'Media power in Europe: the big picture of ownership', 154.
25. Doyle, G., *Media Ownership*, 102.
26. Doyle, G., *Media Ownership*, 102.
27. See Communications Act 2003, Chapter 5 (sections 348–357); see also Humphreys, P., 'Media Freedom and Pluralism in the United Kingdom', in Czepek, A., Hellwig, M., Nowak, E. (eds), *Press Freedom and Pluralism in Europe: Concepts and Conditions* (Intellect Books, 2009), 197–211.
28. See Competition Commission *Carlton Communications Plc/Granada Plc: A Report on the Proposed Merger*, http://www.competition-commission.org.uk.
29. Statement by the Department of Trade and Industry, *Media Guardian*, 7 October 2003.

companies.[30] The Communications Act, 2003 removed the restriction in relation to Channel 5. However, any attempt by a newspaper owner to acquire the Channel 5 license may be subject to review under the 'public interest test'(see below). A newspaper owner with 20% national market share still cannot own an ITV franchise. However, the owner of an ITV license in a particular region may not acquire an interest of 20% or more in a body corporate, running one or more national newspapers with an aggregate market share of 20% or more.[31]

(v) Prohibition of Non-EEA Ownership of UK Terrestrial Television Companies – removed

The removal of the restriction on non-EEA ownership of UK terrestrial television companies has been viewed as one of the most controversial changes introduced by the Communications *Act, 2003*.[32] There is now nothing in UK law preventing the acquisition of British TV companies by large US media conglomerates, such as Rupert Murdoch's News Corporation, which is the largest shareholder of BSkyB. Even though any attempt, by a non-EEA company to acquire a UK terrestrial broadcaster will have to undergo a public interest test,[33] the change is still perceived as detrimental by many due to the possibility of large USA media organizations entering the UK broadcasting market and rendering it 'a dumping ground for cheap, inferior quality programming produced in the USA'.[34]

(vi) Qualified Restriction on Certain Bodies (e.g., Religious Bodies) from Holding Channel 3 and Channel 5 Licenses – upheld

Religious bodies are still prohibited from holding the television licenses of Channel 3 and Channel 5.

(vii) Public Interest Test – extended to the Television Sector

Although the 15% audience share limit was removed by the Communications Act, 2003, concentration in the media sector remains subject to competition regulation under the Enterprise Act,

30. Ward, D., Fueg, O.C., D'Armo, A., 'A Mapping Study of Media Concentration and Ownership in Ten European Countries', 211.
31. European Institute for the Media, Final report of the study on 'The information of the citizen in the EU: obligations for the media and the Institutions concerning the citizen's right to be fully and objectively informed', 205.
32. Open Society Institute, 'Television across Europe: Regulation, Policy and Independence', 1634.
33. Open Society Institute, 'Television across Europe: Regulation, Policy and Independence', 1634.
34. Doyle, G., Vick, D., 'The Communications Act 2003. A New Regulatory Framework in the UK', (2005) Convergence 11, 84.

> 2002.[35] Mergers or acquisitions between media companies are reviewed by a combination of OFCOM and the Office of Fair Trading, which may refer the case to the Competition Commission if they believe the merger may result in a substantial lessening of competition in a relevant market. These bodies also submit their opinions to the Secretary of State, who may issue an intervention notice to the Competition Commission allowing for the assessment of the case on both competition and public interest grounds.[36] The above rules contained in the Enterprise Act with regard to the newspaper and radio sectors have been extended to the television sector by Part V, Chapter 2 (Media Mergers) of the Communications Act, 2003. According to section 58 of the Enterprise Act, in taking a decision to allow or prohibit a media merger, account must now be taken not only of competition issues, but also public interest grounds such as the need for accurate presentation of news and free expression of opinion; the need for a sufficient plurality of views and a sufficient plurality of persons with control of the media enterprises serving that audience; and the need for the availability throughout the United Kingdom of a wide range of broadcasting which is of high quality and is calculated to appeal to a wide variety of tastes and interests.[37]

The extension of the test is a result of a last minute compromise between the Government and the House of Lords during the debates on the Communications Act, 2003. A cross-party group in the House of Lords, led by Lord Puttnam, was concerned about the removal of the cross-media restrictions regarding the acquisition of Channel 5 by large newspaper owners like News Corporation. The group managed to convince the government to accept that, as is the case with newspaper and radio sectors, major mergers and acquisitions in the television sector should be subject to a 'public interest' or a 'plurality' test.[38] OFCOM's rationale for the extension of the public interest test to the broadcasting sector is that television has a special influence which may require public interest considerations, including plurality, to be taken into account in deciding whether or not to allow mergers to go ahead.[39]

---

35. OFCOM, 'Review of Media Ownership Rules', 14 November 2006.
36. OFCOM, 'Review of Media Ownership Rules', 46; See also Open Society Institute, 'Television across Europe: regulation, policy and independence', 1634; European Institute for the Media, Final report of the study on 'The information of the citizen in the EU: obligations for the media and the Institutions concerning the citizen's right to be fully and objectively informed', 205.
37. *Communications Act, 2003*, section 375.
38. European Institute for the Media, Final report of the study on 'The information of the citizen in the EU: obligations for the media and the Institutions concerning the citizen's right to be fully and objectively informed', 205.
39. OFCOM, 'Review of Media Ownership Rules', 23.

Therefore, as it now stands, the public interest test *can* be employed by the Secretary of State in mergers involving television companies. In particular mergers or acquisitions with any of the following characteristics are more than likely to be subject to the public interest test. Mergers involving national newspapers with more than 20% of the market share and the Channel 5 license holder; mergers involving a change of control of the Channel 3 license holder; mergers involving the national Channel 3 license holder and a national radio service; mergers involving the Channel 5 license holder and a national radio service or mergers involving on the one hand, owners outside the EEA, and, on the other hand, any of Channel 3; Channel 5, digital and analogue radio licenses. Mergers involving satellite and cable services are unlikely to be subject to the public interest test and, as the merger of NTL and Telewest in October 2005 illustrated, they will only be analysed under competition criteria.[40] Table 6.1 below summarizes the changes in the UK media legislation brought about by the Communications Act, 2003.

Table 6.1 Media Concentration Regulations in the UK before and after the Communications Act, 2003

Pre-2003	*2003 Communications Act*
Media concentration rules	
15% of market share limit (measured in terms of audience time)	REMOVED – no audience share limit, no restrictions on accumulation of TV licenses*
No joint ownership of the two ITV (Channel 3) London franchises	REMOVED**
No joint ownership of an ITV company and Channel 5	REMOVED with regard to Channel 5
Cross-media concentration rules	
Newspaper owner with a market share of over 20% cannot hold national terrestrial licenses (Channel 3 or Channel 5 licenses)	REMOVED WITH REGARD TO CHANNEL 5 (only subject to Pubic Interest Test); Newspaper owner with 20% market share cannot acquire a Channel 3 license; the holder of a Channel 3 license may not acquire an interest of 20% or more in a body corporate running one or more national newspapers with an aggregate market share of 20% or more

40. Ward, D., Fueg, O.C., D'Armo, A., 'A Mapping Study of Media Concentration and Ownership in Ten European Countries', 217.

Pre-2003	*2003 Communications Act*
Foreign media ownership rules	
Prohibition of non-EEA ownership of UK terrestrial television companies	REMOVED***
Other rules	
Prohibition on certain bodies (*e.g.*, political parties, local authorities, advertising agencies) from holding broadcasting licenses	UPHELD
Qualified restriction on certain bodies (e.g., religious bodies) from holding Channel 3 and Channel 5 licenses	UPHELD
Public interest test for mergers in the newspaper and radio sectors	EXTENDED TO THE TELEVISION SECTOR****
* Allowed for Carlton/Granada merger ** Allowed for Carlton/Granada merger *** Allowed for BSkyB acquiring 17.9% stake in ITV **** Used for the first time in the BSkyB/ITV case [citation]; BSkyB ordered to lower the stake to below 7%; currently under appeal.	

Section 391 of the Communications Act, 2003 requires OFCOM to review media ownership rules at least every three years and, as a result of that review, make recommendations to the Secretary of State if any changes are deemed necessary. OFCOM conducted the first review of the rules in 2006 and recommended that no changes in media ownership rules should be made at this stage.[41] Moreover, OFCOM noted that the media landscape was changing rapidly, and that *further* liberalization of the rules might be needed before long.

6.1.3. The Rules in Practice: BSkyB's Purchase of 17.9% Stake in ITV and News Corp's Bid for the Remaining 61% Shares in BSkyB

The first public interest test intervention in a television merger case followed the recent acquisition by BSkyB of a minority stake in ITV. In November 2006, ITV rejected a merger proposal from the cable company NTL, saying that there was little strategic logic for it to combine with NTL and the offer materially undervalued ITV.[42] Meanwhile, BSkyB purchased a 17.9% stake in ITV for GBP 940 million. Although this was a minority stake it was significant as it would allow Rupert Murdoch to make his views known at

41. OFCOM, 'Review of Media Ownership Rules', 2.
42. BBC News, 'ITV Rejects Merger Move from NTL', BBC News, 21 November 2006.

board meetings.[43] Widespread protest followed the move, most loudly expressed by Sir Richard Branson 10.5% owner of NTL (NTL merged with Telewest in 2005 and changed its name to Virgin Media early in 2007). Following Branson's comments, OFCOM announced that it was considering whether or not there had been a change of control over one or more of ITV's licenses. In addition, OFCOM's analysis would focus on the *Communications Act, 2003* provisions for the prohibition of mergers between Channel 3 license holders and companies which own 20% or more of the national newspaper market. News Corp, the main shareholder in BSkyB, also had a large share of the national newspaper market through News International. The examination of the BSkyB's acquisition of a stake in ITV was later on taken up by the OFT.

In December 2006, the UK's Parliament's All-Party Commons Media Group requested a meeting with Media Minister Tessa Jowell to discuss the implications of BSkyB's acquisition of a 17.9% stake in ITV. The MPs were concerned that the purchase of the stake could restrict ITV's ability or willingness to broadcast rival programmes to those shown by BSkyB, thus lessening media competition and customer choice.[44] They also feared that the acquisition could be the first step towards a takeover of ITV by BSkyB. Although this would not be allowed under the rules at present, a 17.9% stake would leave BSkyB well placed to take advantage of any deregulation in years to come.[45]

On 26 February 2007, the Secretary of State Alistair Darling, intervened in the BSkyB/ITV deal, using for the first time the power provided by section 378 of the *Communications Act, 2003* to apply the public interest test to a merger involving television companies.[46] Darling asked both OFCOM and the OFT to make recommendations allowing him to decide whether to refer the deal to the Competition Commission. The OFT examined the competition issues and OFCOM checked 'whether the case raises public interest concerns about the number of different owners of media enterprises'.[47] In late April, both OFCOM and OFT recommended that the Competition Commission investigate BSkyB's acquisition of the 17.9% stake in ITV. Both regulators agreed with NTL that, although the acquisition of almost 18% of ITV does not amount to a 'change of control', it would allow BSkyB to command a 'material influence' over ITV's content. OFT explained that 'Sky's shareholding means that ITV is no longer fully independent, and this may alter the

43. Hedges, 'It Is a Fight to the Death: Branson v. Murdoch', http://www.followthemedia.com, 28 March 2007.
44. Bosnjak, 'UK's Media Minister in Talks over Sky's ITV Stake', http://www.ovum.com.
45. Vass, 'Murdoch's Empire under Threat As Spotlight Shines on It for the First Time', Sunday Herald, 6 March 2007.
46. Choueka, 'United Kingdom: Competition in the Television Sector', Lawrence Graham's *SmartLaw* Newsletter, March 2007.
47. 'OFCOM Inquiry Awaits BSkyB', Global Competition Review, 27 February 2007.

future competitive landscape, especially as we approach the digital switchover.'[48] The OFT also found that despite the low shareholding, BSkyB could exert significant influence by appointing a member of ITV's board or becoming an uncooperative shareholder, destabilizing ITV's policy. The OFT was also concerned with a possibility of a reduction in strategic rivalry between BSkyB and ITV.[49]

The Competition Commission examined the impact of the deal on competition as well as considered public interest issues that relate to pluralism and diversity.[50] In December 2007, it reached the conclusion that the acquisition harms competition in the UK TV market. In particular, the Commission concluded that BSkyB could seek to influence ITV's strategy in relation to content production and commissioning, as well as investment by ITV in high-definition television (HDTV) or in other services requiring additional spectrum.[51] The Commission, therefore, recommended that BSkyB lowers its stake in ITV to 7.5% (which means a loss of over GBP 200 million for BSkyB).[52]

However, as far as the media public interest test was concerned, the Commission decided that 'regulatory mechanisms, combined with a strong culture of editorial independence within television news production, were likely to be effective in preventing any prejudice to the independence of ITV news'.[53] Therefore, the Commission stated that it did not expect BSkyB's ability materially to influence ITV to have an adverse effect on the plurality of news relative to the position absent the acquisition. The Commission thus concluded that the acquisition would not materially affect the sufficiency of plurality of persons with control of media enterprises servicing audiences for news.[54]

48. 'OFT Calls for Broadcasting Probe', Global Competition Review, 20 April 2007.
49. McGrath of Berwin Leighton Paisner LLP in London quoted by Global Competition Review in 'The UK Competition Commission to investigate BSkyB's merger with ITV, following a referral from the Trade and Industry Secretary, Alistair Darling', 25 May 2007.
50. 'UK government orders investigation into Sky's 17.9% stake in ITV', http://www.followthemedia.com, 25 May 2007.
51. Competition Commission, 'Acquisition by BSkyB of 17.9 per cent of the shares in ITV plc', Report sent to Secretary of State (BERR), 14 December 2007, para. 18.
52. Competition Commission, 'Acquisition by BSkyB of 17.9 per cent of the shares in ITV plc', Report sent to Secretary of State (BERR); See also Global Competition Review, 'BSkyB to divest ITV stake', 29 January 2008.
53. Competition Commission, 'Acquisition by BSkyB of 17.9 per cent of the shares in ITV plc', Report sent to Secretary of State (BERR), para. 41.
54. Competition Commission, 'Acquisition by BSkyB of 17.9 per cent of the shares in ITV plc', Report sent to Secretary of State (BERR).

In January 2008, the Secretary of State for Business, Enterprise and Regulatory Reform, John Hutton, decided to impose the remedies recommended by the Competition Commission.[55] The decision was appealed to the Competition Appeal Tribunal (CAT), both by BSkyB (on competition grounds) and Virgin Media (arguing for even greater lowering of the BSkyB's stake).[56] The Tribunal did not agree with BSkyB's arguments that the purchase of 17.9% stake in ITV was not anti-competitive, and thus it upheld the divestiture order.[57] However, it agreed with Virgin Media that both the Competition Commission and the Secretary of State had misapplied the media public interest test.[58] Nevertheless, the overall conclusion of the Tribunal was that even if on re-examination the Competition Commission were to find that media pluralism had also been affected, this would not alter the divestiture order. Therefore, CAT did not require the Competition Commission to reconsider the media pluralism issue.[59] The Tribunal also refused to grant BSkyB leave to appeal. In March 2009 leave was, however, granted by the Court of Appeal which found that the issues raised in the case were arguable 'and of some general importance'.[60] In January 2010 the Court of Appeal upheld the Competition Appeal Tribunal's decision that BSkyB must lower its stake in ITV from 17.9% to below 7.5%.[61] BSkyB decided not to appeal to the Supreme Court and appointed Morgan Stanley to sell approximately 10.4% of its stake.[62]

News Corp's latest merger activity in the UK involved its bid to acquire the remaining 61% of BSkyB it does not yet own. As discussed in Chapter 4, in December 2010 the takeover bid was approved by the European Commission. In the Commission's opinion, the proposed transaction does

55. Final decisions by the Secretary of State for Business, Enterprise & Regulatory Reform on British Sky Broadcasting Group's acquisition of a 17.9% shareholding in ITV plc dated 29 January 2008.
56. Global Competition Review, 'BSkyB will Appeal', 21 February 2008; Global Competition Review, 'Virgin Asks for Review of BSkyB Decision', 26 February 2008.
57. Cases 1095/4/8/08 and 1096/4/4/08, *BSkyB Group plc v. (1) The Competition Commission, (2) Secretary of State BERR and Virgin Media v. (1) The Competition Commission, (2) Secretary of State BERR*, 29 September 2008.
58. Cases 1095/4/8/08 and 1096/4/4/08, *BSkyB Group plc v. (1) The Competition Commission, (2) Secretary of State BERR and Virgin Media v. (1) The Competition Commission, (2) Secretary of State BERR*, 29 September 2008, paras 198 and 266; see also Craufurd Smith, R., 'Media Ownership and the Public Interest: The Case of Virgin Media, British Sky Broadcasting and Its ITV Shares', (2009) Journal of Media Law 1, 27.
59. Case 1096/4/4/08, para. 36; See also Craufurd Smith, R., 'Media Ownership and the Public Interest: The Case of Virgin Media, British Sky Broadcasting and Its ITV Shares', 27.
60. 'BSkyB Wins Right to Appeal over the Future of Its ITV Stake', 21 March 2009, http://www.telegraph.co.uk.
61. *British Sky Broadcasting PLC v. The Competition Commission*, [2010] EWCA Civ 2 (21 January 2010).
62. 'BSkyB Agrees to Reduce ITV Stake', Times Online, 8 February 2010.

not raise any concerns under the EU competition rules.[63] However, Article 21(4) of the EU Merger Regulation allows the Member States to take appropriate measures, including prohibiting proposed transactions, to protect legitimate interests, such as the plurality of the media. Accordingly, on 4 November 2010 the UK Secretary of State for Business Innovation and Skills issued a European intervention notice which required the relevant UK authorities to investigate and report by the end of 2010 on whether the proposed transaction is or may be expected to operate against the public interest in sufficiency of plurality of persons with control of media enterprises. On 31 December 2010, in a report presented to the Department for Culture Media and Sport, OFCOM recommended that the acquisition should be referred to the Competition Commission. There were reports that News Corp offered to divest Sky News to alleviate any media pluralism concerns, and it seemed that the transaction was set to be cleared by the UK authorities.[64]

However, in July 2011 the so-called Hackergate scandal shook the UK media and political scene. It was discovered that the *News of the World* newspaper owned by News International – a subsidiary of News Corp – used illegal phone hacking techniques to gain access to private information about various people, including the missing teenager Milly Dowler, who was later found murdered. Police questioned the newspaper's senior editors; five people resigned from their positions following the eruption of the scandal;[65] and News Corp's Rupert and James Murdoch were questioned by the House of Commons' Select Committee for Culture, Media and Sport. On 7 July 2011, News International announced the closure of the *News of the World*, which was published since 1843. The scandal shed a different light on the power exercised by News Corp on the UK media market, and questions started to be asked about the relationship between Rupert Murdoch and the UK government. The leader of the opposition party called for News Corp to drop the bid for BSkyB.[66] On 11 July 2011, News Corp announced that it had withdrawn the offer to divest Sky News which left the Secretary for Culture Media and Sport no other choice than to refer the transaction to the Competition Commission. The move by News Corp was seen as a delaying tactic – the Competition Commission's assessment would have taken

63. European Commission, 'Commission clears News Corp's proposed acquisition of BSkyB under EU merger rules', IP/10/1767, 21 December 2010; Commission decision M5932 News Corp/BSkyB.
64. BBC News, 'BSkyB News Corp Bid: Ofcom Calls for Competition Review', 13 January 2011.
65. They are: Andy Coulson, Prime Minister's director of communications; Rebekah Brooks, News International chief executive; Les Hinton, CEO of Dow Jones & Company; Sir Paul Stephenson, Metropolitan police commissioner; and John Yates, Metropolitan police assistant commissioner.
66. Bloomberg, 'Murdoch Should Drop BSkyB Takeover, U.K. Opposition Leader Miliband Says', 10 July 2011.

approximately six months, by which time the phone hacking scandal would not be the front page news anymore. It would have also taken the deal off the hands of the government which was being called by the opposition to check whether News Corp should own any shares at all in BSkyB.[67] However, just two days after the transaction was referred to the Competition Commission, the pressure surrounding the scandal caused News Corp to drop the bid altogether.[68] In this regard, it is interesting to note the recent developments surrounding this case. At the end of April 2012, a special adviser to Culture Secretary Jeremy Hunt resigned from his post after admitting to passing information to News Corp about the Secretary's line of thinking on the takeover bid.[69] This cemented the suspicions of long-term links between the government and Murdoch's company.

6.1.4. Comments and Conclusions

The liberalization of the UK media ownership rules by the *Communications Act, 2003* has been part of a wider liberalization trend in Europe. Over the past decade most European countries, if not all, have liberalized and relaxed their media ownership legislations, or are in the process of doing so. There has been a noticeable shift in the policy-making principles guiding the television sector. There is a distinct move from safeguarding public interests, to fostering competition, market effectiveness and, above all, to support 'national champions'.[70] Just as the EU fights for 'European champions' and argues for light touch regulation, 'at the national level arguments in favour of a more liberal ownership regime are often expressed in terms of the need to match the competitiveness of European media rivals'.[71]

The European Union claims that its role is to fight for the open market, while it is the Member States' role to guard the public interest. However, in reality national governments tend to follow the EU example and increasingly perceive broadcasting as an industry 'like any other',[72] which should only be subject to competition regulations. In addition, firm faith in the benefits that can be derived through the new media, result in hastened adjustments to

67. The Guardian, 'News Corp's BSkyB Bid Referred by Hunt to Competition Commission', 11 July 2011.
68. Reuters, 'Instant View: News Corp Withdraws Bid for BSkyB:, 13 July 2011.
69. The Guardian, 'Adam Smith: Hunt's Aide Accused of Regular Chats with News Corp', 26 April 2012.
70. Ward, D., 'Media Concentration and Pluralism: Regulation, Realities and the Council of Europe's Standards in the Television Sector', UNIDEM Campus Trieste Seminar, 'The role of media freedom and pluralism in strengthening democracy', Trieste, Italy, 24–28 January 2005.
71. Doyle, G., *Media Ownership*, 94.
72. Humphreys, P., 'Regulating for Media Pluralism: Issues in Ownership and Competition', in Andrew, Crook, Holmes, Kolinsky (eds), *Why Europe? Problems of Culture and Identity, Vol. 2: Media, Film, Gender, Youth and Education* (Macmillan, 2000).

regulatory frameworks, in order to facilitate the progress of new technologies.[73] Thus, the recent prevailing trend in Member States has, been to radically overhaul their media ownership regulations in order to submit the sector to market conditions and facilitate the expansion strategies of big media companies.[74] The previously held beliefs surrounding the inadequacy of competition law to regulate on behalf of media pluralism seem to fade.[75] Nowadays, competition policy is slowly becoming the most prominent, if not the only, instrument across Europe, used to counteract excessive media concentration.[76]

It is worth noting that tendencies towards the de-regulation of media ownership rules, 'can be taken as classic illustrations of the degree of political power exercised by powerful media corporations in capitalist democracies'.[77] National politicians have succumbed to the intense lobbying of commercial media companies who argue that 'domestic ownership rules require extensive liberalization in order to promote the new technologies and to provide indigenous media interests with a fair chance of competing in increasingly internationalized markets'.[78] For instance, in the UK, the British Media Industry Group was established by leading media companies, specifically to pressurize the government into liberalizing media ownership rules.[79] Similar trends have been observed in Germany, and other large European countries. As a result, British and German media concentration laws which were previously one of the strictest in Europe, have, been consistently liberalized since the late 1990s.[80] Further, as the UK Communications Act, 2003 demonstrates, there is not only no chance of reversing the trend, there is also no end to liberalization in sight. Judging by the recent OFCOM review

73. Ward, D., 'Media Concentration and Pluralism: Regulation, Realities and the Council of Europe's Standards in the Television Sector'.
74. Humphreys, P., ''Regulating for Pluralism in the Era of Digital Convergence: The Issues of Media Concentration Control and the Future of Public-Service Broadcasting', the ECPR Joint Research Sessions, Mannheim, 26–31 March 1999, Workshop 24: 'Regulating Communications in the Multimedia Age'.
75. Humphreys, P., 'Regulating for Pluralism in the Era of Digital Convergence: The Issues of Media Concentration Control and the Future of Public-Service Broadcasting'.
76. Ward, D., 'Media Concentration and Pluralism: Regulation, Realities and the Council of Europe's Standards in the Television Sector'.
77. Humphreys, P., 'Power and Control in the New Media', paper presented at the ECPR-Workshop, *New Media and Political Communication*, University of Manchester, 1997; see also Doyle, G., 'Convergence: A Unique Opportunity to Evolve in Previously Unthought-of Ways or a Hoax?', in Marsden, C.T., Verhulst, S. (eds), *Convergence in European Digital TV Regulation* (Blackstone Press Limited, 1999), 144; see also Doyle, G., 'Regulation of Media Ownership and Pluralism in Europe: Can the European Union Take Us Forward?', 451–473.
78. Humphreys, P., 'Power and Control in the New Media'.
79. Humphreys, P., 'Power and Control in the New Media'.
80. Humphreys, P., 'Power and Control in the New Media'.

of media concentration rules, further changes may well be introduced in the future.[81]

Doyle observes that growing media concentration accompanied by the 'persistent march towards complete liberalization of national media ownership policies across Europe in recent years is a profound cause for concern'.[82] It is by no means true that the best way to 'drive innovation' in broadcasting is to reduce regulation.[83] One cannot simply replicate a strategy which worked well in the telecommunications sector in the broadcasting environment. The two industries are entirely different. On the contrary, it is the positive forms of regulation in broadcasting that encourage innovation while deregulation almost inevitably leads to 'relentless competition for the mass audience and a corresponding homogenization of programming'.[84] And although it may be too late to reverse some of the effects of de-regulation, there is still room for manoeuvre if only the EU was willed to act. As Humphreys observes:

> In view of the national trends towards the deregulation of media concentration controls, in the context of the diminishing scope for national regulation in the age of transfrontier media operations and the 'deregulatory competition' that has arisen between nations and regions for media investment, the EU presents itself as an obvious locus of harmonising re-regulation.[85]

However, given the intense national lobbying against any EU involvement in this field the prospects for 'restraining any such deregulatory race appear to be highly unpromising'.[86] The most vociferous defender of the right of Member States to do as they please is, not surprisingly, the United Kingdom – the leader of the liberalization race. During the consultation on the revision of the TVWF Directive, the UK submitted a response to the Issues Paper No 6 on media pluralism,[87] in which it declared that it 'strongly shares the view' that no specific action is necessary at the EU level to protect media pluralism. This statement is not surprising, given the enormous liberalization wave which has recently swept through the UK, which sets a worrying example to follow for the rest of the EU Member States.

---

81. Open Society Institute, 'Television across Europe: Regulation, Policy and Independence', 1652
82. Doyle, G., 'Convergence: A Unique Opportunity to Evolve in Previously Unthought-of Ways or a Hoax?', 179.
83. Petley, J., 'The Re-regulation of Broadcasting, or the Mill Owners' Triumph'.
84. Petley, J., 'The Re-regulation of Broadcasting, or the Mill Owners' Triumph'.
85. Humphreys, P., 'Power and Control in the New Media'.
86. Humphreys, P., 'The EU and Audiovisual Regulation: An Agency for De-regulation'.
87. Government of the United Kingdom, Written contribution to the Public Consultation for the review of the 'Television without Frontiers' Directive, Observations on Issues Paper' 6 Media Pluralism 2005.

The UK's Communications Act, 2003 is the result of the 'mercerization' of society, which is a characteristic not only of the UK, but of most European countries. In summary, and as the Communications Act, 2003 clearly exemplifies, the mercerization of the broadcasting sector entails three processes. First of all, as Petley explains, the public interest requirements of regulation are relaxed or removed, and public sector institutions are increasingly replaced by private companies operating according to market realities. Second, market effectiveness criteria such as cost-saving, commercial revenue generation and customer maximization, become the primary yardsticks against which the performance of all organizations including those still formally in the public sector, are evaluated. Third, audiences and users of communications facilities are primarily addressed as consumers with a sovereign right to have their personal needs met, 'rather than as citizens whose right to full social participation carries with it an obligation to recognize and respect the needs and aspirations of others'.[88]

Doyle and Vick summarize the reforms as 'clearly destined to increase concentrations of ownership in the UK radio and television broadcasting sectors',[89] which in turn will inevitably render the diversity and quality of UK broadcasting dependent on the market forces of demand and supply. Worryingly, none of the Government's policy statements surrounding the Communications Act seems to recognize or even mention the dangers posed by facilitating further concentration in the UK's broadcasting market.[90]

The progressive replacement of citizen with consumer, and culture with competition, is also visible in the establishment of OFCOM in the UK. OFCOM is the result of the merger of several regulators with different regulatory goals therefore its remit is contradictory, to say the least.[91] It is required to promote competition and market effectiveness in the television industry whilst at the same time safeguarding public interest and pluralism. Although both concepts should theoretically enjoy equal status in OFCOM's policy approach, the overall deregulatory function of OFCOM[92] suggests that the notion of citizenship will be gradually downgraded and the interests of consumers will be promoted to first place.[93] Indeed, some authors believe that creation of a single regulator is the reform which above all others 'may

88. Petley, J., 'The Re-regulation of Broadcasting, or the Mill Owners' Triumph'.
89. Doyle, G., Vick, D., 'The Communications Act 2003. A New Regulatory Framework in the UK', 84.
90. Doyle, G., Vick, D., 'The Communications Act 2003. A New Regulatory Framework in the UK', 88.
91. Open Society Institute, 'Television across Europe: Regulation, Policy and Independence', 1653.
92. Petley, J., 'The Re-regulation of Broadcasting, or the Mill Owners' Triumph'.
93. Open Society Institute, 'Television across Europe: Regulation, Policy and Independence', 1657.

ultimately facilitate the triumph of a market-driven media policy'.[94] The overall feeling gathered from the entire reform process is that:

> Concerns about pluralism seem to count for little (beyond the level of rhetoric) while the main impetus guiding actual changes of policy is a desire to accommodate the national and international strategic interests and concerns of major UK commercial media players.[95]

And indeed, in his well publicized speech,[96] James Murdoch, currently the deputy Chief Operating Officer of News Corp, compared regulatory intervention in the media sector in the UK to the creationist views rejecting Darwin's theory of evolution. Murdoch believes that media market should be allowed to operate without intervention, just like the natural world. Government involvement in the sector is, according to Murdoch, 'regressive' and 'out of fashion'. The only road to success is, in his opinion, trusting people, that is *consumers*. He, however, believes that the recent liberalizing reforms in the UK do not go *far enough* and elimination of *any* form of regulatory intervention in the sector should be the next step.

However, the complete retreat from the full commitment to public service values is a threat to the future of television broadcasting in Europe.[97] Obviously, the introduction of the 'public interest test' to the merger review by the Communications Act, 2003 is a welcome step and the first 'public interest' intervention in a media merger in the BSkyB/ITV case was spectacular and may in the end indeed prevent a detrimental media concentration. Nevertheless, there is no denying that the overall effect of the replacement of an automatic intervention based on audience share with the case-by-case regime, will lead to less regulatory involvement in media concentration in the UK.[98]

Moreover, as Craufurd Smith observes, the media public interest criteria themselves, are 'problematic on the number of counts'.[99] Most importantly, she notes that the scope of, and interaction between the external and internal media pluralism criteria in section 58 of the Enterprise Act needs to be clarified. In the *BSkyB/ITV* case, the Secretary of State referred solely to the

94. Doyle, G., Vick, D., 'The Communications Act 2003. A New Regulatory Framework in the UK', 89.
95. Doyle, G., Vick, D., 'The Communications Act 2003. A New Regulatory Framework in the UK', 88.
96. Murdoch, J., 'The Absence of Trust', (2009) Edinburgh International Television Festival, MacTaggart Lecture.
97. Open Society Institute, 'Television across Europe: Regulation, Policy and Independence', 1657.
98. European Institute for the Media, Final report of the study on 'The information of the citizen in the EU: obligations for the media and the Institutions concerning the citizen's right to be fully and objectively informed', 205.
99. Craufurd Smith, R., 'Media Ownership and the Public Interest: The Case of Virgin Media, British Sky Broadcasting and Its ITV Shares', 32.

external pluralism considerations of section 58(2C)(a),[100] and left the internal pluralism considerations of section 58 (2C)(b) out of consideration.[101] Craufurd Smith, therefore, recommends revising section 58 to ensure that consideration of media mergers encompasses both ownership and content pluralism concerns.[102]

In addition, the Secretary of State enjoys a large margin of discretion when examining the media public interest criteria. And when media mergers are concerned, the government's self-interest could be at issue, particularly in the pre-election times.[103] Craufurd Smith, notes that 'it would be preferable for an independent regulatory body, such as OFCOM, to be empowered to finally adjudicate on the media public interest considerations'. However, the limitations of OFCOM in relation to media pluralism concerns, as discussed above, may stand in the way of such a solution working in practice. In summary, however, I agree with Craufurd Smith that 'it is questionable whether the media public interest considerations, as currently specified in the Enterprise Act, are fit for purpose'.[104]

There is hope, however, that the recent phone hacking scandal surrounding News Corp's newspaper *News of the World*, will bring the reversal of the liberalization trend. Before the scandal erupted, it all looked set that the biggest newspaper publisher in the UK (News Corp) and the country's largest pay-TV provider (BSkyB) would become one. As explained by Rupert Murdoch himself during the Parliamentary investigation of the hacking scandal, he visited ten Downing Street on many occasions, but was asked to always use the backdoor.[105] It can only be suspected, but the liberalization of ownership rules must have been discussed at some point during one of such visits. The use of the 'back door' is highly symbolic in this regard. Hopefully, the scandal will be the eye-opener for the UK

100. Section 58(2C)a of the Enterprise Act 2002, as amended by section 375 of the Communications Act 2003, specifies the following as one of the public interest considerations for the purpose of the main merger regime: 'The need, in relation to every different audience in the UK or in a particular area or locality of the UK, for there to be a sufficient plurality of persons with control of the media enterprises serving the audience.'
101. Section 58(2C)b of the Enterprise Act 2002, as amended by section 375 of the Communications Act 2003, specifies the following as one of the public interest considerations for the purpose of the main merger regime: 'The need for the availability throughout the UK of a wide range of broadcasting which (taken as a whole) is both of high quality and calculated to appeal to a wide variety of tastes and interests.'
102. Craufurd Smith, R., 'Media Ownership and the Public Interest: The Case of Virgin Media, British Sky Broadcasting and Its ITV Shares', 34.
103. Craufurd Smith, R., 'Media Ownership and the Public Interest: The Case of Virgin Media, British Sky Broadcasting and Its ITV Shares', 36.
104. Craufurd Smith, R., 'Media Ownership and the Public Interest: The Case of Virgin Media, British Sky Broadcasting and Its ITV Shares', 36.
105. The Independent, 'Rupert Murdoch's No 10 Visits Made Through the Back Door', The Independent, 20 July 2011.

government as to the dangers posed by allowing a giant media conglomerate to take over the country's media market.

6.2. IRELAND

6.2.1. STRUCTURE OF THE TELEVISION MARKET

Until the late 1990s, terrestrial television in Ireland was provided only by the public service broadcaster, RTÉ (*Radio Telefís Éireann*). RTÉ, which has a total audience share of over 33%,[106] operates two channels: RTÉ 1 and RTÉ 2. It also cooperates with the Irish language channel TG4 (*Teilifís na Gaeilge*). Ireland has, therefore, three national television channels that receive public funding through an annual license fee payable by those in possession of a television receiver.[107] Commercial broadcasting in Ireland was introduced by the *Radio and Television Act, 1988* which provided for a system of licensing.[108] The first commercial television station in Ireland, was launched in 1998 under the name TV3. It is operated by the TV3 group owned by Tullamore Beta Limited, a subsidiary of a British private equity fund Doughty Hanson & Co, and it enjoys audience share of around 13%.[109]

It is also important to note that Ireland's television landscape is influenced by historical and geographical relations with the United Kingdom.[110] British terrestrial television channels are available to, approximately, 70% of the population, mainly through cable services.[111]

While BSkyB, through Sky Digital, remains the sole provider of digital satellite television services in Ireland,[112] the Irish cable market was recently fundamentally restructured. Ireland used to have two main cable operators: NTL (Éire) and Chorus Communications. In 2004, Chorus was fully taken

106. The most recent audience share data is for 2011 from AC Nielsen Media Research, see http://www.medialive2.com/.
107. European Federation of Journalists, 'Media Power in Europe: The Big Picture of Ownership', 2005, 78.
108. McGonagle, M., *Media Law*; for a full, updated and extended history of the Irish media market see Carolan, E., O'Neill, A., *Media Law in Ireland* (Bloomsbury Professional, 2010).
109. The most recent audience share data is for 2011 from AC Nielsen Media Research, see http://www.medialive2.com/.
110. European Federation of Journalists, 'Media Power in Europe: The Big Picture of Ownership', 78.
111. European Federation of Journalists, 'Media Power in Europe: The Big Picture of Ownership', 79.
112. European Federation of Journalists, 'Media Power in Europe: The Big Picture of Ownership', 79.

over by Liberty Media's affiliate, UGC Europe (now called Liberty Global Europe).

Finally, although this book concentrates mainly on the television sector, it is worth mentioning the Irish press and radio markets here as they are particularly affected by excessive media concentration. The top selling daily newspapers and the two top selling Sunday papers are owned by one company, Independent News and Media (Ireland) Ltd. The company also publishes fourteen local newspapers in counties Cork, Kerry, Dublin, Louth, Wexford and Wicklow.[113] In addition, the Independent News and Media Group has interests across newspaper and magazine publishing, digital media and outdoor advertising in the UK, France, Portugal, South Africa, Australia, and New Zealand.[114] Independent News and Media is dominant in both the daily and Sunday newspaper market segments in Ireland, where it has a 48% and 46% market share respectively. Nevertheless, the Competition Authority concluded that the Irish newspaper industry has sufficient editorial diversity and, thus, media pluralism is not threatened.[115]

However, while it may be true that there is a large degree of editorial diversity, such dominance in any media market is always a threat to media pluralism. There is also a problem with the cross-ownership of newspapers and radio stations. In July 2007, Denis O'Brien's company Communicorp, which owns two Dublin radio stations (98FM and Spin FM), one national radio station (News talk) and a 26% stake in Independent News and Media, acquired national radio station Today FM and Dublin station FM104 from Emap.[116] This acquisition would give Communicorp control over almost 25% of all commercial radio licenses in Ireland and over 53% audience share in Dublin, and this undoubtedly would equate to dominance in this area. In December 2007, the Competition Authority ordered Communicorp to divest FM104.[117] The competition concerns centred on both stations' similar programming format which made them the closest competitors in the Dublin area. At the end of 2007, Communicorp sold FM104 to UTV.[118] However, the cross-ownership issue with Independent News and Media was dismissed by

113. See the company's website at http://www.inmplc.com; See also European Institute for the Media, Final report of the study on 'The information of the citizen in the EU: obligations for the media and the Institutions concerning the citizen's right to be fully and objectively informed', 112.

114. European Institute for the Media, Final report of the study on 'The information of the citizen in the EU: obligations for the media and the Institutions concerning the citizen's right to be fully and objectively informed', 112.

115. European Institute for the Media, Final report of the study on 'The information of the citizen in the EU: obligations for the media and the Institutions concerning the citizen's right to be fully and objectively informed', 112.

116. Shaw, 'O'Brien Bidding to Rule the Airwaves', The Irish Times, 24 July 2007.

117. The Competition Authority, Determination of Merger Notification M/07/040, *Communicorp/SRH*, 7 December 2007.

118. The Competition Authority, Determination of Merger Notification M/07/069, *UTV/FM104*, 17 January 2008.

the Competition Authority which stated that radio and press advertising are two separate markets.

In July 2008, the Broadcasting Commission of Ireland (BCI) investigated the cross-ownership concern between Communicorp and Independent News and Media, but concluded that the interests of Communicorp in Independent News and Media were not substantial.[119] This seemed to have changed in March 2009 when three of O'Brien's long-term associates were appointed to the board of Independent News and Media.[120] In May 2009, the BCI started a review of the new development, and stated promisingly, that the agreement giving Communicorp a number of seats in Independent News and Media provided O'Brien with the ability to influence the strategic direction of the publishing company. In addition, in the Commission's view at the beginning of the investigation, the move gave Communicorp, Independent News' second-largest shareholder, a 'substantial interest' in the newspaper group and raised issues about O'Brien's control of other media in Ireland. Unfortunately, in July 2009, the BCI concluded again that Communicorp does not control an 'undue' share of the country's media market. In April 2012, Gavin O'Reilly, stepped down as Chief Executive of Independent News and Media, the move which ended thirty-nine years of direct control by his family of Ireland's largest media group.[121] His decision followed weeks of speculation in the Irish press that O'Brien would seek to have O'Reilly removed at the annual meeting in June. Reacting to the event, the Irish Prime Minister Enda Kenny commented that 'the Government would consider 'cross-ownership' of the media after an escalation in the battle for control of INM'.[122]

6.2.2. Media Pluralism Legislation

The responsibility for regulating the broadcasting sector in Ireland lies with several different authorities. The Broadcasting Authority of Ireland (BAI) issues licenses and deals with media concentration and pluralism aspects. The Department of Communications, Energy and Natural Resources develops a policy and legislative framework for broadcasting in Ireland and the Department of Enterprise, Trade and Employment takes part in the approval of media mergers from a media pluralism perspective, while the Competition Authority deals with competition issues.[123]

119. Reuters, 'Irish Regulator Reviews O'Brien's Media Empire', 12 May 2009.
120. Reuters, 'Irish Regulator Clears O'Brien Media Empire', 28 July 2009.
121. 'O'Reilly Resigns as IN&M Head', The Irish Times, 19 April 2012.
122. 'O'Reilly Resigns as IN&M Head', The Irish Times, 19 April 2012.
123. The Competition Authority was established by the *Competition Act, 1991* and since the *Competition Act, 2002* it has the power to examine mergers in the media industry.

Before the Broadcasting Act, 2009[124] was adopted, BAI was known as the Broadcasting Commission of Ireland (BCI). BCI replaced the Independent Radio and Television Commission (IRTC), established by the Radio and Television Act 1988 to license and oversee the operation of independent radio and television broadcasting in Ireland.[125] The Broadcasting Act 2001 changed the IRTC's name to the Broadcasting Commission of Ireland.[126]

Broadcasting regulation in Ireland has recently undergone a significant change. In December 2002, the Minister for Communications announced that he intended to create a new structure for regulation in this area, coupled with the creation of a new Broadcasting Authority of Ireland (incorporating the BCI), which would regulate both public and commercial media. The Bill was signed into law on 12 July 2009; however, the provisions relating to the establishment of the Broadcasting Authority of Ireland did not come into force until a Statutory Instrument was adopted on 30 September 2009.

The new Broadcasting Act, 2009 repealed most of the previous legislation in the area.[127] The key features of the reform are, first and foremost, the establishment of a single content regulator for all commercial, community and public service broadcasters in Ireland, to be known as the Broadcasting Authority of Ireland (BAI). The BAI encompasses the existing regulatory functions of the Broadcasting Commission of Ireland, the Broadcasting Complaints Commission and the RTÉ Authority. BAI is not, however, a fully integrated broadcasting and communications regulator similar to OFCOM because the communications regulator (ComReg)[128] and the Competition Authority remain separate. The BAI was established on 1 October 2009 and comprises nine members. Five members, were appointed by the Government a further four were appointed following the nomination of the Joint Oireachtas Committee for Communications, Energy and Natural Resources.

The Act provides for a wider right of reply mechanism than before. Further, the public service remit of RTÉ and TG4 has been extended to include: (i) the broadcasting of public service programming to Irish communities outside the island of Ireland; (ii) the establishment and maintenance of non-broadcast non-linear audio-visual media services, insofar as it is reasonably practicable, which shall have the character of a public broadcasting service; and (iii) the establishment, maintenance and operation of one or

---

124. *Broadcasting Act, 2009* (No. 18 of 2009).
125. *Radio and Television Act, 1988*, (No. 20 of 1988); see also Institute of European Media Law (EMR) *Media Market Definitions – Comparative Legal Analysis. Report for the European Commission*, Chapter 7: Ireland; July/October 2003.
126. *Broadcasting Act, 2001* (No. 4 of 2001), section 10(1).
127. In particular, *Radio and Television Act, 1988* (No. 20 of 1988) and *Broadcasting Act, 2001* (No. 4 of 2001).
128. See *Communications Regulation Act, 2002* (No. 20 of 2002), which established the Commission for Communications Regulation (ComReg), sections 6–38.

more national multiplexes).[129] Finally, the Act provides for the establishment of the two public broadcasters' as limited companies.[130]

The Broadcasting Act, 2009 defines broadcaster very broadly as:

> a person who supplies a compilation of programme material for the purpose of its being transmitted or relayed as a broadcasting service (whether that person transmits or relays that material as such a service or not).[131]

A broadcasting service is defined as:

> a service which comprises a compilation of programme material of any description and which is transmitted, relayed or distributed by means of an electronic communications network, directly or indirectly for simultaneous or near simultaneous reception by the general public, whether that material is actually received or not, and where the programmes are provided in a pre-scheduled and linear order.[132]

However, excluded from the definition of a broadcasting service are services provided in a non-linear manner where each user of the service chooses a programme from a catalogue of programmes (such as video on demand), and audio and audiovisual services provided by way of the internet.

With regard to media concentration, section 25 of the Act generally requires that in performing their functions, BAI and its committees (in particular the Contracts Award Committee responsible for issuing broadcasting licenses), shall endeavour to ensure the provision of open and pluralistic broadcasting services, and that the number and categories of broadcasting services in Ireland best serve the needs of the people, bearing in mind their languages and traditions and their religious, ethical and cultural diversity. Importantly, the Act specifies that in fulfilling the above general duties BAI shall 'promote diversity in control of the more influential commercial and community broadcasting services'.[133]

In addition section 66 of the Act requires BAI to consider if awarding a license to a particular person or a company could operate against the public interest. In particular, the BAI must have regard to the desirability of allowing any person, or group of persons, to have control of, or substantial interests in, an *undue amount* of the communications media in the area;[134] and the desirability of having a diversity of services in the area catering for a wide range of tastes including those of minority interests.[135]

129. *Broadcasting Act, 2009*, section 103.
130. *Broadcasting Act*, 2009, section 79.
131. *Broadcasting Act, 2009*, section 2.
132. *Broadcasting Act, 2009*, section 2.
133. *Broadcasting Act, 2009*, section 25(2)(c).
134. *Broadcasting Act, 2009*, section 66(2)(i), emphasis added.
135. *Broadcasting Act, 2009*, section 66(2)(f).

Under the terms of their contract with the BAI, all radio and television service providers are obliged to notify the BAI, and obtain its consent for changes to their ownership and control structures. Substantial changes are closely examined by the Authority under its Ownership and Control Policy.[136] Under this policy, the BAI (then known as BCI) also defined the 'undue amount of communications media' mentioned previously in section 38(6) of the Broadcasting Act, 2001 (now section 66(2) of the Broadcasting Act, 2009). In the 2012 document 'Ownership and Control Policy',[137] the BAI specified that in order to counteract excessive concentration in the media sector, no license will be given to a company which holds 25% of the total number of broadcasting services licensed in Ireland. Up to 15% of the total number of licenses is deemed 'acceptable' with up to a further 10% ownership of the total number requiring 'more careful consideration by the Authority'. There are no set-percentages for permissible cross-media ownership restrictions in Ireland, although BAI must have regard to 'the desirability of allowing any person … to have control of … an *undue amount* of the communications media in the area specified'. The lack of set-percentages for permissible cross-media ownership has allowed the development of some major players, such as O'Brien's Communicorp, which has interests in the radio and publishing sectors in Ireland. Subsequent moves by Communicorp to grow even further have been consistently accepted by the BAI.

The unique features of the media sector and the concentration thereof have also been recognized by the Irish Competition Act, 2002,[138] which provides for a specific procedure for the review of media mergers. Before the Competition Act, 2002, Irish competition law was regulated by four statutes: (i) the Mergers, Take-overs and Monopolies (Control) Acts, 1978–1996; (ii) the Restrictive Practices (Amendment) Act, 1987; (iii) the Competition Act, 1991; and (iv) the Competition (Amendment) Act, 1996. The Competition Act, 2002 amalgamated the rules into one statute, and introduced significant changes into Irish competition law in order to put it in line with the reforms brought about by the modernization of EC competition law in 2004.[139] The Act moved the majority of competence in competition law enforcement from the Minister for Enterprise, Trade and Employment to the Competition Authority. The Minister retains his/her role in proposing legislation and, most importantly, in evaluating media mergers.

136. See http://www.bai.ie.
137. Broadcasting Authority of Ireland, 'Ownership and Control Policy', 2012.
138. *Competition Act, 2002* (No. 14 of 2002).
139. For instance, the notification regime for agreements between competitors has been abolished.

Generally, mergers have to be notified to the Competition Authority only after certain turnover thresholds are exceeded.[140] However, section 18(5) of the Competition Act provides that the Minister for Enterprise, Trade and Employment can by Order exclude the thresholds from certain classes of mergers or acquisitions, where he/she is of opinion that the exigencies of the common good so warrant. By virtue of the Competition Act, 2002 (section 18(5)) Order 2002,[141] the Minister designated media mergers as such a class of mergers. Pursuant to section 23(10) of the Competition Act, a media merger means a merger or acquisition in which two or more of the undertakings involved carry on a *media business* in Ireland. Media business is defined by the Competition Act as: (i) a business of the publication of newspapers or periodicals consisting substantially of news and comment on current affairs; (ii) a business of providing a broadcasting service;[142] or (iii) a business of providing a broadcasting services platform. Until recently, a notification to the Authority was mandatory where just *one* undertaking involved in a merger carried on a 'media business' in the Republic of Ireland. This stringent approach was putting too much of an administrative burden on companies which had to notify even if there was *no impact* on competition in Ireland. Therefore, on 1 May 2007 the Competition Act, 2002 (section 18(5) and (6)) Order 2007[143] refined the class of media mergers which must be notified to the Competition Authority and the Minister. From that date, a merger must be notified where *two* or more undertakings involved carry on a media business in the Republic of Ireland or where one or more carries on a media business in the Republic of Ireland and one or more of the others carry on a media business elsewhere.

All media mergers must be notified to the Competition Authority, irrespective of the turnover of the merging companies.[144] Pursuant to section

140. Section 18(1) of the Competition Act 2002 provides that each of the undertakings involved is obliged to notify the Competition Authority of the merger or acquisition if in the most recent financial year: (i) the world-wide turnover of each of two or more of the undertakings involved in the merger or acquisition is not less than EUR 40,000,000; ii) each of two or more of the undertakings involved in the merger or acquisition carries on business in any part of the island of Ireland; and (iii) the turnover in the State of any one of the undertakings involved in the merger or acquisition is not less than EUR 40,000,000.
141. *Competition Act, 2002 (section 18(5)) Order 2002*, SI 622 of 2002.
142. Broadcasting service is defined by section 23(10), as 'a service which comprises a compilation of programme material of any description and which is transmitted or relayed by means of wireless telegraphy, a cable system or a multipoint microwave distribution system, a satellite device or any other transmission system, directly or indirectly for reception by the general public, whether that material is actually received or not …, but does not include any such service (whether involving audio-visual material or audio material) that is provided by means of the system commonly known as the Internet'.
143. *Competition Act, 2002 (section 18 (5) and (6)) Order 2007*, SI 122 of 2007.
144. McCarthy, A., Power, V., *Irish Competition Law. The Competition Act, 2002* (Lexis Nexis Butterworths, 2003), 309.

23 of the Competition Act, 2002, within five days of receiving a notification in relation to a media merger, the Competition Authority must forward a copy of the notification to the Minister of Enterprise, Trade and Employment. While the substantive test applied by the Competition Authority in merger analysis is whether the merger would substantially lessen competition in markets for goods and services in Ireland,[145] the Minister evaluates the merger for potential media pluralism issues. The Minister has quite wide ranging powers in this respect. If the Authority decides to approve the merger in the first phase, the Minister may, notwithstanding that determination, within ten days after the date on which that determination is made, order the Authority to open a second phase investigation; that is, to carry out a full investigation. If following the full investigation, the Authority decides to approve the merger or approve it subject to conditions, the Minister may still, within thirty days after the date of the Authority's decision, and notwithstanding that decision, decide that the merger may not be approved. The Minister's decision takes precedence. An appeal may be made to the High Court against the decision prohibiting or approving a merger.

The Competition Act makes it clear that in making his/her decision, the Minister may not have regard to competition criteria and may only consider the relevant public interest, or media pluralism criteria. According to section 23(10) of the Act, the 'relevant criteria' which the Minister must take into account when evaluating a media merger include: (i) the strength and competitiveness of media businesses in Ireland; (ii) the extent to which ownership or control of media businesses in Ireland is spread amongst individuals and other undertakings; (iii) the extent to which the diversity of views prevalent in Irish society is reflected through the activities of the various media businesses; and (iv) the share in the market in Ireland of 'media business' held by any of the undertakings involved in the media merger. There is a significant amount of uncertainty associated with the above criteria. For instance, the Minister may in theory only address the public interest criteria. However, some of the factors mentioned in section 23(10) that he/she is entitled to take into account, resemble the ones taken into account when assessing competition related concerns e.g., 'competitiveness' of media businesses in Ireland mentioned in criterion (i) or 'the share in the market' in criterion (iv).[146]

In March 2008, possibly in order to clarify the existing uncertainties, the Minister for Enterprise, Trade and Employment established the Advisory Group on Media Mergers.[147] The Group's remit was to 'look at the existing

145. Section 20(1)(c) of the *Competition Act, 2002.*
146. McCarthy, A., Power, V., *Irish Competition Law. The Competition Act, 2002*, 319–320.
147. 'Minister Martin announces the establishment of an Advisory Group on media mergers', Department of Enterprise, Trade and Employment, Press Release, 30 March 2008.

criteria and arrangements for considering and assessing how a proposed merger might affect the diversity of views and the concentration of ownership within and across media businesses' and to make recommendations as appropriate.[148] In January 2009, the Minister published the Report of the Group.[149] The main recommendation of the report is that the Competition Act should be amended to incorporate a statutory test to be applied by the Minister in the discharge of his/her function in relation to media mergers, and there should also be a statutory definition of media plurality. The statutory test suggested by the Advisory Group is 'whether the result of the media merger is likely to be contrary to the public interest in protecting plurality in media business in the State'.[150] The recommended definition of 'media plurality' seems to recognize the internal/external pluralism approach to defining the issue, as it states that 'plurality of the media includes both diversity of ownership and diversity of content'.[151] The Report goes on to suggest the definition of diversity of ownership as:

> the spread of ownership and control of media businesses in the State amongst individuals and other undertakings linked to the market share of those media businesses as measured by listenership, readership or other appropriate methods

and the diversity of content as

> the extent to which the broad diversity of views and cultural interests prevalent in Irish society is reflected through the activities of media businesses in the State, including their editorial ethos, content and sources. "Views" includes but is not limited to news and current affairs.[152]

In addition, the Report recommends that (i) there should be a separate system of notification of media mergers to the Minister for clearance; (ii) the Minister for Enterprise, Trade and Employment should continue to be responsible for considering media mergers, but there should be a statutory duty to consult the Minister for Communications, Energy and Natural Resources; (iii) the Minister should publish Guidelines to assist undertakings involved in media mergers in knowing how the Minister would in general apply the relevant criteria; (iv) in the event of the Minister deciding to

148. 'Minister Martin announces the establishment of an Advisory Group on media mergers'.
149. 'Tánaiste publishes Report of the Advisory Group on Media Mergers', Department of Enterprise, Trade and Employment, Press Release, 2 January 2009.
150. Advisory Group on Media Mergers, Report to the Tánaiste and Minister for Enterprise, Trade and Employment, Mary Coughlan T.D., June 2008, para. 6.53.
151. Advisory Group on Media Mergers, Report to the Tánaiste and Minister for Enterprise, Trade and Employment, Mary Coughlan T.D., June 2008, para. 6.55.
152. Advisory Group on Media Mergers, Report to the Tánaiste and Minister for Enterprise, Trade and Employment, Mary Coughlan T.D., June 2008, para. 6.55.

proceed to a detailed investigation of a proposed merger (other than a broadcaster to broadcaster merger), a three to five person Consultative Panel should be established on a statutory basis to provide advice to the Minister on the media merger; (v) the definition of 'media business' should be amended to include publication of newspapers and periodicals over the Internet and broadcast of certain audiovisual material over the Internet. Table 6.2 and 6.3 below illustrate the media merger review procedure in Ireland as provided by section 23 of the *Competition Act, 2002* including the changes suggested by the Report of the Advisory Group on Media Mergers.

Following publication of the Report in 2009, the Minister Mary Coughlan said that legislation will be brought forward to reform aspects of competition law and implement the merger of the National Consumer Agency and the Competition Authority.[153] In June 2011, answering the parliamentary questions asked by Deputy Eamon O'Cúiv, the Minister for Jobs, Enterprise and Innovation, Richard Bruton, confirmed that he will be seeking Government approval shortly for legislation arising from the review carried out by the Advisory Group on Media Mergers.[154] In September 2011, the Minister for Communications, Pat Rabbitte announced that the government is working on a legislation to put the Group's recommendations into practice and it is expected that the draft will be published in 2012.[155]. The rules on media mergers will form part of the new and complex consumer and competition Bill which is due to be published in the end of 2012. In May 2012, Minister Rabbitte attempted to fast-track the media merger legislation by extracting the sections dealing with media mergers from the larger Bill and having a separate Bill on media mergers adopted before the summer recess of the Irish Parliament. Unfortunately, this effort proved unsuccessful.[156]

153. 'Tánaiste publishes Report of the Advisory Group on Media Mergers', Department of Enterprise, Trade and Employment, Press Release, 2 January 2009.
154. See Written Answers, 252–257, http://debates.oireachtas.ie/dail/2011/06/15/00184.asp #N4.
155. 'Media Mergers Plan Outlined', The Irish Times, 19 September 2011.
156. 'Rabbitte Bid to Fast-Track Media Mergers Bill Fails', The Irish Times, 17 May 2012.

Table 6.2 Current Media Merger Review Procedure in Ireland, section 23 Competition Act, 2002. [157]

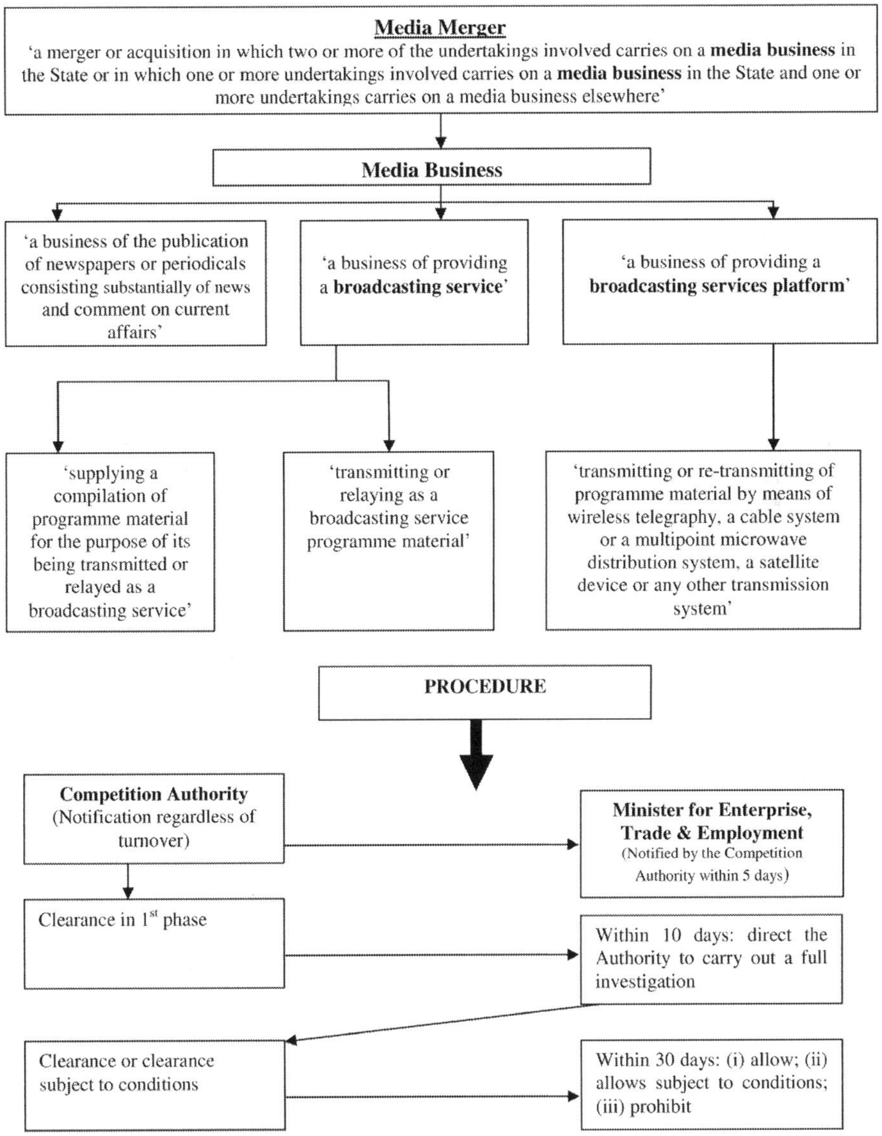

157. Taking into account the *Competition Act 2002 (section 18(5) and (6)) Order 2007*, SI No. 122 of 2007.

Table 6.3 Media Merger Review Procedure in Ireland Showing the Main Changes Recommended by the Advisory Group on Media Mergers (Shaded In Grey).

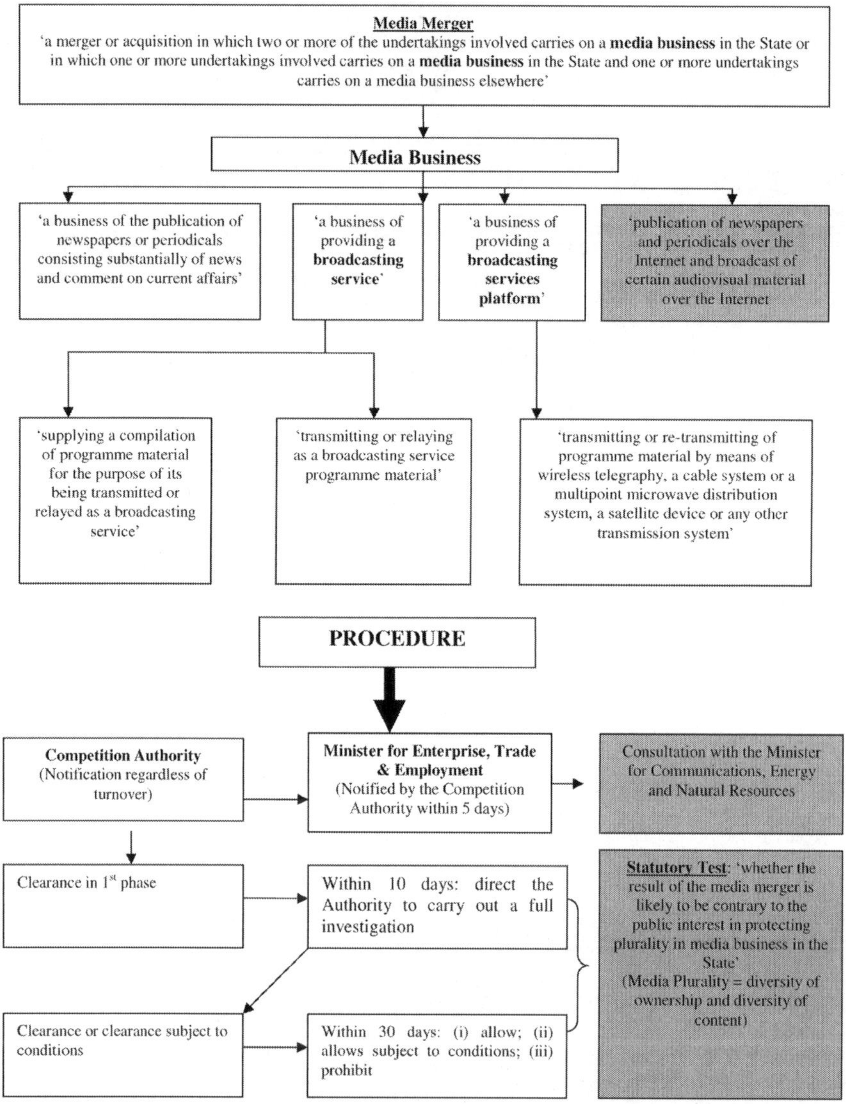

6.2.3. The Rules In Practice: Chorus/NTL Merger

In 2004, the only two cable TV providers, which operated in Ireland at the time, merged. Chorus was fully taken over by Liberty Media's affiliate, UGC Europe. In 2005, NTL announced the sale of its Irish business to Liberty Global *via* financial services firm Morgan Stanley. Morgan Stanley held the stake on Liberty Global's behalf until all regulatory clearances have been achieved. At the time of the notification of the merger to the Competition Authority,[158] Liberty Media had a 16% stake in News Corporation – a parent company of BSkyB. The Competition Authority investigated the NTL/ Chorus merger and noticed that there was a link between News Corporation and Liberty Media. The Authority was concerned that this relationship could result in limiting competition between the combined NTL/Chorus cable network and BSkyB's satellite network. On 4 November 2005, the Competition Authority cleared the merger, subject to nineteen conditions, including the appointment of an independent Director to the board of UPC Ireland and restrictions on the influence of John Malone, Chairman of Liberty Global, in the running of the Irish business.[159] However, these conditions no longer apply since the Authority specified that they should remain in place only for as long as Liberty Media had more than 5% of the voting rights in News Corporation. In December 2006, John Malone and Rupert Murdoch reached a share-swap agreement. News Corporation agreed to exchange its 38.4% stake in DirecTV Group and three regional sports networks for Liberty Media's 16.3% stake in News Corporation.

The merger was also approved by the Minister for Enterprise, Trade & Employment, Micheál Martin in early December 2005, and the deal closed on 12 December 2005. The combined company, named UPC Ireland, is now the parent company of NTL Ireland and Chorus. It provides television, broadband internet and telephone services. According to Liberty Global's second quarter 2009 financial results, the total number of video subscribers in Ireland was 518,000.[160]

158. Pursuant to section 18 of the *Competition Act, 2002*, mergers and acquisitions have to be notified to the Competition Authority if parties to the merger or acquisition achieve turnovers exceeding certain thresholds.
159. Competition Authority assessment M/05/024 – *UGC (Chorus)/NTL*, 4 November 2005, http://www.tca.ie.
160. Liberty Media, Report on the Second Quarter 2009 results.

6.2.4. Comments and Conclusions

There have been over sixty media mergers notified to the Irish Competition Authority since the entry into force of the *Competition Act, 2002*. All have been cleared without the Minister raising any media pluralism concerns.[161] This may have unforeseen long term consequences. If successive Ministers do not intervene, then deals in the media market will be determined solely on competition grounds and will not involve an assessment of public interest issues. However, some may think that the Irish media market, despite some pluralism concerns mainly involving press market, is generally immune from global media concentration trends. As Emmet Oliver wrote in 2005 in The Irish Times:

> When truly global media players like Rupert Murdoch, Ted Turner and Barry Diller sit down for monthly board meetings in New York, London or Los Angeles it is unlikely the Irish media market is listed near the top of the agenda. In other words, most international media tycoons do not spend their days thinking up Machiavellian ways to buy up Irish media assets.[162]

Nevertheless, as Oliver has himself observed, there are subtle changes taking place in the Irish media market, and media pluralism concerns do not centre around Independent News and Media anymore, but apply to other companies as well. Several large British media groups, such as Emap, Johnston Press, Daily Mail and General Trust, not to mention BSkyB and News International or Liberty Global, have entered the Irish market. The 2005 merger between NTL and Chorus, (owned by Liberty Global), is a significant example. After the merger, Ireland was only left with two pay-TV platforms – UPC (cable) and BSkyB (satellite), and as discussed above, there have been substantial links between the two. And yet, this merger did not attract the Minister's intervention. General Irish competition rules on anti-competitive arrangements (section 4 of the Competition Act, 2002) and abuse of a dominant position (section 5 of the Competition Act, 2002) can play only a limited role in alleviating media pluralism concerns in Ireland for the same reasons as Articles 101 and 102 TFEU play a limited role in alleviating media pluralism concerns at the EU level. Prevention of anti-competitive agreements and concerted practices has only an indirect impact on pluralism and diversity of media, and it is already too late if Article 4 has to be used to punish an abuse of dominant position by a media undertaking. Media companies should be prevented from achieving dominant positions, before they can abuse them. The changes to the Irish media market, together with the limited specific media concentration rules, the inadequacy of general competition law to address media pluralism issues and the lack of interest on the part of the

161. See The Competition Authority, Merger Notifications, http://www.tca.ie.
162. Oliver, E., 'Small Media Players Ensure Competition', The Irish Times, 5 September 2005.

subsequent Ministers responsible for evaluating public interest concerns in media mergers, poses a challenge to plurality and diversity in the media in Ireland.[163]

This seems to have been confirmed during a conference entitled 'Media Diversity: Why does it matter?' held in Dublin in February 2012 and organized by an Irish MEP Nessa Childers. In preparation for the conference, Ms Childers commissioned a survey of Irish journalists on media ownership and diversity. The survey, carried out in conjunction with the National Union of Journalists, revealed that 77% of Irish journalists believe that media diversity is at risk in Ireland due to trends in media ownership.[164]

6.3. ITALY

6.3.1. Structure of the Television Market

The Italian media sector is probably one of the most concentrated, contradictory and complex in all of Europe.[165] Although there are fourteen free-to-air national channels and ten to fifteen regional and local channels, the Italian television market is dominated by two players – public service broadcaster, RAI and commercial, Mediaset. Each of them provides three national terrestrial channels – RAI 1, RAI 2 and RAI 3 operated by RAI and CANALE 5, RETEQUATTRO and ITALIA 1 operated by Mediaset. RAI is a public-owned company, financed from both license fees and advertising. It is governed by a board that is appointed by the Chamber of Deputies and the Senate.[166] A controlling 38.6% stake in Mediaset belongs to Fininvest, the company owned by the Italian Prime Minister, Silvio Berlusconi and members of his family. No other individual or company owns more than 2.3% of Mediaset.[167] In addition to broadcasting, Mediaset is active in advertising (Publitalia'80), publishing (Mondadori) and record production. It also controls the Spanish television broadcaster Telecinco and its advertising company Publiespaña. Due to the overwhelming media interests held by Berlusconi, as well as the influence he has had on RAI in his role as Prime

163. Oliver, E., 'Small Media Players Ensure Competition'.
164. 2012 Survey of Irish journalists on media ownership and diversity, http://www.nessachilders.ie.
165. Ward, D., Fueg, O.C., D'Armo, A., 'A Mapping Study of Media Concentration and Ownership in Ten European Countries', 93.
166. European Federation of Journalists, 'Media power in Europe: the big picture of ownership', 84.
167. European Institute for the Media, Final report of the study on 'The information of the citizen in the EU: obligations for the media and the Institutions concerning the citizen's right to be fully and objectively informed', 117.

Minister, he's been nicknamed 'Sua Emittenza'– 'Mr Broadcasting.'[168] There have been attempts to undo the effects of this unprecedented blend of political and media power and the legislative chaos in the media sector, but they proved unsuccessful.

The six channels operated by RAI and Mediaset are complemented by some other minor national networks, such as LA 7 and MTV Italia which is owned by Telecom Italia. Sport Italia (Europa TV) and DFREE (Prima TV) which is owned by Holland Coordinator – TF1. HSE (Home Shopping Europe) which is owned by Fondo Convergenza, Rete A, Elefante TeleMarket (Telemarket) and Rete Capri (TBS).[169] However, the six national channels run by RAI and Mediaset account for almost 90% of audience share, about 85% of net advertising revenues and almost 75% of all the revenues collected in the sector.[170] In addition, the situation is not alleviated by the large number of local television outlets. Despite an estimated 650 local television stations, the development of local television has also been constrained by the duopoly of RAI and Mediaset, in terms of both audience and revenue share.[171]

Multi-channel television is dominated by satellite in Italy. Until 2003, there were two competing pay digital platforms, Stream and Telepiù. Their merger was conditionally approved by the European Commission and in July 2003 an integrated platform, Sky Italia, was launched. It is 80% owned by News Corporation with Telecom Italia having a 19.9% share.

6.3.2. Media Concentration Regulation

As noted by Haraszti in his report on media pluralism prepared for the Council's of Europe Commissioner for Human Rights, although the 'freedom of expression and press freedoms are in a healthy state in Italy, … the television broadcasting market is regularly referred to as the "Italian anomaly"'.[172] Italian example shows that monopolization of the broadcasting

168. European Federation of Journalists, 'Media power in Europe: the big picture of ownership', 82.
169. European Commission for Democracy through Law, 'Opinion on the compatibility of the Laws 'Gasparri and "Frattini" of Italy with the Council of Europe standards in the field of freedom of expression and pluralism of the media' (Opinion No. 309/2004), 13 June 2005, Doc. No. CDL-AD(2005)017, 5.
170. Ward, D., Fueg, O.C., D'Armo, A., 'A Mapping Study of Media Concentration and Ownership in Ten European Countries', 98; European Institute for the Media, Final report of the study on 'The information of the citizen in the EU: obligations for the media and the Institutions concerning the citizen's right to be fully and objectively informed', 117.
171. Ward, D., Fueg, O.C., D'Armo, A., 'A Mapping Study of Media Concentration and Ownership in Ten European Countries', 98.
172. Haraszti, M., 'Media Pluralism and Human Rights'.

sector poses 'acute danger even in older democracies'.[173] Padovani adds that, 'the history of media regulation in Italy serves as an important lesson to learn about the consequences of poor legislation in this sector'.[174]

In 1997, Italy adopted the Broadcasting Law No. 249/97, known as the 'Maccanico Law.' It reformed the audiovisual and telecommunications system and took into account media pluralism.[175] Under its provisions, a single company could not own more than 20% of television or radio networks and digital television or radio programmes. Furthermore, national broadcasters were precluded from achieving more than 30% of advertising revenue in the relevant sector (radio or television). Those who exceeded the thresholds had to move their channels to cable or satellite. The Law also established the *Autorità per le garanzie nelle comunicazioni* (AGCOM) – a regulatory authority for the communications sector. The two main functions of AGCOM are to ensure fair competition in the industry through the application of antitrust rules in the field of communications, and to protect the fundamental rights of all citizens by safeguarding the principles of universal service, quality and distribution of services and products, political and social and economic pluralism in broadcasting.[176]

However, the key ownership rules enshrined in the Maccanico Law have not been successfully enforced. This has mainly been due to the transitional provisions and their subsequent prolongation, which allowed both Mediaset and RAI to exceed the prescribed thresholds. This meant impossibility of a new entry to the market. For instance, in 1999 a company called Centro Europa 7 was granted rights for terrestrial television broadcasting in Italy. However, the national allocation plan for radio frequencies adopted on 30 October 1998 has not been implemented. Therefore, although it had rights according to Maccanico law, Centro Europa 7 has never been in a position to broadcast for lack of radio frequencies. In January 2008, answering the Italian court's request for a preliminary ruling, the European Court of Justice decided that by refusing to release broadcasting frequencies and continually extending transitional periods, Italy was in breach of Article 49 of the EC Treaty and the E-Communications framework.[177]

The situation of unending prolongation of transitional periods for RAI and Mediaset was also severely criticized at national level by the Italian

173. Haraszti, M., 'Media Pluralism and Human Rights'.
174. Padovani, C., 'Pluralism of Information in the Television Sector in Italy: History and Contemporary Conditions', in Czepek, A., Hellwig, M., Nowak, E. (eds), *Press Freedom and Pluralism in Europe: Concepts and Conditions* (Intellect Books, 2009).
175. European Institute for the Media, Final report of the study on 'The information of the citizen in the EU: obligations for the media and the Institutions concerning the citizen's right to be fully and objectively informed', 115.
176. European Institute for the Media, Final report of the study on 'The information of the citizen in the EU: obligations for the media and the Institutions concerning the citizen's right to be fully and objectively informed', 115.
177. Case C-380/05, *Centro Europa 7*, [2008] ECR I-349, para. 116.

President, Carlo Azeglio Ciampi, who in July 2002 requested the Parliament to adopt legislation that would foster media pluralism. In addition in November 2002, the Italian Constitutional Court declared as unconstitutional the undefined transitional periods in the Maccanico Law that protected the programmes transmitted by broadcasters that exceeded the thresholds from being transferred to satellite or cable television. The Court concluded that 'the de facto situation does not guarantee respect for external pluralism of information'[178] and set a final deadline for the introduction of new legislation as 31 December 2003. As a result, the Berlusconi government drafted a new law aimed at the reform of the communications system, known as the Gasparri Law, which was named after the Communications Minister at the time.[179] The legislation was finally adopted in May 2004, despite the objections by President Ciampi, who refused to sign the first draft and returned it to the Parliament for reconsideration.[180]

The objections arose after the Gasparri Law changed the ownership restrictions for the television sector. They were based on a combination of two thresholds, relating to the share of the overall number of available licenses, and the share of revenues. First of all, under the Gasparri Law, one company could not hold licenses allowing it to broadcast more than 20% of all television channels that may be broadcast on terrestrial frequencies at national level and, second, companies registered as communications operators could not, directly or indirectly, earn revenue greater than 20% of the total revenue of the 'integrated communications system'. At first glance, therefore, the Berlusconi government appeared to be tightening media regulations in Italy. The share in revenues was brought down from 30% to 20%. However, the difference was that the threshold no longer applied to each segment of the media market individually, but was calculated for 'an integrated communications sector'. This included profits from television, radio, film, Internet and postal services. This broad definition of the relevant market as a basis for the calculation of one of the thresholds meant that the duopoly of RAI and Mediaset was not brought to an end, but was actually strengthened. Moreover, the Gasparri Law provided for the abolition of

178. European Commission for Democracy through Law, 'Opinion on the compatibility of the Laws "Gasparri" and "Frattini" of Italy with the Council of Europe standards in the field of freedom of expression and pluralism of the media', 10.
179. 'The Principles governing the broadcasting system and RAI-Radiotelevisione Italiana SpA, and the authority delegated to the Government to issue the consolidated legislation on television broadcasting' (The Gasparri Law), CDL(2004) 092.
180. European Commission for Democracy through Law, 'Opinion on the compatibility of the Laws "Gasparri" and "Frattini" of Italy with the Council of Europe standards in the field of freedom of expression and pluralism of the media', 10; see also Padovani, C., 'Pluralism of Information in the Television Sector in Italy: History and Contemporary Conditions', 298.

cross-ownership restrictions between television and press by 2008 and formed a legal basis for the progressive privatization of RAI.[181]

In its opinion on the Gasparri Law, the European Commission for Democracy through Law operating under the auspices of the Council of Europe commented that, the primary beneficiary of the new legislation would not surprisingly, be Mediaset. The concept of an integrated communication system introduced by the new Law as an indicator of the market share diluted the effectiveness of instruments used to protect external pluralism based on the share of revenues 'on individual markets'.[182] Therefore, Gasparri Law would allow Mediaset to expand virtually without any constraint, since it would be almost impossible for any company to be dominant in the integrated communications system. The fact that the general antitrust measures remained applicable[183] did not alleviate the negative consequences of the Gasparri Law as they prohibit the *abuse* of dominant positions and in the media sector dominant positions are forbidden, *as such.* The Commission finished its crushing criticism by concluding that without other indicators such an audience share threshold and a 'relevant market' indicator, the thresholds provided by Gasparri Law are largely redundant as indicators of diversity.[184]

Indeed, Gasparri Law enabled Berlusconi to expand his media empire. Since the value of total revenues collected in the Italian 'integrated communication system' was calculated at EUR 31,814 million in 2002, 20% of that, that is the maximum permissible threshold, equals EUR 6,363 million. This would mean that Fininvest, which had consolidated revenues in 2002 of EUR 4,880 million, would be able to increase its annual turnover by almost EUR 1,889 million.[185] And just as predicted, in 2005, with a turnover of EUR 603.4 million, Mediaset was more powerful than ever.[186] As a direct result of the Gasparri Law, one of Mediaset's channels, Retequattro, was allowed to continue broadcasting on terrestrial frequencies, despite the

181. European Institute for the Media, Final report of the study on 'The information of the citizen in the EU: obligations for the media and the Institutions concerning the citizen's right to be fully and objectively informed', 115.
182. European Commission for Democracy through Law, 'Opinion on the compatibility of the Laws "Gasparri" and "Frattini" of Italy with the Council of Europe standards in the field of freedom of expression and pluralism of the media', 22.
183. Law no. 287 of 10 October 1990, Competition and Fair Trading Act (Official Gazette no. 240 of 13 October 1990) applies to the media sector. The Italian Competition authority (Autorità Garante della Concorrenza e del Mercato) is required to request a non-binding opinion by AGCOM on the draft decisions concerning the communications market.
184. European Commission for Democracy through Law, 'Opinion on the compatibility of the Laws "Gasparri" and "Frattini" of Italy with the Council of Europe standards in the field of freedom of expression and pluralism of the media', 23.
185. Ward, D., Fueg, O.C., D'Armo, A., 'A Mapping Study of Media Concentration and Ownership in Ten European Countries', 106.
186. Cece, B., 'Italy Labours to Rid Itself of Berlusconi', 18 July 2006.

Constitutional Court's judgment that it should be moved to satellite by January 2004.[187]

The second controversial piece of legislation was 'Frattini Law', which was seemingly aimed at counteracting conflicts of interests between business and politics. When Berlusconi became Italian Prime Minister in 1994, the issue of the potential conflicts of interest between his private interests and his public functions came to the fore.[188] Nevertheless, neither of his subsequent governments did anything to tackle the situation by adopting appropriate legislation. When Berlusconi was re-elected in 2001, he committed himself to solving the conflict of interest issue within one hundred days.[189] The result of the commitment is the law on conflicts of interest, known as the Frattini Law.[190] This particular law disqualifies persons holding a government office, from *inter alia* performing *managerial tasks* or other duties in professional societies or associations. Within thirty days of taking office, Government officials must declare to the Competition Authority their disqualifying conditions, as well as, within sixty days of taking office, inform the Authority about their assets, including shareholdings. Despite the government's statements, the Frattini Law did not offer an adequate solution to the problem. On the contrary, it reinforced the *status quo*, because, it actually declared that incompatibility between public office and the *management* was unlawful rather than *ownership,* of a company. And as Berlusconi is the owner, but not the manager, of extensive media interests in Italy, the most important aspect of the conflict of interest in Italy, the very one which indeed made it necessary to adopt the law in the first place, was not resolved.

This resulted in further criticism from the European Commission for Democracy through Law. Apart from stating that the incompatibility with a public post should arise also from ownership of a company, the Commission recalled the 2003 'Guidelines for Managing Conflict of Interest in the Public Service' adopted by the Organization for Economic Co-operation and Development (OECD).[191] The Guidelines defined 'conflict of interest' as one involving 'a conflict between public duty and the private interests of a public official, which could improperly influence the performance of their official duties and responsibilities'. They also listed a number of 'strategies for

---

187. European Federation of Journalists, 'Media power in Europe: the big picture of ownership', 83.
188. European Commission for Democracy through Law, 'Opinion on the compatibility of the Laws "Gasparri" and "Frattini" of Italy with the Council of Europe standards in the field of freedom of expression and pluralism of the media', 36.
189. European Commission for Democracy through Law, 'Opinion on the compatibility of the Laws "Gasparri" and "Frattini" of Italy with the Council of Europe standards in the field of freedom of expression and pluralism of the media', 37.
190. 'Rules for the resolution of conflicts of interest' (the Frattini Law), CDL(2004) 93 rev.
191. European Commission for Democracy through Law, 'Opinion on the compatibility of the Laws "Gasparri" and "Frattini" of Italy with the Council of Europe standards in the field of freedom of expression and pluralism of the media', 39.

positive resolution or management of a continuing or pervasive conflict'. These included divestment or liquidation of the interest by the public official, recusal of the public official from involvement in an affected decision-making process, assignment of the conflicting interest in a genuinely 'blind trust' arrangement, and resignation of the public official from their public office. Meanwhile, none of the above measures were required by the Italian Frattini Law. The government members who found themselves in a situation of conflict of interest only had to inform the competent Authorities, but were put under no other obligation to remove such conflict of interest.[192] The Italian government explained to the Commission that introducing any of the measures mentioned in the OECD Guidelines would be in breach of the provisions in the Italian Constitution protecting private property and the guaranteeing free access to public office.[193] The Commission rebuffed those arguments and noted that if the obligation to sell the business is contrary to the Constitution, then the institution of a 'blind trust' could be an answer. The argument that the Italian law does not provide for such an institution is unfounded as nothing prevents the legislator from introducing it. The Commission rightly observed that entering the political arena is the free choice of each individual. It also entails prerogatives and duties and carries with it some incompatibilities and limitations. Furthermore, as noted by the Commission, 'the mere possibility of suffering some financial loss should not be, in itself, a reason to exclude an activity from the list of activities incompatible with public office'.[194]

Hope for remedying this unhealthy legislative environment in Italy emerged together with the new centre-left government formed by the former President of the European Commission, Romano Prodi, after Berlusconi's electoral defeat in the spring of 2006. In the electoral manifesto, Prodi's party The Union (L'Unione), promised that it would address the two major problems – media concentration regulations and the conflict of interest law. Prodi observed that 'these two issues must be resolved as soon as possible because the current situation does not meet European standards'.[195] However, as reforms had not been quickly introduced or even started, the European Commission felt the need to interject. In July 2006, it sent a formal letter to the Prodi government, urging it to modify the Gasparri Law.[196] The

192. European Commission for Democracy through Law, 'Opinion on the compatibility of the Laws "Gasparri" and "Frattini" of Italy with the Council of Europe standards in the field of freedom of expression and pluralism of the media', 45.
193. European Commission for Democracy through Law, 'Opinion on the compatibility of the Laws "Gasparri" and "Frattini" of Italy with the Council of Europe standards in the field of freedom of expression and pluralism of the media', 45.
194. European Commission for Democracy through Law, 'Opinion on the compatibility of the Laws "Gasparri" and "Frattini" of Italy with the Council of Europe standards in the field of freedom of expression and pluralism of the media', 46.
195. Cece, B., 'Italy Labours to Rid Itself of Berlusconi'.
196. Cece, B., 'Italy Labours to Rid Itself of Berlusconi'.

Commission reminded the government that the law unfairly favours Italy's existing dominant broadcasters and may stifle competition in the nascent digital broadcasting market.[197] Moreover, even though Berlusconi was no longer the Prime Minister he was still the head of the opposition party, and via Mediaset he still had substantial influence over public opinion. The fact that Italy remains the only European country in which a centre-stage politician owns three main national TV channels, renders the need for reform paramount. Communications Minister Paolo Gentiloni promptly embarked on reforming the media regulations aiming at allowing 'more pluralism and more competition'.[198] The 'Gentiloni Law' was expected to be adopted in autumn 2007. The government promised to introduce a cap on advertising whereby no TV company can earn more than 45% of the available advertising revenue. It was also to set a firm provision that companies exceeding the thresholds would be obliged to move their channels to cable or satellite.[199] Both RAI and Mediaset would in any event, have to switch one of their channels to digital TV in 2008 or 2009. This would free up frequencies for digital TV market entrants, such as L'Espresso Editoriale SpA, RCS Media Group SpA and privately-owned De Agostini. Minister Gentiloni admitted that the aim of the reforms is to increase the number of TV players in Italy to three or four, which is the EU average per country.[200]

In addition, the new law was to provide for the reform of RAI. First of all, the public broadcaster was to get an overhaul of its management structure. An eleven-member foundation modelled on the BBC Trust would be set up as RAI's holding company, with four members nominated by the Parliament, two chosen by regional entities, and the remainder named by non-political professional organizations. The foundation would then appoint a five-member board which will oversee RAI's day-to-day operations.[201] Second, the reform plan included having two RAI channels mainly funded by a license fee and the third channel mainly funded by advertising. The reform was expected to be implemented before 2010.[202]

Along with tightening the media ownership regulations, the Prodi government proposed to reform the Frattini Law on the conflict of interests. The new law would render it impossible to combine government positions and the *ownership* of assets exceeding EUR 15 million in value. Furthermore, if elected to government, owners of media companies operating under

---

197. Schomberg, W., Sanderson, R., 'EU Challenges Italy over Berlusconi Media Law', Reuters, 19 July 2006.
198. Padovani, C., 'Pluralism of Information in the Television Sector in Italy: History and Contemporary Conditions'.
199. Vivarelli, N., 'A Year without Berlusconi', Variety, 20 March 2007.
200. 'Italy Govt Plans RAI Reform in Next Stage of TV Revamp', AFX News, 29 November 2006.
201. Vivarelli, N., 'A Year without Berlusconi'.
202. Vivarelli, N., 'A Year without Berlusconi'.

state concessions would have a choice of either selling their companies or handing their management to a blind trust.[203] Berlusconi was quick to brand the new proposal 'an ad hoc attempt to murder Mediaset' and an attempt to prevent him from being the Prime Minister again. He rejected the prospect of handing the management of his company to a blind trust by saying that 'no one can ask me to entrust my entire property to someone I don't know, especially since it's the result of a life of hard work'.[204] In the end, the Gentiloni law which was presented to the Senate in May 2007, was never approved.[205]

Berlusconi has, therefore, remained very vocal and active and despite the long awaited reforms, Mediaset continued to be strong and influential. Thus, commentators have never ruled out Berlusoni's return to the top position in government. Indeed, 'Sua Emmitenza' seemed to be doing everything he can to secure Mediaset's position before the reforms come into full effect. In May 2007, Mediaset led the consortium which purchased Endemol, the Dutch production company and Europe's second-largest TV producer. Using de Mol and Goldman Sachs' private equity arm, Mediaset acquired a 75% controlling stake in Endemol.[206] The acquisition raised concerns in RAI which has recently become heavily reliant on Endemol products. RAI is now facing a situation whereby its top-rated programmes are owned by Mediaset. An informal poll in the newspaper La Repubblica showed that 96% of its readers thought the acquisition of Endemol by Mediaset would 'inevitably penalize RAI'.[207]

The above shows that the danger to media pluralism still looms in Italy. The perseverance and diligence of the current government in pursuing sweeping reforms of Italian media law, which will remain in place and will not be reversed by any future governments, was absolutely crucial. Nevertheless, with the resignation of Prodi government in January 2008 after the loss of the vote of confidence in the Parliament, Berlusconi won the elections in April 2008 and returned to the position of the Italian Prime Minister. He was since replaced in 2011 by the former EU Competition Commissioner, Mario Monti, but remains a centre-stage politician. And with Italy facing austerity measures introduced in an attempt to counteract the worsening economic conditions,[208] the media law reforms arguably slipped from the top position of the Monti government's priorities.

203. 'National Interest and Summer Holidays', Inside Italy, 8 May 2007.
204. 'National Interest and Summer Holidays', Inside Italy.
205. Padovani, C., 'Pluralism of Information in the Television Sector in Italy: History and Contemporary Conditions'.
206. Vivarelli, N., 'RAI Not Sure Which Endemol's Up', Variety, 18 May 2007.
207. Vivarelli, N., 'RAI Not Sure Which Endemol's Up'.
208. 'Italy Senate Passes Monti's Austerity Package', BBC News, 22 December 2011.

6.4. POLAND

6.4.1. STRUCTURE OF THE TELEVISION MARKET

Poland, with almost 40 million inhabitants, has one of the largest and most rapidly developing television markets in Europe. The media sector underwent radical transformation after the fall of the communist regime. It was only after 1989, when censorship was abolished, that independent media started to develop.[209] In addition, it was after this time that foreign media companies began investing in Poland.[210]

Currently, the Polish television market consists of three main players: the public service broadcaster Telewizja Polska (TVP) and the two commercial stations – Polsat and TVN.[211] They are accompanied by a number of smaller players such as TV Puls.

TVP maintains the dominant position in the TV market with an average audience share of over 50%. It operates two terrestrial channels (TVP1 and TVP2), a regional network (twelve channels), an information channel and an International channel TV Polonia. Polsat was the first private broadcaster in Poland. It is owned by Zygmunt Solorz, 'a rare example of an Eastern European media mogul'[212] and was established in 1992 as a satellite station broadcasting from Holland. It began terrestrial broadcasting in March 1994[213] and currently has over 17% market share. Its satellite station Polsat 2 was launched in July 1997, and in November Polsat launched a digital platform. Polsat has interests in the Baltic countries, with shares in Latvian and Lithuanian TV stations. TVN is the second largest commercial television broadcaster in Poland; it covers almost 80% of the country and has an audience share of around 16%. It was established in 1997 by ITI, a Polish financial group set up by former TVP journalist Mariusz Walter and businessman Jan Wejchert, and US broadcasting investor Central European Media Enterprises.[214] It is now 19% owned by ITI Holdings, a subsidiary of Luxembourg based company ITI International. Apart from its terrestrial

209. Open Society Institute, 'Television across Europe: Regulation, Policy and Independence', 1082.
210. European Federation of Journalists, 'Media Power in Europe: The Big Picture of Ownership', 113.
211. Filas, R., Planeta, P., 'Media in Poland and Public Discourse', in Czepek, A., Hellwig, M., Nowak, E. (eds), *Press Freedom and Pluralism in Europe: Concepts and Conditions* (Intellect Books, 2009).
212. European Federation of Journalists, 'Media Power in Europe: The Big Picture of Ownership', 114.
213. Open Society Institute, 'Television across Europe: Regulation, Policy and Independence', 1082.
214. Open Society Institute, 'Television across Europe: Regulation, Policy and Independence', 1082.

operations, TVN provides six satellite television channels: TVN 7 (entertainment), TVN 24 (twenty-four-hour news), TVN Meteo (weather), TVN Turbo (automotive), TVN International and TVN Style. The ITI Group is also active in multiplex cinema operations, home video and theatrical distribution, theatrical production, special events organization and new media (it operates the largest internet portal in Poland, Onet.pl). TVN recently run into financial difficulties and its 60% shares currently owned by the sons of the founders are for sale. In December 2011, one of the global media conglomerates, the French company Vivendi, signed a deal with ITI Holdings, the owner of TVN, taking control of the group's joint pay-TV platform business in Poland and an option to control TVN.[215] The third commercial broadcaster, TV Puls is the successor of TV Familijna, which was launched in 2001 with a license granted to Franciscan fathers for a religious programme. However, this company filed for bankruptcy in 2002. In 2003 Zygmunt Solorz invested in TV Familijna's Antena 1 production company and began transmission through cable networks and on Polsat's digital platform. In June 2005, Polsat became a direct minority shareholder in TV Puls. In 2006, 35% stake in TV Puls was acquired by News Corporation,[216] but in 2008 News Corporation sold the stake to the remaining shareholders.

Poland's cable market is the largest in Central Europe. There has been recent consolidation and the market is dominated by just three companies: UPC TK, Telewizja Kablowa Vectra, and Multimedia Polska.[217] UPC Polska, a subsidiary of the American cable operator UPC which in turn belongs to the media conglomerate Liberty Global, is the largest cable operator in Poland. In 2010 UPC purchased Aster, the fourth biggest cable operator in Poland at the time. Aster fully merged with UPC in 2012.

Pay TV via terrestrial service, cable and satellite is also provided by Canal+ owned by Vivendi Universal. Canal+ launched pay TV in Poland in 1996. It also recently launched its digital platform Cyfra+ which competes with Polsat's digital platform called Polsat Cyfrowy (Digital Polsat).

6.4.2. Media Concentration Regulation

The regulation of the media sector in Poland is currently based on four pieces of legislation, namely, the Press Law (1984), the Broadcasting Act (1992), the Telecommunication Law (2000) and the Act on Competition and

215. Reuters, 'Poland's TVN Signs Partnership Deal with Vivendi', 19 December 2011.
216. Open Society Institute, 'Television across Europe: Regulation, Policy and Independence', 1082.
217. European Institute for the Media, Final report of the study on 'The information of the citizen in the EU: obligations for the media and the Institutions concerning the citizen's right to be fully and objectively informed', 158.

Consumer Protection (2000).[218] There are three regulators involved, the National Broadcasting Council, which is responsible for issuing broadcasting licenses and content regulation, the Office for Telecommunications and Post Regulation with competence to allocate broadcasting frequencies and third, the Competition Authority, which is in charge of assessing mergers.

The Broadcasting Act, 1992, has been amended several times, most recently in 2010. The Act was passed after three years of heated discussion and as a result, the State Radio and Television Committee was dissolved from 1 March 1993, and the National Broadcasting Council began operations in April 1993. Indeed, the Council was the first completely new institution in democratic Poland established after 1989. The role of the Council was further enhanced by the new Polish Constitution of 1997, which in Article 214, recognized the special role of the Council to 'safeguard freedom of speech, the right to information, as well as safeguarding the public interest regarding radio and television broadcasting'. Article 6(1) of the Broadcasting Act specifies that one of the main tasks of the Council is to 'ensure the open and pluralistic nature of radio and television broadcasting'. In fulfilment of its main duties, the Council issues broadcast licenses and binding legal regulations. It also appoints the Supervisory Board of TVP, supervises adherence by all broadcasters to the provisions of the Act, and, in the case of private broadcasters, the fulfilment of their license conditions.[219]

Since the 2005 amendments of the Broadcasting Act, the Council consists of five members.[220] Two are elected by the lower house of the Parliament (the Sejm), one by the Senate and two are appointed by the President.[221] The Constitution requires that no Council member may belong to a political party or trade union or 'perform public activities incompatible with the dignity of his/her function'. The Broadcasting Act further specifies that the Council's members are to be chosen 'from persons with a distinguished record of knowledge and experience in mass media'. However, in practice, things have proven to be very different. Since its establishment, the majority of the members of the Council have been appointed on the basis of their political affiliation to the parties that control the Parliament and the

218. European Institute for the Media, Final report of the study on 'The information of the citizen in the EU: obligations for the media and the Institutions concerning the citizen's right to be fully and objectively informed', 155.
219. European Institute for the Media, Final report of the study on 'The information of the citizen in the EU: obligations for the media and the Institutions concerning the citizen's right to be fully and objectively informed', 155.
220. Until December 2005, the Council consisted of nine members; see http://www.krrit.gov.pl/en/.
221. Open Society Institute, 'Television across Europe: Regulation, Policy and Independence', 1089.

Presidency.[222] Since its establishment, there has only been one non-politically affiliated specialist appointed out of a total of thirty-three members of the Council.[223]

With regard to media concentration rules, the Broadcasting Act provides that a broadcasting license shall not be awarded if transmission of a programme service by the applicant could result in the applicant having a dominant position in mass communications in the given sector. And if the applicant does gain such a dominant position in mass communications in any given area, his/her license shall be withdrawn. However, the Act contains no specific definition of 'dominant position in mass communications', and it provides no thresholds for measuring this dominance. Therefore, a dominant position must be measured, as in other sectors, in accordance with the general provisions of competition law.[224] The Act on Competition and Consumer Protection defines a dominant position as being a share of more than 40% of the market.

In January 2002, the Council proposed a draft amendment to the Act, which included a number of cross-media ownership restrictions. One of them was a ban on the joint ownership of national television and national radio stations as well as disqualification for publishers of national daily newspapers from holding broadcasting licenses. The draft caused a great wave of criticism and debate. While the government was defending the proposals, claiming they would prevent the creation of media monopolies, the private media sector argued that the draft would 'limit the development of electronic private media and would make national companies less competitive than foreign media investors entering the Polish market'.[225] There were also some unclear legislative movements surrounding the draft, which raised the temperature of the discussions somewhat. For instance, an earlier draft had disqualified the publishers of national dailies *or periodicals* from holding broadcasting licenses, but the phrase 'or periodicals' mysteriously disappeared from the subsequent text. This implied that publishers of magazines would not be restricted from entering the broadcasting sector.[226] The controversies culminated in the end of 2003, when the greatest political scandal in the history of democratic Poland erupted.

222. Open Society Institute, 'Television across Europe: Regulation, Policy and Independence', 1092.
223. Open Society Institute, 'Television across Europe: Regulation, Policy and Independence', 1091.
224. European Institute for the Media, Final report of the study on 'The information of the citizen in the EU: obligations for the media and the Institutions concerning the citizen's right to be fully and objectively informed', 162.
225. European Institute for the Media, Final report of the study on 'The information of the citizen in the EU: obligations for the media and the Institutions concerning the citizen's right to be fully and objectively informed', 156.
226. European Institute for the Media, Final report of the study on 'The information of the citizen in the EU: obligations for the media and the Institutions concerning the citizen's right to be fully and objectively informed', 156.

The scandal, nicknamed *Rywingate* after its main actor, was exposed on 27 December 2002 by *Gazeta Wyborcza*, the biggest Polish daily newspaper, and ultimately led to the resignation of Leszek Miller's government in 2004. In July 2002, a well-known Polish film producer Lew Rywin[227] informed Wanda Rapaczynska, the Chief Executive of Agora publishing house which is the owner of *Gazeta Wyborcza,* that the government would be prepared to remove the anti-concentration provisions from the Draft Amendment in exchange for 17.5 million dollars. This would have allowed Agora to purchase commercial broadcaster Polsat, the plans for which have never been a secret of Agora's. A 17.5 million dollars constituted 5% of the value of Polsat at the time estimated at 350 million dollars. Rywin claimed that he acted on behalf of an unidentified 'group in power', but provided a hint that Leszek Miller, the Prime Minister at the time, was the main power behind him. The money was to be transferred to the bank account of Heritage Films – Rywin's production company and used by the then governing party SLD (Democratic Left Alliance). A 30% of the sum was to be paid right after the entry of the new Law into force, and the remaining 70% after the purchase of Polsat by Agora. Additional conditions included no further criticism of the Prime Minister by *Gazeta Wyborcza* and making Rywin the head of Polsat after the acquisition. Rywin informed Rapaczynska that he expected Agora's answer in writing.

Rapaczynska replied that she would now pass the case to *Gazeta Wyborcza*'s Editor-in-Chief, Adam Michnik who would decide on further action. After long talks, Rapaczynska and Michnik decided that Michnik would meet with Rywin and tape-record the entire conversation to expose what would become the greatest corruption scandal in Poland's post-communist history. On 27 December 2002, in an article 'The Law for a Bribe, that is Rywin comes to Michnik',[228]*Gazeta Wyborcza* published the written record of the conversation between Michnik and Rywin. The story raised an immediate and immense public outrage.

On 10 January 2003, Sejm established a special commission to investigate *Gazeta's* allegations, and the public prosecutor started a separate investigation. The work of the parliamentary Culture and Mass Media Committee on amendments to the Broadcasting Act was frozen. The investigation committee's hearings, which were transmitted live by public television, disclosed several serious irregularities concerning legislative procedures. The media pointed to Deputy Culture Minister Aleksandra Jakubowska, the Broadcasting Council's Secretary Włodzimierz Czarzasty, TVP's President Robert Kwiatkowski, Prime Minister Leszek Miller and his

227. He participated in producing such films as Steven Spielberg's *Schindler's List*, Roman Polanski's *The Pianist.*

228. Smolenski, P., 'The Law for a Bribe, That Is Rywin Comes to Michnik', Gazeta Wyborcza, 27 December 2002.

chief aide, Lech Nikolski, as the 'group in power' referred to by Rywin.[229] All five consistently denied any involvement. There were two contradictory reports published by the Commission, by two separate authors. Sejm finally adopted the report claiming that the group in power did indeed exist. This, however, remains controversial to this day. Meanwhile, Rywin was sentenced to two years in prison for bribery and Miller, and his government resigned in May 2004 after Poland's accession to the EU was complete.

In June 2003, and as a direct result of the *Rywingate* scandal, the Government decided to withdraw the draft amendment of the Broadcasting Act from the Parliament.[230] Instead, in March 2004 'a small amendment' was enacted. However, it lacks any anti-concentration clauses, and it does not regulate the control of the transparency of media ownership. It focuses primarily on provisions implementing the TVWF Directive (mainly the independent production and European production quotas).[231] Poland remains without any specific legislative media concentration restrictions.

Rywingate illustrates the influence of political and economic interests when it comes to regulating media market structure.[232] It serves as the best example that, when faced with such powerful and vested interests, Member States cannot cope on their own. Arguably, had there been EU level media concentration restrictions in place, there would have been nothing to bribe anyone for. Poland would simply not be able to introduce or remove media concentration rules as it pleased. It would have to comply with EU law.

As a result of the controversy and scandal surrounding the adoption of the amendment, the provisions relating to media concentration and cross-media ownership were removed from the proposed draft. Instead, in March 2004 'a small amendment' was enacted. However, it lacked any anti-concentration clauses, and it does not regulate the control of the transparency of media ownership. It focused primarily on provisions implementing the then TVWF Directive (mainly the introduction of independent production and European production quotas).[233] Therefore, there are virtually no restrictions on media concentration in the Polish legal system.

Meanwhile, there are examples of excessive media concentration and controversial cross-ownership. As mentioned above, TVP has over 50% of

229. Open Society Institute, 'Television across Europe: Regulation, Policy and Independence', 1097.
230. Open Society Institute, 'Television across Europe: Regulation, Policy and Independence', 1097.
231. Klimkiewicz, B., 'Media Pluralism: European Regulatory Policies and the Case of Central Europe', 11–12.
232. European Institute for the Media, Final report of the study on 'The information of the citizen in the EU: obligations for the media and the Institutions concerning the citizen's right to be fully and objectively informed', 156.
233. European Institute for the Media, Final report of the study on 'The information of the citizen in the EU: obligations for the media and the Institutions concerning the citizen's right to be fully and objectively informed', 156.

the market share. In addition, a company Agora, the owner of the leading daily *Gazeta Wyborcza* is also the owner of twenty-nine local radio stations. Its radio network is the biggest in the market in terms of advertising revenue and audience. In addition, it can be expected that Agora will expand further. The company made no secret of its talks with Polsat about buying a stake in the broadcaster, and although it made no attempt to bid for TVN against Time Warner and Vivendi in 2011, there is nothing in the current legislation preventing it from doing so in the future. In fact, Agora has consistently campaigned against planned restrictions on cross-ownership, arguing that 'threats to media pluralism come from international media giants (particularly American ones) rather than from domestic cross-ownership'.[234]

Other media pluralism concerns in Poland centre at the threats to editorial independence from owners, advertisers and politicians.[235] Although, in theory, the independence of broadcasters from the State is guaranteed by the Constitution and the Broadcasting Act, in practice, public broadcasting has been subject to systematic political influence and pressure. Management positions in TVP have been assigned on the basis of political loyalty and patronage, and news and public affairs coverage have suffered from serious and systematic bias.[236] The rules established by the 2001 TVP Journalists' Code of Ethics[237] do not appear to have been followed in practice.

The situation is not much better in the commercial television sector. There are no specific instruments to help to guarantee the editorial independence of private broadcasters. In the absence of written codes, 'the personality and professional authority of the leading journalists has been of key importance in mapping the boundaries of editorial independence'.[238] General laws protecting journalists are also weak. Large commercial media groups take advantage of this situation and use the legislative limbo to secure their place in the market and develop strategies for the future.[239] This inevitably leads to a growing concentration of media ownership in the commercial sector.[240] There is also evidence that private television channels have tended to avoid highly sensitive political issues.[241]

234. Open Society Institute, 'Television across Europe: Regulation, Policy and Independence', 1135.
235. European Federation of Journalists, 'Media Power in Europe: The Big Picture of Ownership', 113.
236. Open Society Institute, 'Television across Europe: Regulation, Policy and Independence', 1082.
237. TVP Journalists' Code of Ethics, http://www.tvp.pl.
238. Open Society Institute, 'Television across Europe: Regulation, Policy and Independence', 1135.
239. European Federation of Journalists, 'Media Power in Europe: The Big Picture of Ownership', 118.
240. European Federation of Journalists, 'Media Power in Europe: The Big Picture of Ownership', 119.
241. Open Society Institute, 'Television across Europe: Regulation, Policy and Independence', 1082.

Changes in the Polish media legislation were, therefore, inevitable. In 2010, the amendment to the Broadcasting Act changed the way the Supervisory Boards of the public broadcaster TVP are elected. They now have seven members – only two of them appointed by government (minister of culture and minister of treasury). Five remaining ones are appointed by the Broadcasting Council after a competition. The candidates for competition are suggested by universities. Thus elected supervisory board suggests management of TVP which is then appointed by the Broadcasting Council. There is now some hope that TVP will become more independent. However, this will require the universities to select candidates completely independently of any political pressures.

Chapter 7
Case for Action at the EU Level?

7.1 NEED FOR ADDITIONAL EU LEGISLATION ON MEDIA PLURALISM?

The European Commission's current position is that considerations of media pluralism and diversity should be left to the Member States to address. However, as the previous chapter attempted to demonstrate and considering the ongoing 'Italian anomaly', the Hungarian media law of 2010 or the irregularities in the UK brought to light by the 'hacking' scandal in 2011, Craufurd Smith's analogy that 'this is rather like entrusting the friendly fox with the task of looking after the chickens'[1] is rather convincing. Thus, Craufurd Smith adds that 'media pluralism cannot be categorized simply, or primarily, as a domestic or economic issue – it is an issue that foes to the very heart of the democratic legitimacy of the European Union itself'.[2]

To this end, there have been opinions expressed that the European Union is best placed for 'harmonising re-regulation'[3] of the media sector. Member States have to jointly address the issue of media pluralism which currently transcends national borders.[4] As Harcourt noted already in 1998,

---

1. Craufurd Smith, R., 'Rethinking European Union Competence in the Field of Media Ownership: The Internal Market, Fundamental Rights and European Citizenship', 672.
2. Craufurd Smith, R., 'Rethinking European Union Competence in the Field of Media Ownership: The Internal Market, Fundamental Rights and European Citizenship', 672.
3. Humphreys, P., 'Regulating for Pluralism in the Era of Digital Convergence: The Issues of Media Concentration Control and the Future of Public-Service Broadcasting', 10.
4. Arino, M., 'Competition Law and Pluralism in European Digital Broadcasting: Addressing the Gaps', 124.

'the transformation of national mono-media markets into one European multimedia market has been documented by economic analyses ... Thus the regulation of media ownership has become a European issue'.[5]

There are views that regulation of an ever-changing environment is not a bad solution. All in all, as Lord Puttnam explains, 'regulation has to keep up with technology, [but] *ex post facto* law is invariably bad law'.[6] A directive or a regulation would provide a comprehensive and readily accessible legal framework for minimum levels of protection of media pluralism across the EU, in an era of rapidly changing and ever concentrating broadcast media markets. This could have been done during the process of the revision of the TVWF Directive.[7] It is, after all, possible to distinguish between linear broadcasting services to which the regulation on concentration should apply, and the non-linear communications/media services which could be 'left alone' until the market reaches a more mature stage. Gibbons opts for behaviour-based competition regulation, which would impose 'a threshold for media domination that differs from, but complements notions of economic dominance' with the aim of ensuring that 'major media players, do not control more than a significant share of audience's experience'.[8] The answer to the many of the voices is that say it is impossible to find a common denominator for media concentration rules for all twenty-seven Member States, could be a 'tiered' approach to the EU level regulation of media concentration, as suggested by Doyle.[9] A tiered regulation would introduce different levels of diversity of ownership for markets of different sizes.

It has already been noted that the European Parliament insisted on such an outcome of the revision process of the Television Without Frontiers Directive. Nevertheless, media concentration was not on the revision agenda and even more so, almost all of the Parliament's insertions of the words 'media pluralism' after the second reading were deleted from the draft. The European Union de facto follows the first policy option with regard to media concentration, suggested in the 1992 Green Paper on media concentrations and pluralism, i.e., it takes no regulatory action at all. Some claim that the failure to adopt positive EU-level rules against media concentration left 'a fissure between national regulation and European regulation that technically

5. Harcourt, A., 'The European Commission and Regulation of Media Industry'.
6. Puttnam, D., 'The Continuing Need to Advance the Public Interest', in 'Communications. The Next Decade' – a collection of essays prepared for the UK Office of Communications', 131.
7. Bibby, A., 'Global Concentration in the Media', UNI-MEI World General Assembly, Los Angeles, 1–3 October 2003, 16.
8. Gibbons, T., 'Concentrations of Ownership and Control in a Converging Media Industry', 173.
9. Doyle, G., 'Regulation of Media Ownership and Pluralism in Europe: Can the European Union Take Us Forward?'.

allows companies to bypass stringent regulatory demands'.[10] The result is that the internationalizing commercial media sector is increasingly enjoying minimal regulation.[11]

Notwithstanding the claims as to the need for positive EU action in this field, the chances for this to happen are bleak. First of all, the political momentum for the introduction of anti-concentration legislation seems to have faded. Internal Market considerations and the need to level the playing field no longer seem to have any appeal.

As already explained in Chapter 2 above, the current political climate in the European Commission does not favour firm action on media pluralism. The Commission refuses to use its right of initiative to propose legislation in this area and the already mentioned European Citizens Initiative on Media Pluralism, which is to be launched in May 2012,[12] is most likely doomed to fail. Thus, deliberating about the need for a regulation may, on the face of things, seem futile and purely academic.

The Commission seems to believe that the developing and unpredictable nature of an industry such as the media should not be bound by red tape. In this constantly changing environment, concentration should be allowed in order for technologies to develop and progress to take place. Market failures should be corrected by competition law and pluralism safeguarded with other means, preferably at the national level. This belief was best illustrated during the consultation which led to the adoption of the AVMS Directive. In the Issues Paper No 6 for the Liverpool Audiovisual Conference in 2005,[13] the Commission asked the stakeholders for their opinions on what should be the European Union's role in fostering media pluralism. The Issues Paper was constructed in a somewhat guiding manner. It mentioned some of the EU legislative measures which apparently already do promote pluralism actively. It selectively highlighted only those findings of some of the reports prepared for the European Parliament, which concluded that it would be 'difficult to propose any kind of harmonization of rules between the EU Member States';[14] it expressed fear that too restrictive ownership rules in Europe might hinder European companies to compete globally. Lastly, it pointed at the Council of Europe as the proper forum to deal at pan-European level with the human and democratic dimension of communication. It is, therefore, little

10. Ward, D., *The European Union Democratic Deficit and the Public Sphere. An Evaluation of EU Media Policy*, 131.
11. Humphreys, P., 'The EU and Audiovisual Regulation: An Agency for De-regulation', 20.
12. See http://www.mediainitiative.eu/topics/the-campaign-a-european-initiative-for-media-pluralism/.
13. European Commission, 'Media Pluralism – What Should Be the European Union's Role?', Issues Paper, 2005.
14. European Institute for the Media, Final report of the study on 'The information of the citizen in the EU: obligations for the media and the Institutions concerning the citizen's right to be fully and objectively informed'.

wonder that the majority of respondents found little added value in additional EU action in the media concentration field. The general tenet of answers, in particular by the representatives of the commercial media, was along the lines of the ACT submission:

> we share both the Commission analysis that over-restrictive rules will be damaging in a global context, as well as the position of EU Member States that ownership regulation is best left at national level, where tools can be devised to cater for the heterogeneity of European media market.[15]

In addition, one of the priority initiatives of President Barroso is that of 'Better Regulation.'[16] As explained by Commissioner Reding:

> This European Commission under President Barroso strives for *better regulation.* This implies careful political and economical impact assessment of key proposals, ... and the roll-back of unnecessary or outdated legislation if not in line with our competitiveness and jobs goals. Co- or self-regulation has an important part to play especially in [the media] field.[17]

The current reluctance of the European Commission to engage in a discussion on additional EU-level legislative measures for the protection on media pluralism and the belief that 'media pluralism can be realized perfectly adequately by the Member States' is problematic. The liberalization and deregulation trends and the examples of abuses of media pluralism illustrated by the 'Italian anomaly', the UK hacking scandal or the Hungarian media law of 2010 demonstrate that:

> Though Member States are capable of establishing effective media ownership controls, there is a real risk that they will undervalue the importance of media pluralism, with governments prioritising international competitiveness or, at the extreme, their own political survival. Where these failures occur the existing remedies, particularly judicial, are likely to prove slow and of limited effect. The possibility of remedial action at the Community or Union level should consequently be taken seriously.[18]

And although chances for such action *currently* seem remote, when the existing Commission changes, so too might the principles.[19] The history of

---

15. Association of Commercial Television in Europe (ACT), Comments to 'Media Pluralism – what should be the European Union's role?, Issues Paper', 2005.
16. Better Regulation, http://ec.europa.eu/governance/better_regulation/index_en.htm.
17. Reding, V., 'Europe, the Media and European Media Policy'.
18. Craufurd Smith, R., 'Rethinking European Union Competence in the Field of Media Ownership: The Internal Market, Fundamental Rights and European Citizenship', 658.
19. Harcourt, A., *The European Union and the Regulation of Media Markets*, 84.

changing the authority over the media concentration portfolio (Bangemann-d'Archirafi-Monti-Reding) shows that whether a particular initiative is taken up or not, very much depends on the political beliefs of the person in charge. So it is not at all impossible that the new Commission may bring a change in the approach.

However, the next important question to ask is the one about the legal basis. The Council of Europe and the European Parliament believe that there is a legal basis for a specific regulation on media concentration, and they point at the obligation to give full effect to the protection of human rights that was imposed on the European Union in 2000 with the adoption of the Charter of Fundamental Rights. The institutions of the European Union undertook to bring all the legislation in line with the fundamental rights listed therein. The European Parliament emphasizes that the lack of specific regulation on media concentrations aimed at the protection of pluralism means that this commitment has not been fulfilled.[20]

Notwithstanding these arguments, it is true that nowhere in the Treaties is there a firm legal basis for Community action aimed specifically at protecting media pluralism. The previous attempt of the European Commission to introduce a directive on media was based on the internal market considerations remains the only option. However, not only did the political momentum for this kind of intervention seems to have passed, but also the legal basis in the form of the internal market rules was arguably one of the reasons behind the initiative's ultimate failure. Post 1998 the European Commission has consistently used the 'no legal basis' argument as the answer to every call from the European Parliament to return to discussion on the anti-concentration directive. Therefore, this chapter concludes that harmonization legislation on media pluralism in the near future is unfeasible due to the lack of legal basis and the lack of political will to introduce it.

7.2 QUESTION OF A LEGAL BASIS

The Treaties attempt to strike a balance between the legislative powers of the Union and its Member States. The solution adopted is that the European Union has no general law-making power as described by the German term *kompetenz-kompetenz*.[21] It operates on the principle of conferred or attributed powers. Article 5 of the Treaty on European Union (*TEU*) makes it clear that 'the Union shall act only within the limits of the competences conferred upon it by the Member States in the Treaties to attain the objectives set out

20. European Parliament, 'Report on the risks of violation, in the EU and especially in Italy, of freedom of expression and information'.
21. Westphal, D., 'Media Pluralism and European Regulation'; Piris, J.-C., 'Does the European Union Have a Constitution? Does It Need One?', Harvard Jean Monnet Working Paper 5/00.

therein. Competences not conferred upon the Union in the Treaties remain with the Member States'. This means that the EU can only act if there is a specific Treaty provision authorizing it to make a law,[22] and this requirement is strictly monitored by the European Court of Justice.[23]

Article 3 TEU lists the 'aims' of the European Union, which are to be attained through the establishment of an internal market and an economic and monetary union and by implementing common policies. The list of policies has developed significantly since the beginning of European integration and, therefore, 'as the Treaty has expanded … so the number of legal bases [for the EU legislative action] has become ever more voluminous'.[24]

According to Article 3 TFEU, in a small number of common policies[25] the European Union enjoys exclusive competence, which means that the Member States gave up all sovereignty in these areas.[26] On the other side of the EU competence spectrum are the areas of protection and improvement of human health; industry; culture; tourism; education, vocational training, youth and sport; civil protection; and administrative cooperation.[27] In these areas the role of the European Union is limited to supporting, coordinating and supplementing the actions of the Member States.

However, in the majority of the common policies, as enumerated in Article 4 TFEU, the competence is shared between the Union and the States, and any EU action must comply with the principles of subsidiarity and proportionality that are enshrined in Article 5 TEU. Article 5(3) prescribes the dual-aspect[28] test of subsidiarity and provides that:

> in areas which do not fall within its exclusive competence, the Union shall act only if and in so far as the objectives of the proposed action cannot be sufficiently achieved by the Member States, either at central level or at regional and local level, but can rather, by reason of the scale or effects of the proposed action, be better achieved at Union level.

---

22. Chalmers, D., et al., *European Union Law: Text and Materials*, 131.
23. Piris, J.-C., 'Does the European Union Have a Constitution? Does It Need One?'.
24. Chalmers, D., et al., *European Union Law: Text and Materials*, 131.
25. The EU has exclusive competence in the following areas: customs union; the establishing of the competition rules necessary for the functioning of the internal market; monetary policy for the Member States whose currency is the euro; the conservation of marine biological resources under the common fisheries policy; common commercial policy.
26. Orebech, P., 'The EU Competency Confusion: Limits, "Extension Mechanisms", Split Power, Subsidiarity, and "Institutional Clashes"', (1999) Journal of Transnational Law & Policy 13(1).
27. Article 6 TFEU.
28. Arnull, A.M., et al., *European Union Law* (Sweet & Maxwell, 2000), 159.

Subsidiarity was added as a general principle of Community law by the Treaty of Maastricht in 1993. Protocol 30 annexed to the Treaty of Amsterdam in 1997 further clarified that for Community action to be justified, both aspects of the subsidiarity principle shall be met: the objectives of the proposed action cannot be sufficiently achieved by Member States' action in the framework of their national constitutional system and can therefore be better achieved by action on the part of the Community.

The Protocol also provided guidelines which should be used in examining whether the subsidiarity test is passed with regard to a Community measure: (i) the issue under consideration has transnational aspects which cannot be satisfactorily regulated by action by Member States; (ii) actions by Member States alone or lack of Community action would conflict with the requirements of the Treaty; and (iii) action at Community level would produce clear benefits by reason of its scale or effects compared with action at the level of the Member States. Further, Protocol 30 orders the European Commission to provide a justification as regards subsidiarity, in the Explanatory Memorandum accompanying a legislative proposal on a matter for which the Community does not have exclusive competence.

In addition to the principle of subsidiarity, Article 5(4) TEU provides that any action by the EU must be proportionate, that is, 'the content and form of Union action shall not exceed what is necessary to achieve the objectives of the Treaties'. Legislative action at the EU level is, therefore, limited not only by the attribution of powers principle, but also in the area of shared competencies, which means that the EU has to first check whether the aim it is trying to achieve could not be equally effectively achieved by national legislation.[29]

De Búrca has, therefore, suggested that the subsidiarity principle embraces three related ideas – the first two entail a 'test of comparative efficiency' and the third one is a proportionality test.[30] Thus, first, the EU can only take action if the objectives of that action cannot be sufficiently achieved by the Member States. Second, due to the action's scale and effects, the EU can better achieve the action. And third, if it is the EU that takes the action then this should not go beyond what is necessary to achieve the Treaty objectives. De Búrca has also suggested elsewhere that the most important feature brought by the principle of subsidiarity is 'the imposition of a certain onus of justification – a kind of public reason requirement – on the various EU institutions when they act'.[31]

29. Alston, P., Weiler, J.H.H., 'An "Ever Closer Union" in Need of Human Rights Policy', (1998) European Journal of International Law 9, 683.
30. Craig, P., de Búrca, G., *EU Law. Text, Cases, and Materials*, 3rd edn (Oxford University Press, 2003), 135.
31. De Búrca, G., 'Reappraising Subsidiarity's Significance after Amsterdam', Harvard Jean Monnet Working Paper 7/99.

The principle of subsidiarity therefore places a burden on the EU institutions to carefully consider whether a particular action is indeed necessary to be taken at the EU level. However, it is worth noting that once the action is taken by the EU it is very difficult to argue before the European Court of Justice that it is in breach of Article 5. The Court has been persistently reluctant to annul a Community measure for breach of the principle of subsidiarity.[32] As proven by the case *Germany v. European Parliament and Council,*[33] the European Court of Justice will generally interpret EU legislation as compatible with the principle of subsidiarity. In this case, the Court held that there is no requirement that EU measures contain an express reference to the subsidiarity principle. It is sufficient that the recitals to the measure made clear why the EU institutions believe that the aims of the measure could be best attained by EU action.

Knowing when the European Union can act, the next question is: does it have any legal competence to regulate for media pluralism? The main texts of the Treaties do not mention the term 'media pluralism'.[34] The European Union does not have a common media policy and, although the respect for rich, cultural and linguistic diversity is mentioned as one of the aims of the Union, respect for media pluralism is not. Nevertheless, the Commission and the Parliament, as well academic literature have discussed several possible 'candidates' for the legal basis for EU action in the media pluralism field. There have even been attempts to base legislation in this area on some of them (e.g., Articles 56 (ex 49) and 114 (ex 95)). Others have only been suggested but never relied on in practice (e.g., Article 167 (ex 151) or 352 (ex 352)). In addition, since the entry into force of the Treaty of Lisbon in 2010, the Charter of Fundamental Rights gained equal status to the Treaties and its Article 11(2) requires freedom and pluralism of the media to be respected. This prompted some opinions that the EU legislative action on media pluralism may be based on this provision. It is worthwhile to analyse in greater detail the chances of success of the EU-level media concentration legislation given the current scope of EU competence.

7.2.1 Legal Bases Used

7.2.1.1 Article 56 TFEU: Broadcasting as a Service?

Article 56 reads as follows:

32. Chalmers, D., et al., *European Union Law: Text and Materials*, 220.
33. Case C-233/94, *Germany v. European Parliament and Council*, [1997] ECR I-2405, paras 26–28.
34. Apart from Article 11(2) of the Charter on Fundamental Rights and the Protocol 32 on the system of public broadcasting in the Member States.

> Within the framework of the provisions set out below, restrictions on freedom to provide services within the Union shall be prohibited in respect of nationals of Member States who are established in a Member State other than that of the person for whom the services are intended.

In the already mentioned *Sacchi*[35] judgment back in the 1970s the European Court of Justice expressed its seminal view that:

> In the absence of express provision to the contrary in the Treaty, a television signal must, by reason of its nature, be regarded as *provision of services*'[36] and 'trade in material, sound recordings, films, apparatus and other products used for the diffusion of television signals are subject to the rules relating to freedom of movement for goods.[37]

This and a later judgment in *Debauve*[38] paved the way for the adoption of the Television Without Frontiers Directive in 1989. The Directive mentioned Articles 47(2) and 55 of the EC Treaty as legal bases for its adoption. Article 47(2) allowed the Council to issue directives for the coordination of national laws concerning the taking-up and pursuit of activities as self-employed persons, and Article 55 extended this permission to the area of services. The AVMS Directive mentions Articles 53(1) and 62 TFEU as its legal bases – the equivalents of Articles 47 and 55 in the EC Treaty. However, as Westphal rightly points out, 'even if one follows the generally accepted approach of EU competence to regulate broadcasting in principle, this does not automatically mean that the EU is also competent to regulate for media pluralism'.[39] Admittedly, the TVWF Directive, by establishing the 'country of origin principle', harmonized first and foremost, the economic aspects of providing broadcasting services. However, the EU has managed to slip into the Directive some rules safeguarding relevant public interests, such as rules on protection of minors, rule against incitement to racial hatred and against surreptitious advertising. The rules on European and independent production quotas contribute to the protection of internal media pluralism. In addition, these provisions have arguably been strengthened in the AVMS Directive.

Moreover, the Commission itself admitted that they fall into the category of legislative tools introduced by the EU to *actively* safeguard media pluralism.[40] Therefore, not only can Article 56 *potentially* be used to introduce measures protecting pluralism, in fact in practice, has already happened. In this situation, Westphal's diagnosis that 'the EU has no regulatory competence in the area of media pluralism on the basis of the

35. Case C-155/73, *Sacchi*, [1974] ECR 409.
36. Case C-155/73, *Sacchi*, [1974] ECR 409, para. 6 (emphasis added).
37. Case C-155/73, *Sacchi*, [1974] ECR 409, para. 7.
38. Case C-52/79, *Procureur du Roi v. Debauve*, [1980] ECR 833.
39. Westphal, D., 'Media Pluralism and European Regulation', 481.
40. European Commission, 'Media Pluralism – What Should Be the European Union's Role?', Issues Paper, 2005.

Articles 49 ff EC Treaty [now 56 ff TFEU]',[41] is questionable. Westphal explains his findings by highlighting the ECJ judgments in *Gouda*[42] and in the *Commission v. Netherlands.*[43] In these cases, the Court held that a national cultural policy aimed at the maintenance of media pluralism may constitute 'an overriding requirement relating to the general interest which justifies a restriction on the freedom to provide services'.[44] From this, Westphal arrives at the conclusion that the EU cannot regulate for media pluralism on the basis of Article 56, because national laws are doing this.

What, therefore, of the production quotas? The Commission itself sees them as aimed at contributing to the protection of media pluralism. They, therefore, constitute a public interest dictated fissure in the general economically driven orientation of the Directive. Therefore, the EU *has acted* on the basis of Article 56 to introduce measures contributing to internal pluralism, and there has been no protest either from the Member States' side, nor from the European Court of Justice. In fact, one of the suggestions of the 1992 Green Paper on 'Pluralism and media concentration in the Internal Market'[45] was to adopt a directive based on, what is now Article 53, that is the legal basis for the harmonization of national rules on services.[46]

Admittedly, however, independent or European production requirements are more similar to the rules on advertising or the rules on protection of minors and prohibiting incitement to racial hatred, since they can be seen as closely related to the provision of the broadcasting service itself. Introducing provisions on structural pluralism however, would be much different since they do not relate to the provision of a service but regulate the size and number of the providers of services.

7.2.1.2 Article 114 TFEU: Pluralism via Backdoor of the Internal Market?

The backdoor of the internal market provisions was opened back in the mid 1990s. Indeed, the Commission almost succeeded in squeezing media concentration legislation through this unlikely opening.

Article 114 TFEU is the main legal basis for the harmonization of national measures in order to achieve a properly functioning Internal Market. It allows the European Parliament and the Council to 'adopt the measures for

41. Westphal, D., 'Media Pluralism and European Regulation', 482.
42. Case C-288/89, *Stichting Collectieve Antennevoorziening Gouda and others v. Commissariaat voor de Media*, [1991] ECR I-4007.
43. Case C-353/89, *Commission v. The Netherlands,* 25 July 1991, [1991] ECR I-4069.
44. Case C-288/89, *Stichting Collectieve Antennevoorziening Gouda and others v. Commissariaat voor de Media*, n. 1090, para. 23; Case C-353/89, *Commission v. The Netherlands,* n. 1091, para. 30.
45. European Commission, 'Pluralism and Media Concentration in the Internal Market: An Assessment of the Need for Community Action (Green Paper)'.
46. Article 47(2) applies to self-employed persons. Article 55 makes it applicable to services.

the approximation of the provisions laid down by law, regulation or administrative action in Member States which have as their object the establishment and functioning of the internal market'. The Article is used in situations when, in the absence of action at Community level, the development of the laws and practices of the different Member States would impede the proper functioning of the Internal Market.[47] However, as de Búrca points out, the EU has also in the past relied on Article 114 to propose legislation in 'borderline' areas such as culture or public health.[48] For instance, the Directive on tobacco advertising,[49] was adopted under the then Article 95 (now Article 114). The reasoning was that the differences between the Member States' laws on the advertising and sponsorship of tobacco products are likely to give rise to barriers to the movement between Member States of the products which serve as the media for such advertising and sponsorship and the freedom to provide services in this area, as well as to distort competition, thereby impeding the functioning of the Internal Market. Therefore, the Directive declares in Article 1 that its objective is to approximate the laws, regulations and administrative provisions of the Member States relating to the advertising of tobacco products and their promotion. However, the main outcome of the harmonization exercise is the general ban of tobacco advertising and promotion (Articles 3 and 4). And this can only be seen as a measure aimed at the reduction of smoking, and thus – at protection of public health.

Similarly, when in the mid 1990s the Commission made an attempt to adopt a media concentration directive, which would lie on the border between the internal market and cultural considerations, the legal basis chosen was the then Article 95 EC Treaty (now Article 114 TFEU). As has been already discussed in Chapter 2, the first Green Paper released in December 1992 entitled 'Pluralism and media concentration in the Internal Market'[50] suggested that media pluralism could be achieved through the realization of the Internal Market, by creating opportunities for media companies.[51] Hence, the promotion of pluralism at the EU level was treated by the Green Paper as a positive 'side effect' of the realization of the Internal Market. The Green Paper suggested that the need for a harmonizing directive

47. See, for instance, Case C-377/98, *Kingdom of the Netherlands v. European Parliament and Council of the European Union*, ECR [2001] I-07079, para. 33.
48. De Búrca, G., 'Reappraising Subsidiarity's Significance after Amsterdam'.
49. Directive 2003/33/EC of the European Parliament and of the Council of 26 May 2003 on the approximation of the laws, regulations and administrative provisions of the Member States relating to the advertising and sponsorship of tobacco products OJ (2003) L152/16, repealing Directive 98/43/EC of the European Parliament and of the Council of 6 July 1998 on the approximation of the laws, regulations and administrative provisions of the Member States relating to the advertising and sponsorship of tobacco products, OJ (1998) L213/9.
50. European Commission, 'Pluralism and Media Concentration in the Internal Market: An Assessment of the Need for Community Action (Green Paper)'.
51. Hitchens, L.P., 'Media Ownership and Control: A European Approach', 591.

arose from the existing 'patchwork' of media ownership rules across Europe, which causes legal uncertainty and, therefore, is an impediment to cross-border investment and constricts the growth of the Information Society within the Internal Market. Given all that, one of the solutions suggested by the Green Paper was to base the legislation on Article 95 of the EC Treaty (now Article 114 TFEU). Although the European Parliament supported by the European Economic and Social Committee and DG Culture voiced serious concerns about basing Community action on the Internal Market and industry arguments and treating protection of pluralism on the EU level as a mere 'side effect',[52] the tenet of the whole debate until the ultimate failure in 1997 was not altered.

The failure of the attempt to base media concentration legislation solely on the Internal Market considerations was, however, quite edifying. Arguably, this was one of the main reasons for the collapse of the whole debate. While it is undeniably true that 'Article 95 EC Treaty [now Article 114 TFEU] ... confers powers upon the European Union in extraordinarily wide and undefined terms [and] it has been of central importance in the making of the Internal Market',[53] it proves impossible to maintain that the need for EU-level measures for structural pluralism is by no means dictated by cultural concerns, but is a purely Internal Market issue. The failure of the directive in the mid 1990s actually excludes any future possibility of basing EU potential media concentration legislation on Article 114. The discussions and tensions surrounding the debate back then, made it clear that it is impossible to use the internal market as the legal basis if the 'dominant purpose' of the legislation is to protect the cultural issue of structural media pluralism. As Chalmers explains 'in determining the predominant purpose of a measure, the Court will look at the principles on which it is based and its ideological content rather than its effects'.[54] He gives an example of the *Framework Directive on Waste*[55] case, in which the ECJ ruled that the Directive should be based on Article 175(1) EC (now Article 192 TFEU) (the environmental base) rather than Article 95 EC (now Article 114 TFEU) (the Internal Market provision). It noted that the central tenets of the Directive were those of environmental management rather than securing the Internal Market objectives of free movement of waste.

Similarly, as de Búrca explains, a measure aimed at the regulation of media concentration, although it may be in part responsible for facilitating the Internal Market in media services, is mainly a measure 'of cultural import in the sense of attempting to ensure media pluralism, the quality of

---

52. European Parliament, Resolution on Pluralism and Media Concentration, 72; The Economic and Social and Committee 'Opinion on Commission Green Paper', 93/C304/07.
53. Chalmers, D., et al., *European Union Law: Text and Materials*, 212.
54. Chalmers, D., et al., *European Union Law: Text and Materials*, 143.
55. Case C-155/91, *Commission v. Council*, [1993] ECR I-939.

programming and the provision of information'.[56] Therefore, even if it was labelled as an internal market measure, it would have a predominantly cultural dimension. Under Article 167 TFEU the Member States retain considerable autonomy in cultural matters, while the Union's role is purely supportive and complementary. It follows that, since the area of media pluralism is so much more sensitive than tobacco advertising and there is no widespread agreement between Member States as to the necessity of legislation, it would be much more difficult to convince the stakeholders once again that internal market considerations underlie the need for a media pluralism directive.

Therefore, any future proposal to adopt a media concentration directive on the basis of Article 114 runs a serious risk of being flawed on the basis of the 'dominant purpose' principle. As Westphal rightly observes, a media concentration directive based on Article 114 would aim to harmonize national media concentration laws 'with the objective of protecting the Internal Market, whereas the national laws it seeks to harmonize will have been primarily initiated to protect the non-economic objective of media pluralism'.[57] This intrinsic tension and disparity of purposes makes Article 114 an unsuitable legal basis for media concentration legislation.

7.2.2 Legal Bases Suggested

7.2.2.1 Article 167 TFEU: Pluralism as a Cultural Matter?

Since it has been established that legislation on media concentration is mainly concerned with the cultural issue of protecting structural media pluralism, rather than the realization of the Internal Market, it has to be considered to what extent is the EU empowered to act on cultural matters.

The only Treaty provision dealing with culture is Article 167, which was added to the Treaty by the Amsterdam amendment. It provides that 'the Union shall contribute to the flowering of the cultures of the Member States, while respecting their national and regional diversity and at the same time bringing the common cultural heritage to the fore'. Article 167 clarifies, however, that Community action in cultural matters may be aimed only at *encouraging cooperation* between Member States and, if necessary, *supporting and supplementing* their action in four, strictly delineated areas: (i) the improvement of knowledge and dissemination of the culture and history of the European peoples; (ii) the conservation and safeguarding of cultural the heritage of European significance; (iii) non-commercial cultural exchanges;

56. De Búrca, G., 'Reappraising Subsidiarity's Significance after Amsterdam'.
57. Westphal, D., 'Media Pluralism and European Regulation', 484.

and (iv) artistic and literary creation, including in the audiovisual sector. In addition, paragraph 5 of Article 167 limits the Union's legislative action to *incentive measures* and *recommendations*, and it expressly excludes any harmonization of the laws and regulations of the Member States.

Therefore, culture is not even in the area of 'shared competences' of the European Union. In this field, the subsidiarity principle requires the EU to opt for Member State level decisions.[58] The only power of incentive measures, recommendations or guidelines which may be adopted under Article 167 lies in their potential interpretative force. As Chalmers explains, national courts are to have regard to these measures 'when interpreting national legislation, implementing them, or when interpreting binding EU measures which supplement them'.[59]

The scope of Article 167 is therefore, strictly limited,[60] and it cannot provide a strong legal basis for EU legislation on media concentration. Harcourt suggests that a ruling by the European Court of Justice on Article 167 could provide a legitimate basis for legislation, without a revision of the EC Treaty.[61] However, as Harcourt herself admits, it is unlikely that the Court would go as far as to interpret Article 167 as providing an appropriate legal basis for media concentration legislation without an explicit Treaty statement from EU Member States.[62]

7.2.2.2 Article 103: Pluralism as a Side-effect of Effective Competition?

Article 103 gives the EU the right to adopt appropriate regulations or directives to give effect to the principles set out in Articles 101 (anticompetitive agreements) and 102 (abuse of a dominant position). The EU Merger Regulation[63] is based on this Article, and as has already been explained in Chapter 4, it explicitly rules out its applicability to media pluralism matters. Article 21(4) leaves the media pluralism concerns of media mergers to the exclusive competence of the Member States. Competition legislation necessarily deals with market efficiency and the competitiveness of the industry. It is also an *ex post* regulation of market failures. Media concentration legislation, however, should aim at *preventing* significant positions being built preferably through the introduction of acceptable thresholds of audience share. This can by no means be achieved on the basis of Article 103.

58. Orebech, P., 'The EU Competency Confusion: Limits, "Extension Mechanisms' Split Power", Subsidiarity, and "Institutional Clashes"'.
59. Chalmers, D., et al., *European Union Law: Text and Materials*, 193.
60. Westphal, D., 'Media Pluralism and European Regulation', 482.
61. Harcourt, A., *The European Union and the Regulation of Media Markets*, 72.
62. Harcourt, A., *The European Union and the Regulation of Media Markets*, 72.
63. Council Regulation (EC) No. 139/2004 of 20 January 2004 on the control of concentrations between undertakings (the EC Merger Regulation), 1.

Westphal quotes Commissioner Monti who said that 'plurality and diversity – fundamental to the health of an open, democratic society – may not be assured by a simple free market approach'.[64]

7.2.2.3 Article 352 TFEU: A 'Rubber Provision'?

Article 352 TFEU is designed to come to the rescue when there is no other clear legal basis for intended legislation. And as it seems that this is the situation with the legal basis for media concentration legislation, it is worth considering the usefulness of this Article in greater detail. It allows the Council to act (unanimously) on a proposal from the Commission and after obtaining the consent of the European Parliament, 'If action by the Union should prove necessary, within the framework of the policies defined in the Treaties, to attain one of the objectives set out in the Treaties, and the Treaties have not provided the necessary powers.'

Article 352 allows EU action only to attain an *objective* of the Union. As has already been mentioned earlier, the Union's objectives are listed in Article 2 TEU, and they are to be attained by common policies. The Union's action on the basis of Article 352 is therefore limited. However, since the formulation of this Article is not very precise,[65] Craig and de Búrca pose the statement that 'the breadth of the Treaty objectives and ... the ECJ's purposive mode of interpreting Community aims' mean that the Article has been used very extensively. In fact, it is often called a 'rubber paragraph' because the EU has stretched it in order to allow for the creeping jurisdiction of the EU.[66] Piris even refers to the 'great period of Article 308 [now 352 TFEU]' which lasted between 1972 and 1998. At the 1972 Paris European Council, the Heads of Government 'agreed that in order to accomplish the tasks laid out in different action programmes, it was advisable to use *as widely as possible* all the provisions of the Treaties including [Article 352]'.[67] The golden era ended in 1988 with the adoption of Single European Act, and it was further frustrated by the ECJ's Opinion 2/94 (see below).

The example of the use of Article 352 is the already mentioned EU Merger Regulation itself. It is based on Article 103 in conjunction with Article 352. Article 103 allows for regulations and directives in order to give effect to the principles set out in Articles 101 and 102. None of these Articles deals with mergers. However, it is clear that one of aims of the European Union mentioned in Article 3 TEU is 'a highly competitive social market

64. Monti, M., 'Does EC Competition Policy Help or Hinder the European Audiovisual and Telecoms Industries?'.
65. Piris, J.-C., 'Does the European Union have a Constitution? Does It Need One?'.
66. Orebech, P., 'The EU Competency Confusion: Limits, "Extension Mechanisms", Split Power, Subsidiarity, and "Institutional Clashes"'.
67. Piris, J.-C., 'Does the European Union Have a Constitution? Does It Need One?'.

economy' and regulating large mergers clearly contributes to this objective. There is, therefore, a Union objective, supported by a common policy, but the Treaty has not provided a clear-cut legal basis for the regulation of all its aspects.

Nonetheless, it is not that simple with media pluralism, or speaking in even wider terms – with media policy. However far Article 352 may be stretched, it is not entirely 'devoid of meaning',[68] and its use to achieve goals which fall outside the scope of the Treaty is not possible either politically or legally.[69] The area of human rights provides a telling example. It has been argued in the past that since media pluralism is a cultural issue, it is closely related to a human right of freedom of expression guarded by Article 10 of the European Convention on Human Rights. Based on that assumption, some authors have drawn an analogy with the protection of equality between men and women, which is not only protected by Article 14 the European Convention on Human Rights, but also by EU law.[70] The Directive on the implementation of the principle of equal treatment for men and women as regards access to employment, vocational training and promotion, and working conditions[71] was adopted in 1976. This was at the time when the equality objective was not yet expressed in the Treaty itself. It was added in 1997 by the Treaty of Amsterdam. Therefore, by analogy, there could possibly be room for a media pluralism directive on the basis of Article 352.

Nevertheless, this argument seems weak. First of all, even if the broad equality objective was not directly mentioned in the EC Treaty, Article 141 (now Article 157 TFEU) already then provided for the more limited equal pay principle. There was, therefore, a starting point. However, as regards media pluralism, the Treaty has always been silent. The term *pluralism of the media* is not used in the main texts of the Treaties. It is only mentioned in the Charter and the protocol on public service broadcasting. There is, therefore, no point of departure. Second, one must not forget that the Equal Treatment Directive was adopted in 1976 – in the 'golden era' of Article 352 when there was a wide consensus between the EU institutions and the Member States as to the need to progress European integration at whatever cost. The same cannot be said about the current mood in the European Union.

As already mentioned, the last nail in the coffin of the 'golden era' of Article 352 and the symbol of the changing mood, was the ECJ's *Opinion 2/94* regarding the Accession of the Community to the European Convention

---

68. Craig, P., de Búrca, G., *EU Law. Text, Cases, and Materials*, 125.
69. Piris, J.-C., 'Does the European Union Have a Constitution? Does It Need One?'.
70. De Búrca, G., 'Reappraising Subsidiarity's Significance after Amsterdam'.
71. Council Directive 76/207/EEC of 9 February 1976 on the implementation of the principle of equal treatment for men and women as regards access to employment, vocational training and promotion, and working conditions, OJ 1976 L39, amended by Directive 2002/73/EC.

on Human Rights.[72] The Opinion was rendered after the Council had asked the European Court of Justice for advice on the legality of using Article 352 to facilitate the European Union's possible accession to the European Convention on Human Rights. The ECJ observed that the Treaty confers no specific powers on the Community in the field of human rights. Such rights are protected only by way of general principles of Community law. The Court, therefore, proceeded to consider Article 352 as the possible legal basis for the EU's accession to the European Convention on Human Rights. It provided a useful definition of Article 352 by saying that the Article

> is designed to fill the gap where no specific provisions of the Treaty confer on the Community institutions express or implied powers to act, if such powers appear none the less to be necessary to enable the Community to carry out its functions with a view to attaining one of the objectives laid down by the Treaty.[73]

However, the ECJ was still adamant that Article 352 could not serve as a basis for widening the scope of Community powers beyond the general framework created by the provisions of the Treaty. Furthermore under no circumstances could it be used as a basis for the adoption of provisions, the effect of which would be to amend the Treaty without following the procedure which it specifically provides for that purpose.[74] As the Court noted, the accession of the EU to the Convention would 'entail the entry of the Community into a distinct international institutional system as well as integration of all the provisions of the Convention into the Community legal order'.[75] Such an outcome would be of constitutional significance and would therefore go beyond the scope of Article 352. The ECJ's conclusion was that the EU could only lawfully accede to the Convention after the Treaty had been amended.[76]

7.2.2.4 Article 11(2) Charter of Fundamental Rights of the European Union?

The Treaty has since been amended, with the Treaty of Lisbon making it mandatory for the European Union to accede to the European Convention on Human Rights and, thus, providing an express legal basis for the accession

72. European Court of Justice, Opinion 2/94 regarding the Accession of the Community to the European Human Rights Convention (Opinion 2/94), [1996] ECR I-1759.
73. European Court of Justice, Opinion 2/94 regarding the Accession of the Community to the European Human Rights Convention, para. 29.
74. European Court of Justice, Opinion 2/94 regarding the Accession of the Community to the European Human Rights Convention, para. 30.
75. European Court of Justice, Opinion 2/94 regarding the Accession of the Community to the European Human Rights Convention, para. 34.
76. European Court of Justice, Opinion 2/94 regarding the Accession of the Community to the European Human Rights Convention, para. 35.

in the form of Article 6(2) TEU.[77] The Treaty of Lisbon also provided the Charter on the Fundamental Rights with a binding legal effect, equal to the Treaties. Therefore, the European Union seems to be increasingly embracing the human rights considerations in its work. This prompted some authors to suggest Article 11(2) of the Charter, which provides that 'the freedom and pluralism of the media shall be *respected*', as a possible legal basis for the binding EU legislative action on media pluralism.

Already in 2004 the European Parliament drew a conclusion that EU-level legislation on media concentration could be adopted on the basis of what was then Article 6(2) TEU.[78] Back then the Article provided that that 'the Union respects fundamental rights, as guaranteed by the European Convention for the Protection of Human Rights and Fundamental Freedoms, as general principles of Community law'. The Parliament noted that following the proclamation of the Charter of Fundamental Rights in 2000, the approval of the Copenhagen criteria for the accession countries, the strengthening of the provisions on European citizenship, the development of an area of freedom, security and justice, the promotion of transparency and privacy, and the prevention of discrimination, the protection of human rights became the *priority objective* of the European Union.[79] The Parliament further concluded that even if the issue of pluralism in the media could at that time only be dealt with indirectly, as there was no specific provision in the Treaties, the situation changed after Amsterdam and Nice Treaties were incorporated which elevated the protection of fundamental rights to 'one of the defining elements and priority objectives of both the Union and the Community'.[80] In the European Parliament's view, there was consequently a need to review the existing competencies and legislation of the Union in the light of the obligation of the EU to ensure the respect of fundamental rights within its internal legal system. In fact, the 1992 Green Paper on 'Pluralism and media concentration in the Internal Market'[81] had already considered in Part IV, Chapter I (IV) the respect of fundamental rights as a Community objective and recognized the close links between the question of protecting pluralism, and freedom of expression.

Nevertheless, and as the Parliament's suggestion has never received an answer, the human rights provisions of EU law cannot serve as a legal basis for

77. Article 6 TEU reads: 'The Union shall accede to the European Convention for the Protection of Human Rights and Fundamental Freedoms. Such accession shall not affect the Union's competences as defined in the Treaties.'
78. European Parliament, 'Report on the risks of violation, in the EU and especially in Italy, of freedom of expression and information'.
79. European Parliament, 'Report on the risks of violation, in the EU and especially in Italy, of freedom of expression and information', 8.
80. European Parliament, 'Report on the risks of violation, in the EU and especially in Italy, of freedom of expression and information', 25.
81. European Commission, 'Pluralism and Media Concentration in the Internal Market: An Assessment of the Need for Community Action (Green Paper)'.

EU media pluralism legislation. First, although the Charter of Fundamental Rights requires that all EU legislation must be adopted with fundamental rights in mind, Article 11(2) cannot serve as a legal basis per se. The wording of the Article is weak. It just declares that pluralism of the media shall be *respected*. It is worth noting that initially the word was *guaranteed*. However, it was weakened following 'concerns that this formulation could become the basis of a 'creeping' EU competence'.[82] Thus, the history of the drafting process itself provides an answer on whether Article 11(2) could be a legal basis for media concentration legislation. Moreover, Article 6(1) TEU provides that 'the provisions of the Charter shall not extend in any way the competences of the Union as defined in the Treaties' and Article 51(2) of the Charter confirms that 'the Charter does not extend the field of application of Union law beyond the powers of the Union or establish any new power or task for the Union, or modify powers and tasks as defined in the Treaties'. In summary, as Westphal notes, Article 11(2) does not 'play a new, significant role for the interpretation of the various freedoms of communication'.[83]

It is worth noting, that in the already mentioned *Centro Europa 7* case, the Italian Ministry of Communications asked for a preliminary ruling on the following question:

> Does Article 10 of the ECHR, as referred to in Article 6 of the TEU, guarantee pluralism in the broadcasting sector, thus requiring the Member States to secure pluralism and competition in the sector based on an antitrust system which, in relation to technological development, secures network access and multiplicity of operators and renders duopolistic market behaviours unlawful?[84]

There was some hope that in answering this question the ECJ may provide further guidance on the question of a legal basis for EU-level legislation on media pluralism. Unfortunately, the Court refused to answer this question by saying that since Italy was in breach of other provisions of the EU law (notably Article 56 TFEU and the E-Communications framework), there was no need to answer the question on Article 10 ECHR.[85]

7.2.2.5 Conclusions on the Question of a Legal Basis

The above analysis of potential legal bases for EU action on media concentration can lead to only one conclusion: there is no *obvious*, clear-cut,

82. Westphal, D., 'Media Pluralism and European Regulation', 486.
83. Westphal, D., 'Media Pluralism and European Regulation', 486.
84. Case C-380/05, *Centro Europa 7*, [2008] ECR I-349.
85. Case C-380/05, *Centro Europa 7*, paras 121–122.

legal basis in either the TEU or the TFEU, for EU legislative action aimed solely at the protection of pluralism and diversity in the media.[86]

If it is ever concluded that the binding EU action on media pluralism is needed, it will be necessary to amend the Treaties in order to extend EU competences in the media industry[87] and to introduce the legal basis. Arino points out that with the shift of the competence balance which was originally drafted in 1950s, the Community competence has gradually widened and EU law 'has gradually restricted the capacity of [the Member States] to regulate their media'.[88] Therefore, the introduction of a legal basis for media pluralism legislation would be taking 'one step forward' in a journey that has already started. And with the broadcast media industry becoming increasingly pan-European, 'the question of the European competence for broadcasting regulation needs to be addressed sooner rather than later'.[89]

However, there is obviously the problem of no political will to introduce such a legal basis.[90] In a 2009 speech to the European Parliament, the then Media and Information Society Commissioner Viviane Reding admitted although one could arrive at a 'generous interpretation of the Treaty to allow the EU to tackle the matter', it would require the political support of the Parliament and the Member States.[91] The Commissioner, arguably rather rhetorically, asked the Parliament whether this seems possible … In this context, practical difficulties associated with the Treaty amendment are illustrative. It took a very long tome to negotiate the Constitution, and it was rejected by France and the Netherlands who felt that it was taking European integration too far. The more cautious Lisbon Treaty still provoked a 'No' vote in the first referendum in Ireland in 2008.[92] It is, therefore, clear that it is not the best time to suggest further changes to the Treaty leading to expanding EU powers to the area which has traditionally been left in the exclusive competence of the Member States.

However, even if the political climate is unfavourable now, the topic should not be abandoned. Awareness raising should continue in order to keep the matter on the agenda. And since, as admitted by Commissioner Reding

86. Westphal, D., 'Media Pluralism and European Regulation', 481.
87. Varney, E. 'Regulating the Digital Television Infrastructure in the EU. Room for Citizenship Interests?', 240; Arino, M., 'Competition Law and Pluralism in European Digital Broadcasting: Addressing the Gaps', 124; Arino, M., 'Pluralism in Digital Broadcasting: Myths, Realities and the Boundaries of European Intervention'.
88. Arino, M., 'Competition Law and Pluralism in European Digital Broadcasting: Addressing the Gaps', 124.
89. Arino, M., 'Competition Law and Pluralism in European Digital Broadcasting: Addressing the Gaps', 124.
90. Craufurd Smith, R., 'Rethinking European Union Competence in the Field of Media Ownership: The Internal Market, Fundamental Rights and European Citizenship', 666.
91. Reding, V., 'Freedom of Expression and Information in Italy: Declaration in the European Parliament Plenary', 8 October 2009.
92. BBC News, 'Ireland Rejects EU Reform Treaty', 13 June 2008.

herself, doing nothing is not an option,[93] Chapter 8 discusses the possible solutions which could currently be utilized or strengthened to augment the active promotion of media pluralism at the EU level.

93. Reding, V., 'Empowering Citizens – The Magazine Media'.

Chapter 8

Solutions to Augment Current EU Action in the Media Pluralism Field

There can be little doubt that it is a pluralistic, rather than a consolidated media market should remain the key priority for the European Union. However, as discussed in the previous chapters, the introduction of a binding EU-level legislation on media pluralism is unlikely in the near future, due to a lack of an express legal basis and a lack of political will to introduce one. Therefore, it is worth considering some non-legislative solutions which could be utilized or strengthened at the EU level to complement the actions taken by the Member States. As noted by Craufurd Smith, 'the choice is not simply between the action at the European level or at the domestic level, but … there is considerable scope for co-ordinated action at both levels'.[1]

The European Parliament, as well as the existing academic literature,[2] have suggested several possible solutions for more involvement of the European Union in safeguarding media pluralism. This chapter discusses and develops some of the particularly noteworthy suggestions. They include:

(i) Strengthening *transparency and the monitoring* of media concentrations. The Parliament suggested introducing rules requiring the transparency of ownership in the media, in particular, in relation to cross-border ownership and for the publication of information on significant interests in the media industry. A Europe-wide media

1. Craufurd Smith, R., 'Rethinking European Union Competence in the Field of Media Ownership: The Internal Market, Fundamental Rights and European Citizenship', 657.
2. Craufurd Smith, R., 'Rethinking European Union Competence in the Field of Media Ownership: The Internal Market, Fundamental Rights and European Citizenship'; Barnett, S., 'Media Ownership Policy in a Recession: Redefining the Public Interest', 217–232.

concentration monitoring body, such as European Media Pluralism Observatory or a European Media Council, should also be considered.[3]

(ii) Soft law, including communications or recommendations, with proposals of actions to be taken at the national and EU level with a view to protecting and enhancing media pluralism. I refer to this solution as developing *soft law with 'hard statements*'.

(iii) *Media specific merger review.* An examination of the need to introduce a 'pluralism test' into the EU Merger Regulation and to establish a European Media Council to assist DG Competition in the analysis of media merger cases.[4]

(iv) Active *promotion of public service media***.** The Parliament has, *inter alia,* recommended the Commission to consider the establishment of EU-wide minimum conditions to ensure that the public service broadcaster is independent and free from interference by the government. I propose to discuss additional support measures for PSB that could be adopted.

In addition, two existing EU measures: the promotion of *media literacy*, and *subsidizing European media production* could be strengthened.

Almost all of the above measures have been suggested by the Council of Europe and acknowledged by the European Parliament. The 1994 Recommendation on measures to promote media transparency,[5] the 1996 Recommendation on the guarantee of the independence of public service broadcasting,[6] or the system of exchange of information between the Council's Member States could be seen as effective sources of inspiration for the EU.

8.1 TRANSPARENCY REQUIREMENTS AND CONSTANT MONITORING

Before any discussion on the ways to combat excessive media concentration can start, it is important to establish what point levels of media concentration actually cross the 'excessive' threshold. The examination of the full picture of media ownership should, therefore, be the first step before *any* measures

3. European Institute for the Media, Final report of the study on 'The information of the citizen in the EU: obligations for the media and the Institutions concerning the citizen's right to be fully and objectively informed'.
4. European Institute for the Media, Final report of the study on 'The information of the citizen in the EU: obligations for the media and the Institutions concerning the citizen's right to be fully and objectively informed'.
5. Council of Europe, Recommendation No. R(94) 13 on Measures to promote media transparency, 22 November 1994.
6. Council of Europe, Recommendation No. R(96) 10 on the guarantee of the independence of public service broadcasting, 11 September 1996.

are taken to regulate it, be it by regulation or soft law. As noted by Commissioner Reding:

> I firmly believe that in order to preserve our pluralist and free societies, we need the monitoring of freedom of the media and of media pluralism. Only this will demonstrate in a convincing manner that legislation is really not needed at EU level. It is therefore in your own interest that there is a regular, objective and fair monitoring.[7]

There is currently a lack of transparency in media ownership patterns across Europe. In many Member States only public companies are required to report changes in shareholding. There is no such requirement at the EU level. Moreover, there is no central data collection of audience share, which should be collected not only at the national level, but also at the European level. The result is that companies in the media sector are not used to complying with transparency requirements and this, therefore, inevitably hinders the application of media concentration laws.[8]

Meanwhile, Noveck is right that transparency of media ownership,

> assumes greater significance with the proliferation of media outlets and concentration of ownership. The globalisation of the media business makes it more difficult for consumers to know who their providers are and to secure a means of communication and redress.[9]

Albarran and Mierzejewska add:

> The situation in Europe is confusing. Each nation treats concentration differently, and follows different guidelines. Even though regulators hope to position Europe as a common market, the reality is there is no effective way to measure concentration across European Union. Data is hard to find, and in some cases, does not even exist.[10]

This makes monitoring and regulating media concentration at European level a near impossible task. Without official and centralized data collection, 'researchers can only provide an anecdotal picture of media concentration in Europe'.[11] There is, therefore, a need for an up-to-date European level collection of data on European media firms, their ownership and audience share. It is also necessary for the EU to join forces and collaborate on a greater scale with the US, given the fact that global media conglomerates,

---

7. Reding, V., 'Empowering Citizens – The Magazine Media'.
8. Sanchez-Tabernero, A., Carvajal, M., *Media Concentration in the European Market. New Trends and Challenges* (Media Markets Monographs, University of Navarra, 2002), 131.
9. Noveck, B.S., 'Thinking Analogue about Digital Television? Bringing European Content Regulation into the Information Age', 51.
10. Albarran, A.B., Mierzejewska, B.I., 'Media Concentration in the US and European Union: A Comparative Analysis'.
11. Albarran, A.B., Mierzejewska, B.I., 'Media Concentration in the US and European Union: A Comparative Analysis'.

such as Time Warner, Viacom, NBC, News Corporation, Liberty Global and Disney, increasingly invest in European media.[12]

Only after a precise and up-to-date picture of media concentration in Europe is available, can proper mechanisms for regulation and control be developed. As noted by Craufurd Smith and Stolte, full picture of media ownership structures in the EU 'would enable the Commission to take concrete steps to address a problem that to date has largely eluded it'.[13]

The Council of Europe has for several years raised the issue of the need to increase media ownership transparency in Europe. In the 1994 Recommendation on measures to promote media transparency,[14] the Committee of Ministers noted that the current development of media concentration is likely to create difficulties for media transparency, given that:

> the growing internationalisation of the capital and activities of firms in the media sector, the development of multimedia groups and the appearance in the media sector of new actors from other branches of economic activity, and the gradual integration of the media into much bigger entities covering the whole of the media production and distribution process from beginning to end.[15]

The Council then identified a two-fold problem that the growing media concentration poses for transparency. First, the public will find it increasingly difficult to identify who are the owners of the media. This is particularly vital as viewers have the right to know the identity and the motives of the owners of the media and of those who may be behind them. This is because with that knowledge it is easier to form an opinion on the value of the news and programmes broadcast by these media players. Second, growing media concentration complicates the activities of the authorities responsible for implementing legislation relating to the control of media concentrations.

In light of the above, the Council of Europe recommended its Member States to consider the inclusion in their domestic legislation of provisions intended to guarantee or promote media transparency, as well as to facilitate exchanges of information between Member States on this issue. The Committee of Ministers provided the Member States with a set of guidelines from which Member States may choose those measures which they feel necessary and appropriate in light of their own specific context. With regard to the broadcasting sector, the Council of Europe suggests introducing

---

12. Albarran, A.B., Mierzejewska, B.I., 'Media Concentration in the US and European Union: A Comparative Analysis'.
13. Craufurd Smith, R., Stolte, Y., 'The European Union and Media Ownership Transparency: The Scope for Regulatory Intervention' (2010); http://mediapolicy.org/wp-content/uploads/the-european-union-media-ownership-transparency.pdf.
14. Council of Europe, Recommendation R(94) 13 on measures to promote media transparency.
15. Council of Europe, Recommendation R(94) 13 on measures to promote media transparency, para. 2.

provisions obliging applicants for broadcasting licenses to provide the regulator with wide-ranging information on the ownership structure. Furthermore, information should also be provided on the interests held by the owners in other media companies, as well as information on other persons or bodies likely to exercise a significant influence on the programming policy of the applicant, by the provision of certain kinds of resources. Any subsequent changes to the above information should also be notified to the regulator. The regulator should then make this information accessible to the public, as well as be prepared to exchange it with regulators from other Member States.

Since 1994, when the Council of Europe's Recommendation on media transparency was adopted, levels of media concentration have increased significantly with a correlating decrease in the transparency of ownership structures. As a result of the internationalization of the broadcasting industry, individual States are incapable of securing transparency in the media sector. In addition, the sector has undergone a significant change since the date of the first Recommendation in 1994. Thus, the 2007 Recommendation on media pluralism and diversity of media content, provides an updated position of the Council in the area of media transparency. The requirements of transparency have not changed significantly, and the Council still recommends its Member States to ensure that the public have access to the following types of information on existing media outlets: (i) information concerning the persons or bodies participating in the structure of the media and on the nature and the extent of the respective participation of these persons or bodies in the structure concerned and, where possible, the ultimate beneficiaries of this participation; (ii) information on the nature and the extent of the interests held by the above persons and bodies in other media or in media enterprises, even in other economic sectors; (iii) information on other persons or bodies likely to exercise a significant influence on the programming policy or editorial policy; (iv) information regarding the support measures granted to the media; and (v) information on the procedure applied in respect of the right of reply and complaint.

In addition, the European Parliament in paragraph 35 of the already mentioned 2008 Resolution on concentration and pluralism in the media in the European Union,[16] encouraged 'the disclosure of ownership of all media outlets to help achieve greater transparency regarding the aims and background of the broadcaster and publisher'.

However, none of the recommendations by the European Parliament or the Council of Europe and the European Parliament have been acted on by the European Commission.[17] Admittedly, the publication of the Media Pluralism Monitor as a second step in the 'Three-Step-Approach' to media

16. European Parliament, Resolution on concentration and pluralism in the media in the European Union, 25 September 2008 (2007/2253).
17. Craufurd Smith, R., Stolte, Y., 'The European Union and Media Ownership Transparency: The Scope for Regulatory Intervention'.

pluralism initiative may suggest the beginning of a more proactive approach on the Commission's part. In fact, the MPM has been praised by its authors as 'a *first step* in the development of an EU-wide standardized monitoring system for detecting and dealing with societal risks in the area of media pluralism and the first attempt to apply risk analysis to media policy'.[18] The MPM, however, is a diagnostic tool to be utilized by the Member States with no obligation to do so and no EU-level monitoring mechanism.

Thus the next step could be to make the MPM part of the *European-level* action aimed at centralized monitoring of dangerous trends and increasing media transparency. To ensure as wide pan-European monitoring as possible, the European Audiovisual Observatory, which operates within the legal framework of the Council of Europe, could play a role of a central European body responsible for monitoring media concentration. According to the Observatory's Statute:

> The aim of the European Audiovisual Observatory shall be to improve the transfer of information within the audiovisual industry, to promote a clearer view of the market and greater transparency. In doing so, the Observatory shall pay particular attention to ensuring reliability, compatibility and comparability of information.[19]

The Observatory has, therefore, a clearly defined task, that is, to create transparency in the European audiovisual sector by improving the transfer of and access to information. The tasks could be broadened to include the collection of data on media ownership and audience share and the monitoring media concentration.

However, one could also envisage the creation of a separate body under the auspices of the European Union, which would specialize only in the collection of media ownership and audience share data and monitor media concentration levels in Europe. The European Parliament has consistently called on the European Commission to consider structured monitoring of media concentration as one of its main tasks in the audiovisual field, in view of the trend towards concentration of media ownership, both 'horizontally' and 'vertically'. The Parliament further warned the Commission that 'in the absence of such monitoring and without a strengthening of national rules, this development risks undermining media diversity, freedom of expression and free access to information'.[20]

---

18. Valcke, P., et al., 'The European Media Pluralism Monitor: Bridging Law, Economics and Media Studies as a First Step towards Risk-Based Regulation in Media Markets', 85–113, 86 (emphasis added).
19. European Audiovisual Observatory, Mission Statement, http://www.obs.coe.int.
20. European Parliament, Report on the application of Articles 4 and 5 of Directive 89/552/EEC (the 'TV without Frontiers' Directive), as amended by Directive 97/36/EC, for the period 2001–2002, 21 June 2005, Final A6-0202/2005 (Weber Report), 14.

During the consultation on the revision of the TVWF Directive, a suggestion was made to establish a European Media Pluralism Observatory. In its 2004 Report for the European Parliament,[21] the European Institute for the Media (EIM), debated the ways in which to increase media ownership transparency in Europe and concluded that:

> the establishment of an Observatory focusing on media markets and concentration, with the provision of a data-base of information on EU Member States, would go a long way towards providing such transparency and enhancing national systems of regulation.[22]

During the consultation that took place before the Liverpool Audiovisual Conference, EBU agreed with EIM and added that for the Observatory 'to work successfully it might be necessary, as a complementary measure, to ensure that Member States make the requisite data available'.[23] The creation of the Observatory could, therefore, be a good starting point for the Commission. Once it starts monitoring the situation in an organized way, it could realize what exactly the level of concentration is. This could possibly lead the Commission to conclude that media concentration in Europe has reached dangerous levels, and that the time has come for positive action at the EU level. As Wallis explains:

> by making both decision-makers and the general public aware of a decreased range of choice, pressure could be brought to bear on media channels and their management to increase diversity, maybe even to convince decision-makers that 'diversity is a profit-making strategy.[24]

The European Commission has not openly opposed the proposal to establish the European Media Pluralism Observatory. In fact, in the final report from the 2005 Liverpool Audiovisual Conference, the Working Group on Media Pluralism declares that the idea to create European Observatory was in theory, supported.[25] Through the creation of the Observatory, the postulated enhancement of the EU's role in monitoring, exchanging information and

---

21. European Institute for the Media, Final report of the study on 'The information of the citizen in the EU: obligations for the media and the Institutions concerning the citizen's right to be fully and objectively informed'.
22. European Institute for the Media, Final report of the study on 'The information of the citizen in the EU: obligations for the media and the Institutions concerning the citizen's right to be fully and objectively informed', 251.
23. European Broadcasting Union, 'Position on Issues Papers for the Liverpool Audiovisual Conference, 2005', 18.
24. Wallis, R., 'Diversity in Media – Pluralism through Privatisation Or?', Conference on Cultural Diversity, Copenhagen, 2002.
25. European Commission, Liverpool Audiovisual Conference, 22 September 2005, 'Final Report', 26.

comparing legislation on media concentration could be achieved. Furthermore, having a supra-national monitoring body, would guarantee transparency, independence and neutrality of the data collection exercise. The Observatory could work with the Council of Europe to draw up a minimum set of standards for media pluralism which would be observed by all Member States.[26] In addition, the European Parliament has tabled an interesting suggestion, which is to organize a European Year of Television with the aim of drafting a European Audiovisual Pact to ensure a balance between competition, innovation, quality, culture and plurality.[27] These tasks could, in theory all fall within the competence of the European Media Pluralism Observatory. Otherwise, Stolte and Craufurd Smith suggest that the sphere of competence of the already existing European Agency for Fundamental Rights could be broadened to include responsibility for the EU-level monitoring of media concentration and stimulating debate on media transparency.[28] However, as the potential scope for action of the Agency is limited, the establishment of a separate EU-level body tasked solely with monitoring the European media market should not be dismissed.

Finally, Craufurd Smith and Stolte suggest that it would be beneficial and, in theory, feasible under the current scope of the EU's competence, to adopt a Media Transparency Directive.[29] They note that although the adoption of a comprehensive media ownership directive in the mid-1990s proved unsuccessful due to the lack of legal basis and political support, a more contained directive focused only on transparency could potentially be envisaged. In fact, certain transparency requirements are already present in two EU legislative acts: the AVMS Directive (Article 3a) and the Transparency Directive.[30] Still, they are not sufficient to achieve a full media market transparency in the European Union and there is scope for additional action. The AVMS Directive requires the Member States to ensure that audiovisual service providers *under their jurisdiction* provide a minimum set of information (name, address, contact details) which should be accessible to the recipients of the service. However, as noted by Craufurd Smith and

26. Commission of the Bishops' Conferences of the European Community, Comments on 'Media Pluralism – what should be the European Union's role?', Issues Paper, 1.
27. European Parliament, Report on the application of Articles 4 and 5 of Directive 89/552/EEC (the 'TV without Frontiers' Directive), as amended by Directive 97/36/EC, for the period 2001–2002, 21 June 2005, Final A6-0202/2005 ('Weber Report'), 15.
28. Craufurd Smith, R., Stolte, Y., 'The European Union and Media Ownership Transparency: The Scope for Regulatory Intervention'.
29. Craufurd Smith, R., Stolte, Y., 'The European Union and Media Ownership Transparency: The Scope for Regulatory Intervention'.
30. Directive 2004/109/EC of the European Parliament and of the Council on minimum transparency requirements for listed companies.

Stolte, these requirements are more complaint, than information and ownership transparency oriented.[31]

The Transparency Directive, however, does require information relating to major shareholdings in companies listed in regulated markets to be made publicly available. The weaknesses of the directive from the media transparency perspective are two-fold. First of all, not all media organizations will fulfil the requirements in the Directive, and second, often the ownership is 'obscured behind a chain of companies that lie behind a listed shareholder'.[32]

Therefore, Craufurd Smith and Stolte conclude that there is scope for EU action to support transparency of media ownership preferably on the internal market basis. They believe that it is possible to prove that action at the EU level is required, because there has been no concerted effort by Member States to ensure transparency, and that the existing patchwork of transparency rules creates a barrier to the proper functioning of the internal market.[33]

However, the European Commission's continuous resistance to introduce binding legislation, or, as will be discussed below, even soft law in the media pluralism and ownership field, makes it rather unlikely that it will propose a Media Transparency Directive any time soon. The Media Pluralism Monitor seems to be the first and only step taken in this area as even the third step from the 'Three-Step-Approach' to media pluralism initiative, i.e., the Communication on pluralism indicators, has not been taken. However, as the Media Transparency Directive is arguably within the European Union's scope of competence, Craufurd Smith and Stolte suggest that the case for a European Citizen's Initiative (ECI) as regulated by Article 11 of the Treaty on European Union could be promoted. As explained in more detail in Chapter 2.2.1, the current ECI demanding a broad media pluralism directive intended for launch in May 2012[34] will probably be regarded inadmissible due to the lack of legal basis. When this happens, attention should be drawn to the possibility of re-launching the ECI with a more contained proposal of a Media Transparency Directive. As Craufurd Smith and Stolte note,

> After all, nothing could be more important to Europe's citizens than knowing who owns the media on which they depend for information.[35]

31. Craufurd Smith, R., Stolte, Y., 'The European Union and Media Ownership Transparency: The Scope for Regulatory Intervention'.
32. Craufurd Smith, R., Stolte, Y., 'The European Union and Media Ownership Transparency: The Scope for Regulatory Intervention'.
33. Craufurd Smith, R., Stolte, Y., 'The European Union and Media Ownership Transparency: The Scope for Regulatory Intervention'.
34. See http://www.mediainitiative.eu/topics/the-campaign-a-european-initiative-for-media-pluralism/.
35. Craufurd Smith, R., Stolte, Y., 'The European Union and Media Ownership Transparency: The Scope for Regulatory Intervention'.

8.2 SOFT LAW WITH 'HARD' STATEMENTS

As already discussed in Chapter 2, the Barroso Commission's 'Better Regulation Strategy' aims to simplify and improve the existing regulation in order to 'reinforce the respect and the effectiveness' of EU law.[36] This implies a roll-back of unnecessary or outdated legislation if it is not in line with competitiveness and jobs goals. In addition, the introduction of new binding legislation should be very carefully considered.

However, notwithstanding this negative attitude towards adding to the EU's legislative omnipresence, resorting to soft law would possibly be acceptable. In fact, the adoption of soft law may be welcome as part of the new 'better regulation' paradigm.[37] The European Parliament has suggested that the EU should begin a journey towards comprehensive EU policy on media concentration with developing recommendations with a view to paving the way for the adoption of binding regulations in the future. Moreover, Commissioner Reding herself emphasized in one of the speeches, that the Commission 'should explore all the possibilities of using "soft law"'.[38]

In fact, in other policy areas this has already happened. For instance, the development of Community social regulation has been restricted by the Member States, which have constrained the expansion of the legislative competence of the Community in this area.[39] The Commission, therefore, turned to soft law as an alternative to formal legislation. Soft law has been defined in the academic literature as 'rules of conduct that are laid down in instruments which have not been attributed legally binding force as such, but nevertheless may have certain – indirect – legal effects, and that are aimed at and may produce practical effects'.[40]

Senden has offered an interesting classification of EC soft law into three categories of instruments: (i) preparative and informative (e.g., Green Papers, White Papers, action programmes and informative communications); (ii) interpretative and decisional (e.g., communications, notices, guidelines,

---

36. European Commission, Better Regulation Initiative, http://ec.europa.eu/governance/better_regulation/index_en.htm.
37. Barani, L., 'Hard and Soft Law in the European Union: The Case of Social Policy and Open Method of Coordination', Webpapers on Consitutionalism & Governance beyond the State 2/2006.
38. Reding, V., 'The European Commission and Media Industry: The Need for a New Partnership'.
39. Snyder, F., 'The Effectiveness of European Community Law: Institutions, Processes, Tools and Techniques', (1993) The Modern Law Review 56(1), 19–54, 32.
40. Senden, L., 'Soft Law, Self-regulation and Co-regulation in European Law: Where Do They Meet?', (2005) Electronic Journal of Comparative Law 9(1), 23; See also generally in soft law, Senden, L., *Soft Law in European Community Law* (Hart Publishing, 2004); see also Snyder, F., 'The Effectiveness of European Community Law: Institutions, Processes, Tools and Techniques', 32.

codes); and (iii) steering instruments (e.g., recommendations, declarations, conclusions).[41]

It is the third category – steering instruments – which is of greatest interest for the purposes of this chapter. And of the instruments belonging to this category, the most valuable is a recommendation as it is a 'formal' steering instrument mentioned as one of the sources of secondary EU law in Article 288 TFEU. The value of recommendations stems from the fact that, as observed by Senden, they may fulfil a dual function: (i) a *para-law* function, when they are used as temporary or permanent alternatives to legislation; or (ii) the *pre-law* function when they pave the way for the adoption of future legislation 'by providing or increasing the basis of support for the rules contained therein'.[42]

There are a number of advantages soft law offers over formal legislation. First of all, it provides for lower 'contracting' costs as it lowers the stakes for the negotiating parties.[43] Second, it also lowers 'sovereignty' costs. As noted by Abbott et al., 'even the most powerful states recognize that legalization will circumscribe their autonomy'.[44] By opting for soft law, States can reduce sovereignty concerns by 'opting for escape closes, imprecise commitments or "political" forms of delegation that allow them to maintain future control if adverse circumstances arise'.[45] Third, soft law is better equipped than hard law to cope with diversity between the States. It may serve as a tool for compromise when it would be impossible to adopt a formal piece of legislation due to overly divergent national interests.[46] Fourth, soft law offers flexibility as it allows for easier modification if circumstances change. And finally, the stated advantage of soft law over hard law is the simplicity and speed – to a large extent, it allows to avoid formal and cumbersome legislative procedures.[47]

Turning now to how soft law can support regulation of media concentration at the EU level, it is interesting to observe that what we can currently observe in the EU in the area is the existence of hard law (Merger Regulation, AVMS Directive, the E-Communications Framework's Directives), but with relatively weak statements. In all public statements and in the majority of legislative measures, the EU limits itself to at best *accepting*,

41. Senden, L., 'Soft Law, Self-regulation and Co-regulation in European Law: Where Do They Meet?', 23–24.
42. Senden, L., 'Soft Law, Self-regulation and Co-regulation in European Law: Where Do They Meet?', 24.
43. Case C-322/88, *Grimaldi v. Fonds des Maladies Professionnelles* [1991] ECR 4402.
44. Abbott, K.W., Snidal, D., 'Hard and Soft Law in International Governance' (2000) International Organization 54(3), 421–456, 435.
45. Abbott, K.W., Snidal, D., 'Hard and Soft Law in International Governance', 435.
46. Abbott, K.W., Snidal, D., 'Hard and Soft Law in International Governance', 444.
47. Trubek, D.M., Cottrell, P., Nance, M., 'Soft Law, Hard Law, and European Integration: Toward a Theory of Hybridity', Jean Monnet Working Paper 02/05, 15–16.

tolerating or allowing national measures to prevent excessive media concentration or otherwise supporting media pluralism. Given the lack of a legal basis for EU action on media pluralism, EU law *allows* Member States to keep their media concentration rules, but does not require the introduction of such rules if they are lacking (as in Poland) or does not do anything if these laws are ignored (as in Italy), liberalized (as in the UK) or is almost powerless if new laws are introduced which threaten media freedom and pluralism (as in Hungary). The Treaty also allows Member States to provide for the funding of public service broadcasting, but only insofar as such funding is granted to for the fulfilment of the public service remit, and insofar as such funding does not affect trading conditions and competition in the Community. Further, it is only up to the Member States to avail themselves of Article 21(4) of the Merger Regulation. It is also up to them to designate network operators with significant market power, and those companies may, but do not have to, be subject to access remedies. Article 31 of the Universal Service Directive merely *allows* Member States to introduce reasonable must-carry rules, and only within strictly delineated limits. Similarly, according to the AVMS Directive, lists of events of major importance are not compulsory, and production quotas are required only 'where practicable'.

The result is that the Member States are not making an extensive use of the measures *allowed under* EU law. Many Member States have not introduced any control measures for media concentration. After the *Newspaper Publishing* case, there has been no further instances of the use of Article 21(4) of the Merger Regulation. Not all Member States have introduced must-carry rules and production quotas, and only very few have submitted lists of events of major importance to the society, to be broadcast on free TV. One cannot help but think, what the outcome would be if the situation was reversed: if we had 'soft' law with 'hard' statements.

There is an interesting example in the form of a 2006 Recommendation on the protection of minors and human dignity.[48] The legal basis for this Recommendation is Article 157 TFEU which deals with the competitiveness of the Community's industry and only requires qualified majority voting in the Council.

The Recommendation declares, at the outset, that because Article 1 of the Charter of Fundamental Rights of the European Union provides that human dignity must be respected and protected, the European Union should gear its political action to preventing any form of violation of that principle. Therefore, the Member States are recommended, in the interests of promoting the development of the audiovisual and on-line information services *industry*, to take the necessary measures to ensure the protection of minors

48. European Parliament and the Council, Recommendation of 20 December 2006 on the protection of minors and human dignity and on the right of reply in relation to the competitiveness of the European audiovisual and on-line information services industry, OJ (2006) L378/72.

and human dignity in all audiovisual and on-line information services. If it was possible to reach that conclusion in relation to one of the fundamental rights protected by the Charter, it should in theory be possible for all the other rights. The statement from the 2006 Recommendation could be paraphrased as follows:

> Article 11(2) of the Charter of Fundamental Rights of the European Union provides that the freedom and pluralism of the media shall be respected. The European Union should, therefore, gear its political action to preventing any form of violation of that principle. Therefore, Member States are recommended, in the interests of promoting the development of the audiovisual and on-line information services *industry*, to take the necessary measures to ensure the protection of media pluralism and diversity, in particular by maintaining or introducing anti-concentration legislation, actively supporting public service broadcasting and promoting open CAS.

Just like there is no legal basis in EU law allowing EU action on media pluralism other than the Charter, there is equally no legal basis for EU action on human dignity other than the Charter. And yet, the EU chose to stretch the EC Treaty so as to protect the minors and human dignity as necessary preconditions for the proper development of the European broadcasting industry; however, it continually refuses to do the same for media pluralism. As proven by the above paraphrase, the arguments used in the Recommendation on measures to promote media pluralism could be almost identical as the arguments of the Recommendation on the protection of minors and human dignity.

'Soft law with hard statements' may also potentially build political momentum for binding action. And EU law knows a precedent in the form of sex equality legislation. As G. Monti reminds us:

> The pace of sex equality legislation stalled in the 1980s and 1990s, in part because of the reluctance of Member States to take equality further. The Commission responded to this hiatus by drafting a range of soft law measures to encourage Member States' action [e.g. Recommendation 84/635 on the promotion of positive action for women]. It has been suggested that the increased legislative output in the 1980s and 1990s was in part motivated by the need for the EC to show that it was not merely about achieving economic goals.[49]

Moreover, which is particularly helpful, the European Court of Justice has offered support for recommendations in the *Grimaldi* judgment.[50] The Court held that the national courts 'are bound to take recommendations into

49. Chalmers, D., et al., *European Union Law: Text and Materials*, 886.
50. Case C-322/88, *Grimaldi v. Fonds des Maladies Professionnelles* [1991] ECR 4402.

consideration in order to decide disputes submitted to them, in particular where they cast light on the interpretation of national measures adopted in order to implement them or where they are designed to supplement binding Community provisions'.[51]

Nevertheless, one must not overlook the weaknesses of soft law which lacks features such as 'obligation, uniformity, justiciability (and) sanctions'.[52] In addition, as noted by Trubek et al., soft law lacks clarity and precision needed to provide predictability and a reliable framework for action, it bypasses normal systems of accountability and 'undermines EU legitimacy because it creates expectations, but cannot bring about change'.[53] Therefore, 'soft law with hard statements' suggested here may possibly exercise the pre-law function. In fact, the European Parliament has suggested that the EU may begin its journey towards binding measures on media pluralism by developing recommendations, and it may move on to the adoption of *binding regulations* in the future.

However, this is all provided that the Commission is willing to adopt the soft law in this area in the first place. As already mentioned, the third step of the 'Three-Step Approach' to the issue of media pluralism launched by then-Information Society Commissioner Reding in 2007,[54] was supposed to be a Commission Communication on the indicators for media pluralism in the EU Member States, on which a broad public consultation was to take place. It was not taken under the Commissioner's Reding term. The initial plan was to hold public consultation following the publication of the Communication and, should the consultation reveal such a need, to commission a second study in order to systematically apply the media pluralism indicators to all EU Member States. In 2009, Commissioner Reding commented that the Communication would be presented by the next Commission.[55] However, it seems that under the new Commissioner Kroes, the third step has been abandoned altogether. Instead, two new advisory bodies have been created: the High Level Group on Media Freedom and Pluralism and a Centre for Media Pluralism and Media Freedom within the Robert Schuman School of the European University Institute. They are both

---

51. Case C-322/88, *Grimaldi v. Fonds des Maladies Professionnelles* [1991] ECR 4402, para. 18.
52. Trubek, D.M., et al., 'Soft Law, Hard Law, and European Integration: Toward a Theory of Hybridity', 5.
53. Trubek, D.M., et al., 'Soft Law, Hard Law, and European Integration: Toward a Theory of Hybridity', 6; see also Klabbers, J., 'The Undesirability of Soft Law', (1998) 1 Nordic Journal of International Law 36.
54. See European Commission, DG Media and Information Society, 'Media Pluralism: The need for transparency, freedom and diversity in Europe's media landscape', http://ec.Europa.eu/information_society/media_taskforce/pluralism/index_en.htm.
55. Reding, V., 'Empowering Citizens – The Magazine Media'.

a valuable answer to the calls for more EU-level research in the area,[56] but an opportunity for a soft law instrument in the form of a Communication which could possibly contain several 'hard' statements was once again not realized.

8.3 MEDIA SPECIFIC MERGER REVIEW

In its 2004 Report for the European Parliament,[57] the European Institute for the Media (EIM) suggested that:

> competition policy should recognise the specific cultural and democratic importance of the media industries as opposed to other industries when examining merger and acquisitions. An assessment of the UK 'public interest test' and its application, or the assessment of other systems dealing with the impact of ownership changes on pluralism, would be useful as a step in this direction.[58]

The public interest test used in the UK was already described in detail in Chapter 6, section 6.1. One of the ways of transplanting it to the EU level would be to require DG Competition to take pluralism and diversity concerns into account while examining the impact of media mergers. Even if DG Competition is ultimately not empowered to make binding decisions concerning media pluralism, the effect of using the public interest test in competition analysis could be an obligation on DG Competition that would suggest to a Member State concerned, to use Article 21(4) of the Merger Regulation. This solution is, however, rather unfeasible. Media pluralism issues of a pan-European dimension are very complex, and the European competition authority probably lacks the requisite expertise and furthermore is not adequately resourced to deal with them.

Therefore, a better method would be to implement the British and Irish solution of shared competences coupled with the European Parliament's suggestion from its 1992 Resolution[59] to create an independent European Media Council responsible for safeguarding diversity of opinion. The 'division of labour' between DG Competition and the Member States, which characterizes current EC merger control in the media sector, would thus be

56. Craufurd Smith, R., 'Rethinking European Union Competence in the Field of Media Ownership: The Internal Market, Fundamental Rights and European Citizenship'.
57. European Institute for the Media, Final report of the study on 'The information of the citizen in the EU: obligations for the media and the Institutions concerning the citizen's right to be fully and objectively informed'.
58. European Institute for the Media, Final report of the study on 'The information of the citizen in the EU: obligations for the media and the Institutions concerning the citizen's right to be fully and objectively informed', 251.
59. European Parliament, Resolution on media concentration and diversity of opinions, OJ (1992) C-284/44.

shifted to the European level. DG Competition would continue examining the economic effects of media mergers with a Community dimension, while the European Media Council, with the support of the national regulatory bodies, would assess the impact the merger would have on pluralism and diversity in the European media market, and produce a possibly binding report or an opinion.[60] Not to multiply institutions dealing with media concentration and pluralism issues, the European Media Council could also perform the tasks of the Media Pluralism Observatory mentioned above (transparency issues and drafting European Audiovisual Pact). As Scheuer and Strothmann argue, 'in view of the numerous media companies currently being formed, the need for Europe-wide measures is obvious', and in this regard 'the idea of a European media concentration authority with comprehensive powers is highly topical'.[61] They are, however, quick to point out two arguments against this idea. First of all, the well-known lack of legal basis argument that is, the fact that 'the Community has no specific power to set objectives or requirements to guarantee diversity of opinion'.[62] Second, since there is no obligation to protect Europe-wide pluralism or diversity, the establishment of a European Media Council would contravene the principles of subsidiarity and proportionality.[63]

It could, however, be argued that the European Media Council, or whatever else the body would be called, would not have to possess decision making powers. It could be composed of the representatives of the Member States, and initially it could act as a kind of 'advisory committee' to DG Competition. It could only analyse cases of transnational media concentration, for instances 'when a large media network strongly present in one or more European countries enters the market of another Member State',[64] and it would therefore suggest DG Competition to, in turn advise a Member State concerned to use Article 21(4). This would not be anything that DG Competition is not able to do itself today, and it is simply not doing it due to merger review time pressures and the lack of adequate resources. Although a body with no decision making powers may seem somewhat toothless, the

60. Arino, M., 'Pluralism in Digital Broadcasting: Myths, Realities and the Boundaries of European Intervention'.
61. Scheuer, A., Strothmann, P., 'Media Supervision on the Threshold of the 21st Century. What Are the Requirements of Broadcasting, Telecommunications and Concentration Regulation?', 7.
62. Scheuer, A., Strothmann, P., 'Media Supervision on the Threshold of the 21st Century. What Are the Requirements of Broadcasting, Telecommunications and Concentration Regulation?', 7.
63. Scheuer, A., Strothmann, P., 'Media Supervision on the Threshold of the 21st Century. What Are the Requirements of Broadcasting, Telecommunications and Concentration Regulation?', 7.
64. European Broadcasting Union, 'Position on Issues Papers for the Liverpool Audiovisual Conference, 2005'.

fact that there was actually a case where Article 21(4) was suggested,[65] proves that such a recommendation mechanism can indeed be effective.

The introduction of an EU-level media specific merger review would ensure that in the application of competition law to media mergers, full account would be taken of the public interest of maintaining sufficient levels of media pluralism in Europe. And this is notwithstanding the fact that the Commission has never acted on this suggestion and, thus, it largely remains on the European Parliament's 'wish list'. In fact, as noted by Craufurd Smith:

> Member States are unlikely to back such a proposal, given their limited influence in the field of Community competition law, and any moves in this direction would probably be seen as an illegitimate attempt to do indirectly what could not be agreed directly through the 'appropriate' regulatory procedures.[66]

8.4 ACTIVE PROMOTION OF PUBLIC SERVICE MEDIA AS GUARANTORS OF CONTENT DIVERSITY

As already mentioned. Napoli[67] and Valcke identify the so-called diversity chain. The three links of the chain can in simplified terms be described as: (i) source/supplier diversity (structural pluralism); (ii) content diversity (internal pluralism); and (iii) and exposure diversity. In order for any given media market to be truly pluralistic and diverse, safeguards are needed at each level of the 'diversity' chain.

The main answer in Europe to the need for content diversity has been 'public service broadcasting, with its objective of universality'.[68] Indeed Tongue corroborates by highlighting that the democratic objectives, to provide a society with a full range of information, debate and expression, is the mission and the *raison d'être* of public service broadcasting.[69] Therefore, a large number of EU Member States have established their own public service broadcasters and imposed on them a set of obligations, known as a public service remit, which 'technically guarantee that a wide range of programmes are available to the public and these programmes are of

---

65. Case IV/M.423, *Newspaper Publishing*, 14 March 1994.
66. Craufurd Smith, R., 'Rethinking European Union Competence in the Field of Media Ownership: The Internal Market, Fundamental Rights and European Citizenship', 670.
67. Napoli, P.M., 'Deconstructing the Diversity Principle', 7–34; Valcke, P., 'Looking for the User in Media Pluralism Regulation: Unraveling the Traditional Diversity Chain and Recent Trends of User Empowerment in European Media Regulation'.
68. Gibbons, T., 'Pluralism, Guidance and the New Media', in Marsden, C.T. (ed.), *Regulating the Global Information Society* (Routledge, 2000), 307.
69. Tongue, C., 'Culture or Monoculture? The European Audiovisual Challenge', 135.

sufficient quality and diversity so as to be representative of the views and needs of a democratic state'.[70]

Public Service Broadcasters are broadcasters with a public service mandate or remit. The 2009 Commission Communication on the application of State-aid rules to public service broadcasting,[71] which will be discussed in more detail below, explains that in general definition of the public service remit falls within the competence of the Member States, which can decide at national, regional or local level. The Communication further clarifies that it is possible to adopt a wide definition of the PSB remit, entrusting a broadcaster with the task of providing *balanced and varied programming* to fulfilling the democratic, social and cultural needs of a particular society and guaranteeing pluralism, including cultural and linguistic diversity.[72] Further guidance as to the understanding of the public service remit has been provided by the Committee of Ministers of the Council of Europe. The 2007 Recommendation on the remit of public service media in the information society[73] explains the Council's understanding of the remit of public service broadcasting as consisting of five elements: (i) a reference point for all members of the public, offering universal access; ii) a factor of social cohesion and integration for all individuals, groups and communities; iii) a source of impartial and independent information and comment, and of innovatory and varied content which complies with high ethical and quality standards; iv) a forum for pluralistic public discussion and a means of promoting broader democratic participation for individuals; and v) an active contributor to audiovisual creation and production and greater appreciation and dissemination of the diversity of national and European cultural heritage.

In summary, therefore, public service broadcasters in Europe, regardless of their 'nationality', should posses several key common features. They should provide universal access to programmes that are free at the point of use; present accurate and independent news, education and entertainment; express the full range of political views and cultural values; be independent from political and economic pressures; compete for good programming not for audience share; and be publicly financed.[74]

---

70. Ward, D., 'Media Concentration and Pluralism: Regulation, Realties and the Council of Europe's Standards in the Television Sector'.
71. Communication from the Commission on the application of State aid rules to public service broadcasting, OJ (2008) C-257/1.
72. Communication from the Commission on the application of State aid rules to public service broadcasting, OJ (2008) C-257/1.
73. Recommendation CM/Rec(2007)3 of the Committee of Ministers to Member States on the remit of public service media in the information society, adopted by the Committee of Ministers on 31 January 2007 at the 985th meeting of the Ministers' Deputies.
74. Tongue, C., 'Culture or Monoculture? The European Audiovisual Challenge', 135; O'Mahony, C., 'A Future for Public Service Broadcasting: New Challenges, New Pressures, New Approaches', paper presented to the Irish Media Research Network Conference, 16 June 2006; Rumphorst, W., 'Public Service Broadcasting in an Enlarging Europe: Contributing to European Policy Objectives', Amsterdam, 2 September 2004.

Given all of the above, several authors have suggested that relying on strong public service broadcasters, who act as a 'counterweight'[75] to the large commercial profit-oriented media conglomerates, may be a way to ensure internal media pluralism in Europe.[76] As noted by Ward, while the commercial sector may provide a diversity of outlets, the public broadcasters provide the backbone of pluralism by offering a diversity of programmes that serve the whole of the public.[77] And the provision of a wide range of quality programmes is not only a feature of public service broadcasters, but it is also their *obligation.*

For instance, section 114(3) of the Irish Broadcasting Act 2009 requires the public service broadcaster, RTE to

> ensure that the programme schedules of the broadcasting service ... (a) provide a comprehensive range of programmes in the Irish and English language that reflect the cultural diversity of the whole island of Ireland and include, ... programmes that entertain, inform and educate, provide coverage of sporting, religious and cultural activities and cater for the expectations of the community generally, as well as members of the community with special or minority interests and which, in every case respect human dignity.

The 'quality' obligation has resulted in public service broadcasters providing significant investment in European media creativity, impartial information, more European-originated content and overall – very high quality programmes for the society as a whole.[78] For these reasons, in its 2004 Report for the European Parliament,[79] the European Institute for the Media (EIM) recommends that strong, independent and financially secured public service broadcasting should be supported in all EU Member States, *in particular* in the new digital age. This may be a little surprising given the fact that the new Information Age brings with it countless channels and websites which should in theory satisfy the thirst for a wide range of information, news, opinions and views of the world we live in. However, in the current digital environment, public services broadcasters are not becoming obsolete, but they add a new role to their portfolio. They help to build bridges over the

75. Cavallin, J., European Policies and Regulations on Media Concentration', 13.
76. Gibbons, T., 'Concentrations of Ownership and Control in a Converging Media Industry'; Tongue, C., 'Culture or Monoculture? The European Audiovisual Challenge'.
77. Ward, D., 'Media Concentration and Pluralism: Regulation, Realties and the Council of Europe's Standards in the Television Sector'.
78. Tongue, C., 'Public Service Broadcasting and European Community Policy', address to the Experts Meeting on Public Service Broadcasting in Europe, Amsterdam, 17 February 1997.
79. European Institute for the Media, Final report of the study on 'The information of the citizen in the EU: obligations for the media and the Institutions concerning the citizen's right to be fully and objectively informed', 252.

divide between the 'information rich' and the 'information poor', which is deepened by the multiplying sources of communication.

8.4.1 THE EUROPEAN UNION AND PSB

The 'romance' between the European Union and PSB started in September 1995 when the then Competition Commissioner Karel van Miert, appeared before the Culture Committee of the European Parliament and declared public service broadcasting to be an essential tool in preserving pluralism. He also proclaimed the need to ensure that the conditions for its continued existence were maintained at Community level.[80] The next step was taken in 1996 when during a meeting in Galway, the EU Culture Ministers expressed 'considerable and strong' support for the concept of a public service, and that funding of public broadcasters should be 'adequate and guaranteed, and not subject to review under competition and state aid regime'.[81] This led to an official engagement in 1996 when the EP's Committee on Culture, Youth, Education and the Media, led by the UK socialist MEP Carole Tongue, drafted a Report on public service broadcasting, known as the Tongue Report.[82] The Report resulted in the Resolution which then formed the basis for the subsequent inclusions of the 'Protocol on public service broadcasting to the 1997 Treaty of Amsterdam'.[83] The fate of the EU-PSB relationship, seemed sealed.

The Tongue Report was nothing less than a song of praise for PSB. Its self proclaimed core was to answer the question as to why PSB is so crucial for democracy and to explain the rationale behind the continued support from national governments for PSB.[84] The Report noted that television is still the dominant mass medium and the main source influencing thought and imagination in the Member States of the EU. It also acknowledged the changes brought about by the digital technology and rejected the claim that the multiplication of television channels would render PSBs obsolete. On the contrary, it praised PSB as 'an aid to informed citizenship and an agency of representative pluralism bringing together different groups in society in a common conversation that shapes public opinion'.[85] It enumerated the virtues of PSB, for example, offering a wide range of quality production in all genres to the whole population, setting quality standards in popular

---

80. Humphreys, P., 'The EU and Audiovisual Regulation: An Agency for De-regulation', 13.
81. Levy, D., *Europe's Digital Revolution: Broadcasting Regulation, the EU and the Nation State*, 48.
82. European Parliament, 'Report on the Future of Public Service Television in a Multi-channel Digital Age (Tongue Report)', 11 July 1996, A4-0243/96.
83. Humphreys, P., 'The EU and Audiovisual Regulation: An Agency for De-regulation', 13.
84. European Parliament, 'Report on the Future of Public Service Television in a Multi-channel Digital Age (Tongue Report)', n. 1320, Explanatory statement, 1.
85. European Parliament, 'Report on the Future of Public Service Television in a Multi-channel Digital Age (Tongue Report)', n. 1320, Motion for a Resolution, para. B.

programmes followed by mass audiences, serving minority interests, providing unbiased and fully independent information, pioneering innovative programme types, genres and services, etc. Indeed, given all of the above, the Report called on the Commission to propose adjustments in the Treaty allowing the Union to develop a positive policy on PSB 'recognizing its crucial importance in building national and European citizenship rather than a policy which is based exclusively on exceptions to provisions on competition and Internal Market policy'.[86]

The Commission's response to this call was to append a Protocol on PSB to the EC Treaty during the 1997 Amsterdam Treaty amendment. In comparison to the Tongue Report, the Protocol is short and concise. Yet, it marked the first instance, where the term 'media pluralism' was mentioned expressly in the Treaty context. The Protocol declares that 'the system of public broadcasting in the Member States is directly related to the need to preserve media pluralism', and that 'the provisions of the Treaty establishing the European Community shall be without prejudice to the competence of Member States to provide for the funding of public service broadcasting insofar as such funding is granted to broadcasting organizations for the fulfilment of the public service remit as conferred, defined and organized by each Member State'.

The Protocol requires is that the Member States spell out clearly the remit of public service broadcasting, that they provide funding *only* in support of that remit, and that they introduce adequate monitoring and control mechanisms to ensure the fulfilment of the public service remit.[87] If Member States fail to meet these demands, they render their PSBs vulnerable to an adverse ruling on competition grounds, that is a finding that a public service broadcaster is making inappropriate use of state aid and needs to pay back the public money it received.[88]

Following the insertion of the Protocol, commercial broadcasters started to complain to the European Commission alleging infringements of Article 87 if the EC Treaty (now 107 TFEU) in relation to the public funding schemes established in favour of public service broadcasters. Complaints surfaced in France, Spain, Portugal, Germany, the UK and Italy. Initially the Commission tried to avoid taking decisions by ordering studies on PSB funding in the Member States. However, under pressure, the Commission eventually decided on several of the pending PSB cases.[89] The decisions were all in favour of the PSBs.[90] The *News 24* case is an interesting example.

86. European Parliament, 'Report on the Future of Public Service Television in a Multichannel Digital Age (Tongue Report)', n. 1320, Motion for a Resolution, para. 11.
87. Humphreys, P., 'The EU and Audiovisual Regulation: An Agency for De-regulation', 14.
88. Humphreys, P., 'The EU and Audiovisual Regulation: An Agency for De-regulation', 14.
89. For instance Case NN-70/98, *Kinderkanal/Phoenix*; Case NN-88/98, *News 24*.
90. Harcourt, A., *The European Union and the Regulation of Media Markets*, 55.

In 1997, BSkyB accused the UK government of granting illegal state aid to BBC News 24 – the BBC's new special interest channel. Preliminary consent was granted by the Secretary of State in March 1997 to offer BBC News 24 on the digital platforms, in particular the BSkyB's satellite platform, which was at the time being developed. However, given the delay of the launch of the digital satellite network, the BBC asked for a second consent, this time to launch News 24 on the existing analogue cable infrastructure. BSkyB's complaint relates to this second consent granted by the Secretary of State in October 1997. BSkyB alleged that financing the News 24 channel by the use of part of the license fee constituted state aid, which was not notified, and thus unlawful. Furthermore, BskyB alleged that it could not be justified by any of the conditions listed in Article 87(2), 87(3) or 86(2) (now 107(2), 107(3) or 106(2) TFEU).

Having established that the measures in question could indeed constitute State aid, and they could not be justified by any of the provisions in Article 87(2) or (3) (now 107(2) or (3) TFEU), the Commission turned to examine whether they could benefit from the derogation provided for in Article 86(2) (now 106(2) TFEU) in cases of companies entrusted with the provision of 'services of general economic interest'. The Commission analysed all four conditions for the derogation and concluded that funding of BBC News 24 could be justified on the basis of Article 86(2) (now 106(2) TFEU).

First, the Commission rejected BSkyB's argument that BBC News 24 was considered a commercial channel and must, therefore, be financed only with market revenues. The Commission concluded that the News 24 service is a service of general economic interest, since it addresses the democratic and social needs of society by ensuring a wider coverage of news topics and providing a greater degree of depth in the analysis of events.[91] Moreover, when giving consent to the launching of this service, the Secretary of State explicitly stated that the provision of BBC News 24 is a public service, provided it is financed solely by the license fee. The Commission also rejected BSkyB's claim that BBC News 24 cannot be considered a public service as it is not available to the whole UK population, but instead only to a limited number of viewers (those connected to the analogue cable services, i.e., roughly 10% of all households). The Commission noticed that the preliminary consent of 21 March, which was not contested by BSkyB, was also given for a limited distribution platform, i.e., the digital satellite platform, which would not have been available to the whole population for a number of years.[92] In this regard, the Commission warned BSkyB about being too hypocritical. It pointed out that BSkyB started to contest the channel's nature of the public service only when the BBC decided to make

91. Case NN-88/98, *News 24*, n. 1201, para. 50.
92. Case NN-88/98, *News 24*, n. 1201, para. 60.

the channel available on all possible platforms without awaiting the launch of the BSkyB's digital satellite platform.[93]

Second, the Commission confirmed that the BBC had officially been entrusted by the UK with the provision of the service of general economic interest.[94] Third, the Commission determined that the application of the state aid ban would obstruct the performance of the News 24 service. In fact, without the public funds the provision of the service would be impossible.[95] Finally, the Commission was satisfied that the exemption from the state aid clause in this particular case, would not affect competition to the extent that it would be contrary to the interests of the Community. This was because, although the competitors of BBC News 24, such as Sky News and CNN suffered a reduction in their market shares, they were still able to maintain a large part of their customer base.[96]

The *News 24* case is an exemplification of what the Commission's approach was to PSB in the 1990s. On the face of things, the Commission proclaimed the need to strictly apply State aid rules to PSBs just like to any other undertakings. In practice, however, all the decisions were favourable towards PSB, even if it meant stretching the rules a bit. The Commission was challenged on its new attitude towards the funding of PSB in two cases brought before the Court of First Instance (renamed the General Court by the Treaty of Lisbon). In one of the cases, the Court declared that the Commission took too long to take a decision and therefore 'failed to act',[97] and in the second case the Court annulled the Commission's decision declaring that funding of a Portuguese PSB did not constitute state aid, within the meaning of Community law.[98] The Court, however, did not openly rule what kind of funding of PSB would be allowed under Community state aid rules. This called for clarification from the Commission.

The clarification, at least in theory, came in 2001 when the Commission issued a Communication on the application of state aid rules to public service broadcasting.[99] This also marked the beginning of the third phase in the EU-PSB relations – the global cooling phase.

The Communication started by stating that PSB is not comparable to a public service in any other economic sector, because there is no other service that at the same time has access to such a wide sector of the population, provides it with so much information and content, and by doing so conveys

93. Case NN-88/98, *News 24*, n. 1201, para. 56.
94. Case NN-88/98, *News 24*, n. 1201, para. 70.
95. Case NN-88/98, *News 24*, para. 74.
96. Case NN-88/98, *News 24*, para. 94.
97. Case T-17/96, *Télévision française 1 SA (TF1) v. European Commission,* [1999] ECR II-1757.
98. Case T-46/97, *SIC v. European Commission*, [2000] ECR II-2125.
99. European Commission, 'Application of state aid rules to public service broadcasting (Communication)', 2001; revised in 2009.

and influences both individual and public opinion.[100] This made the Commission issue a specific Communication on PSB in addition to its horizontal Communication on services of general interest adopted just one year earlier.[101] The stated reason for the adoption of the Communication was to foster the PSB, but at the same time also to answer the concerns of private broadcasters about the level playing field.[102] The Commission adopted a broad definition of state aid for PSB, stating that national financing of public service broadcasters will *normally* be regarded as state aid. This was followed by a very narrow definition of 'culture's' a possible justification of state aid for PSB on the basis of Article 87(3)(d) (now 107(3)(d) TFEU). The Commission explained that the educational and democratic needs of a Member State, which are to a large extent fulfilled by PSBs, have to be regarded as distinct from the promotion of culture which is a possible defence under Article 87(3)(d) (now 107(3)(d) TFEU).[103] Therefore, as state aid to PSBs often does not differentiate between the educational, democratic and cultural needs, state aid for PSB will in general not be approved under Article 87(3)(d). The only other possible way is Article 86(2), which provides for a derogation from a state aid ban for companies entrusted with the provision of services of general interest. The Commission reminds us of the four criteria necessary for the derogation to apply (as explained in the analysis of *News 24* case above) and further reminds that the finding for PSBs must also satisfy the proportionality test. Although, the Commission has clarified that any assessment under Article 86(2) of the compatibility of state aid to public broadcasters can only be made on a case-by-case basis, in general state financing of PSBs may be regarded as justified under three conditions: (i) a clear remit for public service broadcasting must be set out in a formal act; (ii) independent national monitoring of the fulfilment of the PSB remit must be ensured; and (iii) the funding of the PSB must be proportionate.[104]

The Communication has been criticized by the EBU for several reasons.[105] First of all, in the EBU's opinion the broad definition of state aid

100. European Commission, 'Application of state aid rules to public service broadcasting (Communication)', 2001, para. 6.
101. European Commission, Services of general interest in Europe (Communication), COM (2000) 580.
102. European Commission, Services of general interest in Europe (Communication), COM (2000) 580, para. 3.
103. European Commission, Services of general interest in Europe (Communication), COM (2000) 580, para. 26.
104. European Commission, 'Public service broadcasting and state aid – frequently asked questions', 3 March 2005, MEMO/05/73.
105. European Broadcasting Union, 'Comments on the Communication from the Commission on the application of State aid rules to public service broadcasting', http://www.ebu.ch, 8 May 2002.

for PSBs is unjustified and against established EU case-law. In the *Ferring*[106] judgment, the European Court of Justice held that 'only advantages which exceed the necessary cost for ensuring the public service obligation constitute state aid'.[107] Therefore, as EBU rightly points out, the funding necessary for the fulfilment of the public service remit of a broadcaster should not qualify as state aid. This is despite the Commission's belief that in none of the PSB cases, have the *Altmark*[108] judgment's conditions been fulfilled.[109] The ECJ established in the *Altmark* case that compensation for the costs incurred in the discharge of a public service obligation do not qualify as state aid if the following four conditions are cumulatively met: (i) clear public service obligations; (ii) pre-established parameters for determining the compensation; (iii) no overcompensation; and (iv) either selection of an operator through tender procedure or determination of compensation with reference to costs of a typical, well-run undertaking.[110] The Commission justifies its belief that these conditions were not fulfilled in any of the PSB cases by saying that in none of the cases were there any objective pre-established parameters for determining the compensation, public service broadcasters were not been selected by way of a tender procedure, and the compensation was not determined on the basis of an analysis of the costs of a typical well-run undertaking.[111] This is why the Commission claims that public financing of PSBs will *normally* be regarded as state aid. However, PSBs are a special class of public service companies and, therefore, some of the *Altmark* conditions should be interpreted more flexibly.

Second, a narrow definition of culture excluding the possibility of justifying aid for PSB on the basis of Article 87(3) (now 107(3)) is also problematic. EBU observed that:

> Cultural, democratic and social needs of society are closely interrelated, and the usual meaning of 'culture' includes public service broadcasting. In mentioning the cultural, democratic and social needs of society, the Amsterdam Protocol makes reference to the broad, dynamic character of

106. Case C-53/00, *Ferring SA v. Agence centrale des organismes de sécurité sociale (ACOSS)*, [2001] ECR I-9067.
107. Case C-53/00, *Ferring SA v. Agence centrale des organismes de sécurité sociale (ACOSS)*, [2001] ECR I-9067, para. 33.
108. Case C-280/00, *Altmark Trans and Regierungspräsidium Magdeburg*, [2003] ECR I-7747.
109. European Commission, 'Public service broadcasting and state aid – frequently asked questions'.
110. Case C-280/00, *Altmark Trans and Regierungspräsidium Magdeburg*, n. 1220, paras 89–93.
111. European Commission, 'Public service broadcasting and state aid – frequently asked questions'.

> the public service remit but in no way requires the three aspects of the remit to be separated.[112]

In summary, therefore, the 2001 Communication with its broad definition of state aid for PSBs combined with the narrow definition of culture as a possible justification, marks the changed approach of the Commission to PSB. Instead of full and active support, the EU policy towards PSB became a narrow exemption from the general ban on state aid. And this is probably not the reality that Tongue MEP or even 'the authors of the Amsterdam Protocol had in mind'.[113]

The new approach was tested very quickly. The Communication was followed by an investigation into the funding of PSB in Germany, Ireland, the Netherlands, France, Italy and Spain. The Commission's 'sophisticated and sympathetic approach to the question of public service broadcasting'[114] indeed had changed. The results of the investigations were considerably harsher than those of the pre-2001 Communication era. France, Italy and Spain have accepted measures to introduce greater transparency and proportionality in their funding systems. This is supposed to help to guard against cross-subsidies for activities not related to public service broadcasting.[115] Following complaints by commercial broadcasters in March 2005, Germany, Ireland and the Netherlands were requested by the Commission for clarification about the role and the financing of their PSBs. The Commission's preliminary view was that the current financing system in these countries was no longer in line with the EU rules on state aid. In order to remedy the situation, the Commission requested the three countries to implement the following principles: (i) a clear definition of the PSB remit; (ii) a separation of accounts distinguishing between public service and other activities and adequate mechanisms to prevent the overcompensation of public service activities; and (iii) the establishment of an independent authority that would check compliance with these rules.[116]

In April 2007, the Commission closed the investigation into the financing of the German PSB following a number of commitments presented by the German government. The amendments included a more precise definition and a proper entrustment of the public service mission, in particular as regards new media activities, adequate safeguards against

112. European Broadcasting Union, 'Comments on the Communication from the Commission on the application of State aid rules to public service broadcasting', 3.
113. European Broadcasting Union, 'Comments on the Communication from the Commission on the application of State aid rules to public service broadcasting', 3.
114. Ward, D., 'State Aid or Band Aid? An Evaluation of European Commission's Approach to Public Broadcasting', (2003) Media, Culture and Society 25, 233.
115. European Commission, 'Commission closes inquiries into French, Italian and Spanish public broadcasters following commitments to amend funding systems, 20 April 2005, IP/05/458.
116. European Commission, 'Commission requests Germany, Ireland and The Netherlands to clarify role and financing of public service broadcasters', 3 March 2005, IP/05/250.

overcompensation and cross-subsidization, the respect of market principles in commercial activities and more transparency as regards the sublicensing of sports rights.[117] Similarly, the Irish case was closed in February 2008 after the Irish government undertook to clarify the remit and financing of RTE in the Broadcasting Bill which ultimately became Broadcasting Act 2009.[118] Finally, the most severe sanction was applied to the Netherlands for the ad hoc financing of PSBs between 1994 and 2005. In addition to the regular financing through license fees obligations, nineteen Dutch PSBs received ad hoc payments from several funds held by the Dutch State. The Dutch government was ordered by the Commission to recover EUR 76.3 million plus interest from NOS, the umbrella organization of public broadcasters in the Netherlands.[119]

This is all against the background of continuous support for the *idea* of public service broadcasting as such. In the Media Pluralism Issues Paper on Media Pluralism prepared for the Liverpool Audiovisual Conference the Commission observed that:

> PSB has an important role to play in ensuring media pluralism. The Commission's policy recognises the importance and special role of PSB as well as the Member States' freedom to define the public service tasks as stated in the Amsterdam protocol and spelled out in the Communication on PSB. This leaves the possibilities open for the Member States to support PSB in order to promote media pluralism actively.[120]

Similarly, in her 2006 speech on the role of public service broadcasters 'in a vibrant and pluralist digital media landscape', Commissioner Reding emphasized that:

> Public broadcasters have to be given stable resources such as those ensured by a licence fee regime. The need for public service broadcasters to remain strong players in the digital media landscape only reinforces this challenge of stable, predictable resources.[121]

117. European Commission, 'Commission closes investigation regarding the financing regime for German public service broadcasters', 24 April 2007, IP/07/543.
118. European Commission, 'Commission welcomes proposed changes to financing of Irish public service broadcasters and closes investigation',27 February 2008, IP/08/317.
119. European Commission, 'Commission orders Dutch public service broadcaster NOS to pay back €76.3 million excess ad hoc funding', 22 June 2006, IP/06/822.
120. European Commission, 'Media Pluralism – what should be the European Union's role?', Issues Paper, 2005.
121. Reding, V., 'The Role of Public Service Broadcasters in a Vibrant and Pluralist Digital Media Landscape', speech at joint EBU-MTV's conference 'From secret service to public service', Budapest, 3 November 2006.

However, the reality is that 'the status and independence of public service broadcasting is in no way secured in many of the countries in the EU'.[122] Moreover, in none of the 'official' documents on the financing of PSB, is the need for securing such financing emphasized. As the European Parliament has noted, both the Commission Communication and the *Altmark* judgment provide criteria for the compatibility of public funding to public broadcasting, but they do not require Member States to *ensure* adequate funding for the public service broadcasters.[123]

The revised Communication adopted in July 2009 did not bring change in this regard. The main novelty of the new Communication is the discussion of the PSB remit in relation to new media. Thus, the Communications deals with *ex ante* review of new services launched by public service broadcasters (the key feature being balancing the market impact of such new services with their public value),[124] and the inclusion of pay services within the public service remit. In addition, the 2009 Communication has sharpened the focus on accountability and more effective control of overcompensation and enhanced supervision of the public service mission at the national level.

8.4.2 From Public Service Broadcasting to Public Service Media?

Even if the need for the existence of PSB continues to be generally accepted, the hotly contested question is: what kind of public-service broadcasting? Will the PSB as we know it – a single company with a public service remit – be the thing of the past? Perhaps what is needed today, in the digital era, is public funding for public service *programmes* or *channels*, which may just as well be broadcast by commercial companies. The economists Motta and Polo observe:

> Many private channels today offer the kind of news, cultural or scientific programmes which would have been considered as minority programmes some years ago. The range of programmes now considered as not profitable has been considerably reduced, further narrowing the scope of public television. However, there are types of programmes that serve the public interest (e.g. those with educational content, or those which defend the right of expression of certain minorities) would probably not exist without public intervention. The question is whether

122. European Institute for the Media, Final report of the study on 'The information of the citizen in the EU: obligations for the media and the Institutions concerning the citizen's right to be fully and objectively informed'.
123. European Parliament, 'Report on the risks of violation, in the EU and especially in Italy, of freedom of expression and information'.
124. See http://ec.europa.eu/avpolicy/reg/psb/index_en.htm.

a public company should provide these programmes or whether instead private channels should be obliged to carry them.[125]

Within the European Commission, DG Competition and DG Information Society have already posed and analysed this very question. In the 1997 Convergence Green Paper,[126] DG Information Society had already concluded that the PSB mission could be fulfilled purely by commercial operators. A year later, DG Competition came up with its 'Discussion Paper on the application of Articles 90, paragraph 2, 92 and 93 of the Treaty in the broadcasting sector'. The Paper confirmed the Member States' authority to decide on public service funding however, it endorsed the Convergence Green Paper's idea of competition between the private and the public sectors where public funding would only be used for those *programmes* clearly defined as being of general interest.[127] The Discussion Paper suggested that DG Competition would not regard sports and entertainment shows as public service broadcasting, and that it would not necessarily so regard films and drama.[128]

The idea of public service media rather than PSB has been picked up by some Member States. For instance, a report by the Broadcasting Policy Group in the UK released in 2004 and entitled 'Beyond the Charter'[129] suggested potential alternative approaches to funding public service television. One of the recommendations was to reserve public funding for a small number of channels and replace the rest with a voluntary subscription system. Furthermore, the report also suggested creating a Public Broadcasting Authority, that would be funded through the Treasury and would oversee the diminution of public service funding through television license fees from 2007 onwards.[130] Although these proposals were at the time rejected, they are gathering more momentum these days. In the collection of essays entitled 'Communications. The next decade',[131] prepared in 2006 for OFCOM, Chris

125. Motta, M., Polo, M., 'Concentration and Public Policies in the Broadcasting Industry: The Future of Television', 323.
126. European Commission, 'Convergence of the Telecommunications, media and Information Technology, and the Implications for Regulations, towards an Information Society Approach (Green Paper)', 28.
127. European Audiovisual Observatory, 'Developments of digital television in European Union', 4 December 1999, http://www.obs.coe.int, 42.
128. Humphreys, P., 'Regulating for Pluralism in the Era of Digital Convergence: The Issues of Media Concentration Control and the Future of Public Service Broadcasting', 13–14.
129. Broadcasting Policy Group, 'Beyond the Charter', 2004; see also O'Mahony, C., 'A Future for Public Service Broadcasting: New Challenges, New Pressures, New Approaches', 10.
130. O'Mahony, C., 'A Future for Public Service Broadcasting: New Challenges, New Pressures, New Approaches', 10.
131. 'Communications. The next decade. A collection of essays prepared for the UK Office of Communications', 27.

Giles examines the possible alternatives for BBC.[132] He analyses six possible scenarios for the future of PSB in the UK: (i) an 'Arts Council of the Air' which would fund individual *programmes* having public service value; BBC could apply for funding like any other broadcaster and it could seek additional funding through advertising or subscription; (ii) fully contestable funding at broadcaster level – broadcasters would compete for block funding for a specified period; (iii) fully contestable funding at the broadcaster level for a specific franchise – broadcasters would compete to run a PSB-style *channel*; (iv) the BBC competing with ITV/C4/C5 for public money; (v) the BBC alone as a commissioner without any production – BBC would act as the 'Arts Council of the Air'; (vi) the BBC as it is.[133] Giles then ranks the suggestions taking into account the following factors: competition in production, competition in commissioning, oversight of public money and brand awareness. Fully contestable funding at broadcaster level scored the highest of all options, with BBC 'as it is' taking the last place in the ranking.

Given the fact that the 'Communications. The Next Decade' was prepared for and by OFCOM, it has not been ruled out that the proposals put forward in the essays will be taken into account by the UK authorities. And this is despite the fact that the new BBC Charter has already been agreed for the period 2007–2016 and the license fee already detailed for the period 2007–2013. After that, anything could happen. In its recent and ongoing review of public service broadcasting,[134] OFCOM notes that the important feature of PSB following the digital switchover will be 'competition for quality', which in essence means plurality of PSB commissioning and production. Currently, OFCOM still sees BBC as the cornerstone of PSB in the UK, with 'plurality' relating to the existing broadcasters beyond BBC which are equipped with some form of PSB remit (Channels 4 and 5 and ITV1). However, OFCOM suggests that, especially after the current BBC Charter period expires and following the digital switchover the plurality of PSB provision may also begin to relate to other commercial broadcasters which could be provided with some kind of PSB status.[135]

Therefore, we may be slowly witnessing the erosion of the PSB model as we know it. Some argue that 'public television is likely to ensure better quality for [public service] programme than commercial channel under

132. Giles, C., 'The Public Interest Challenges for the Communications Sector over the Next 10 Years: Contestable Public Service Funding', in 'Communications. The next decade. A collection of essays prepared for the UK Office of Communications', 27, 101–111.
133. Giles, C., 'The Public Interest Challenges for the Communications Sector over the Next 10 Years: Contestable Public Service Funding', 109.
134. OFCOM, 'Review of Public Service Broadcasting (PSB) Television', http://www.ofcom.org.uk
135. OFCOM, Review of public service television broadcasting, Phase 3 – 'Competition for quality', http://www.ofcom.org.uk, 8.

obligation to produce and broadcast the programme'.[136] However, advocates of public service media believe that this will result in television broadcasting as a whole becoming more public service oriented. To this end, Craufurd Smith suggested that 'there is some scope for the [EU] to help finance new and innovative media projects' in addition to the currently existing MEDIA programme. The Irish Broadcasting Fund introduced by the Broadcasting Act 2009 could serve as a template. Its purpose is to offer an independent source of funding for high quality original or public service programming. The Act contains rules specifying which programmes qualify for funding and requires that the programmes must be broadcast during peak viewing times on a free television service which provides near-universal coverage in the State.

8.5 POWER TO THE USERS! FOSTERING MEDIA LITERACY

Valcke notes that 'it may be that increases in content diversity should be considered essentially meaningless from a policy perspective if the additional content is ignored by the audience'.[137] Therefore, safeguards are needed also at the last link of the 'diversity chain'– the exposure diversity. This may be achieved by promoting media literacy.

As noted by Commissioner Reding, 'today, media literacy is as central to active and full citizenship as literacy was at the beginning of nineteenth century'.[138] Unlike in the past, we are today awash with information. The problem is, however, as Naughton observes, we are not getting much wiser as a result, on the contrary, we are living in a state of 'informed bewilderment'.[139] The way out of this information rut is to become media literate, that is, as the European Commission defines, to be able 'to access, analyse and evaluate the power of images, sounds and messages ... and to communicate competently in media available on a personal basis'.[140] All in all, a media literate citizen is the one who is a master rather than a slave of

136. Motta, M., Polo, M., 'Concentration and Public Policies in the Broadcasting Industry: The Future of Television', 323.
137. Valcke, P., 'Looking for the User in Media Pluralism Regulation: Unraveling the Traditional Diversity Chain and Recent Trends of User Empowerment in European Media Regulation', 301.
138. European Commission, 'Making sense of today's media content: Commission begins public media literacy consultation', 6 October 2006, IP/06/1326.
139. Naughton, J., 'Our Changing Media Ecosystem', in 'Communications. The next decade. A collection of essays prepared for the UK Office of Communications', 41.
140. European Commission, Audiovisual and Media Policies, Media Literacy, http://ec.Europa.eu/avpolicy/media_literacy/index_en.htm.

technology, an active participant in democratic life and able to contribute to political debate.[141]

Thus, media literacy is not only about how to access the content in the multiplying media outlets and how to use the ever changing technology and find your way in the jungle of new services and gadgets. It is also about how to understand the forces behind media industry. Being media literate is to understand that process, be critical of the way the media shape our understanding of the world and know how to look for alternative sources of news in the Information Age. As the European Commission explained, media literacy:

> should help citizens to recognise how the media filter their perceptions and beliefs, shape popular culture and influence personal choices. It should empower them with the critical thinking and creative problem-solving skills to make them judicious consumers and producers of information. Media Education is part of the basic entitlement of every citizen, in every country in the world, to freedom of expression and the right to information and it is instrumental in building and sustaining democracy.[142]

Media literacy programmes are providing safeguards at the last link of the 'Diversity Chain'. They pave the way to make people more media savvy, more technology confident and more media aware. It is of vital importance to put those programmes in place as soon as possible. This is because, the new Internet era, called Web 2.0, is all about throwing our personal messages out there in the open with the use of blogs, Twitter and websites like YouTube, Facebook and the multitude of similar. TIME magazine decided that the 2006 Person of the Year should be 'You'– that is an ordinary person, who 'controls the Information Age'.[143] TIME anticipated that we will soon be less reliant on traditional media to get news, and we will form our view about the events in the world. The power of mass media is thus predicted to be gradually diminishing and, therefore, the threat of concentrated media power is slowly becoming obsolete. While the new forms of communication will probably not completely replace traditional broadcasting, it is true that they widen the horizons and contribute to pluralism of voices and diversity of opinions presented in the public. As noted by Valcke:

> The image of viewers as powerless eyeballs has … started to fade as a result of recent technical and market developments that trigger waves of

141. UK Film Council, 'Comments on "Media Pluralism" – What Should Be the European Union's role?', Issues Paper, 2005.
142. Communication from the Commission to the European Parliament, the Council, the European Economic and Social Committee and the Committee of the Regions, 'A European approach to media literacy in the digital environment', COM(2007) 833 final.
143. Time Magazine, 'Person of the Year Complete List 1927–2004', http://www.time.com.

user empowerment in the form of increasing tools for active choice and selection of content, as well as for active participation in media production and distribution.[144]

Media literacy is mentioned in one of the recitals of the AVMS Directive. Recital 47 states that media literacy refers to 'skills, knowledge and understanding that allow consumers to use media effectively and safely'. Therefore, the Directive recommends that 'the development of media literacy in all sections of society should be promoted and its progress followed closely'.

In view of the above, in 2007 the Commission adopted a Media Literacy Communication,[145] which is a complement to the Directive adopted in the same year.[146] The Commission declared that the Communication provides a further building block to European audiovisual policy (the other being the AVMS Directive and MEDIA 2007 Programme). It provides a European definition of media literacy as 'the ability to access the media, to understand and to critically evaluate different aspects of the media and media contents and to create communications in a variety of contexts'.[147] It then expand on it by saying that there are several 'aspects' to media literacy, including (i) feeling comfortable with all existing media; (ii) actively using media; (iii) having a critical approach to media as regards both quality and accuracy of content; (iv) using media creatively, and most importantly for this thesis; (v) understanding the economy of media and the *difference* between pluralism and media ownership.

Apart from the work of the Expert Group and the public consultation, the Commission has undertaken other activities aimed at fostering media literacy in Europe. It has organized three workshops on Media Literacy and, through the eLearning initiative, provided EUR 3.5 million of financial support to some thirty projects focusing on *inter alia* analysing media representations and media values in a multimedia perspective, stimulating the use of media in order to improve participation in social and community life or implementing media literacy initiatives.

The Member State so far most inspired by the Commission's work is the United Kingdom. Section 11 of the 2003 Communications Act imposes

144. Valcke, P., 'Looking for the User in Media Pluralism Regulation: Unraveling the Traditional Diversity Chain and Recent Trends of User Empowerment in European Media Regulation', 304.

145. Communication from the Commission to the European Parliament, the Council, the European Economic and Social Committee and the Committee of the Regions, 'A European approach to media literacy in the digital environment', COM(2007) 833 final.

146. Valcke, P., 'Looking for the User in Media Pluralism Regulation: Unraveling the Traditional Diversity Chain and Recent Trends of User Empowerment in European Media Regulation', 305.

147. Communication from the Commission to the European Parliament, the Council, the European Economic and Social Committee and the Committee of the Regions, 'A European approach to media literacy in the digital environment', COM(2007) 833 final, 3.

a duty on OFCOM to promote media literacy. In the Strategy and Priorities for the Promotion of Media Literacy published on its website,[148] OFCOM lays down its priorities in the area. It declares that in an increasingly converged communications world, where people face constantly changing technology and greater media choice, it will work with stakeholders to help focus on the present and future media literacy needs of all members of society. In its work to promote media literacy in the UK, OFCOM will focus on three key strands: (i) research; (ii) connecting, partnering and signposting; and (iii) labelling. The research is expected to drive OFCOM's agenda for action. Connecting, partnering and signposting means stimulating debate at conferences and debates as well as funding projects to foster media literacy. Finally, labelling will be used to ensure that viewers and listeners have 'clear, accurate and timely information about the nature of content'.[149]

In addition to the official work of OFCOM, as a result of a private initiative in the UK, the European Charter for Media Literacy was drafted.[150] It was the idea of the UK Film Council, the British Film Institute, Channel Four and the BBC, to establish a Steering Group which would prepare the Charter. The Group represents major institutions in several European countries[151] who have committed to promoting the Charter within their own nations and, therefore, to spreading awareness of the Charter across Europe. The Charter may be signed by individuals, organizations, companies and regulators who are either supporters, sponsors or providers of media literacy initiatives. It is supposed to provide a framework for organizations to develop and deliver coherent media literacy strategies.[152]

Initiatives such as these, need to be openly and actively supported by the European Commission. The Media Literacy Communication was a first step in this direction. Currently, enhancing digital literacy, skills and inclusion is one of the actions taken by the Commission under the Digital Agenda for Europe,[153] which is one of the flagship initiatives of the Europe 2020 Strategy[154] – the successor of the Lisbon Strategy.

However, Valcke calls for 'caution in shifting the regulatory focus too enthusiastically or radically from source and content diversity to exposure

148. OFCOM, 'Strategy and Priorities for the Promotion of Media Literacy – A Statement', http://stakeholders.ofcom.org.uk/consultations/strategymedialit/.
149. OFCOM, 'Strategy and Priorities for the Promotion of Media Literacy – A Statement'.
150. European Charter for Media Literacy, http://www.Euromedialiteracy.eu.
151. Austria, Belgium, France, Germany, Portugal, Spain, Sweden, United Kingdom.
152. UK Film Council, 'Comments on "Media Pluralism – What Should Be the European Union's role?" (Issues Paper)', 2005.
153. Digital Agenda for Europe, http://ec.europa.eu/information_society/digital-agenda/index_ en.htm.
154. Europe 2020 Strategy, http://ec.europa.eu/europe2020/index_en.htm.

diversity'.[155] Fostering media literacy is the way to promote exposure diversity which is the third link in the 'diversity chain'. It does not render safeguards for source and content diversity obsolete. In order for the European media market to be truly pluralistic and diverse, it continues to be necessary to make sure that all three links in the chain remain solid.

155. Valcke, P., 'Looking for the User in Media Pluralism Regulation: Unraveling the Traditional Diversity Chain and Recent Trends of User Empowerment in European Media Regulation', 287.

Chapter 9
Conclusions

The preservation of a pluralistic structure of the European media market continues to be a stated key priority for modern integrated Europe. However, the lost battle for harmonizing legislation in the mid-1990s is illustrative of the complexity and sensitivity of the issue. Although the Council of Europe and the European Parliament have continued to call for the EU legislative action in the media pluralism field, not only did the political momentum for this kind of intervention seems to have passed, but there is also no firm legal basis for it in the Treaties. Post 1998, the European Commission has consistently used the 'no legal basis' argument as the answer to every call from the European Parliament to return to discussion on the media pluralism directive.

In addition, the technological change of the recent years resulting from digitalization, convergence and the proliferation of 'new media outlets' marked a paradigm shift in the European approach to media pluralism regulation. As noted by Valcke, currently 'the growing role of the user is frequently used as an argument to relax existing regulations in the area of source and content diversity'.[1]

As a result, there is no specific and comprehensive legislation aimed specifically at safeguarding media pluralism at the European level. The existing tools in the form of competition law and scattered legislative measures are not without their weaknesses. Competition law *by definition* cannot be used to guarantee media pluralism. This is so, not only because media pluralism and diversity depend on more factors than access to key

1. Valcke, P., 'Looking for the User in Media Pluralism Regulation: Unraveling the Traditional Diversity Chain and Recent Trends of User Empowerment in European Media Regulation', 307.

'gateways', but mainly because competition law and media concentration rules have fundamentally different focuses.[2] As noted by the Commission itself, 'competition rules alone may not be sufficient to ensure cultural diversity and media pluralism',[3] because fighting a 'dominant market position' on a relevant market differs from counteracting the development of a 'dominant power of opinion' in the media sector.[4]

The EU legislative measures aimed at directly or indirectly safeguarding media pluralism do exist, but they are fragmented and imperfect. This applies in particular to safeguards for structural media pluralism. First of all, there are still no EU rules on the supply diversity. The existing measures contributing to a larger or lesser extent to structural media pluralism are economic in focus and have only a passing effect on media pluralism. Access rights regulated in the Access Directive apply only in situations when an operator is designated with significant market power. Therefore, they are effective only in situations of dominance and they have an inevitable *ex post* effect, which for media pluralism is not ideal. Second, the E-Communications framework also does little in terms of securing interoperability as there are no binding EU standards on CAS and APIs. Finally, the country of origin principle which is the cornerstone of the AVMS Directive, can indeed contribute to structural pluralism, but it can also lead to situations where operators purposefully locate themselves in countries with liberal regulatory regimes and thus avoid stricter regulations in countries to which they actually intend to broadcast.

Measures supporting internal media pluralism are somewhat more numerous and with a more specific public interest focus. However, they too are not free from weaknesses. The imperfections of must-carry rules include the much too narrow definition of public interest, the lack of preferential access to associated facilities, and the fact that they should be implemented with must-offer and must-distribute rules on other levels of the broadcasting value chain. Lists of events and short reporting rights focus on citizens' right to information and only in an indirect manner contribute to media pluralism. And finally, although the production quotas have probably the greatest potential, they too have their shortcomings in being non-binding (the 'where practicable' clause) and insufficiently monitored, executed and sanctioned.

---

2. Scheuer, A., Strothmann, P., 'Media Supervision on the Threshold of the 21st Century. What Are the Requirements of Broadcasting, Telecommunications and Concentration Regulation?'.
3. European Commission, Media Concentration in the Internal Market: An Assessment of the Need for Community Action (Green Paper); Directive 2002/19/EC of the European Parliament and of the Council of 7 March 2002 on access to, and interconnection of, electronic communications networks and associated facilities (Access Directive), Rec. 10.
4. Scheuer, A., Strothmann, P., 'Media Supervision on the Threshold of the 21st Century. What Are the Requirements of Broadcasting, Telecommunications and Concentration Regulation?'.

With regard to the MEDIA programme, it is still rather modestly financed, and in practice it has little impact on increasing diversity of content available on European television.

The European Commission's current stance is that media pluralism 'can be realized perfectly adequately by the Member States acting alone'[5] with a minimal help and guidance from the European Union. Meanwhile, the problem of increasing media concentration has long ago crossed national borders and slipped out of the control of the individual States. Despite the fact that the majority of EU Member States have some form of media pluralism regulation, it is by no means sufficient in the current era of cross-border broadcasting and global media empires. Moreover, the liberalization sentiments which have taken over media regulators in Europe mean that the rules are being relaxed or, in some cases, done away with completely. The situations such as the continuing 'Italian anomaly', the *Rywingate* scandal in Poland in 2002, the Hungarian media law of 2010 or the hacking scandal in the UK in 2011 only seem to strengthen the argument that Member States alone are not able to deal with pressures of regulating media markets in order to guarantee pluralism and diversity.

This, combined with the weaknesses and fragmentation of the currently available EU-level legislative tools supporting media pluralism has led to one conclusion: there is a need for positive additional action at the EU level aimed at safeguarding media pluralism in the European media market. However, it is highly unlikely that the additional action will take a form of a *binding* legislative intervention in the near future. As explained in detail in Chapter 7, there is no firm legal basis in the Treaties for the EU legislative action aimed specifically at the protecting pluralism.

There is also no political will to introduce such a legal basis.[6] In a 2009 speech to the European Parliament, the then-Media and Information Society Commissioner Reding admitted that although one could arrive at a 'generous interpretation of the Treaty to allow the EU to tackle the matter', it would require the political support of the Parliament and the Member States'.[7] In another speech she added:

> I know well that Media Pluralism is a perennial favourite for many members of the European Parliament. I personally am rather sceptical about any harmonised 'one size fits all' approach to media governance

5. Craufurd Smith, R., 'Rethinking European Union Competence in the Field of Media Ownership: The Internal Market, Fundamental Rights and European Citizenship', 656.
6. Craufurd Smith, R., 'Rethinking European Union Competence in the Field of Media Ownership: The Internal Market, Fundamental Rights and European Citizenship', 666.
7. Reding, V., 'Freedom of Expression and Information in Italy: Declaration in the European Parliament Plenary, 8 October 2009.

> in the EU. That's why I set out the three step plan for monitoring media pluralism. Note: I said monitoring, not regulating.[8]

The 'Three-Step Plan' mentioned by Commissioner Reding and launched in 2007 has indeed been the most concrete response of the European Commission to the Parliament's calls for EU-level action on media pluralism.[9] The three steps were intended to comprise of: (i) a Commission Staff Working Paper on Media Pluralism; (ii) an independent study on media pluralism; and (iii) a Commission Communication on the indicators for media pluralism in the EU Member States, on which a broad public consultation was to take place. The Staff Working Paper published in 2007[10] clarified that the intended result of the 'Three-Step Approach' was the identification of indicators of media pluralism in the Member States. It did not mention any possibility for a change in the European legislation in this area.[11]

The outcome of the second step, an independent study called 'Indicators for Media Pluralism in the Member States – Towards a Risk-Based Approach' published in 2009,[12] was a prototype for a Media Pluralism Monitor (MPM) described as a 'risk-based, holistic, user-friendly and evolving monitoring tool'.[13] The MPM uses three types of indicators (legal, socio-demographic and economic) to identify risks for media pluralism across six domains: (i) basic domain, (ii) pluralism and media ownership and control, (iii) pluralism of media types and genres, (iv) political pluralism in the media, (v) cultural pluralism in the media, and (vi) geographic pluralism in the media.[14]

The MPM has been praised by its authors as 'a *first step* in the development of an EU-wide standardized monitoring system for detecting and dealing with societal risks in the area of media pluralism and the first

---

8. Reding, V., 'Empowering Citizens – The Magazine Media'.
9. See European Commission, DG Media and Information Society, 'Media Pluralism: The need for transparency, freedom and diversity in Europe's media landscape', http://ec.Europa.eu/information_society/media_taskforce/pluralism/index_en.htm.
10. European Commission, 'Media pluralism in the Member States of the European Union (Staff Working Document)'.
11. Beunderman, M., 'Brussels Reluctant to Regulate National Media Rules', n. 361; Beunderman, M., 'Brussels Wary of Rules on National Media', BusinessWeek.com, 18 January 2007.
12. Independent Study on Indicators for Media Pluralism in the Member States – Towards a Risk-Based Approach, Final Report, viii.
13. Independent Study on Indicators for Media Pluralism in the Member States – Towards a Risk-Based Approach, Final Report, ix.
14. For a detailed discussion on MPM see Valcke, P., et al., 'The European Media Pluralism Monitor: Bridging Law, Economics and Media Studies as a First Step towards Risk-Based Regulation in Media Markets', 85–113.

attempt to apply risk analysis to media policy'.[15] The MPM, however, is a diagnostic tool to be utilized by the Member States with no obligation to do so and no EU-level monitoring mechanism.

The third step – the Commission Communication on indicators for media pluralism in EU Member States was not taken under the Commissioner's Reding term. The initial plan was to hold public consultation following the publication of the Communication and, should the consultation reveal such a need, to commission a second study in order to systematically apply the media pluralism indicators to all EU Member States. However, it seems that under Commissioner Kroes, the third step had been abandoned altogether. Instead, two new advisory bodies have been created: the High Level Group on Media Freedom and Pluralism and a Centre for Media Pluralism and Media Freedom within the Robert Schuman School of the European University Institute. They are both valuable answer to the calls for more EU-level research in the area,[16] but an opportunity for a soft law instrument in the form of a Communication which could possibly contain several 'hard' statements was not realized.

The overall conclusion is that the aim of the Commission's 'Three-Step-Approach' was to finally respond to a decade of the Parliament's calls for positive action. However, even though the Media Pluralism Monitor may prove a useful tool in monitoring media pluralism in the Member States, there will be no change in EU legislation resulting from the 'Three-Step-Approach' exercise.

It must be noted that even if the political climate for legislative intervention is currently unfavourable, the topic should not be abandoned. Awareness raising should continue in order to keep the matter on the agenda since there is a case for more EU rules on media pluralism. As admitted by Commissioner Reding herself, doing nothing is not an option.[17] Therefore, in light of the EU's current competence, it is possible to suggest some solutions which could be introduced *now* to provide additional safeguards at every level of 'diversity chain'.[18] This book has examined several possible solutions, including the following:

15. Valcke, P., et al., 'The European Media Pluralism Monitor: Bridging Law, Economics and Media Studies as a First Step towards Risk-Based Regulation in Media Markets', 86 (emphasis added).
16. Craufurd Smith, R., 'Rethinking European Union Competence in the Field of Media Ownership: The Internal Market, Fundamental Rights and European Citizenship', 652–673, 670.
17. Reding, V., 'Empowering Citizens – The Magazine Media'.
18. Valcke, P., 'Looking for the User in Media Pluralism Regulation: Unraveling the Traditional Diversity Chain and Recent Trends of User Empowerment in European Media Regulation'.

(i) Strengthening transparency and the monitoring of media concentrations. A suggestion has been made for the establishment of a Europe-wide media concentration monitoring body, such as European Media Pluralism Observatory. It could also be possible to make the MPM part of the *European-level* action aimed at centralized monitoring of dangerous trends and increasing media transparency. In addition, Craufurd Smith and Stolte suggest that it would be beneficial and, in theory, feasible under the current scope of the EU's competence, to adopt a Media Transparency Directive.[19]

(ii) Adopting 'soft law with hard statements'. An example could be a Recommendation on measures to promote media pluralism, modelled on the recently adopted Recommendation on the protection of minors and human dignity.

(iii) The introduction of a media specific merger review by introducing a 'pluralism test' to the EU Merger Regulation and establishing an agency to assist DG Competition in the analysis of media merger cases.

(iv) The promotion of public service media as guarantors of content diversity. Financing new and innovative media projects in addition to the currently existing MEDIA programme could be considered.

(v) Fostering media literacy. Open and active support of the EU is necessary for initiatives promoting media literacy which contributes to exposure diversity.[20] The 2007 Media Literacy Communication was a first step in this direction. Currently, enhancing digital literacy, skills and inclusion is one of the actions taken by the Commission under the Digital Agenda for Europe,[21] which is one of the flagship initiatives of the Europe 2020 Strategy[22] – the successor of the Lisbon Strategy.

Constant raising of awareness of the need to safeguard pluralism in the European media is vital. Current reluctance of the European Commission to introduce any strong-worded recommendations, much less a legislation in this area, should not prevent searching for ways to augment the currently utilized tools aimed at safeguarding media pluralism. Situations such as the

19. Craufurd Smith, R., Stolte, Y., 'The European Union and Media Ownership Transparency: The Scope for Regulatory Intervention'.
20. Valcke, P., 'Looking for the User in Media Pluralism Regulation: Unraveling the Traditional Diversity Chain and Recent Trends of User Empowerment in European Media Regulation'.
21. Digital Agenda for Europe, http://ec.europa.eu/information_society/digital-agenda/index_ en.htm.
22. Europe 2020 Strategy, http://ec.europa.eu/europe2020/index_en.htm.

continuing 'Italian anomaly', the Hungarian media law of 2010 or the hacking scandal in the UK in 2011 indicate that a stronger EU voice is needed. In the end, as noted by Craufurd Smith, 'the choice is not simply between the action at the European level or at the domestic level, but … there is considerable scope for co-ordinated action at both levels'.[23]

23. Craufurd Smith, R., 'Rethinking European Union Competence in the Field of Media Ownership: The Internal Market, Fundamental Rights and European Citizenship', 657.

Bibliography

Abbott, K.W., Snidal, D., 'Hard and Soft Law in International Governance', (2000) International Organization, 54(3), 421–456.

Albarran, A.B., Mierzejewska, B,I., 'Media Concentration in the US and European Union: A Comparative Analysis', 6th World Media Economics Conference, 12–15 May 2004.

Alger, D., *Megamedia. How Giant Corporations Dominate Mass Media, Distort Competition, and Endanger Democracy* (Rowman & Littlefield Publishers, 1998).

Alston, P., Weiler, J.H.H., 'An "Ever Closer Union" in Need of Human Rights Policy', (1998) European Journal of International Law.

Alter, K., Meunier-Aitsahalia, S., 'Judicial Politics in the European Community: European Integration and the Path Breaking Cassis de Dijon Decision', (1994) Comparative Political Studies 26.

Arino, M., 'Competition Law and Pluralism in European Digital Broadcasting: Addressing the Gaps', (2004) 54 Communications and Strategies.

Arino, M., 'Pluralism in Digital Broadcasting: Myths, Realities and the Boundaries of European Intervention', in Preissl, B., Muller, J. (eds), *Governance of Communications Networks. Connecting Societies and Markets with IT* (Physica-Verlag, 2006).

Arino, M., Valcke, P., 'The Future (or Non-future) of Must-Carry', *OfcomWatch*, 11 April 2005.

Arnull, A.M., et al., *European Union Law* (Sweet & Maxwell, 2000).

Bagdikian, B., *The Media Monopoly*, 6th edn (Beacon Press, 2000).

Bagdikian, B., *The New Media Monopoly* (Beacon Press, 2004).

Baker, C.E., 'Media Concentration: Giving up on Democracy' (2002) Florida Law Review 5455.

Barani, L., 'Hard and Soft Law in the European Union: The Case of Social Policy and Open Method of Coordination', Webpapers on Consitutionalism & Governance beyond the State 2/2006.
Barendt, E., *Broadcasting Law. A Comparative Study* (Clarendon Press, 1993).
Barendt, E., *Freedom of Speech*, 2nd edn (Oxford University Press, 2005).
Barendt, E.M., Hitchens, L.P., *Media Law: Text, Cases and Materials* (Longman, 2000).
Barnett, S., 'Media Ownership Policy in a Recession: Redefining the Public Interest', (2010) Interactions: Studies in Communication and Culture, 1(2).
Bekkers, R., *Mobile Telecommunications Standards: UMTS, GSM, TETRA, & ERMES (Artech House, 2001), 95.*
Beltrame, F., 'Lawmaking in the European Union', paper prepared for the W.G. Hart Legal Workshop, Institute of Advanced Legal Studies, 1996.
Berlin, I., *Four Essays on Liberty* (Oxford Paperbacks, 1969).
Bibby, A., 'Global Concentration in the Media', UNI-MEI World General Assembly, Los Angeles, 1–3 October 2003.
Campaign for Quality Television, 'Serious Documentaries on ITV: An Endangered Species', 1999.
Carolan, E., O'Neill, A., *Media Law in Ireland* (Bloomsbury Professional, 2010).
Cavallin, J., 'European Policies and Regulations on Media Concentration', (1998) International Journal of Communications Law and Policy 1.
Chalmers, D., et al., *European Union Law: Text and Materials* (Cambridge University Press, 2006).
Coen, D., 'Business-Regulatory Relations: Learning to Play Regulatory Games in European Utility Markets', (2005) Governance 18(3).
Coen, D., 'The European Business Interest and the Nation State: Large-Firm Lobbying in the European Union and Member States', (1998) Journal of Public Policy 18.
Collins, R., 'Realising Social Goals in Connectivity and Content', in Marsden, C.T. (ed.), *Regulating the Information Society* (Routledge, 2000).
Cowie, C., Marsden, C.T., 'Convergence, Competition and Regulation', (1998) International Journal of Communications Law and Policy 1.
Craig, P., de Búrca, G., *EU Law. Text, Cases, and Materials*, 3rd edn (Oxford University Press, 2003).
Craufurd Smith, R., *Broadcasting Law and Fundamental Rights* (Clarendon Press, 1997).
Craufurd Smith, R., 'Rethinking European Union Competence in the Field of Media Ownership: The Internal Market, Fundamental Rights and European Citizenship', (2004) European Law Review 29, 652–73

Craufurd Smith, R., 'Media Ownership and the Public Interest: The Case of Virgin Media, British Sky Broadcasting and Its ITV Shares', (2009) The Journal of Media Law 1, 21–37.

Craufurd Smith, R., Stolte, Y., 'The European Union and Media Ownership Transparency: The Scope for Regulatory Intervention', (2010) http://mediapolicy.org/wp-content/uploads/the-european-union-media-ownership-transparency.pdf.

De Avillez Pereira, M. (ed.), *Antitrust and New Media* (Kluwer Law International, 2000).

De Búrca, G., 'Reappraising Subsidiarity's Significance after Amsterdam', Harvard Jean Monnet Working Paper 7/99.

Didizian, M., Romer, J., 'The Communications Bill – The Place of the BBC', (2003) Computer and Telecommunications Law Review 9(4).

Doyle, G., 'From "Pluralism" to "Ownership": Europe's Emergent Policy on Media Concentrations Navigates the Doldrums', (1997) The Journal of Information Law and Technology 3.

Doyle, G., 'Regulation of Media Ownership and Pluralism in Europe: Can the European Union Take Us Forward?', (1998) Cardozo Arts & Entertainment Law Journal 16.

Doyle, G., 'Towards a Pan-European Directive? From Concentrations and Pluralism to Media Ownership', (1998) Communications Law 3(1).

Doyle, G., 'Convergence: "A Unique Opportunity to Evolve in Previously Unthought-of Ways or a Hoax?"', in Marsden, C., Verhulst, S. (eds), *Convergence in European Digital TV Regulation* (Blackstone Press Limited, 1999).

Doyle, G., *Media Ownership* (SAGE Publications, 2002).

Eeckhout, P., Tridimas, T. (eds), *Yearbook of European Law 1999–2000* (Oxford Clarendon Press, 2000).

European Audiovisual Observatory, 'Developments of Digital Television in European Union', 4 December 1999.

European Audiovisual Observatory, Iris Special: 'Television and Media Concentration. Regulatory Models on the National and European Level' (Strasbourg 2001).

European Audiovisual Observatory, Iris Special: 'To Have or not to Have – Must Carry Rules', (Strasbourg 2005).

European Commission for Democracy through Law, 'Opinion on the Compatibility of the Laws 'Gasparri and "Frattini" of Italy with the Council of Europe Standards in the Field of Freedom of Expression and Pluralism of the Media'(Opinion No. 309/2004), 13 June 2005, Doc. No. CDL-AD(2005)017.

European Federation of Journalists, 'Media Power in Europe: The Big Picture of Ownership' (2005).

European Institute for the Media (EIM), 'Transparency of Media Control' (1994).

European Institute for the Media, Final report of the study on 'The information of the citizen in the EU: obligations for the media and the Institutions concerning the citizen's right to be fully and objectively informed', Düsseldorf, 31 August 2004.

Fairbairn, C., 'Serving the Public Good in the Digital Age: Implications for UK Media Regulation', in 'Communications. The next decade. A collection of essays prepared for the UK Office of Communications'.

Feintuck, M., Varney, M., *Media Regulation, Public Interest and the Law* (Edinburgh University Press, 2006).

Filas, R., Planeta, P., 'Media in Poland and Public Discourse', in Czepek, A., Hellwig, M., Nowak, E. (eds), *Press Freedom and Pluralism in Europe: Concepts and Conditions* (Intellect Books, 2009).

Fraser, M.W., 'Television', in Kassim, H., Menon, A. (eds), *The European Union and National Industrial Policy* (Routledge, 1996).

Garzaniti, L., *Telecommunications, Broadcasting and the Internet* (Thomson, Sweet & Maxwell, 2003).

Geradin, D., 'Competition Law Problems Raised by the Entry of Incumbent Telecommunications Operators in the Media Content Delivery Market' (University of Zurich, 7 September 2005).

Gerl, M., Slovenian Broadcasting Council, Working Group II, 'Licensing Local Broadcasters', EPRA, Barcelona, 19–20 April 2001.

Gibbons, T., 'Concentrations of Ownership and Control in a Converging Media Industry', in Marsden C., Verhulst, S. (eds), *Convergence in European Digital TV Regulation* (Blackstone Press Limited, 1999).

Gibbons, T., 'Pluralism, Guidance and the New Media', in Marsden, C. (ed.), *Regulating the Global Information Society* (Routledge, 2000).

Giles, C., 'The Public Interest Challenges for the Communications Sector over the Next 10 Years: Contestable Public Service Funding', in Communications. The next decade. A collection of essays prepared for the UK Office of Communications (30 November 2006).

Goldberg, D., Prosser, T., Verhulst, S. (eds), *Regulating the Changing Media. A Comparative Study* (Clarendon Press, 1998).

Goldberg, D., Prosser, T., Verhulst, S., 'Regulating the Changing Media', in Goldberg, D., Prosser, T., Verhulst, S. (eds), *Regulating the Changing Media. A Comparative Study* (Clarendon Press, 1998).

Goldberg, D., Prosser, T., Verhulst, S., *EC Media Law and Policy* (Longman, 1998).

Goodhall, Alexander, O'Hare (GAH), Feasibility of Using Audience Measures to Assess Pluralism (1997).

Graham A., Davies G., *Broadcasting, Society and Policy in the Multimedia Age* (John Libbey Media, 1997).

Grande, E., 'The State and Interest Groups in a Framework of Multi-level Decision-Making: The Case of the European Union', (1996) Journal of European Public Policy, 3(3).

Hallin, D., Mancini, P., *Comparing Media Systems* (Cambridge University Press, 2004).

Haraszti, M., 'Media Pluralism and Human Rights', Discussion paper prepared for the Council's of Europe Commissioner for Human Rights, 6 December 2011.

Harcourt, A., *The European Union and the Regulation of Media Markets* (Manchester University Press, 2005).

Harcourt, A., 'The European Commission and Regulation of the Media Industry', (1998) Cardozo Arts & Entertainment Law Journal 16(2).

Harcourt, A., 'EU Media Ownership Regulation: Conflict over the Definition of Alternatives', (1998) Journal of Common Market Studies 36(3).

Harcourt, A., 'Support for Regulation and Transparency of Media Ownership and Concentration – Russia, Study of European Approaches to Media Ownership', Russia, Department for International Development (1999).

Harcourt, A., 'European Policy and Legal Framework for Media Ownership – Aims, Obstacles and Effectiveness', Regional Conference for South-East European and New EU Member Countries on 'Concentration of Media Ownership and Its Impact on Media Freedom and Pluralism, Bled, Slovenia, 11–12 June 2004.

Helberger, N., *Controlling Access to Content: Regulating Conditional Access in Digital Broadcasting* (Kluwer Law International, 2005).

Helberger, N., 'The "Right to Information" and Digital Broadcasting: About Monsters, Invisible Men and the Future of European Broadcasting Regulation', (2006) Entertainment Law Review 2.

Herman, E.S., *Beyond Hypocrisy: Decoding the News in an Age of Propaganda* (South End Press, 1992).

Hitchens, L.P., 'Media Ownership and Control: A European Approach', (1994) The Modern Law Review 57.

Hoffman-Riem, W., *Regulating Media. The Licensing and Supervision of Broadcasting in Six Countries* (The Guilford Press, 1996).

Humphreys, P., 'The Changing Nature of the Broadcast Media in Europe: Some Key Policy Issues' (1995), http://www.psa.ac.uk/journals/pdf/5/1995/hump.pdf.

Humphreys, P., *Mass Media and Media Policy in Western Europe* (Manchester University Press, 1996).

Humphreys, P., 'Power and Control in the New Media', paper presented at the ECPR-Workshop 'New Media and political Communication' (University of Manchester, 1997).

Humphreys, P., 'Regulating for Pluralism in the Era of Digital Convergence: The Issues of Media Concentration Control and the Future of Public-Service Broadcasting', the ECPR Joint Research Sessions, Mannheim, 26–31 March 1999, Workshop 24: 'Regulating Communications in the Multimedia Age'.

Humphreys, P., 'Regulating for Media Pluralism: Issues in Ownership and Competition', in Andrew, J., Crook, M., Holmes, D., Kolinsky, E. (eds), *Why Europe? Problems of Culture and Identity, Vol.2: Media, Film, Gender, Youth and Education* (Macmillan, 2000).

Humphreys, P., 'The EU and Audiovisual Regulation: An Agency for De-regulation' (2005).

Hunt, J., 'The Court of Justice as a Policy Actor in the Development of the EC Labour Law Regime: The Case of the Acquired Rights Directive', (1998) Legal Studies 18(3).

Jakubowicz, K., 'Legislative Guarantees of Plurality of Information Sources', Implementation of constitutional provisions regarding mass media in a pluralist society, Collection Science and Technique of Democracy (1994) 13.

Jakubowicz, K., 'PSB in Post-communist Countries: Finding the Right Place on the Map', the 2007 Spry Memorial Lecture, Montreal, 27 November 2007.

Janis, M.W., Kay, R.S., Bradley, A.W., *European Human Rights Law. Text and Materials*, 2nd edn (Oxford University Press, 2000).

Jones, C.A., 'Television without Frontiers', in Eeckhout, P., Tridimas, T. (eds), *Yearbook of European Law 1999–2000* (Oxford Clarendon Press, 2000).

Kaitatzi-Whitlock, S., 'Pluralism and Media Concentration in Europe: Media Policy as Industrial Policy', (1996) European Journal of Communication 11(4).

Karppinen, K., 'Against Naïve Pluralism in Media Politics: Some Implications of the Radical-Pluralist Approach to the Public Sphere', Public Spheres and Their Boundaries, Tampere 25–27 May 2006.

Katsirea, I. *Public Broadcasting and European Law: A Comparative Examination of Public Service Obligations in Six Member States* (Kluwer Law International, 2008).

Kevin, D., 'Media Ownership and Pluralism: Regulatory Trends and Challenges in the European Union Member States', presentation at the 20th EPRA meeting, Istanbul 2004.

Klimkiewicz, B., 'Media Pluralism: European Regulatory Policies and the Case of Central Europe', European University Institute Working Paper, RSCAS No. 2005/19.

Klimkiewicz, B., 'Is the Clash of Rationalities Leading Nowhere? Media Pluralism in European Regulatory Policies', in Czepek, A., Hellwig, M., Nowak, E. (eds), *Press Freedom and Pluralism in Europe: Concepts and Conditions* (Intellect Books, 2009).

Knee, J.A., 'Should We Fear Media Cross-Ownership?', (2003) Regulation 26(3).

Komorek, E., 'European Attempts to Regulate Media Concentrations. Persisting Conflict of Interests', (2004/2005) Hibernian Law Journal 1.

Komorek, E., 'Is Media Pluralism a Human Right? The European Court of Human Rights, the Council of Europe and the Issue of Media Pluralism', (2009) European Human Rights Law Review 3, 395–414.

Kroes, N., 'Strengthening the European Creative Industries in the Light of the i2010 Strategy', Opening address at the Austrian Presidency Expert Seminar: Content for competitiveness, 2 March 2006.

Kuhne, H., 'Critical Examination of the Green Paper on the Convergence of the Telecommunications, Media and Information Technology Sectors and the Implications for Regulation', cited by Tongue, C., in 'Culture or Monoculture? The European Audiovisual Challenge' in Marsden, C., Verhulst, S. (eds), *Convergence in European Digital TV Regulation* (Blackstone Press Limited, 1999).

Kumar, D., 'Media, War, and Propaganda: Strategies of Information Management During the 2003 Iraq War', (2006) Communication and Critical/Cultural Studies 3(1).

Lang, M., 'Entering the Digital Age. The Promise of Pluralism and the Danger of Monopoly Control', article presented at the ECPR-Workshop on *New Media and Political Communication* in Bern, 27 February 1997.

Lange, A., Van Loon, A., *Multimedia Concentration Regulation in Europe* (IDATE, Montpelier and Institute for Information Law, 1990).

Levy, D., *Europe's Digital Revolution. Broadcasting Regulation, the EU and the Nation State* (Routledge, 1999).

Llorens-Maluquer, C., 'European Responses to Bottlenecks in Digital Pay-TV: Impacts on Pluralism and Competition Policy', (1998) Cardozo Arts & Entertainment Law Journal 16(2–3).

Lorimer, R., Scannel, P., *Mass Communications: A Comparative Introduction* (Manchester University Press, 1994).

Lowe, P., 'Media Concentration and Convergence: Competition in Communications', Oxford Media Convention, 13 January 2004.

Mac Síthigh, D., 'Death of a Convention: Competition between the Council of Europe and European Union in the Regulation of Broadcasting', Paper presented at SLS Annual Conference, Cambridge, September 2012 (unpublished).

Marsden, C., Verhulst, S. (eds), *Convergence in European Digital TV Regulation* (Blackstone Press Limited, 1999).

Marsden, C., Verhulst, S., 'Convergence: A Framework for Discussion', in Marsden, C., Verhulst S. (eds), *Convergence in European Digital TV Regulation* (Blackstone Press Limited, 1999).

Marsden, C.T. (ed.) *Regulating the Information Society* (Routledge, 2000).

Marsden, C.T., 'Pluralism in the Multi-channel Market – Suggestions for Regulatory Scrutiny' (1999/2000) International Journal of Communications, Law and Policy 4.

Mastrolonardo, R., 'Media Concentration: The Italian Case-Study', Open Democracy 14 March 2002.

McCallum, L., 'EC Competition Law and Digital Pay Television', Competition Policy Newsletter (1996), 1.

McCarthy, A., Power, V., *Irish Competition Law. The Competition Act, 2002* (LexisNexis, 2003).

McGonagle, M., *Media Law*, 2nd edn (Thomson, Round Hall, 2002).

McGougan, J., 'The Challenge of Convergence to Audiovisual Regulation: Is the Current Regulatory Framework Approaching Its Sell-By Date?', in Marsden, C., Verhulst, S. (eds), *Convergence in European Digital TV Regulation* (Blackstone Press Limited, 1999).

McLuhan, M., *The Gutenberg Galaxy* (University of Toronto Press, 1962).

McQuail, D., Siune, K. (eds), *Media Policy. Convergence, Concentration and Commerce* (SAGE Publications, 1998).

Mendes Pereira, M., 'Vertical and Horizontal Integration in the Media Sector and EU Competition Law', Conference on the ICT and Media Sector within the EU Policy Framework, Brussels, April 2003.

Monti, M., 'Pluralism and Media Concentration', speech to the European Parliament's Committee on Culture, Youth, Education and the Media, 26 September 1995.

Monti, M., 'Does EC Competition Policy Help or Hinder the European Audiovisual and Telecoms Industries?', British Screen Advisory Council, The Cavendish Conference Centre, London, 26 November 2001.

Moonen, S., 'News Corp/BSkyB and the Boundaries of Merger Review', (2011) Journal of Competition Law and Practice 2(4), 351.

Motta, M., Polo, M., 'Concentration and Public Policies in the Broadcasting Industry: The Future of Television', (1997) Economic Policy 12.

Mowbray, A., *Cases and Materials on the European Convention on Human Rights* (Butterworths, 2001).

Moyers, B., 'Keynote Address to the National Conference on Media Reform', Madison, Wisconsin (8 November 2003).

Murdoch, J., 'Net Age Has No Place For Archaic TV Regulation', *Financial Times*, 22 September 2005.

Napoli, P.M., 'Deconstructing the Diversity Principle', (1999) Journal of Communication 49(4), 7–34.

Naughton, J., 'Our Changing Media Ecosystem', in 'Communications. The next decade. A collection of essays prepared for the UK Office of Communications'.

Nicol, A., Millar, G., Sharland, A., *Media Law and Human Rights* (Blackstone Press Limited, 2001).

Nieto, A., *Time and the Information Market: The Case of Spain* (Media Markets Monographs, University of Navarra, 2001).

Nitsche, I., *Broadcasting in the European Union: The Role of Public Interest in Competition Analysis* (T.M.C. Asser Press, 2001).
Noveck, B.S., 'Thinking Analogue about Digital Television? Bringing European Content Regulation into the Information Age', in Marsden, C., Verhulst, S. (eds), *Convergence in European Digital TV Regulation* (Blackstone Press Limited, 1999).
O'Mahony, C., 'A Future for Public Service Broadcasting: New Challenges, New Pressures, New Approaches', paper presented to the Irish Media Research Network Conference, 16 June 2006.
O'Malley, T., 'The State of the Media – Media Policy and the Need for Reform', The Campaign for Press and Broadcasting Freedom, 6 December 2001.
Open Society Institute, 'Television across Europe: Regulation, Policy and Independence' (Monitoring Report) 11 October 2005.
Orebech, P., 'The EU Competency Confusion: Limits, "Extension Mechanisms," Split Power, Subsidiarity, and "Institutional Clashes"', (1999) Journal of Transnational Law & Policy 13(1).
Organization for Economic Co-operation and Development 'Media Mergers', 19 September 2003.
Ovey, C., White, R.C.A., *Jacobs and White: The European Convention on Human Rights*, 3rd edn (Oxford University Press, 2002).
Padovani, C., 'Pluralism of Information in the Television Sector in Italy: History and Contemporary Conditions', in Czepek, A., Hellwig, M., Nowak, E. (eds), *Press Freedom and Pluralism in Europe: Concepts and Conditions* (Intellect Books, 2009).
Peters, B., 'Corporate Media Trends in Europe', Contribution to the CPBF conference on the 'Communications Revolutions – who benefits?' (2001).
Petley, J., 'The Re-regulation of Broadcasting, or the Mill Owners' Triumph', (2002) Journal of Media Practice 13(3).
Piris, J.-C., 'Does the European Union Have a Constitution? Does It Need One?', Harvard Jean Monnet Working Paper 5/00.
Pons, J.F., 'The Application of Competition and Anti-trust Policy in Media and Telecommunications in the European Union', speech at International Bar Association,14 September 1998, Vancouver, Speech 1998/41.
Puttnam, D., 'The Continuing Need to Advance the Public Interest', in 'Communications. The next decade' – a collection of essays prepared for the UK Office of Communications' (November 2006).
Randall, H., 'Commercial Speech under the European Convention on Human Rights: Subordinate or Equal?', (2006) Human Rights Law Review 6 53.
Reding, V., 'Sport and Television: Ready to Face New Challenges?', Sportel Monaco, 11 October 2004.

Reding, V., 'The European Commission and Media Industry: The Need for a New Partnership', Luxembourg, Opening of the European Newspaper Publishers' Association Congress, 5 November 2004.

Reding, V., 'Better Regulation for Europe's Media Industry: The Commission's Approach', Audiovisual Conference – Between Culture and Commerce, Liverpool, 22 September 2005.

Reding, V., 'Europe, the Media and European Media Policy', Congress of the Federal Association of German Newspaper Publishers, Berlin, 26 September 2005.

Reding, V., 'New Rules for a Convergent Multi-Media World: The Need for a 'Light Touch'', IIC and Chatham House 36th annual conference, London, 10 October 2005.

Reding, V., 'The Role of Public Service Broadcasters in a Vibrant and Pluralist Digital Media Landscape', speech at joint EBU-MTV's conference 'From secret service to public service', Budapest, 3 November 2006.

Reding, V., 'Empowering Citizens – The Magazine Media', FAEP Gala Reception, 8 October 2009.

Rifkin, J., *The Age of Access* (Penguin Putnam, 2001).

Robertson, G., Nicol, A., *Media Law*, 4th edn (Penguin Books, 2002).

Roukens, T., 'What Are We Carrying across the EU These Days? Comments on the Interpretation and Practical Implementation of Article 31 of the Universal Service Directive', in European Audiovisual Observatory, *Iris Special: To Have or Not to Have – Must Carry Rules* (2005).

Rumphorst, W., 'Public Service Broadcasting in an Enlarging Europe: Contributing to European Policy Objectives', Amsterdam, 2 September 2004.

Samuelson, P., 'Five Challenges for Regulating the Global Information Society', in Marsden, C.T. (ed.), *Regulating the Global Information Society* (Routledge, 2000).

Sanchez-Tabernero, A., Carvajal, M., *Media Concentration in the European Market. New Trends and Challenges* (Media Markets Monographs, University of Navarra, 2002).

Sanchez-Tabernero, A., 'Media Concentration in Europe. Commercial Enterprise and the Public Interest' (The European Institute for the Media, 1993).

Sarikakis, K., 'Defending Communicative Spaces: The Remits and Limits of the European Parliament', in Harrison, J., Wessels, B. (eds), *Mediating Europe. New Media, Mass Communications, and the European Public Sphere* (Berghahn Books, 2009).

Sauter, W., 'The Rejection of the ONP Voice Telephony Directive by the European Parliament', (1994) Utilities Law Review 5, 176.

Scheuer, A., Strothmann, P., 'Media Supervision on the Threshold of the Twenty-First Century. What Are the Requirements of Broadcasting, Telecommunications and Concentration Regulation?', Iris Plus, Legal Observations of the European Audiovisual Observatory, Issue 2002-2.

Schoental, M., 'Major Events and Reporting Rights', IRIS-plus, 2006-04.

Senden, L., *Soft Law in European Community Law* (Hart Publishing, 2004).

Senden, L., 'Soft Law, Self-regulation and Co-regulation in European Law: Where Do They Meet?', (2005) Electronic Journal of Comparative Law 9(1).

Smith, P., 'The Politics of UK Television Policy: The Introduction of Digital Television', paper presented at Workshop 24, Regulating Communications in the 'Multimedia Age', European Consortium of Political Research, 27th Joint Sessions of workshops, University of Mannheim, Germany, 26–31 March 1999.

Snyder, F., 'The Effectiveness of European Community Law: Institutions, Processes, Tools and Techniques' (1993) The Modern Law Review 56(1), 19–54.

Tambini, D., 'What Citizens Need to Know. Digital Exclusion, Information Inequality and Rights', in 'Communications. The next decade. A collection of essays prepared for the UK Office of Communications'.

Thierer, A., 'A Brief History of Media Merger Hysteria: From AOL-Time Warner to Comcast-NBC', Progress & Freedom Foundation, Progress on Point, 16(25) December 2009

Tongue, C., 'Public Service Broadcasting and European Community Policy', address to the Experts Meeting on Public Service Broadcasting in Europe, Amsterdam, 17 February 1997.

Tongue, C., 'Culture or Monoculture? The European Audiovisual Challenge', in Marsden C., Verhulst, S. (eds), *Convergence in European Digital TV Regulation* (Blackstone Press Limited, 1999).

Trager, R., Dickerson, D.L., *Freedom of Expression in the 21st Century* (Pine Forge Press Inc., 1999).

Trubek, D.M., Cottrell, P., Nance, M., 'Soft Law, Hard Law, and European Integration: Toward a Theory of Hybridity', Jean Monnet Working Paper 02/05.

Ungerer, H., 'Competition Policy and the Issue of Access in Broadcasting Markets: The Commission Perspective', Vision in Business, Broadcasting Competition Law, Brussels, 14–15 January 2003.

Ungerer, H., 'Legal and Regulatory Aspects of Public Service Broadcasting – Panel Contribution', Conference on Public Service Broadcasting, International Press Institute and Romanian Radio Broadcasting Corporation, Bucharest, 19–20 September 2003.

Ungerer, H., 'Why Can't the Market Decide?', Oxford IPPR Media Convention, 13 January 2004.

Ungerer, H., 'Legal Framework to Secure Open Media Markets and the Independence of the Press – The Role of EU Competition Law', Conference on Democracy and Human Rights in the EU, Opole (Poland), 5 June 2004.

Ungerer, H., 'Application of Competition Law to Media – Some Recent Issues', Nera Conference, Brussels, 22 June 2004.

Ungerer, H., 'Application of EU Competition Rules to Broadcasting – The Transition from Analogue to Digital', Universita di Napoli, Naples, 20 September 2004.

Ungerer, H., 'Impact of European Competition Policy on Media', IESE Business School & School of Communication of the University of Navarra, Centre for Media Studies, Madrid, 15 February 2005.

Ungerer, H.,' Competition Rules and the Media: Are They Determinant or Complementary?', Panel contribution at European Media Law and Practices. Radio and Television Broadcasters, Istanbul, 1 April 2005.

Valcke, P., 'The Future of Must Carry. From Must-Carry to a Concept of Universal Service in the Info-Communications Sector', in European Audiovisual Observatory, *Iris Special: To Have or Not to Have – Must Carry Rules*' (2005).

Valcke, P., et al., 'The European Media Pluralism Monitor: Bridging Law, Economics and Media Studies as a First Step towards Risk-Based Regulation in Media Markets', (2010) Journal of Media Law 2(1), 85–113.

Valcke, P., 'Looking for the User in Media Pluralism Regulation: Unraveling the Traditional Diversity Chain and Recent Trends of User Empowerment in European Media Regulation', (2011) Journal of Information Policy 1, 287–320.

Van Heffen, O., Kickert, W.J.M., Thomassen, J.J.A. (eds), *Governance in Modern Society: Effects, Change and Formation of Government Institutions* (Springer, 2000).

Van Loon, A., 'Freedom versus Access Rights in a European Context', in Marsden, C.T. (ed.), *Regulating the Global Information Society* (Routledge, 2000), 287.

Varney, E., 'Regulating the Digital Television Infrastructure in the EU. Room for Citizenship Interests?', (2006) SCRIPT-ed 3:3.

Varney, M., 'Must-Carry Obligations in the New European Regulatory Framework for Communications: A True Guardian of Pluralism and Diversity?', (2004/2005) Utilities Law Review 14.

Varney, M., 'Must-Carry Provisions and Digital Broadcasting: An Effective Means of Protecting Pluralism and Diversity in Media Output?', paper presented at SLS Annual Conference in Keele, September 2006 (unpublished).

Wallis, R., 'Diversity in Media – Pluralism through Privatization Or?', Conference on Cultural Diversity, Copenhagen, 2002.

Ward, D., *The European Union Democratic Deficit and the Public Sphere. An Evaluation of EU Media Policy* (IOS Press, 2004).

Ward, D., 'State Aid or Band Aid? An Evaluation of European Commission's Approach to Public Broadcasting', (2003) Media, Culture and Society 25.

Ward D., 'Media Concentration and Pluralism: Regulation, Realties and the Council of Europe's Standards in the Television Sector', UNIDEM Campus Trieste Seminar 'The role of media freedom and pluralism in strengthening democracy', Trieste, Italy, 24–28 January 2005.

Ward, D., Fueg, O.C., D'Armo, A., 'A Mapping Study of Media Concentration and Ownership in Ten European Countries', published by the Commissariaat voor de Media, 2004.

Westphal, D., 'Media Pluralism and European Regulation', (2002) European Business Law Review 5.

Wheeler, M., 'Supranational Regulation: The EU Competition Directorate and the European Audio-Visual Marketplace', in Harrison, J., Wessels, B. (eds), *Mediating Europe. New Media, Mass Communications, and the European Public Sphere* (Berghahn Books, 2009).

Whiddington, C., 'European Union', in De Avillez Pereira, M. (ed.), *Antitrust and New Media* (Kluwer Law International, 2000).

White, A., 'Public Media, Democratic Values: Challenges Facing Public Service Broadcasting in the Age of Transition', Regional Meeting on Public Broadcasting, 15–17 February 2002, Budapest.

Wiedermann, V., 'The Future of Public Service Broadcasting in Europe and the Commonwealth', VLV's 10th International Conference, London, February 11th 2005, cited in O'Mahony, C., 'A Future for Public Service Broadcasting: New Challenges, New Pressures, New Approaches'.

Zeno-Zencovich, V., 'Plurality of Political Opinions and the Concentration of Media', Italia National Reports to the XVIIIth International Congress of the International Academy of Comparative Law, Washington 2010, The Cardozo Electronic Law Bulletin, 16(1) Special Issue.

Table of Cases

European Court of Human Rights

European Court of First Instance

European Court of Justice

European Commission

Case M.553, *RTL/Veronica/Endemol*, OJ (1996) L134/3, 113, 114
Case M.709, *Telefonica/Sogecable/Cablevision*, OJ (1996) C-167/3, 117
Case IV/M.938, *Guiness/Grand Metropolitan*, OJ (1998) L228/24, 98
Case IV/M.794, *Coca-Cola Enterprises/Amalgamated beverages*, OJ (1997) L218/15, 98
Case M.993, *Bertelsmann/Kirch/Premiere*, OJ (1999) L53/1, 99, 109–110
Case M.1027, *Deutsche Telekom/BetaResearch*, OJ (1999) L53/31, 111
Case JV.37, *BSkyB/KirchPayTV*, OJ (2000) C-45/3, 123, 124
Case M.1845, *AOL/Time Warner*, OJ (2000) C-130/06, 122
Case M.1943, *Telefonica/Endemol*, OJ (2000) C-170/5, 122
Case M.2050, *Vivendi/Seagram/Canal Plus*, OJ (2000) C-311/3, 122
Case M.2845, *Sogecable/Canalsatélite Digital /Vía Digital*, OJ (2002) C-166/6, 119, 126
Case M.2876, *Newscorp/Telepiù*, OJ (2004) L110/73, 75, 111–11383, 124–126
Case M.5932, *News Corp/BSkyB*, 127, 206
Case NN-70/98, *Kinderkanal/Phoenix,* 289
Case NN-88/98, *News 24,* 289–291
Case NN 631/01, *BBC Licence Fee,* 159

House of Lords

R. v. Independent Television Commission, Ex Parte TV Danmark 1 Ltd, [2001] UKHL, 173

Index

A

N

O

P

R

INFORMATION LAW SERIES

1. Egbert J. Dommering & P. Bernt Hugenholtz, *Protecting Works of Fact: Copyright, Freedom of Expression and Information Law,* 1991 (ISBN 90-654-4567-6).
2. Willem F. Korthals Altes, Egbert J. Dommering, P. Bernt Hugenholtz & Jan J.C. Kabel, *Information Law Towards the 21st Century,* 1992 (ISBN 90-654-4627-3).
3. Jacqueline M.B. Seignette, *Challenges to the Creator Doctrine: Authorship, Copyright Ownership and the Exploitation of Creative Works in the Netherlands, Germany and The United States,* 1994 (ISBN 90-654-4876-4).
4. P. Bernt Hugenholtz, *The Future of Copyright in a Digital Environment, Proceedings of the Royal Academy Colloquium,* 1996 (ISBN 90-411-0267-1).
5. Julius C.S. Pinckaers, *From Privacy Toward a New Intellectual Property Right in Persona,* 1996 (ISBN 90-411-0355-4).
6. Jan J.C. Kabel & Gerard J.H.M. Mom, *Intellectual Property and Information Law: Essays in Honour of Herman Cohen Jehoram,* 1998 (ISBN 90-411-9702-8).
7. Ysolde Gendreau, Axel Nordemann & Rainer Oesch, *Copyright and Photographs: An International Survey,* 1999 (ISBN 90-411-9722-2).
8. P. Bernt Hugenholtz, *Copyright and Electronic Commerce: Legal Aspects of Electronic Copyright Management,* 2000 (ISBN 90-411-9785-0).
9. Lucie M.C.R. Guibault, *Copyright Limitations and Contracts: An Analysis of the Contractual Overridability of Limitations on Copyright,* 2002 (ISBN 90-411-9867-9).
10. Lee A. Bygrave, *Data Protection Law: Approaching its Rationale, Logic and Limits,* 2002 (ISBN 90-411-9870-9).
11. Niva Elkin-Koren & Neil Weinstock Netanel, *The Commodification of Information,* 2002 (ISBN 90-411-9876-8).
12. Mireille M.M. van Eechoud, *Choice of Law in Copyright and Related Rights: Alternatives to the Lex Protectionis,* 2003 (ISBN 90-411-2071-8).
13. Martin Senftleben, *Copyright, Limitations and the Three-Step Test: An Analysis of the Three-Step Test in International and EC Copyright Law,* 2004 (ISBN 90-411-2267-2).
14. Paul L.C. Torremans, *Copyright and Human Rights: Freedom of Expression – Intellectual Property – Privacy,* 2004 (ISBN 90-411-2278-8).
15. Natali Helberger, *Controlling Access to Content: Regulating Conditional Access in Digital Broadcasting,* 2005 (ISBN 90-411-2345-8).
16. Lucie M.C.R. Guibault & P. Bernt Hugenholtz, *The Future of the Public Domain: Identifying the Commons in Information Law,* 2006 (ISBN 978-90-411-2435-7).

17. Irini Katsirea, *Public Broadcasting and European Law: A Comparative Examination of Public Service Obligations in Six Member States,* 2008 (ISBN 978-90-411-2500-2).
18. Paul L.C. Torremans, *Intellectual Property and Human Rights: Enhanced Edition of Copyright and Human Rights,* 2008 (ISBN 978-90-411-2653-5).
19. Mireille van Eechoud, P. Bernt Hugenholtz, Stef van Gompel, Lucie Guibault & Natali Helberger, *Harmonizing European Copyright Law: The Challenges of Better Lawmaking,* 2009 (ISBN 978-90-411-3130-0).
20. Ashwin van Rooijen, *The Software Interface between Copyright and Competition Law: A Legal Analysis of Interoperability in Computer Programs,* 2010 (ISBN 978-90-411-3193-5).
21. Irini A. Stamatoudi, *Copyright Enforcement and the Internet,* 2010 (ISBN 978-90-411-3346-5).
22. Wolfgang Sakulin, *Trademark Protection and Freedom of Expression: An Inquiry into the Conflict between Trademark Rights and Freedom of Expression under European Law,* 2011 (ISBN 978-90-411-3415-8).
23. Stef van Gompel, *Formalities in Copyright Law: An Analysis of their History, Rationales and Possible Future,* 2011 (ISBN 978-90-411-3418-9).
24. Nadezhda Purtova, *Property Rights in Personal Data: A European Perspective,* 2012 (ISBN 978-90-411-3802-6).
25. Brad Sherman & Leanne Wiseman, *Copyright and the Challenge of the New,* 2012 (ISBN 978-90-411-3669-5).
26. Ewa Komorek, *Media Pluralism and European Law*, 2013 (ISBN 978-90-411-3894-1).